CONTEMPORARY STUDIES IN SCRIPTURE

An exciting new series from Greg Kofford Books featuring authors whose works engage in rigorous textual analyses of the Bible and other LDS scripture. Written by Latter-day Saints for a Latter-day Saint audience, these books utilize the tools of historical criticism, literature, philosophy, and the sciences to celebrate the richness and complexity found in the standard works. This series will provide readers with new and fascinating ways to read, study, and re-read these sacred texts.

Textual Studies of the Doctrine and Covenants

Textual Studies of the Doctrine and Covenants

The Plural Marriage Revelation

William Victor Smith

GREG KOFFORD BOOKS
SALT LAKE CITY, 2018

Paperback ISBN: 978-1-58958-690-1
Hardcover ISBN: 978-1-58958-691-8
Also available in ebook.

Greg Kofford Books
P.O. Box 1362
Draper, UT 84020
www.gregkofford.com
facebook.com/gkbooks
twitter.com/gkbooks

Library of Congress Cataloging-in-Publication Data

Names: Smith, William V. (William Victor), 1948- author.
Title: Textual studies of the Doctrine and Covenants : the plural marriage revelation / William Victor Smith.
Description: Salt Lake City : Greg Kofford Books, 2017. | Series: Contemporary studies in scripture. | Includes bibliographical references and index.
Identifiers: LCCN 2017061708| ISBN 9781589586901 (pbk.) | ISBN 9781589586918
(hardcover)
Subjects: LCSH: Doctrine and Covenants. Section 132--Criticism, interpretation, etc. | Polygamy--Religious aspects--Mormon Church--History of doctrines.
Classification: LCC BX8643.P63 S66 2017 | DDC 289.3/23--dc23 LC record available at https://lccn.loc.gov/2017061708

For Eric

Contents

Acknowledgements

A number of people kindly assisted me in reading early drafts of this work. They offered keen insights, saw matters I failed to address, recognized when I wandered too far afield, and identified other flaws in my work. Many very generously offered source material or questions that opened up further ideas. In particular, John Dallon, Frederick Edvalson, Steve Evans, and Kristine Haglund kindly consented to read various forms of the manuscript. Other patient scholars read excerpts and provided important feedback. Robin Jensen assisted me with several archival issues. Stephen Taysom pointed out source material and helped me understand aspects of Joseph F. Smith's ideas. Samuel Brown and John Turner helped me address some questions regarding polygamy in Nauvoo and evolving ideas within Mormonism. Jonathan Stapley pointed out a number of relevant documents and references in addition to reading an early draft. The bloggers at *By Common Consent* politely put up with my blogging on the subject and offered several keen insights on the subject. Brad Kramer warmly suggested the need for the present volume. Loyd Isao Ericson, on behalf of Greg Kofford Books, provided essential editorial advice.

The staff of the Church History Library of The Church of Jesus Christ of Latter-day Saints, in particular Jenny St. Clair, Anne Barrett, Diane Matson, and Anya Bybee, assisted with accessing certain manuscripts and provided expert help on bibliographic matters. Staff members of the Joseph Smith Papers Project generously shared and verified information pertaining to manuscripts related to Doctrine and Covenants 132. Barbara Jones Brown graciously allowed me to read an advance copy of her article, "The Rise and Demise of Latter-day Saint Polygamy in Mexico," in Jason Dormady and Jared Tamez's edited volume *Just South of Zion: The Mormons in Mexico and Its Borderlands* (University of New Mexico Press, 2015).

The L. Tom Perry Special Collections and Manuscripts Library at Brigham Young University, the Special Collections division of the Marriott

Library at the University of Utah, and the Merrill-Cazier Library at Utah State University also provided generous and competent help. In spite of the kind help of friends and colleagues, errors of thought and fact may remain, and for these I assume full responsibility. Finally, I express deep gratitude to my wife for her patience during this project.

Chapter One

Introduction

Section 132 of the Doctrine and Covenants is perhaps Joseph Smith's most historically influential revelation after the Book of Mormon. Its significance flows from its language of deification—tied closely to the notion of "sealing"—and its explicit promotion of polygamy. Though disclosure of the revelation was limited at first, the resulting rumors about it had a powerful effect on cognizant Church leaders and members in Nauvoo, Illinois. It would fracture Church leadership at the highest levels and set the stage for acts that both led to the assassination of Joseph Smith and elevated the Twelve Apostles to the summit of Church leadership. Beyond this, the plural marriage revelation, delivered on July 12, 1843, has had a profoundly important interpretive and textual history that reflects a complex internal structure with several interwoven themes. Fundamental to the revelation is polygamy: its justification, purpose, regulation, and salvific force.[1] Embedded within the revelation's narrative of plural marriage[2] and sealing is the fusion of two sacerdotal arcs launched early in Joseph Smith's career:

---

1. I speak mostly of its immediate (1843) and nineteenth-century context. The revelation's role in Church discourse has varied considerably. One public strategy in use from the beginning, used by Joseph Smith himself, was to claim the revelation was only tangentially concerned with polygamy as ancient artifact. Minutes of Nauvoo City Council for June 10, 1844, reported in "To the Public," *Nauvoo Neighbor Extra* (June 17, 1844): 1. Even contemporary critics gave a bipolar picture, though they were careful to note the revelation's emphasis on the perseverance of sealing. On the revelation's interaction with history and culture, see Stephen C. Taysom, "A Uniform and Common Recollection: Joseph Smith's Legacy, Polygamy, and the Creation of Mormon Public Memory," 121–52; and Newell G. Bringhurst, "Section 132 of the Doctrine and Covenants: Its Complex Contents and Controversial Legacy," 59–86.

2. While "plural marriage" was a common term for polygamy in Mormon discourse after Joseph Smith, Joseph does not seem to have ever referred to the relation between himself and wives other than Emma with the term "marriage."

the 1831 high priesthood to "seal up to eternal life" (D&C 68:12) and the angel Elijah's part in the delivery of "the keys of this dispensation" (D&C 110:16). The high priesthood was a realization of Melchizedek's position in biblical and Book of Mormon theology. First introduced in June 1831 among the Latter-day Saints (those so ordained were then and are yet called "high priests"), it was a feature of some forms of Freemasonry.[3] The high priesthood and visitation of Elijah together offered men and women a durable marriage union persisting beyond death in a felicity of domestic exaltation. Though polygamy did not endure in normative Mormonism, its sealing subtext still occupies the apex of Mormon liturgical emphasis today—an emphasis manifested in the bumper sticker phrase "families are forever."

While frequently separated in modern LDS discourse, the revelation fuses polygamy and sealing into a single tributary to the stream of the 1843 Mormon narrative of salvation. Because of the seeming inseparability of polygamy and eternal sealing, the promise of the latter (and its associated blessings) was frequently a gateway for devoted couples to enter into polygamy. Those who accepted the invitation to engage plurality were eligible to have their present unions sealed, while refusing the invitation to polygamy generally barred the opportunity (at least for a time).

As the new order of marriage became more broadly known, and the plural marriage revelation became a part of Mormon identity in Utah, polygamy and sealing became symbols out of which much of the cultural pattern (and perception) of Mormonism was built. At the same time, the forces of frontier reality and the dynamics of a post-Joseph Smith era of Mormon leadership formed an interpretative superstructure that saw the revelation as a framework of future heavenly life and the general cosmic order. That superstructure built on Joseph Smith's other work as well, but it also diverged from much of his later theological expansions in important ways. This divergence led to fascinating interactions as the contrasting theological concepts of Utah and Nauvoo history collided in the decades following the 1890 Manifesto as the LDS Church began to distance itself from plural marriage.[4]

If the plural marriage revelation was a formal confirmation of a "domestic heaven," it went much further, seeing such unions as parts of a larger

---

They were "sealed"—and it is clear that practically this was true. Domesticity was never a part of Smith's relationships to wives other than Emma.

3. See the discussion of verses 6–15 in Chapter 4; and William V. Smith, "Early Mormon Priesthood Revelations: Text, Impact, and Evolution," 1–84.

4. On cosmological and ontological issues, see the discussions of verses 28–45 and 58–66 in Chapters 6, 9, and 10.

framework of communal salvation, even God-like in nature. It wrote those unions into a story that made them part of human and biblical history from its beginnings, a trend that characterized much of Joseph Smith's religion making.[5] Moreover, through a series of polygamous unions, the revelation created an expanding network of interconnected familial sealings with dynastic overtones. This new temple theology, centered in binding husband and wife for time and eternity, contributed to a refurbished vision of Zion.

In addition, sermons by Smith in Nauvoo made clear the expanse of the new Zion and subtly reckoned with relieving the increasing pressures brought by clandestine polygamy and the growing Mormon population of Hancock County, Illinois.[6] Realizing that their goals could not be achieved in the United States as it was, Smith established the "Kingdom of God" (or Council of Fifty) in March 1844 to both campaign for Joseph Smith's run for the United States presidency and, if necessary, to explore ways to relocate the Latter-day Saints beyond the reach of the Union.[7] Reaching out to Sam Houston, the Council sought a land grant in the disputed buffer territory of western Texas. They also looked toward Oregon and California as possibilities. The Mormon move was not unusual in America, where private citizens and groups were not shy about seeking new territory to expand the United States or even to establish their own nations. The movement's principals were called Filibusters, and the Council was following a well-trodden path.[8]

---

5. The Book of Mormon and Smith's Bible revision work saw Christianity as a lost part of an archetypal text of the Hebrew Bible. Terryl L. Givens, *By the Hand of Mormon: The American Scripture That Launched a New World Religion*, 47; and John G. Turner, "More than a Curiosity: Mormonism and Contemporary Scholarship," 239.

6. For the text of these July 19, 1840, April 16, 1843, and April 8, 1844, sermons, see Andrew F. Ehat and Lyndon W. Cook, *The Words of Joseph Smith*, 415–20, 362–65. Sources for Joseph Smith's sermons may be found on those dates at the online resource, William V. Smith et al., eds., "The Parallel Joseph."

7. On Joseph Smith's presidential aspirations, see Newell G. Bringhurst and Craig L. Foster, *The Mormon Quest for the Presidency*, ch. 1. See also Brent M. Rogers, *Unpopular Sovereignty: Mormons and the Federal Management of Early Utah Territory*, ch. 1.

8. Michael Scott Van Wagenen, *The Texas Republic and the Kingdom of God*, ch. 1. The Fifty as government played over and against Smith's position that the national government had failed in its duty to the citizenry, largely due to its political nature. They were subject to vigorous *internal* debates, but unlike the constitutional republic, there were no crippling shackles to a fractured constituency and inflexible laws that could prevent the protection of the socially

The plural marriage revelation had set in motion a reconceived notion of Zion, with polygamy at its center. Among its practitioners it could be neither a temporary nor a local feature of Mormonism.

The plural marriage revelation impacted Mormon theology in multiple other ways as well. The reconceptualized Zion was theologically, if not topologically, more temple-centric than Missouri had been. It was paradoxically less focused on gathering believers to a central location, a vision that took many decades to bear circumstantial fruit.[9] The revelation further entailed a refined vision of eternal life, shifting from being merely a kind of shorthand for living in the eternal, post-mortal presence of God to being an all-encompassing term for God's salvation work. It also provided brief textual support for the lesser-known doctrine of adoption and for further implicit refinement of the high priesthood.

With so much of Mormon theology being centrally tied to plurality, the discontinuation of polygamy made it vital but difficult to separate the new theological vision from the practice.[10] In the textual analysis of the revelation I will briefly treat such impact issues.

To explore the structure of the revelation's text in a historical and documentary fashion, I consider successive portions of the text in their

---

or religiously downtrodden. In that sense, the Fifty shared an already occupied stage with other antebellum American groups like abolitionists, feminists, and Catholics. On the role of the Fifty in Utah especially see Jedediah S. Rogers, *The Council of Fifty: A Documentary History*; and Matthew J. Grow et al., eds., *Administrative Records: Council of Fifty, Minutes, March 1844–January 1846*.

9. William Victor Smith, *Every Word Seasoned with Grace: A Textual Study of the Funeral Sermons of Joseph Smith*, ch. 8. The Zion theology of Nauvoo was perpetuated for a time after Smith's death, but it gradually changed to suit the conditions of migration to Utah. In October 1844, Brigham Young repeated Smith's theology: "Nauvoo will be the head stake for the Saints to come and receive their endowment. . . . [T]here will also be many more stakes or places for the gathering for the Saints of God." Brigham Young, sermon, October 4, 1844, Journal, 1844 September 28–1846 February 3.

10. As historian Kathleen Flake has noted, one of the possibly unintentional but fortuitous engines deployed in this effort at separation was the printing of the six volume History of Joseph Smith during 1902–1912, edited by B. H. Roberts as *History of the Church of Jesus Christ of Latter-day Saints*. The history manuscript and its planned sources were largely written (ca. 1840s–50s) at or about a time when polygamy was unknown, secret, or dangerous. Hence its printing referenced the July 12 revelation but little else regarding polygamy. Kathleen Flake, *The Politics of American Religious Identity: The Seating of Senator Reed Smoot, Mormon Apostle*, 44.

evolving contexts. This method creates some topical disjuncture and repetition but has the advantage of approaching the text from a reader's perspective. The Epilogue draws together and expands on some matters to give a somewhat smoother historical overview.

In addition to a general analysis of the text of the revelation, several theses will be explored that serve to organize the historical and typological substrata of the revelation. These include the following:

1. The nature of the revelation (that is, its text and context) suggests that its present form results from a fusion of several revelations and ideas that developed during Joseph Smith's lifetime. But the prehistory of the revelation is only tangential: its topics had immediate connection to Joseph Smith in 1843 and are mostly driven by the immediate purpose of the text.[11]

2. The revelation was not intended for public circulation and reflects aspects of the relationship between Joseph Smith and Emma Smith that were meant to remain between them, or at least in a narrow circle of insiders. Indeed, the revelation may be considered part of the epistolary genre: in effect it is a letter to Emma. It was because of Hyrum Smith's persuasion and enthusiasm that the text of the revelation was produced and subsequently distributed.[12]

3. The revelation represents the textual completion of what I call the high priesthood cycle, a cycle that began in 1831 and ended in the final ritualization of sealing and anointing. The end of that cycle saw a combined re-centering of the high priesthood in both its ecclesial and temple forms within the President of the High Priesthood. Joseph Smith's office of President of the High Priesthood began and ended, in a sense, as an office without assistants or counselors. I see the nature of the high priesthood and its cycle as an interpretive subtext for various portions of the revelation. While Brigham Young and the apostles who succeeded Smith retold the story in terms of apostleship, even attempting to redefine the high priest-

---

11. Danel W. Bachman considered the text as historically generated, answering questions that Smith had at different points in his career. See Danel W. Bachman, "New Light on an Old Hypothesis: The Ohio Origins of the Revelation on Eternal Marriage," 19–32. See also B. Carmon Hardy, *Solemn Covenant: The Mormon Polygamous Passage*, 10; and Lyndon W. Cook, *The Revelations of the Prophet Joseph Smith: A Historical and Biographical Commentary of the Doctrine and Covenants*, 293.

12. There is intentional evidence in parallel literature, environmental considerations, and the personalities connected to the text.

hood as apostleship at one point, the endpoint remained the same: Young held tightly to two sets of reins—ecclesial leadership and temple liturgical regulation (see Chapter 4). The apostles are part of what I call the apostolic cycle.[13]

4. Evolving interpretations of the revelation text began to see it as reflexive. Effectively a map to ultimate reward, subsequent experience and cultural forces helped it to be seen as a reflection of God's own life. Within the revelation there is the outline of an eschatological framework, a space for "ultimate" things that allowed for different salvific narratives whose foundations depended on two rather distinct cosmologies. Early Mormon accounting for the beginnings of things (protology) by different cosmologies meant the revelation might fund different accounts of end things (eschatology), each within the parameters of the revelation. Attempts at fusing the different cosmologies in the latter nineteenth and early twentieth centuries still linger in Latter-day Saint thought and provide distinct readings of the revelation.

Delivery and Original Manuscript

At the time the revelation was delivered, scribal culture in Mormonism stood at the edge of revolution. In only a few years, stenography significantly changed the problem of reporting the words and pronouncements of Church leaders. But until the 1850s, longhand reports of events were the essential reality. It was in longhand that William Clayton, confidant and scribe of Joseph Smith, observed the following in his second Nauvoo diary on July 12, 1843:

> Wednesday 12th This A.M, I wrote a Revelation consisting of 10 pages on the order of the priesthood, showing the designs in Moses, Abraham, David and Solomon having many wives & concubines &c. After it was wrote Prests. Joseph & Hyrum presented it and read it to E[mma]. who said she did not believe a word of it and appeared very rebellious. J[oseph] told me

---

13. Both of these terms (high priesthood cycle, apostolic cycle) participate in a serviceable myth: that Joseph Smith or other principal characters in Mormonism held chronologically self-consistent views of these concepts and the acts and words associated with them. The archival traces of those words and acts show that such organizational memes may have some value to distant observers, but it is unlikely that Smith and his associates would have found them useful if they had been consulted in their past states.

to Deed all the unincumbered lots to E[mma] and the children He appears much troubled about E[mma].[14]

Clayton's reference to "ten pages" probably refers to ten half-foolscap pages or possibly pages cut from a blank ledger book (not an unknown practice).[15]

Three decades later, Clayton wrote a much longer affidavit detailing his July 12, 1843, experience, wherein he sought to defend the Mormon practice of polygamy against RLDS (Reorganized Church of Jesus Christ of Latter Day Saints) critics who denied that Joseph Smith engaged in and instituted polygamy.[16] Because of the affidavit's importance in understanding the revelation, I include it here in its entirety:[17]

Inasmuch as it may be interesting to future | generations of the members of the Church of Jesus Christ of | Latter Day Saints, to learn something of the first teachings of | the principle of plural marriage by President Joseph Smith, | the Prophet, Seer, Revelator and Translator, of said church, | I will give a

---

14. Clayton combined events from the day of the revelation and the day following here. This and most of the other quotations from Clayton's diaries that appear here may be found online at Robert Fillerup, "William Clayton's Nauvoo Diaries and Personal Writings." Clayton's diaries also appear in part in George D. Smith, ed., *An Intimate Chronicle: The Journals of William Clayton* and *The Nauvoo Diaries of William Clayton, 1842–1846, Abridged.* The latter two are organized by date and may be easily consulted under the dates supplied in the text and notes herein. For more information on Clayton's records see James B. Allen, "William Clayton and the Records of Church History," 83–114; and James B. Allen and George D. Smith, "Editing William Clayton and the Politics of Mormon History," 129–56.

15. The Kingsbury manuscript is discussed in the Addendum. It may suggest the physical format of Clayton's original.

16. Aside from annoyance over RLDS missioning in Utah, the so-called "Temple Lot" court case required testimony on polygamy, the July 12 revelation, and Joseph Smith's participation in plural marriage. Affidavits were generated from Nauvoo participants in polygamy to verify that Smith initiated the practice, delivered the plural marriage revelation, and engaged in plurality himself. Joseph F. Smith was the engine behind collecting much of this testimony. See Ron Romig, "The Temple Lot Suit After 100 Years," 3–15; S. Patrick Baggette II, "The Temple Lot Case: Fraud in God's Vineyard," 121–36; Joseph F. Smith, Letter to George A. Smith, July 11, 1872; Brian C. Hales, *Joseph Smith's Polygamy,* 2:app. C; Roger D. Launius, *Joseph Smith III: Pragmatic Prophet,* 124, 207, ch. 10; Newell G. Bringhurst, "RLDS Church Reaction to the LDS Doctrine and Covenants' Section 132: Conflicting Responses and Changing Perceptions."

17. William Clayton, Affidavit, February 16, 1874. The affidavit was published in Andrew Jenson, *Historical Record,* 6:225. I use a diplomatic transcription of the original document here. The "|" mark indicates a line end in the original manuscript.

short relation of facts which occurred within my | personal knowledge, and also matters related to me by | President Joseph Smith.

I was employed as a clerk in President Joseph | Smith's office under Elder Willard Richards, and | commenced to labor in the office on the 10th day of | February 1842.[18] I continued to labor with Elder Richards | until he went East to fetch his wife to Nauvoo.

After Elder Richards started East I was necessarily | thrown constantly into the company of President Smith, | having to attend to his public and private business,- | receiving and recording tithings and donations, attending | to land, and other matters of business.[19] During this period, | I necessarily became well acquainted with Emma Smith, | the wife of the Prophet Joseph, and also with the | children—Julia M. (an adopted daughter,) Joseph, | Frederick and Alexander, very much of the business being transacted at the residence of the Prophet.

On the 7th of October 1842, in presence of Bishop | Newel K. Whitney and his wife Elizabeth Ann, President | Joseph Smith appointed me Temple Recorder, and also his | private clerk, placing all records, books, papers &c. in | my care, and requiring me to take charge < of >[20] and preserve | them, his closing words being, "when I have any | Revelations to write you are the one to write them.[21]

During this period the Prophet Joseph frequently | visited my house in my company, and became well[22] acquainted with my wife Ruth, to whom I had been | married five years.

One day in the month of February 1843, date not | remembered,[23] the Prophet invited me to walk with him. | During our walk, he said he had learned that there was | a sister back in England to whom I was very much attached. | I replied there was, but nothing farther than an attachment | such as a brother and sister in the church might rightfully | entertain for each other. He then said, "why don't you send for | her?" I replied, "in the first place I have no authority to send for | her, and if I had, I have not the means to pay expenses." To this | he answered, "I give you authority to send for here, and

---

18. Clayton recorded in his diary for the day, "Brother Kimball came in the morning to say that I must go to Joseph Smiths office and assist Brother Richards. I accordingly got ready and went to the office and commenced entering tithing for the Temple. I was still shaking with the Ague [malaria] every day but it did not much disable me for work." Fillerup, "William Clayton's Nauvoo Diaries."

19. Clayton kept the "Book of the Law of the Lord," during this period. See Andrew H. Hedges, Alex D. Smith, and Richard Lloyd Anderson, eds., *Journals, Volume 2: December 1841–April 1843*, 2–9.

20. The pointed brackets indicate an insertion in the text. This is Clayton's insertion.

21. Clayton did not close the quote.

22. Page 1 (recto of leaf one, the document is not paginated) ends here.

23. The event took place on March 9, 1843, according to Clayton's diary.

I will furnish | you the means," which he did.[24] This was the first time the | Prophet Joseph talked with me on the subject of plural | marriage. He informed that the doctrine and principle | was right in the sight of our Heavenly Father, and that it | was a doctrine which pertained to Celestial order and glory. | After giving me lengthy instructions and information | concerning the doctrine of celestial or plural marriage, | he concluded his remarks by the words, "It is your | privilege to have all the wives you want."

After this introduction, our conversations on the subject | of plural marriage were very frequent, and he | appeared to take particular pains to inform and | instruct me in respect to the principle. He also | informed me that he had other wives <u>living</u>, besides | his first wife Emma, and in particular gave me to | understand that Eliza R. Snow, Louisa Beman, | S. P. Sessions[25] and Desdemona C. Fullmer, and others | were his lawful wives in the sight of Heaven.

On the 27th of April 1843 the Prophet Joseph Smith | married to me Margaret Moon, for time and eternity[26] at the residence of Elder Heber C. Kimball; and on the 22nd of | July 1843, he married to me, according to the order of the | church, my first wife Ruth.

On the first day of May 1843, I officiated in the | office of an Elder by marrying Lucy Walker to the Prophet | Joseph Smith, at his own residence.[27]

During this period the Prophet Joseph took several | other wives. Amongst the number I well remember Eliza | Partridge, Emily Partridge, Sarah Ann Whitney, Helen | Kimball and Flora Woodworth. These all, he acknowledged | to me, were his lawful, wedded wives, according to the | celestial order. His wife Emma was cognizant of the | fact of some, if not all, of these being his wives, and she | generally treated them very kindly.

On the morning of the 12th of July, 1843, Joseph and | Hyrum Smith, came into the office, in the upper story of | the brick store, on the bank of the Mississippi River. They | were talking on the subject of plural marriage. Hyrum | said to Joseph, "if you will write the revelation on Celestial marriage, | I will take, and read it to Emma, and I believe I can convince | her of its truth, and you will hereafter have peace." Joseph | smiled and remarked, "you do not know Emma as well | as I do." Hyrum repeated his opinion and further remarked, | "the doctrine is so plain I can convince any reasonable man | or woman of its truth, purity and heavenly origin," or | words to their effect. Joseph then said,

---

24. Clayton's diary for March 9, 1843, has the following: "Thursday 9. At prest. Josephs office. Walked out in the P. M. he told me it was lawful for me to send for Sarah & said he would furnish me money."

25. Sylvia Porter Sessions Lyon. Lyon was civilly married to Windsor P. Lyon at the time. Lyon was left out of published versions of Clayton's affidavit.

26. Page 2 of Clayton's affidavit ends here.

27. Clayton's diary: "May 1st A.M. At the Temple. At 10 married Joseph to Lucy Walker. P. M. at Prest. Joseph's; he has gone out with Woodworth."

"well, I will write | the revelation, and we will see." He then requested me | to get paper and prepare to write. Hyrum very urgently | requested Joseph to write the revelation by means of the | Urim and Thummim, but Joseph, in reply, said he did | not need to, for he knew the revelation perfectly from | beginning to end.[28]

Joseph and Hyrum then sat down, and Joseph commenced | to dictate the Revelation on Celestial marriage, and I wrote it, | sentence by sentence, as he dictated. After the whole was written, | Joseph asked me to read it through, slowly and carefully, | which I did, and he pronounced it correct. He then remarked | that there was much more that he could write, on the same | subject, but what was written was sufficient for the present.

Hyrum then took the Revelation, to read to Emma. Joseph | remained with me in the office until Hyrum returned. | When he came back, Joseph asked him how he had succeeded. | Hyrum replied that he had never received a more severe | talking to in his life, that Emma was very bitter and full | of resentment and anger.

Joseph quietly remarked, "I told | you, you did not know Emma as well as I did." Joseph | then put the Revelation in his pocket and they both | left the office.

The revelation was read to several of the authorities | during the day. Towards evening Bishop Newel K. | Whitney asked Joseph if he had any objections to his | taking a copy of the revelation; Joseph replied that | he had not, and handed it to him. It was carefully | copied the following day by Joseph C. Kingsbury.

Two or three days after the Revelation was written, | Joseph related to me and several others that Emma had | teazed, and urgently entreated him for the privilege | of destroying it; that he became so weary of her | teazing, and to get rid of her annoyance, he told her | she might destroy it, and she had done so, but he | had consented to her wish in this matter to pacify | her, realizing that he knew the Revelation perfectly, | and could re-write it at any time, if necessary.

The copy made by Joseph C. Kingsbury is a true[29] and correct copy of the original in every respect. The copy was | carefully preserved by Bishop

---

28. Page 3 of the affidavit ends here. Clayton's reference to "the Urim and Thummim" here is important for a number of reasons. First, it illustrates that Smith's use of revelatory instrumentality had never really ceased, as is sometimes suggested. This was a catchall term in early Mormonism for various stones that assisted revelation, not just the spectacles associated with the Book of Mormon. W. W. Phelps was perhaps the first to suggest the title for these objects, Urim and Thummim. (When early revelations were published, the term was back-written into them.) On Smith's early use of such objects see Mark Ashurst-McGee, "A Pathway to Prophethood: Joseph Smith as Rodsman, Village Seer, and Judeo-Christian Prophet."

29. Page 4 of the affidavit ends here. Page 5 is the final page of the affidavit. By nature of the writing medium, pages 6, 7, and 8 are blank.

Whitney, and but few knew of | its existence until the temporary location of the Camp of Israel | at Winter Quarters, on the Missouri River, in 1846.

After the Revelation on celestial marriage was written | Joseph continued his instructions, privately, on the doctrine, | to myself and others, and during the last year of his life we were | scarcely ever together, alone, but he was talking on the | subject, and explaining that doctrine and principles | connected with it. He appeared to enjoy great liberty[30] and | freedom in his teachings, and also to find great relief in | having a few to whom he could unbosom his feelings | on that great and glorious subject. From him I learned | that the doctrine of plural and celestial marriage is | the most holy and important doctrine ever revealed to | man on the earth, and that without obedience to that | principle no man can ever attain to the fulness | of exaltation in celestial glory.[31]

Salt Lake City,   Wm Clayton.[32]

         js

February 16th 1874
Territory of Utah
County of Salt Lake.

On this sixteenth day of February, A.D. 1874, before the | undersigned a Notary Public in and for said County and | Territory, personally came Wm Clayton, who, being sworn in due form of law, says, | that the foregoing

---

30. "Liberty" was a common term among preachers of the era, meaning that the speaker enjoyed uninterrupted flow of thought and ease of expression, which was generally ascribed to inspiration. For example, 1870s Seventh Day Adventist preacher Joseph Waggoner reported, "Most of the time I enjoyed great liberty in speaking." J. H. Waggoner, "Report of Meetings," 175.

31. Clayton's claims at this point are supported by his diary. Joseph Smith focused a lot of his time with Clayton discussing polygamy and the angst they both felt over the domestic strains it fostered. (The male-centeredness of these reports is, of course, evident.) Additionally, there is no doubt that both Clayton, Smith, and the others involved in the practice engaged in sexual activity with their multiple marriage partners. Of course, Smith had more wives than any of the other participants in Nauvoo, and it appears that the linkage aspect was globally more important than sex, though, as the revelation suggests, the latter had a vital religious meaning too. It is naïve to divorce Joseph Smith from physical desire. There are clear dynastic elements (see the discussion of verses 49–50 in Chapter 7). But some unions seem designed as loyalty hurdles (Smith's marriages to the wives of leader associates) trying to drive commitment to levels that would avoid the devastating betrayals of Missouri and Ohio. Others may have been largely motivated by desire.

32. Clayton underscored both his name and the date with a flourish.

statement is true in every particular, and where the facts are | related as coming under his own personal observation, and where the language of others | is quoted the exact sentiments, and as near as possible the exact words, are given in every | instance.

[Notary seal applied] In testimony whereof I have hereunto subscribed my name | and affixed my notarial seal, at my office in Salt Lake City, | Utah Territory, the day and year aforsaid.

John T. Caine
Notary Public

Clayton admits that his affidavit is correct in outline ("words to their effect"), but that it should not be taken as a transcript of the event. Clayton's diary entry and his affidavit hint at the strained relationship between Joseph and Emma Smith at the time, as well as Emma's confused and angry feelings over her husband's marriages.[33] Emma felt vulnerable to disgrace and insecurity. She had ambivalent feelings over the legitimacy of polygamy, but avoided direct public action.

Clayton was living his own drama over polygamy, with one wife fending off (or ambivalent about) an ignorant suitor, confused or upset "in-laws," and so forth. Smith made promises of support but had to be careful over his own situation. Meanwhile, Joseph Smith's sermons at this point are in part a reflection of this stormy background, meant partly to support those in the know and perhaps to prepare others.[34]

The July 12 revelation, however, was not the final revelation on this topic from Smith.[35] For instance, two months later, on September 15, 1843, Clayton recorded the following:

---

33. The day after the revelation was given, Clayton was called to a meeting of Joseph and Emma who had come to some agreement over their differences. Joseph perhaps hoped to either keep her from leaving him by offering stability tied to city property or fulfill already discussed alternatives. See Clayton's diary entry for July 13, 1843. A month later Clayton recorded that Emma had found two letters from one of Joseph's wives, Eliza Roxcy Snow, in his coat pocket. In anger, she asked Clayton if he was the delivery service. See his entries for August 21, 23, 1843. For Kingsbury's memory of copying the revelation, see Chapter 9 and the Epilogue.

34. See Smith's July and August 1843 sermons in William V. Smith et al., "The Parallel Joseph." In particular, see Clayton's interpretive account of Smith's August 27, 1843, sermon.

35. Clayton's affidavit above reports that Smith claimed more information was available at the time. There is no record of a specific continuation of the July 12 plural marriage revelation text.

Prest. J. told me he had lately had a new item of law[36] revealed to him in relation to myself. He said the Lord had revealed to him that a man could only take 2 of a family except by express revelation and as I had said I intended to take Lydia he made this known for my benefit. to have more than two in a family was apt to cause wrangles and trouble. He finally asked if I would not give L[ydia] to him I said I would so far as I had any thing to do in it. He requested me to talk to her.

The patriarchal language of give and take reflects the plural marriage revelation but was probably more optimistic than warranted. Lydia Ann Moon was reluctant to marry Smith, though she was apparently comfortable about marrying Clayton. However, at the time, William Clayton was already married to two of the Moon sisters, Margaret and Ruth. Thus, this new revelation prevented Clayton from marrying a third sister. In the end, Lydia would marry neither and instead monogamously married Clayton's younger brother James, who died soon after at Winter Quarters (Florence, Nebraska).[37] This regulation reported by William Clayton was either unknown or ignored in later instances of marriages, where several daughters and even a widowed mother might be married to the same man.[38]

---

36. "Law," "Priesthood," and "order of the priesthood" were often, as they are in the plural marriage revelation, code words for plural marriage; as Clayton saw it, that law had to be lived if it was "revealed" to a man or woman (meaning, apparently, that the person was introduced to the practice and invited to participate). The text of the revelation suggests this and lies at the foundation of nineteenth-century Mormon claims that the highest heaven was closed to those who rejected the practice. See Smith et al., "Parallel Joseph," August 27, 1843.

37. Lydia and James had one child, Hirum James Clayton. Lydia remarried after Clayton's death in 1847 but never entered polygamy in life. She died at Rock Creek, California, in 1897. She was sealed to James by proxy in 1915 and to other husbands in 1994 and 2010. William Clayton made a rather dreary assessment of Lydia in his diary entry for January 23, 1846: "She went to Burlington last year but previous to her going she agreed to be sealed to me for time and eternity. She refused to be sealed to Joseph. While at Burlington she wrote pledging herself to her contract. When she came home she faultered and went out to fathers where she got entangled with my brother James and has resolved to marry him. She has lost her faith in the Church and is on the road to ruin, but so determined that no argument is of any use. The family feel sorry but cannot change her feelings. Her mother frets much about it."

38. Theodore Turley married three sisters in March and April 1844, hence the regulation was either Clayton's alone, or Smith rethought it. Nancy R. Turley and Lawrence R. Turley, *The Theodore Turley Family Book*, 56. On such practice, see also Gary James Bergera, "Identifying the Earliest Mormon Polygamists 1841–1844," 39; Kathryn M. Daynes, *More Wives Than One: Transformation of*

Dating the Revelation

While the July 12, 1843, dating of the plural marriage revelation is not in dispute, an issue that has always surrounded the revelation is the chronology of when Joseph Smith first understood, taught, and practiced plural marriage. A common view is that this revelation is connected to Smith's revisions of the Bible between 1830 and 1833. In tension with this view is the internal and external context of the revelation itself. The text of the revelation is largely contemporary to 1843 in the sense that it is a product of that year. On the other hand, at least some of its ideas were shared with members of Smith's inner circle much earlier.

One reason to support the revelation's connection to Smith's efforts to revise the Bible is the revelation's points of contact with the Bible. First, as Clayton summarized in his diary: "I wrote a Revelation . . . on the order of the priesthood, showing the designs in Moses, Abraham, David and Solomon having many wives & concubines." Thus, much of the text of the revelation references polygamous figures from the Hebrew Bible. The other two obvious points of contact are from the teachings of Jesus: one being Jesus's parable of the talents (Matt. 25), and the other being his response to the Saducean puzzle of the Levirate husbands (Matt. 22:23–33, Mark 12:18–27, Luke 20:27–39).

This last point of contact is prominent in Smith's explanation of the revelation as the Nauvoo City Council (most of whom were previously unaware of the practice) debated how to respond to the *Nauvoo Expositor*'s leaking of Smith's secretive polygamous marriages in June 1844. Not wanting to confirm the *Expositor*'s allegations, Joseph Smith claimed that the revelation's intersection with polygamy was merely historical and that the driving force behind the revelation was his own concern with the levirate puzzle.[39] It is unclear from the council minutes whether this referred to his work with Sidney Rigdon in the Bible revision effort more than a decade before the revelation or some other encounter with the text.[40]

---

the Mormon Marriage System, 1840–1910, 69–70; and John D. Lee, *Mormonism Unveiled or the Life and Confessions of the Late Mormon Bishop John D. Lee*, ch. 14.

39. "To the Public," 1. The change of story was not unnoticed by those who were taught that the revelation marked a restoration of polygamy, not just an historical commentary. Danel W. Bachman, "The Authorship of the Manuscript of Doctrine and Covenants Section 132," 35–36.

40. Samuel Brown argues that Smith's early 1830s revisions to the story of the Sadducees indicate a beginning for Smith's thought on both eternal marriage and

Manuscript Copies of the Revelation

The original Clayton manuscript of the revelation did not survive the disgust of Emma Smith, who apparently burned it.[41] However, other copies were made and shared among those in Smith's inner circle.

Of the several copies of the revelation made, the two most prominent and influential for later imprints are those of Joseph C. Kingsbury and Willard Richards. According to Clayton, Newel K. Whitney, one of Smith's closest confidantes on the subject,[42] asked for a copy of the revelation and recruited Kingsbury to produce it.[43] Willard Richards, acting in his position as Church historian, produced the other important handwritten copy of the revelation. Both the Kingsbury and Richards manuscripts show markup, with those on the Kingsbury manuscript suggesting that it was employed in setting type for the first imprint, and those on the Richards manuscript indicating that it may have been used for the Manuscript History of the Church.[44] See the Addendum at the end of this volume for a transcription of the Kingsbury manuscript with comparisons to the Richards manuscript.

Additional copies of the revelation were also made and distributed. Both Brigham Young and Hyrum Smith seemed to have copies of the

---

polygamy. See Samuel Morris Brown, *In Heaven as It Is on Earth: Joseph Smith and the Early Mormon Conquest of Death,* 230.

41. One story circulated that she used fire tongs to put it to the flames so that she could say she never touched it. Robert J. Woodford, "The Historical Development of the Doctrine and Covenants," 1735.

42. Newel Whitney was not only one of those to whom the revelation was read after its delivery, he was already well-acquainted with the practice of polygamy. His daughter, Sarah Ann, was married to Smith.

43. Kingsbury, by Clayton's affidavit, copied the revelation the day after it was delivered. However, an examination of the manuscript suggests it may have been copied in two episodes. The Kingsbury copy is cataloged in Revelations Collection, circa 1829–1876, MS 4583, Box 1, fd. 75, LDS Church History Library. See Chapter 9 and the Addendum.

44. The Manuscript History of the Church was a project begun by Joseph Smith, Sidney Rigdon, and clerks in 1838. In Nauvoo, after several more attempts, the project was turned over to Willard Richards. When Richards died in 1854, having brought the history to 1838, George A. Smith then helmed the project to its completion, winding up at Joseph Smith's death. As noted elsewhere, the history project generally made no reference to polygamy, except its citation of the plural marriage revelation.

revelation, though whether those copies still exist is unknown.[45] Aside from these, two other copies are known to exist, both in the handwriting of Newel K. Whitney's oldest son, Horace Kimball Whitney.[46]

Despite its secrecy, some street knowledge of the revelation certainly existed in Nauvoo.[47] Hyrum showed the revelation to various people, including some members of the Nauvoo high council. William Law related his introduction:

> I hereby certify that Hyrum Smith did, (in his office,) read to me a certain written document, which he said was a revelation from God, he said that he was with Joseph when it was received. He afterwards gave me the document to read, and I took it to my house, and read it, and showed it to my wife, and returned it next day. The revelation (so called) authorized certain men to have more wives than one at a time, in this world and in the world to come. It said this was the law, and commanded Joseph to enter into the law. —And also that he should administer to others. Several other items were in the revelation, supporting the above doctrines.[48]

Similarly, James Allred reminisced to a clerk:

> At a meeting of the High council in Nauvoo, Sept 23 1843 Br Hirum Smith read the revilation relating to the plurality of wives, he said he did not believe it at first, it was so contrary to his feelings, but he said he knew Joseph was a profit of God, so he made covenant that he would not eat, drink, or sleep

---

45. "A Special Conference of the Elders of the Church of Jesus Christ of Latter-Day Saints," *Deseret News—Extra* (September 14, 1852): 25. On Hyrum having a copy, see David Fullmer's June 15, 1869, affidavit in *40 Affidavits on Celestial Marriage, Book number 1, 1869*, 27; Hales, *Joseph Smith's Polygamy*, 2:142.

46. See the Addendum. The Horace Whitney copies are catalogued as MS 7876, LDS Church History Library, and MS 3497, LDS Church History Library. Horace (1823–1884) was the oldest child of Newel and Elizabeth Ann Whitney.

47. M. Guy Bishop, "Eternal Marriage in Early Mormon Marital Beliefs," 85; Orson Pratt, October 7, 1869, *Journal of Discourses*, 13:193.

48. Law's affidavit was published in the single issue of the *Nauvoo Expositor*. Austin Cowles, former counselor in the Nauvoo stake presidency, gave similar testimony. The *Expositor* offered heated criticism of Smith and the other practitioners of polygamy in Nauvoo, styling them "heaven daring, hell deserving, God forsaken villains" and offering the reports of women who had been shocked by proposals of plural marriage. See also Nauvoo vs. O. F. Bostwick, February 26, 1844. Richard Bushman, *Joseph Smith: Rough Stone Rolling*, 490–95.

untill he knew for himself, that he had got a testimony that it was true, that he had even had the voice of God concerning it."[49]

Since Hyrum Smith learned of polygamy prior to the writing of the revelation, "it" in Allred's statement has "plurality of wives" as antecedent, not the July 12 revelation. Leonard Soby recalled that Hyrum read the revelation to the council around August 12.[50]

Such reports of reading the revelation suggest the idea that several contemporary copies were made, though precisely how many other manuscript copies existed in Nauvoo is unknown.

Printing the Plural Marriage Revelation

In 1866, Brigham Young (already a polygamist by July 12, 1843) discussed his being introduced to the revelation:

> If it is wrong for a man to have more than one wife at a time, the Lord will reveal it by and by, and he will put it away that it will not be known in the Church. I did not ask Him for the revelation upon this subject. When that revelation was first read to me by Joseph Smith, I plainly saw the great trials and the abuse of it that would be made by many of the Elders, and the trouble and the persecution that it would bring upon this whole people. But the Lord revealed it, and it was my business to accept it.[51]

Assuming the accuracy of this report, the soonest this might have happened was October 23, 1843, when the apostles returned to Nauvoo from a mission through parts of the east coast of the United States.

Young collected and kept the Kingsbury copy himself three years after Joseph Smith's death.[52] This would be used for the first imprint of the

---

49. James Allred, "Statement," October 15, 1854. Allred's report is substantively different from Brigham Young's, who claimed that he convinced Hyrum of the divinity of polygamy a year earlier in 1842, during Hyrum's attempts to entrap those he thought were engaged in illicit polygamy. Hales, *Joseph Smith's Polygamy*, 2:44–45. Hyrum, himself, gave different accounts. See Thomas Bullock's minutes in *Historian's Office General Church Minutes: 1839–1845*, April 8, 1844 (quoted in the Epilogue, below). On the circulation of the revelation see Richard S. Van Wagoner, *Mormon Polygamy: A History*, 63–64; and Hardy, *Solemn Covenant*, 10–11.

50. Leonard Soby, Statement, November 14, 1883.

51. Brigham Young, August 19, 1866, *Journal of Discourses*, 11:267.

52. See Young's remarks in "A Special Conference of the Elders," 25. The provenance of the Kingsbury copy is mostly complete and its textual influence is traceable without much difficulty. With the death of Joseph and Hyrum Smith,

revelation, which appeared in a special edition of the Church's Salt Lake City weekly newspaper, the *Deseret News Extra*, on September 14, 1852. This was a part of the Church's public announcement of plural marriage as a practice in the faith, an announcement made in the wake of federally appointed territorial officials who were also making public claims about the practice in Utah.[53] The *Extra* was not the first public defense of polygamy. Six weeks prior to the August conference that brought the public announcement of polygamy at Church headquarters, Parley P. Pratt responded in print to accusations of polygamy by a San Francisco editor, John Nugent. In Pratt's pamphlet, *"Mormonism!" "Plurality of Wives!" An especial chapter, for the especial edification of certain inquisitive news editors, etc.*, he admitted to and defended polygamy with a series of arguments that set the standard for Mormon preaching on its justification: 1) polygamy was a biblical practice, 2) it was practiced by a majority of mankind at the present time, 3) it protected the virtue of women by eliminating the need and opportunity for prostitution, fornication, and adultery. Pratt did not mention the plural marriage revelation directly but told of the "law of God . . . from Zion."

Beginning with the public announcement, the major imprints of the revelation are as follows:

Church historian Willard Richards assumed control of those materials in Joseph Smith's office and the historian's collections, while Emma Smith held ownership of materials in the Smith residence (known as the Mansion House), such as the Egyptian mummies and papyri connected to the Book of Abraham, and the Bible revision manuscripts. Whitney may not have had custody of the Kingsbury copy in October 1843 when Joseph Smith apparently read the revelation to Brigham Young. Smith may have returned the Kingsbury copy after that. At any rate, Whitney held the Kingsbury copy in 1847 when Brigham Young requested it in March of that year. Young kept it in his possession (except for its use in publishing the *Extra*). Richards may have copied the revelation sometime after August 1852. Joseph C. Kingsbury's own affidavit (dated May 22, 1886) on copying the Clayton original appears as Joseph C. Kingsbury, affidavit, 1886 May 22. Probably before the manuscript passed to Young, Whitney's son, Horace K. Whitney, made a copy (and perhaps two copies—one of the two may be a copy of the other). See the bibliographic notes on these copies at the end of the Addendum.

53. Jonathan H. Moyer, "Dancing with the Devil: The Making of the Republican/Mormon Pact," 18–22; Peter L. Crawley, *A Descriptive Bibliography of the Mormon Church*, 2:357–58. This was the fourth *Extra* published by the *Deseret News* since its inaugural in 1850. A January 1852 *Extra* detailed a defense of the Territory against claims made by federal appointees who had fled Salt Lake City the previous year. Rogers, *Unpopular Sovereignty*, 45–54.

1. *Deseret News Extra* (Sept. 14, 1852): 25–27. Salt Lake City, Utah.[54]
2. *Deseret News Extra. Great Salt Lake City, U. T., September 14, 1852.* Horace S. Eldredge, presiding elder in St. Louis, Missouri, had item 1 reprinted at the "Valley Farmer" print shop in St. Louis in December 1852.[55]
3. *The Seer* 1, no. 1 (January 1853): 7–11, Washington, D.C. Based on item 1. Orson Pratt introduced verse numbers here for the first time. Pratt renumbered the verses to their present form in his 1876 edition of the Doctrine and Covenants.[56]
4. *Latter-Day Saints' Millennial Star* (January 1, 1853), 5–8. Liverpool, UK. Based on item 1.[57]
5. *Millennial Star Supplement* (January 22, 1853).[58] A reprint of item 1 with an editorial postscript by Samuel W. Richards, calling for a fair hearing of the pamphlet.[59]
6. *Deseret News* (January 21, 1857): 361–62. Based on the Manuscript History of the Church version of the revelation.
7. *Millennial Star* (November 5, 12, 1859): 715–16, 729–31. Reprint of item 6.
8. *Millennial Star* (April 28, 1866): 257–61. Based on item 4.

---

54. The *Deseret News Extra* gave minutes of the August 28–29, 1852, special conference when polygamy was publicly announced, and the resulting pamphlet was edited by Thomas Bullock, Brigham Young, and Willard Richards. Young redacted the pamphlet on several occasions prior to publication. See Church Historian's Office Journal, August 29–September 16, 1852, 15:272–92. See also Crawley, *Descriptive Bibliography*, 2:354–57.

55. Eldredge made some changes in the *Extra,* but the revelation itself is duplicated without additional comment. Crawley, *Descriptive Bibliography*, 2:357–58.

56. For Joseph Smith's revelation corpus in general, see Robin Scott Jensen, "'Rely Upon the Things Which are Written': Text Context and the Creation of Mormon Revelatory Records."

57. Hereafter abbreviated *Millennial Star.*

58. Crawley, *Descriptive Bibliography*, 3:41.

59. Rumors of polygamy had long circulated in Britain, but missionaries were instructed to deny the practice or were simply ignorant of it. (For example, see Crawley, *Descriptive Bibliography*, 2:114–15.) Now that the rumors had in essence been acknowledged, a number of staunch members became disaffected. An active program ensued to explain the revelation and offer arguments for previous Church policy. The 8,000 copies of the supplement sold out during the year. This was remarkable in the sense that the first edition of the Pearl of Great Price published in 1851 in 12,000 copies still had several thousand copies on the shelf in 1876.

9. George A. Smith's pamphlet, "Answers to Questions," published initially in 1869 and reprinted twice (in 1872 and 1873).

10. *Millennial Star*, "An Answer" (February 13, 1869): 107–11. Reprint of the material in item 9, but subtitled, "*Deseret News*" in reference to item 1.

11. *Millennial Star*, "The Resurrection" (November 22, 1875): 746–50. Has the verse numbering matching that of the *Seer* (item 3), but this is probably accidental since both simply placed digits at the beginning of the paragraphs of item 1.

12. The next five imprints of the revelation appeared in the 1878, 1879, 1882, 1888, and 1891 editions of the Pearl of Great Price (canonized in 1880).[60]

13. Doctrine and Covenants 1876, 1879, etc. The revelation first appeared as a part of the Doctrine and Covenants in Pratt's 1876 edition, where it received the same number (132) as in the current (2013) edition. The 1921 edition followed the format of item 14 below.[61]

14. B. H. Roberts ed., *History of the Church of Jesus Christ of Latter-day Saints*, 5:501–7. Roberts submitted occasional redactions of the texts of the revelations to the Church presidency and his work then formed a standard for later editions until 1981.[62]

While viewed as authoritative by believers since its initial delivery, the plural marriage revelation was officially canonized in the October 1880 General Church Conference when Pratt's 1880 edition of the Doctrine and Covenants and his 1878 Pearl of Great Price were accepted by the Church.[63]

---

60. On editions to 1930 see Chad J. Flake and Larry W. Draper, *A Mormon Bibliography, 1830–1930: Books, Pamphlets, Periodicals, and Broadsides Relating to the First Century of Mormonism*.

61. An episode of the "History of Joseph Smith" series that appeared five years after the *Extra*, once again in the *Deseret News*, contained the plural marriage revelation. The *Deseret News* History was edited for inclusion in the *Millennial Star* in Liverpool, which formed the basis for B. H. Roberts's *History of the Church of Jesus Christ of Latter-day Saints* published between 1902 and 1912.

62. Roberts often consulted Church Historian Anthon H. Lund in person on the history. For examples, see John P. Hatch, ed., *Danish Apostle: The Diaries of Anthon H. Lund, 1890–1921*, 157, 169, 194, 197.

63. "Fiftieth Semi-Annual Conference, Fifth Day," 724.

Organization of the Revelation

This study will examine the text of the revelation through the lens of topics suggested by the following outline of its structure:

1. The Revelation Heading. Most imprints of the revelation text add a summary heading. Over the years, the length and emphasis of the heading has changed as its social and religious meaning has evolved.
2. The Ancient Roots of Polygamy (vv. 1–5). The revelation begins with an explanation for its existence. It shows modern polygamy as an extension of ancient practice, one that has salvific overtones.
3. The Permission to Seal (vv. 6–15). Priesthood sacraments may bestow permanence on mortal relationships, and hence it forms a fundamental theme in polygamy. Here the revelation demonstrates itself as the endpoint in a developing chain of ritual instruction in Mormonism.
4. Unconditional Sealing and Eternal Damnation (vv. 16–27). Sealing bonds as conceived by the revelation and in Nauvoo practice were nearly unconditional. Parties to a sealing might crack that seal only with the most dread transgressions.
5. Polygamy and the Afterlife (vv. 28–45). Kingdoms of God and polygamy in the accumulation of afterlife glory.
6. The "Sealing" Keys of the Kingdom (vv. 46–48). The Patriarchal Priesthood and the complex historical narrative over the distribution of authority for sealing and polygamy.
7. Joseph Smith's Exaltation (vv. 49–50). "All that he gives me I shall take with me." Smith's guarantee of salvation gave him standing in his role as temple priest and the discussion of the validity of the plural marriage revelation.
8. The Secret of Emma (vv. 51–57). A mystery surrounding the revelation and its relation to Emma.
9. The Mechanics of Plurality (vv. 58–63). Parable of the Ten Virgins, polyandry, and the basis for priesthood status in the "transfer" of plural wives.
10. The Law of Sarah (vv. 64–66). An ultimatum to Emma Smith that would not be an empty threat in later practice.

The genesis of the July 12, 1843, revelation on plural marriage may have been Emma Smith's resistance to polygamy, but below its disturbing surface it captured, reformulated, and originated many of Joseph Smith's ideas about the ancient world and modern doctrine. Publicly announced nine years later in response to claims by appointed territorial officers, it played a major and continuing role in the politics and culture of the Intermountain West. Additionally, it had consequences for important Mormon ideas about earthly and heavenly salvation. It was and is in many ways the textual foundation for much of nineteenth and twentieth-century Mormonism.

Chapter Two: The Revelation Heading

Evolving Context

The Doctrine and Covenants is not a narrative work but a compilation of somewhat independent texts largely consisting of revelations dictated by Joseph Smith. To help readers appreciate the original meaning and purpose of those revelations, or understand how a revelation was or is presently interpreted, short introductions of varying complexity have been supplied over the years.[1]

The first imprint (1852) of the plural marriage revelation merely provided the place and the date that the revelation was received and dictated:

REVELATION
Given to Joseph Smith, Nauvoo, July 12th, 1843.[2]

Orson Pratt's 1853 printing of the revelation in his Washington DC *The Seer* carried the preamble:

CELESTIAL MARRIAGE:
A Revelation on the Patriarchal Order of Matrimony, or Plurality of Wives. Given to Joseph Smith, the Seer, in Nauvoo, July 12th, 1843.

The term "Celestial Marriage" was almost universally synonymous with polygamy in Mormonism until 1890, after which it gradually came to refer exclusively to sealing.[3] Pratt makes no separate mention of sealing,

---

1. See Newell G. Bringhurst, "Section 132 of the Doctrine and Covenants: Its Complex Contents and Controversial Legacy," and Stephen C. Taysom, "A Uniform and Common Recollection: Joseph Smith's Legacy, Polygamy, and the Creation of Mormon Public Memory," 124.

2. See the Addendum. This heading matches the text added by Thomas Bullock to page 1 of the Kingsbury manuscript.

3. For examples of the former, see George A. Smith's interesting summary of Church principles in George A. Smith, May 7, 1874, *Journal of Discourses*, 17:60; also Joseph F. Smith in *Report of the Semi-Annual Conference of the Church of Jesus Christ of Latter-day Saints*, October 6, 1902, 87 (hereafter cited as *Conference Report*). For the latter, see William C. Parkinson, *Conference Report*,

and his use of "Patriarchal Order of Matrimony" is a reference to the Abrahamic context of the revelation.[4] That term also would be repurposed after the end of plural marriage, and would lose its contextual sense.

The 1875 *Star* imprint echoed Pratt's heading, and introduced the revelation simply as the following:

> Revelation on Celestial Marriage.

In both the 1876 Doctrine and Covenants and his 1878 edition of the Pearl of Great Price, Orson Pratt prefaced the revelation with this heading:

> Revelation on the Eternity of the Marriage Covenant, Including Plurality of Wives. Given Through Joseph, the Seer, in Nauvoo, Hancock County, Illinois, July 12th, 1843.

From these headings it is clear that for the first several decades of its existence, the revelation's purpose was understood to be both an introduction to and insurer of the practice of polygamy, and that polygamy is one and the same with "Celestial Marriage." However, Pratt's 1876 Doctrine and Covenants and 1878 Pearl of Great Price headings suggest a separate emphasis on sealing, with plurality as a secondary aspect of the revelation. This separation corresponded naturally with the Mormon marriage ritual practice from the early 1850s, when sealings were performed for both first marriages and plural unions.[5]

A major revision in format and liminal text for the Doctrine and Covenants appeared well after the death of plurality in Mormonism, beginning with the heading for the 1921 edition:

> REVELATION given through Joseph Smith the Prophet, at Nauvoo Illinois, recorded July 12, 1843, relating to the new and everlasting covenant, including the eternity of the marriage covenant, as also the plurality of wives.

April 6, 1917, 80; Charles W. Penrose, *Conference Report,* October 6, 1918, 16; Stephen L. Richards, *Conference Report,* April 6, 1937, 48. The usage was a source of tension over continuing rogue polygamists for Heber J. Grant. See Heber J. Grant, *Conference Report,* April 7, 1932, 121; and Matthew Bowman, *The Mormon People: The Making of an American Faith,* 161–63.

4. The *Seer*'s preamble appeared in broader circulation. For example, see S. N. Carvalho, *Incidents of Travel and Adventure in the Far West with Col. Fremont's Last Expedition Across the Rocky Mountains: Including Three Months' Residence in Utah, and a Perilous Trip Across the Great American Desert, to the Pacific,* 251–61.

5. The 1851 Council House was used for the purpose along with other buildings. See Lisle G. Brown, "'Temple Pro Tempore': The Salt Lake City Endowment House," 1–68.

Here, the "new and everlasting covenant" appears as an umbrella term that encompassed both sealing and polygamy, with the latter having a reduced status. This heading remained with the revelation until 1981 when the LDS Church produced comprehensive new editions of its English scriptures with new headings and annotations. Since the 1981 edition and the more recent 2013 edition show interesting and important heading changes compared to each other as well as the 1921 edition, I will place the most recent two texts in parallel:

1981	2013
Revelation given through Joseph Smith the Prophet, at Nauvoo, Illinois, recorded July 12, 1843, relating to the new and everlasting covenant, including the eternity of the marriage covenant, **as also plurality of wives. HC 5:501–507**. Although the revelation was recorded in 1843, it is evident **from the historical records that the doctrines and** principles involved in this revelation **had been** known by the Prophet **since** 1831.	Revelation given through Joseph Smith the Prophet, at Nauvoo, Illinois, recorded July 12, 1843, relating to the new and everlasting covenant, including the eternity of the marriage covenant **and the principle of plural marriage**. Although the revelation was recorded in 1843, evidence indicates that **some of the** principles involved in this revelation **were** known by the Prophet **as early as** 1831. **See Official Declaration 1**.

An important difference in the 2013 edition is the reference to Official Declaration 1, the 1890 Manifesto of President Wilford Woodruff that officially ended the public practice of polygamy. Another important difference is that it softens the dating of when "principles" surrounding polygamy were first "known by the Prophet." This is an acknowledgement of the existing historical record and the fraught question of when Joseph Smith became familiar with ideas in the revelation. Both headings give voice to the Church's current position on polygamy: it was a revealed system of marriage and its practice was divinely approved. As with most of the section headings in the 2013 editions, the reference to *History of the Church* was removed due to weaknesses in relation to new sources, such as the recent *Joseph Smith Papers*. In this case, the *History* added little in the way of explanation beyond the citation of a date. Because the various texts of the plural marriage revelation have shown little variation over its published or manuscript life and because that is the text most available to readers, I will use the current section 132 text in the discussion of the revelation with appropriate annotation.[6]

---

6. See the Addendum for an annotated diplomatic transcription of the Kingsbury manuscript. Variations in the 2013 text from the Kingsbury text are noted in this volume. In dealing with the text, I assume that Joseph Smith dictated the revelation. I think the evidence for this is strong and in my view virtually irrefutable. I'm aware of critics of the revelation who find evidence in the text that Joseph Smith was not its source—by virtue of what they see as contradiction with other scripture or Church literature.

The Ancient Roots of Polygamy

Like most of Joseph Smith's revelations found in the Doctrine and Covenants, section 132 is dialogic in nature—Joseph Smith poses (or relays) questions to God, and the revelation text communicates answers to those questions in the voice of Deity. In this manner, the revelation opens with a prologue explaining its origin:

1 Verily, thus saith the Lord unto you my servant Joseph, that inasmuch as you have inquired of my hand to know and understand wherein I, the Lord, justified my servants Abraham, Isaac, and Jacob, as also Moses, David and Solomon, my servants, as touching the principle and doctrine of their having many wives and concubines—

2 Behold, and lo, I am the Lord thy God, and will answer thee as touching this matter.[1]

3 Therefore, prepare thy heart to receive and obey the instructions which I am about to give unto you; for all those who have this law revealed unto them must obey the same.

4 For behold, I reveal unto you a new and an everlasting covenant; and if ye abide not that covenant, then are ye damned; for no one can reject this covenant and be permitted to enter into my glory.

5 For all who will have a blessing at my hands shall abide the law which was appointed for that blessing, and the conditions thereof, as were instituted from before the foundation of the world.

This preamble does at least three things. First, it frames the revelation as a response to Joseph's inquiries concerning the plural marriages of early Israelite patriarchs, prophets, and kings. Second, it links the "doctrine of

---

1. In the early parlance of Mormonism, this text qualifies as both *commandment* and *revelation*. Robin Scott Jensen, Robert J. Woodford, and Steven C. Harper, eds., *Revelations and Translations: Manuscript Revelation Books, Facsimile Edition*, xxv note 3. The words "Lord thy God" and "Lord your God" echo the declaration at Mount Sinai; taken together, they occur more frequently in this revelation than any other.

their having many wives and concubines" (v. 1) with "a new and an everlasting covenant" (v. 4). Third, verses 3 through 5 establish the revelation as a threshold of knowledge beyond which one cannot reverse course: "for all those who have this law revealed unto them must obey the same" (v. 3). Once this threshold is crossed, failure to accept and obey the covenant opens the door to damnation (a theme repeated in other parts of the revelation).[2] While the notion that increased knowledge implies increased jeopardy was nothing new (see Mosiah 3:11–12), this threat of possible damnation was especially directed toward Emma Smith.[3]

Evidence that the revelation was used as a convincing tactic on other occasions in Nauvoo is sparse, though other expressions about jeopardy may have been deployed. Smith is reported to have told prospective wives that their salvation and that of their family would be assured by accepting his proposal. Martha Brotherton, a young convert who came to Nauvoo with her family in 1842, found herself the object of a marriage proposal by Brigham Young. Smith's explanation of the legality of the proposal echoes portions of the plural marriage revelation, in particular verses 46 through 48 and verses 61 through 62. Brotherton was shocked by the situation and her faith was devastated. She wrote an account of the proposal for the St. Louis *American Bulletin*, where she suggests that romantic attraction was a part of the conversation—at least whether or not she felt attracted to Young.[4] Unfortunately, when a woman publicly disclosed such adventures, she could be labeled as a prostitute or otherwise slandered. The tactic worked to some degree among Church members who were ignorant of polygamy, but failed to draw attention away from Joseph Smith in the press.[5]

---

2. William Clayton interpreted verse 3 to mean that polygamy was necessary for exaltation and that "there can be no blessings for the human family only through a polygamist." William Clayton, letter to Madison M. Scott, November 11, 1871.

3. Richard S. Van Wagoner, *Mormon Polygamy: A History,* 39; Richard Lyman Bushman, *Joseph Smith: Rough Stone Rolling,* 463; Merina Smith, *Revelation, Resistance and Mormon Polygamy,* 84.

4. Martha H. Brotherton, "St. Louis, July 13th, A. D. 1842," 1.

5. Lyman Wight voiced support for such treatment as a legitimate response to a woman who complained about insulting behavior. Melvin C. Johnson, *Polygamy on the Pedernales: Lyman Wight's Mormon Villages in Antebellum Texas, 1845–1858,* 47–48. Women who rejected polygamy in Nauvoo and kept silent seemed to endure no penalty other than the shock to their understanding.

"Inasmuch as You have Inquired of My Hand"

Verse 1 has been the basis for parts of the heading descriptions in various (especially later) imprints of the revelation that tie it to Smith's early career, when his actions are often perceived as founded on closely-packed miraculous events. (For example, the 1981 heading states that "the doctrines and principles involved in this revelation had been known by the Prophet since 1831.") In Utah, stories were propagated that both Oliver Cowdery and Joseph Smith knew of the "principle"[6] as early as 1830 or 1831, with some believing that Cowdery had early on taken a plural wife without Smith's permission.[7]

It is natural to assume that the revelation may have been prompted by Smith's inquisitiveness during his revision of the Hebrew Bible, as other revelations and events during that time were prompted by questions had during this revision and other translation efforts. For example, according to Cowdery, the restoration of authority to baptize was prompted by Smith's translating of the Book of Mormon, and the sweeping vision of heaven in Doctrine and Covenants 76 occurred "while translating St.

---

6. This was a common, insider term for polygamy. For example, William Clayton learned from Smith that polygamy is the "most holy . . . principle." See Clayton's affidavit in the introduction to this volume. Fundamentalist Mormon polygamists are fond of the word. Three years before the affidavit, Clayton wrote that "Polygamy is a Celestial order, the most sacred and holy that was ever revealed from Heaven to man." Clayton, letter to Madison M. Scott, November 11, 1871.

7. These stories may have been founded on rumors surrounding Oliver Cowdery's behavior when the 1830 "Lamanite" missionaries left New York for Missouri. Before leaving New York, Cowdery was engaged to Elizabeth Whitmer, who played a founding role in the early Church. While in Ohio, Cowdery became enamored with another young woman, to whom he apparently proposed marriage. The breach of faith resulted in some discussion and discipline in May 1832. See The Conference Minutes and Record Book of Christ's Church of Latter Day Saints, 1838–1839, 1844, May 26, 1832. Van Wagoner, *Mormon Polygamy*, 13; Orson Pratt, June 23, 1878, *Journal of Discourses*, 20:29; Joseph F. Smith, "Celestial Marriage," *Ogden Herald*, May 21, 1886, 2. "They had a revelation that . . . Patriarchal Marriage . . . was right. . . . Joseph said, 'Oliver if you go into this thing it is not with my faith or consent.' . . . Oliver Cowdery took to wife Annie Lyman, cousin to Geo. A. Smith. From that time he went into darkness and lost the spirit." Comments by Brigham Young, July 26, 1872, in Charles Lowell Walker journals, 1854–1899, 8:118. D. Michael Quinn, *The Mormon Hierarchy: Origins of Power*, 17. Scott G. Kenney, ed., *Wilford Woodruff's Journal, 1833–1898 Typescript*, 5:84.

John's Gospel."[8] Reminiscent reports, however, suggest that it was Hyrum who asked for clarification on the Old Testament Patriarchs and that verse 1 acknowledges this more recent conversation—not an early question of Joseph Smith during his revision of the Bible a decade earlier.

While the text of the revelation may not have been prompted by Joseph Smith's earlier efforts to revise the Bible, he had made claims to Hyrum and others that revelation dictated his course in polygamy. Sarah Kimball reported that when Smith proposed marriage to her early in 1842 (a proposal she rejected) he claimed that God had given two revelations on polygamy. The first one he characterized as given "many years before as a privilege with blessings" but the new revelation in Nauvoo was a commandment.[9] Given the volatility of public knowledge of the practice, Smith may have had safety concerns that prevented earlier revelations on it from being written down. This was not an unusual restriction. For example, the endowment ceremonies, according to Heber C. Kimball, were "not to be written" (though they would later be transcribed in Utah).[10] Similarly, Joseph Smith's revelation on war (now section 87) was concealed during his lifetime and his shared vision of April 3, 1836 (now Doctrine and Covenants 110), remained unmentioned until August 1852 and unpublished until November 1852. Perhaps Smith's much earlier relationship with Fanny Alger depended on this "first" revelation rather than on an early version of July 12, 1843, revelation. William Clayton's 1874 affidavit claims that Smith had known the content of the revelation, if not the precise and full text, for some time. There is little doubt that Smith had been thinking about the parameters of such a text, and the language of the revelation appears in several contexts prior to July 12, 1843. While any previous and unrecorded revelation on the topic may have had general connections to the 1843 revelation, a close examination of the text reveals it to be a compilation of various thematic elements that were modified and brought together in a July dictation that was mainly relevant to 1843.[11]

---

8. The quotation appears in the heading of the current edition of Doctrine and Covenants 76. On Cowdery, see Oliver Cowdery, "Dear Brother," 14–16.

9. Sarah Kimball, "Auto-Biography," 51.

10. Heber C. Kimball, Letter to Parley P. Pratt, June 17, 1842.

11. On Alger's puzzling place in the polygamy panorama, see B. Carmon Hardy, *Doing the Works of Abraham, Mormon Polygamy: Its Origin, Practice, and Demise*, 42–44; Bushman, *Rough Stone Rolling*, 323–27; Don Bradley, "Mormon Polygamy Before Nauvoo? The Relationship of Joseph Smith and Fanny Alger," 14–58; Brian C. Hales, *Joseph Smith's Polygamy*, 2:85–152.

As mentioned earlier, the question often assigned to Joseph Smith in verse 1 seems to have originated with Hyrum Smith. Unaware of his brother's own involvement, Hyrum was previously a leader in the effort to detect and expose polygamy in Nauvoo up to May 1843. It was during this time that he may have been converted to the idea of plural marriage by Brigham Young, who had (according to Young) disclosed the news to Hyrum of Joseph's own polygamous marriages. In a reminiscent account, Mercy Fielding Thompson tells of a revelation Joseph reported to his brother on proxy sealing of marriages. Joseph apparently informed Hyrum that polygamy meant he could be sealed to both his deceased wife, Jerusha Barden, and his living wife, Mary Fielding.[12] The prospect of preserving both unions in the hereafter was a side of polygamy Hyrum had not considered, and it reflects the developing nature of sealing concepts as they connected to baptism for the dead, which was the initial foray into a theology of proxy sacraments.[13] In a marriage for mortal life only, Mercy Fielding (Mary Fielding's sister and a widow of Joseph Smith's clerk and early polygamist Robert Thompson) became, with her sister Mary, Hyrum's wife.[14] Mercy

---

12. Unfortunately, the only report of Young informing Hyrum Smith comes twenty-three years after the fact, in which Young added comments that placed Hyrum in a somewhat unflattering light, perhaps still reflecting Young's anxiety over the perceived legitimacy of his own position. Elden J. Watson, ed., *Brigham Young Addresses: A Chronological Compilation of Known Addresses of the Prophet Brigham Young*, 5:52–54. Hyrum's own report suggests that his brother introduced him to the idea. Hyrum, Jerusha, and Mary were sealed in May 1843 after Joseph informed Hyrum of a new revelation that made such proxy sealings possible. Carol Cornwall Madsen, ed., *In Their Own Words: Women and the Story of Nauvoo*, 194–95. It seems unlikely that this April or May revelation claimed by Mercy was the text of the plural marriage revelation, and it is unclear whether the revelation Mercy mentions was written. In her undated account, Mercy mentions the Presiding Bishop of the Church. In 1843 no presiding bishop was in place. She may have meant future presiding bishop Newel K. Whitney, suggesting a collation of various memories. On Hyrum's story, see James Allred's statement in Chapter 1 and Hyrum's unpublished remarks at the April 8, 1844, Church conference. Joseph Smith began actively preaching about the virtues of sealing in May 1843, and this continued through the fall.

13. Bushman, *Rough Stone Rolling*, 495–96; Linda King Newell and Valeen Tippetts Avery, *Mormon Enigma: Emma Hale Smith*, 141–42. John G. Turner, *Brigham Young: Pioneer Prophet*, 97–98.

14. Mercy was unaware of husband Robert's participation in polygamy. She was apparently sealed to him by proxy in May 1843. Mercy stated that Robert's

was taken into the Smith home, where for the remaining year of Hyrum's life she lived in relative security and was treated with kindness.

Despite its 1843 purpose and construction, the plural marriage revelation contained ideas that were circulating years before its dictation. For example, William W. Phelps wrote to his wife Sally in 1835:

> A new idea, Sally, if you and I continue faithful to the end, we are certain to be one in the Lord throughout eternity; this is one of the most glorious consolations we can have in the flesh.[15]

Phelps's letter hints at an early conceptual leakage of high priesthood sealing to familial bonds, though there was no corresponding liturgy in evidence.[16]

Other reports of earlier knowledge of eternal marital sealing were rarely contemporary and at times seem to conflate various later events or teachings. For example, in his posthumously published autobiography, Parley P. Pratt wrote that Smith taught him about sealing while the two were in the Washington, DC area in 1839:

> During these interviews he taught me many great and glorious principles concerning God and the heavenly order of eternity. It was at this time that I received from him the first idea of eternal family organization, and the eternal union of the sexes in those inexpressibly endearing relationships which none but the highly intellectual, the refined and pure in heart, know how to prize, and which are at the very foundation of everything worthy to be called happiness.

---

spirit appeared to Joseph Smith several times in the summer of 1843 requesting she be married "for time" to Hyrum. When Mercy was introduced to polygamy in July or August 1843, she rejected it until she was able to take and contemplate a copy of the July revelation. Mercy Fielding Thompson, *Autobiography*. 195.

15. W. W. Phelps, Letter to Sally Phelps, May 26, 1835. See also Samuel Brown, *In Heaven as It Is on Earth: Joseph Smith and the Early Mormon Conquest of Death*, 145–48, 214–17, 228–36.

16. The plural marriage revelation follows this idea in a strictly textual sense: it makes no mention of Elijah, and Phelps's remarks preceded the April 3, 1836, vision (Doctrine and Covenants 110) by a year. Regulation of sealing in the mid-twentieth century required that men assigned to perform sealing be high priests, and current practice assures that the same condition exists by default. Heber J. Grant, Letter to Lewis R. Anderson, March 5, 1935, and Devery S. Anderson, *The Development of LDS Temple Worship, 1846–2000: A Documentary History*, 255. Phelps claimed some special knowledge of the 1836 vision in 1851, reporting: "I was present when the keys were delivered to Joseph." Thomas Bullock, booklet (#10), February 2, 1851.

Till then I had learned to esteem kindred affections and sympathies as appertaining solely to this transitory state, as something from which the heart must be entirely weaned, in order to be fitted for its heavenly state.

It was Joseph Smith who taught me how to prize the endearing relationships of father and mother, husband and wife; of brother and sister, son and daughter.

It was from him that I learned that the wife of my bosom might be secured to me for time and all eternity; and that the refined sympathies and affections which endeared us to each other emanated from the fountain of divine eternal love. It was from him that I learned that we might cultivate these affections, and grow and increase in the same to all eternity; while the result of our endless union would be an offspring as numerous as the stars of heaven, or the sands of the sea shore.

It was from him that I learned the true dignity and destiny of a son of God, clothed with an eternal priesthood, as the patriarch and sovereign of his countless offspring. It was from him that I learned that the highest dignity of womanhood was, to stand as a queen and priestess to her husband, and to reign for ever and ever as the queen mother of her numerous and still increasing offspring.[17]

With some irony, Pratt's wife at the time of the Washington interviews, Mary Ann Frost Stearns Pratt, initially accepted sealing in 1843 but later rejected it and became estranged from her husband upon discovering in 1846 that he had married other wives without her knowledge. (A month later, Brigham Young would convince her to be sealed to Parley for time and to the deceased Joseph Smith for eternity by proxy.) It is possible that Smith introduced sealing to Pratt without the context of polygamy, perhaps knowing that Pratt might be repulsed by the latter—Pratt was apparently working against Smith regarding polygamy early in 1843[18]—however Pratt's inclusion of likely post-Nauvoo thought (such as the detailed nature of the heavenly family) points to his recital almost surely compressing a number of experiences and feelings over a considerable period.

---

17. Parley P. Pratt, *The Autobiography of Parley Parker Pratt*, 329–30.

18. Willard Richards, Letter to Brigham Young, July 18, 1843. Terryl L. Givens and Matthew J. Grow, *Parley P. Pratt: The Apostle Paul of Mormonism*, 202–10. Pratt's admission of a classically Puritan attitude is instructive regarding the way early Latter-day Saints who persevered from the New York period may have seen plurality and sealing.

Claiming that knowledge of polygamy came even earlier, Parley Pratt's brother, Orson Pratt, taught that Smith was quietly discussing polygamy as early as 1832:

> In the forepart of the year 1832, Joseph told individuals, then in the Church, that he had inquired of the Lord concerning the principle of plurality of wives, and he received for answer that the principle of taking more wives than one is a true principle, but the time had not yet come for it to be practiced. . . . The Lord has His own time to do all things pertaining to His purposes in the last dispensation; His own time for restoring all things that have been predicted by the ancient prophets.[19]

Whether or not Orson Pratt's claim is correct, Smith's vision of the enterprise of restoration was prominent in his preaching and his coreligionists were ready to believe that almost any biblical precedent was fair game to Mormonism.

"A New and an Everlasting Covenant"

Though he was oriented by a Protestant world, Joseph Smith did not feel bound by the scriptural interpretations of that tradition. Protestants frequently viewed Abraham, Isaac, and Jacob as men whose moral weakness or cultural tradition made them examples of the foibles of human nature. For example, in his 1830 edition of *A Theological Dictionary*, Charles Buck wrote that the Patriarchs' polygamy was a reflection of the

---

19. Orson Pratt, October 7, 1869, *Journal of Discourses*, 13:193. Pratt relates a story that may have circulated for thirty years. Given the way Cowdery's misstep followed him, it seems unlikely that such a conversation in 1832 broached anything like a specific suggestion. Even the broad suggestion that an Abram-Hagar union was God-approved let alone God-commanded may have bordered on scandalous. Phelps wrote to Brigham Young in 1861 that Joseph gave an 1831 revelation to the effect that the "Lamanites" would become "white" by virtue of the Mormon men taking Indian women as wives (a not unheard of idea at the time, outside of Mormonism). Phelps may have been exaggerating or misremembering for several reasons, and the structure of his remembered text may reflect this. See Hardy, *Works of Abraham*, 34–37 for Phelps's reconstruction of this revelation. Phelps's claim is supported in part by Ezra Booth, "Mormonism—Nos. VIII–IX," 1. On Booth's letters, see Dennis Rowley, "The Ezra Booth Letters," 135–41. Polygamy did not go beyond implication in this Missouri revelation. David J. Whittaker, "Mormons and Native Americans: A Historical and Bibliographical Introduction," 35. On Phelps, see Samuel M. Brown, "The Translator and the Ghostwriter: Joseph Smith and William Phelps," 26–62.

"hardness of their heart."[20] Instead, Smith's revelation rehabilitated the ancient Patriarchs, making them exemplars of not only righteous living but of meeting the necessary ritual requirements to achieve the fullest exaltation.[21] Thus, Abraham, Isaac, and Jacob in particular are depicted as having become "gods" (v. 37). Protestants often preached that Abraham's lie about Sarah was a fault, whereas Smith dictated a revelation absolving Abraham's character (Abr. 2:22–25). The Book of Abraham assigns the lie to God's commandment—not an unusual position in Nauvoo where community morals and church law might be ignored under special conditions. The plural marriage revelation marks Abraham's taking Hagar as divine command, not Sarah's response to a childless marriage. John Cook Bennett's claims that Joseph Smith argued for a divine command ethic isn't at odds with the text of the revelation, or for that matter, the Book of Mormon itself.[22]

Based on this understanding of the Patriarchs being exemplars of righteous obedience to law, verse 5 (compare vv. 11, 28) is interesting for its allusion to Smith's April 2, 1843, declaration found in Doctrine and Covenants 130:20–21: "There is a law irrevocably decreed in heaven before the foundations of this world, upon which all blessings are predicated— And when we obtain any blessing from God, it is by obedience to that law upon which it is predicated." Bringing this all together, the implication could be easily drawn that in order to be exalted in God's presence one must fulfill all of the sacraments including, in this case, participation in polygamy. Smith's sermon of June 11, 1843, was one of the more important instances where he considered the necessity of performance completeness, and it formed a vital link in the logic of proxy ordinances like baptism for the dead. Orson Pratt canonized the idea by adding one of Smith's 1842 open letters to the Saints to the Doctrine and Covenants (section 128).[23]

The revelation's connecting the "new and an everlasting covenant" of marital sealing with the practice of plural marriage, and Joseph Smith's tendency to present them together, suggest a related question: Were there

---

20. B. Carmon Hardy, *Solemn Covenant: The Mormon Polygamous Passage*, 40. Wilson H. Kimnach, ed., *Sermons and Discourses, 1743–1758*, 25:444, 453.

21. Charles Buck, *A Theological Dictionary Containing Definitions of All Religious Terms*, s.v. polygamy.

22. See the discussion of verses 28 through 45 in Chapter 6. Van Wagoner, *Mormon Polygamy*, 29–32.

23. For reports of the sermon, see William V. Smith et al., "The Parallel Joseph," June 11, 1843.

any non-polygamous Nauvoo couples simultaneously civilly and eternally married while Smith was still alive? Some Church members who were already civilly united and heard of sealing through the Nauvoo grapevine apparently requested (and were granted) sealing without being introduced to polygamy.[24] However, during that time there does not seem to be any officially-recorded, simultaneous sealing and marriage that did not involve polygamy. This should be expected though, as Smith, either himself or through an intermediary, seems to have rarely broached sealing with a person outside the context of polygamy.[25]

After Smith's death and before the trek west, there were a small number of simultaneous sealings and marriages not involving plurality. Brigham Young married and sealed Truman Leonard to Orlensia White, as well as his own son, William Goodall Young, to Adelia Clark on January 1, 1846. William Clayton recorded the latter couple's ceremony, which bears similarity to verse 19 of the plural marriage revelation. A more typical example of non-plural sealing was Charles Lambert and Mary Alice Cannon, who were civilly married by John Taylor in November 1844 but not sealed until 1846 in the Nauvoo temple (again by Taylor).[26] A much less typical example is that of Joseph C. Kingsbury, who was married and sealed to Caroline Dorcas by Heber C. Kimball on March 4, 1845. Kingsbury was a widower but was previously engaged in a faux public marriage with Sarah Ann Whitney, a plural wife of Joseph Smith.[27]

---

24. Hales, *Joseph Smith's Polygamy*, 2:173.

25. Sealing may have been a (silent) subtext for Smith's sermon on hearing of the death of perennial missionary Lorenzo Dow Barnes. Barnes fell in love with Philadelphia convert Susan Conrad; when Barnes died in late 1842, Smith seemed to suggest the possibility of sealing. See William V. Smith, "A Documentary Note on a Letter to Joseph Smith. Romance, Death, and Polygamy: The Life and Times of Susan Hough Conrad and Lorenzo Dow Barnes." Smith, *Every Word Seasoned with Grace*, ch. 3; Andrew H. Hedges, Alex D. Smith, and Richard Lloyd Anderson, eds., *Journals, Volume 2: December 1841–April 1843*, 361.

26. On the Young and Clark sealing, see Heber C. Kimball journal entries in George D. Smith, *An Intimate Chronicle: The Journals of William Clayton*, 246; and Lisle G. Brown, ed., *Nauvoo Sealings Adoptions and Anointings*, 355. On the Lambert and Cannon marriage and sealing, see Charles Lambert, Autobiography. On sealing among those already legally married in Nauvoo, see Gary James Bergera, "The Earliest Sealings for Civilly Married Couples Living and Dead," 49–74.

27. Kingsbury's sham marriage was meant to protect Joseph Smith from suspicion—perhaps in case of pregnancy—by participating in a public marriage

"If Ye Abide not that Covenant, then Are Ye Damned"

The meaning of the word "law" in this particular revelation was historically interpreted as referring to authorized polygamy. This is important in understanding other portions of the revelation. The law is connected with sealing, but its main thrust centered on a threshold of knowledge. While polygamy, sealing, and exaltation were implicitly linked in the revelation, it was only "those who have this law revealed unto them" (v. 3) who had passed that threshold of knowledge. Those who had such knowledge revealed to them but failed to "abide . . . that covenant" would be "damned" (v. 4).

This threat of damnation for failure to live the law that one had knowledge of was inconsistent in practice. While William Clayton anguished over the ambivalence of his second wife, Margaret, his first wife, Ruth, did not seem to complain (at least by Clayton's record), even though the difficult emotions that so often surrounded polygamy were no doubt present in Ruth. Conversations between Clayton and Joseph Smith revealed no salvific threat over revoking the marriage (covenant) with Margaret. A single rule is difficult to apply perhaps. On the other hand, if things were not properly done, either against Smith's rulings about who took whom in marriage, how many, how often (see v. 44), or other deeper matters, Smith said that there could be extreme penalties, including death. In his June 23, 1843, journal, a few weeks before the revelation, Clayton wrote:

> [Joseph] said [Robert B.] Thompson professed great friendship for him but he gave way to temptation & he had to die. Also bro [Vinson] Knight he gave him one [wife] but he went to loose conduct and he could not save him. Also [Brigham Young] had transgressed his covenant & he pled with the Lord to spare him this end & he did so, other wise he would have died.[28]

The statements about death may play into the seriousness of the "destroyed" clauses later in the revelation (vv. 26, 41, 52, 54, 63–64). However, *destruction* is more explicitly presented there as the denial of the highest joy in heaven or being "delivered unto the buffetings of Satan" (v. 26), a phrase that appears in several of Smith's revelations and borrows from 2 Corinthians 12:7.[29]

---

to one of Joseph Smith's wives, Sarah Ann Whitney, on April 29, 1843. Todd M. Compton, *In Sacred Loneliness: The Plural Wives of Joseph Smith,* 351.

28. Robert Fillerup, ed., "William Clayton's Nauvoo Diaries and Personal Writings," June 23, 1843.

29. It also appears in a number of early Mormon ecclesiastical court minutes, and it echoes the events of the Jewish and Roman trials of Jesus, as measured by

The idea of a death penalty, however, certainly fits the Old Testament context of polygamy, which associated sexual misconduct (adultery with a married woman, rape, consensual loss of virginity by a betrothed woman, etc.) with death. Smith apparently entrusted Robert B. Thompson with the secrets of polygamy some time before Thompson died in August 1841. According to Clayton, Smith believed that Thompson's death was a result of his giving "way to temptation."

The context suggests that Thompson went out on his own in taking a wife or perhaps was expressing a sexual freedom not authorized or sanctioned by Smith.[30] Clayton reported Smith saying that, "the way he knew in whom to confide, God told him in whom he might place confidence."[31]

Clayton's interview with Smith was in fact a personal caution about proper boundaries:

> J[oseph] took me and conversed considerable concerning some delicate matters. said [Emma] wanted to lay a snare for me. He told me last night of this and said he had felt troubled. He said [Emma] had treated him coldly & badly since I came and he knew she was disposed to be revenged on him for some things she thought that if he would indulge himself she would too.[32]

The underground Nauvoo process of marrying and giving in marriage contained generous sprinklings of revelation reports confirming, denying, or introducing the practice to men and women, but the complete boundaries of engagement were nowhere to be found. Instead, participants seemed to feel their way through a forest of oral or aural perception and cultural interpretation. Consistency was difficult to achieve when personalities interfaced with secrecy and a crucial lack of common knowledge.

---

an 1829 revelation to Smith (Doctrine and Covenants 19).

30. This was not an unknown problem even after polygamy became public knowledge. The rules were not always clear. See the case of Gustavus Hills discussed in Chapter 9, note 11. The cause of Thompson's death was linked to malaria. Knight was singled out in Smith's January 1841 revelation as the first "presiding" bishop of the Church (Doctrine and Covenants 124:141). His death meant that the office was not filled until after the exodus of the Mormons from Nauvoo. After Smith, the mystique of a death penalty is not in evidence when participants overstepped Brigham Young's boundaries. Young might have required a penitent heart for such things among his closest associates, but none of them seemed to be in danger of death over it. See the discussion of verse 37 in Chapter 6.

31. Fillerup, "William Clayton's Nauvoo Diaries," May 16, 1843.

32. Ibid., June 23, 1843.

The Permission to Seal

The LDS Church today frequently advertises the Quorum of the Twelve Apostles as being the collective custodians of the sealing authority between the passing of a Church President and the sustaining and ordination of his successor. Although this has been a part of the succession tradition since the crisis following the death of Joseph Smith, there is nothing in the textual history of restored priesthood authority that establishes this. Rather, that narrative was constructed out of Smith's teachings and the conferral of temple rites before his death.[1] The Nauvoo apostles, or most of them, stood at the center of four converging streams that finally placed them at the pinnacle of Nauvoo leadership: polygamy, temple sacraments,[2] ecclesial stature,

---

1. For modern examples of this constructed narrative, see Neal A. Maxwell, "My Servant Joseph," 37–39; and Bruce R. McConkie, "The Keys of the Kingdom," 21–22. The 1845 Nauvoo apostles temporarily wrote themselves into the high priesthood narrative, proclaiming "the great and eternal High Priesthood, after the Order of His Son, even the Apostleship, has been restored.... This High Priesthood, or Apostleship, holds the keys of the kingdom of God." James R. Clark, ed., *Messages of the First Presidency of the Church of Jesus Christ of Latter-day Saints*, 1:253–54.

2. The term "ordinance" was preferred in Mormonism, following the Protestant tradition that associated "sacrament" with Catholic theology, particularly the idea that sacraments had salvific powers independent of the faith or penitence. Mormonism partook of Protestant sacramental ethics, but those ethics were more difficult when placed in the context of Mormon legal administrator theology. For Protestants generally, it is the faith of the individual that matters and much less so the authoritative genealogy of sacramental administrators or even the sacraments themselves. See Joseph Smith's preaching of January 17, 1843, January 22, 1843, January 29, 1843, July 23, 1843, in William V. Smith et al., "The Parallel Joseph." These sermons emphasize Smith's kingdom of God thinking in contrast to one of his well-known critics, Alexander Campbell. Doctrine and Covenants 20:60 adds complexity here since it subscribes to a moral theory where ordinances (ordination in this case) are valid only when the administrator has "the power of the Holy Ghost."

and the Council of Fifty.[3] The first carried the strongest motivation to continue Joseph Smith's plan, priesthood, and keys; and the apostles as a group, even while coming to grips with Joseph Smith's death, felt confident that the work of Mormonism would roll on. As Orson Hyde said in a Boston sermon on the eve of returning to Nauvoo after hearing of the assassination of the Smith brothers, "Their is a secret Joy in the hearts of the Priest and many people that the Prophet and Patriarch is murdered and some manifest their joy openly. It is always a dark time Just before day. It is a dark time now but it will soon be light."[4]

Central to the motivation tying polygamy to the apostles' claim of succession was the revelation's decree that polygamous unions were essential to a restoration of the fullness of the gospel and that those unions could only be performed by those with divine authorization:

> 6 And as pertaining to the new and everlasting covenant, it was instituted for the fulness of my glory; and he that receiveth a fulness thereof must and shall abide the law, or he shall be damned, saith the Lord God.
>
> 7 And verily I say unto you, that the conditions of this law are these: All covenants, contracts, bonds, obligations, oaths, vows, performances, connections, associations, or expectations, that are not made and entered into and sealed by the Holy Spirit of promise, of him who is anointed, both as well for time and for all eternity, and that too most holy, by revelation and commandment through the medium of mine anointed, whom I have appointed on the earth to hold this power (and I have appointed unto my servant Joseph to hold this power in the last days, and there is never but one on the earth at a time on whom this power and the keys of this priesthood are conferred), are of no efficacy, virtue, or force in and after the resurrection from the dead; for all contracts that are not made unto this end have an end when men are dead.
>
> 8 Behold, mine house is a house of order, saith the Lord God, and not a house of confusion.

A year later, section 42 founded valid ordination in public knowledge of hierarchy approval. See Michael Hubbard MacKay, Gerrit J. Dirkmaat, Grand Underwood, Robert J. Woodford, and William G. Hartley, eds., *Documents, Vol. 1: July 1828–June 1831*, 245; and Robin Scott Jensen, Robert J. Woodford, and Steven C. Harper, eds., *Revelations and Translations: Manuscript Revelation Books, Facsimile Edition*, 95.

3. See William V. Smith, "Early Mormon Priesthood Revelations: Text, Impact, and Evolution," 39–43; Andrew F. Ehat, "Joseph Smith's Introduction of Temple Ordinances and the 1844 Mormon Succession Question."

4. Orson Hyde, sermon, July 18, 1844, in Scott G. Kenney, *Wilford Woodruff's Journal, 1833–1898 Typescript*, 2:426. See also Brigham Young's remarks recorded in Woodruff's journal the same day.

9 Will I accept of an offering, saith the Lord, that is not made in my name?

10 Or will I receive at your hands that which I have not appointed?

11 And will I appoint unto you, saith the Lord, except it be by law, even as I and my Father ordained unto you, before the world was?

12 I am the Lord thy God; and I give unto you this commandment—that no man shall come unto the Father but by me or by my word, which is my law, saith the Lord.

13 And everything that is in the world, whether it be ordained of men, by thrones, or principalities, or powers, or things of name, whatsoever they may be, that are not by me or by my word, saith the Lord, shall be thrown down, and shall not remain after men are dead, neither in nor after the resurrection, saith the Lord your God.

14 For whatsoever things remain are by me; and whatsoever things are not by me shall be shaken and destroyed.

15 Therefore, if a man marry him a wife in the world, and he marry her not by me nor by my word, and he covenant with her so long as he is in the world and she with him, their covenant and marriage are not of force when they are dead, and when they are out of the world; therefore, they are not bound by any law when they are out of the world.

This is the newly defined "new and everlasting covenant," a divine system of oaths, obligations, and ordinances that supersedes any earthly institutions and enables participants to partake in the "fullness of [God's] glory." It builds on the notion of kingdom expansion and bridges its temporal and eternal duality (that is, an expansion of one's kingdom in life and afterlife).

"The Keys of this Priesthood"

Verse 7 is important in understanding (in part) the modern use of the term "priesthood keys" in Mormonism. It establishes Joseph Smith as the one "to hold this power in the last days" and mandates that "there is never but one on the earth at a time on whom this power and the keys of this priesthood are conferred." Thus, it was a challenge for anyone who hoped to succeed Smith, as there is no instruction in the revelation on how and to whom they were to be given after the death of Joseph (though the unpublished—at that point—Doctrine and Covenants sections 110 and 112 may have been understood as giving the apostles a legitimate place in the line of ecclesial succession). Smith's revelations and acts during his life indicate several different ideas regarding a successor. By the Nauvoo period he appears to have settled on keeping it in the family with one or the other of his brothers. (William was probably not his first choice.) Unfortunately, all the brothers but William died before they could be considered. William did attempt to exercise the familial prejudice—partly through the patriarchal office he inherited—but this was too late to be very effective.[5]

The language of the revelation highlights the evolving and refining narrative within Mormonism regarding authority and its fluctuating terminology. The phrase "keys of this priesthood" is easily misunderstood in this context. The revelation places high value on what is essentially the office of chief temple priest, the one and only hierarch who could authorize sealing and polygamy—an office that is distinct from, or at least not entirely synonymous with, the ecclesial office of the President of the Church. Smith is designated as being God's "anointed" (vv. 7, 18–19), but that is used here metaphorically rather than liturgically, positioning him as priest of both temple and Church. Priesthood was a versatile word and concept throughout Smith's tenure. In the plural marriage revelation, Smith deploys "priesthood" as the act of sealing (another evolving term and concept, which in this case is used to denote an eternal relationship between persons). The particular act of sealing is *a* priesthood in Smith's parlance, a kind of speech common to his preaching and earlier revelations. Synonyms for priesthood in this sense could be sacrament, ordinance, or ministry.[6]

Just as "priesthood" does not have a fixed meaning, the "keys" of priesthood (or more often, "keys of the kingdom") went through considerable and wide-ranging changes and bifurcations of meaning during Smith's lifetime. In the beginning, the phrase "keys of the kingdom" was strongly linked with the notion of a *seer*, someone who had the ability to both see into heaven and observe the otherwise invisible happenings around us.[7] The narrative of keys

---

5. See Christine Elyse Blythe, "William Smith's Patriarchal Blessings and Contested Authority in the Post-Martyrdom Church," 60–95; Robert Fillerup, ed., "William Clayton's Nauvoo Diaries and Personal Writings," July 12, 1844, August 15, 1844; Irene M. Bates, "William Smith, 1811–93: Problematic Patriarch," 20–2; and E. Gary Smith, "The Patriarchal Crisis of 1845," 24–36. For William Smith's criticism of Young and his allied apostles, see William Smith, "A Proclamation," 1.

6. For example, Doctrine and Covenants 124:132 calls the deceased Seymour Brunson's position as a high councilor a "priesthood." In the first few years of Church life, "priesthood" and "lesser priesthood" were used as a term for what today is considered an office: priest in the Aaronic Priesthood. See Smith, "Early Mormon Priesthood Revelations," 12–13.

7. On the earliest meanings, see, for example, the narration of Edward Partridge's February 1833 sermon on Joseph Smith's powers reported in Salmon Sherwood, "The Mormons," 1. On later meanings, see Smith, "Early Mormon Priesthood Revelations," 17.

later paralleled that of the changing narrative of salvation in Mormonism. After early twentieth-century Mormon polygamy ran aground in the Reed Smoot senate hearings,[8] an important story began to surface to the effect that the Church president now lacked authority to enact new plural marriages. The loss of such power would mean that the Church had somehow been deprived of a "priesthood" in Joseph Smith's terms. The plural marriage revelation makes this level of separation of sealing and plurality unlikely, even impossible, given other statements to the effect that the current Church president holds the same authority that Joseph Smith received.[9]

By the Nauvoo period, "keys" referred to the authority to direct Church entities, secret knowledge, and the right to direct the sacred rite of sealing.[10] The notion of keys in modern Mormon discourse defies a consistent, single, historical meaning. Ecclesiastically, it now signifies (usually limited) executive authority over a specified fraction of those acting in a lower level of the Church organizational chart and exercised especially in terms of sacramental functions. Thus, certain keys authorize a priest to bless the bread and water of the LDS sacrament, and other keys authorize a deacon to administer them. In some twentieth-century Church literature, ecclesial keys were tied to the notion of "quorum," based on Smith's teachings that divine revelation respected mortal priesthood office, such that someone lower on the organizational chart would not receive direction for a superior.[11] Since the word has become vested with a kind of

---

8. LDS Apostle Reed Smoot was elected to the U.S. Senate for Utah on January 20, 1903. Senate hearings went on for several years on whether Smoot should be seated, partly driven by public suspicion that the Church still secretly practiced polygamy. Kathleen Flake, *The Politics of American Religious Identity: The Seating of Senator Reed Smoot, Mormon Apostle*. Anthon H. Lund diary, March 21, 1903, in John P. Hatch, ed., *Danish Apostle: The Diaries of Anthon H. Lund, 1890–1921*, 226–27.

9. See Joseph F. Smith, *Report of the Semi-Annual Conference of the Church of Jesus Christ of Latter-day Saints*, April 1911, 9 (hereafter cited as *Conference Report*). Moreover, Church presidents or their agents had approved plural marriages for two decades after 1890. The lack of authority served the public face of the Church in the difficult politics of the first decade of the twentieth century. For more on this separation, Smoot, and the revelation's interpretive evolution, see the Chapter 5 and the Epilogue.

10. See the discussion of verses 46 through 48 in Chapter 7.

11. Smith learned the lesson of leadership chaos early on. See MacKay et al., *Documents*, 1:183–86; Bushman, *Joseph Smith: Rough Stone Rolling*, 120–21; and Joseph Smith's October 5, 1840, and January 21, 1844, sermons in Smith et al., "The Parallel Joseph." On the twentieth-century relationship of keys and

divine duality, the situation is more complex than a simple business top-down turf diagram, and it is not coextensive with leadership charts, given that women provide direction to Church organizations but are not seen (at present) as vendors or receivers of keys.

"Sealed by the Holy Spirit of Promise"

The term "sealing" has also gone through a fluctuation, evolution, and refinement of meaning in Mormonism. When the Church made its blockbuster public announcement of polygamy in 1852, it included the first public reference to Joseph Smith's April 3, 1836, visitation of Elijah in the Kirtland temple—when, according to Orson Pratt, "the keys of sealing, to bind the hearts of the fathers to the children, and the children to the fathers" were restored. The full April 3 vision itself (which would be first published three months later in November 1852) makes no explicit reference to sealing and only links Elijah with "turn[ing] the hearts of the fathers to the children, and the children to the fathers" (D&C 110:15). This would be more congruent with the Bible, in which it is the apostle Peter to whom the "keys of the kingdom" are given so that "whatsoever [he] shalt bind on earth shall be bound in heaven" (Matt. 16:19). Given the continued emphasis in Mormonism of Elijah's role in restoring the sealing keys, it is somewhat remarkable that the plural marriage revelation makes no mention of that figure.[12] Instead, the central personality in the revelation is Abraham. This is reflected in Orson Pratt's public announcement of polygamy, which mentions Elijah in a single sentence but spends multiple paragraphs discussing Abraham—the patriarch who symbolizes what I call the high priesthood cycle.

Following the death of Smith, Brigham Young and the apostles believed that they were the ones given temple authority—not just as dispensers of endowments and overseers of baptisms for the dead, but also (eventually) with Young as the singular holder of the power to determine

---

quorums, see, for example, the *General Handbook of Instructions 24* (1989), 3-2; and *1991 Supplement to the 1989 General Handbook of Instructions*, 4.

12. While the plural marriage revelation does not reference Elijah or the usual Malachi verses, shortly after the Bennett scandal and exposé, the Church's *Times and Seasons* press published a pamphlet under a pseudonym (possibly Smith himself or his secretary Willard Richards) that connected polygamy with Elijah and the turning of the hearts of the fathers. Lawrence Foster, *Religion and Sexuality: The Shakers, the Mormons, and the Oneida Community*, 174–77.

sealing. Young did not come to this understanding of being the single person with sealing authority in a formal way through the high priesthood tradition. This claim or realization came as a consequence from the post-1840 rise of the apostles among Joseph Smith's trusted insiders and the simultaneous deaths of Smith and his immediate anointed successor: his brother Hyrum. Young's account of his reaction to the assassination of the Smith brothers should be read in terms of this sealing authority and, more broadly, the endowment. A few days after the news of the death of Joseph and Hyrum Smith came to Young, Wilford Woodruff reported that, "Elder B Young arose and Said he felt disposed to add his testimony. . . . When God sends a man to do a work all the devils in hell cannot kill him untill he gets through his work. So with Joseph. He prepared all things [and] gave the keys to men on the earth."[13] Young understood ecclesial office as a tool and not as an end in itself, and his later investment in the theology of apostolic office was a very overt nod to the practicalities of succession.[14] For fellow apostle Heber Kimball, all Smith's official acts were founded in an ordination as an apostle by angelic visitors. However, twentieth-century narratives discounted Smith as an office holder prior to the April 6, 1830, founding of the Church. These narratives seem partly based on Joseph F. Smith's interpretations of Doctrine and Covenants 107 and a vacuum of early textual evidence on the nature of Joseph Smith and Oliver Cowdery's encounter with the angels, Peter, James, and John. Doctrine and Covenants 27 mentions Smith being ordained an apostle by the angels, but the words "ordain" and "apostle" in early Mormonism are difficult to map onto their later evolved meanings. Complicating this reading is the question of when section 27 was written down in its present form (1835).[15]

---

13. Wilford Woodruff journal, July 18, 1844, in Kenney, ed., *Wilford Woodruff's Journal*, 2:428. See also "History of Brigham Young," 1.

14. See Young's remarks at the August 1852 Church conference that announced polygamy as a public doctrine of Mormonism reported in "A Special Conference of the Elders of the Church of Jesus Christ of Latter-Day Saints," 25.

15. See Heber C. Kimball's remarks at the 1852 conference, who reviewed the historical record without any reference to Smith as President of the High Priesthood (ibid., 1). On section 27, see MacKay et al., *Documents*, 1:245–56. Seventy years later, discussions were still at play over meanings. Anthon H. Lund diary, December 31, 1902, in Hatch, ed., *Danish Apostle*, 216. Doctrine and Covenants 21 also calls Smith "a seer, a translator, a prophet, an apostle of Jesus Christ, an elder of the church through the will of God the Father," echoing Paul in 1 Corinthians 1:1–2.

The answers to the questions of succession after the death of Smith were, however, far from clear, and several themes in the Kirtland and Nauvoo narrative of Church leadership were somewhat problematic for Young and the apostles. In Kirtland, an April 1835 revelation (D&C 107) characterized the top leadership as "three presiding high priests." After Smith's death, the apostles worked in various ways to reduce the value of high priesthood language.[16] Themes connected to this section of the plural marriage revelation include the statement that "there is never but one on the earth at a time on whom this [sealing] power and the keys of this priesthood are conferred" (D&C 132:7). While the singular limitation seems to be made clear here, two years earlier (January 1841) Smith had delivered a revelation that seemed to contradict this: "First, I give unto you Hyrum Smith to be a patriarch unto you, to hold the sealing blessings of my church, even the Holy Spirit of promise, whereby ye are sealed up unto the day of redemption, that ye may not fall notwithstanding the hour of temptation that may come upon you" (D&C 124:14).[17] The difference between the 1843 plural marriage revelation and Hyrum Smith's 1841 designation as Patriarch lies in the heritage and cycle of the high priesthood.

When high priests were ordained in 1831, a part of their collective assignment was "sealing up to eternal life."[18] Among Protestants at this time, "eternal life" took meaning from its numerous usages in the New Testament and was viewed ultimately as a description of heaven. Hence, sealing to eternal life played into the vigorous religious debates over salvation assurance. To be sealed to eternal life was to have one's own salvation guaranteed to some degree. With the establishment of a Church patriarch

---

16. See Smith, "Early Mormon Priesthood Revelations."

17. This sealing is markedly different from the July revelation, in which sealing does not keep one from transgression and instead merely guarantees final reward. When Parley and Mary Ann (Frost) Pratt came to accept polygamy, Joseph Smith was away from Nauvoo. Hyrum sealed the couple in June 1843. When Smith returned, he declared the act illegal, a reflection of the idea in the plural marriage revelation and its relation to the January 1841 revelation (D&C 124). Hyrum evidently received his brother's permission for Pratt's sealing to plural wife Elizabeth Brotherton in the next month and read the July 12 plural marriage revelation at the sealing. On Pratt's marriage, see Elizabeth Brotherton, "Autobiography of Elizabeth B. Pratt," 94–95.

18. For example, see Doctrine and Covenants 68:12. While this revelation was modified significantly prior to its 1835 printing, verse 12 was an early (November 1831) text. See Jensen et al., *Manuscript Revelation Books, Facsimile Edition*, 199–201; MacKay et al., *Documents*, 1:98–101.

in 1834 as a division of the high priesthood, sealing now found its home in the new office. Hyrum Smith's 1841 patriarchal office—following the death of his father and previous Church patriarch, Joseph Smith Sr.—is merely a restatement of patriarchal praxis in Mormonism. Sealing to eternal life was (and is) common language in patriarchal blessings.[19] The sealing discussed in the plural marriage revelation, however, was something different.

Without context, Joseph Smith's various revelations over the years brought some confusion after his death. The acontextual fusion of meanings in tradition and text began with William Smith's attempt to claim the Church presidency from the other apostles in 1845,[20] to John Taylor's possible authorization of some Church patriarchs to seal couples, continuing with Joseph F. Smith's twentieth-century ideas about succession in the presidency of the Church and the relative position of the patriarch and other Church leaders. For example, Joseph F. Smith had his half-brother and Church patriarch, John Smith, set him apart as Church president. Smith also proposed that the patriarch be sustained in the conference before all the other authorities, referencing Doctrine and Covenants 124:124. The

---

19. Joseph Smith Sr. began using "sealing" language specifically from the time of his earliest blessings. For example, he used this word in his patriarchal blessing of his daughter Lucy, given December 9, 1834. (From the beginning, patriarchal blessings were written down and kept in Church records.) Not every blessing carried the imprimatur of sealing to eternal life, and many did so in a pessimistic fashion. Others, like Lucy Mack Smith's, had no faithfulness clause implied. See H. Michael Marquardt, *Early Patriarchal Blessings of the Church of Jesus Christ of Latter-Day Saints*, 18–19. As another example, see Julia (Ives) Pack's blessing: "I seel the[e] up to Eternal life being Spokemon for thy Father." The phrase became so common in such blessings that blessing books copying records submitted by patriarchs in nineteenth-century Utah merely noted it by "&c" (and so on). In the latter part of the twentieth century, at least some apostles instructed patriarchs against unconditional sealing language, placing it outside their ability to use such language, possibly with reference to temple ritual. See Delbert L. Stapley, "Outline of Instructions to Patriarchs."

20. A claim supported by William Smith's mother, evidently based on Joseph Smith's Nauvoo ideas of succession. See Lavina Fielding Anderson, *Lucy's Book: A Critical Edition of Lucy Mack Smith's Family Memoir*, epilogue. On this aspect of succession see Robin Scott Jensen and Benjamin Park, "Debating Succession, March 1846: John E. Page, Orson Hyde, and the Trajectories of Joseph Smith's Legacy," 181–205; and Blythe, "William Smith's Patriarchal Blessings," 60–95.

other leaders rejected the idea, but Smith inserted the sustaining of the patriarch between the First Presidency and the apostles.[21]

While the language of "time and eternity" seems to have been deployed by Joseph Smith in at least some marriages before 1843,[22] formal sealing in the mode of the plural marriage revelation may have waited until that year—though before the July 12 revelation was dictated.[23] For example, William Clayton was sealed to his first wife, Ruth Moon, on July 22, 1843, three months after his marriage and sealing to his second wife, Margaret Moon, on April 27, 1843. (Sealings between Clayton and the Moon sisters were repeated as a kind of ratification in the Nauvoo temple January 26, 1846.)[24] Joseph and Emma Smith were sealed in May along with a number of others.[25] The words "time and eternity" or "eternity" were employed in at least some of these ceremonies. However, it does not seem that these early ceremonies employed the "sealing" words that appeared in later ceremonies and there is no way of determining if all such marriages entailed time and eternity. Indeed, some did not.[26] The revealed language of Sarah Ann Whitney's July 27, 1842, marriage to Joseph Smith (read by her father as he performed the ceremony) is instructive, though not a universal pattern for other marriages:

> Verily, thus saith the Lord unto my servant N. K. Whitney, the thing that my
> servant Joseph Smith has made known unto you and your family and which

---

21. D. Michael Quinn, *The Mormon Hierarchy: Extensions of Power*, 122–23. Compare Joseph F. Smith's inaugural address on November 10, 1901, in *Conference Report*, 71. On the meaning of "high priesthood" as it is used here, as well as sealing, see Smith, "Early Mormon Priesthood Revelations."

22. Testimony of its use was delivered long after those events for the specific purpose of demonstrating that it was used.

23. Mercy Thompson's recollection was that sealing as codified in the plural marriage revelation first occurred in May 1843 when she was sealed (by proxy) to her dead husband Robert Thompson. Mercy Thompson, Autobiography.

24. These repeated rituals served a number of purposes. Perhaps the most important one in Nauvoo was the solidifying of apostolic status in the temple order. See Brigham Young, Letter to William Smith, August 10, 1845; Linda King Newell and Valeen Tippetts Avery. *Mormon Enigma: Emma Hale Smith*, 350 note 29.

25. Bushman, *Rough Stone Rolling*, 492–96. Smith, *An Intimate Chronicle*, 99–107.

26. Compare Orson Pratt's imprint of the ceremony in Orson Pratt, "Celestial Marriage," 31; also Hubert H. Bancroft, *History of Utah, 1540–1886*, 353–54. Joseph Smith's levirate marriage to Agnes Smith was apparently not for eternity, and there were other examples. See Gary James Bergera, "The Earliest Sealings for Civilly Married Couples Living and Dead," 54n61.

you have agreed upon is right in mine eyes and shall be rewarded upon your heads with honor and immortality and eternal life to all your house, both old and young because of the lineage of my Priesthood, saith the Lord, it shall be upon you and upon your children after you from generation to generation, by virtue of the holy promise which I now make unto you, saith the Lord. These are the words which you shall pronounce upon my servant Joseph and your daughter S. A. Whitney. They shall take each other by the hand and you shall say, You both mutually agree, calling them by name, to be each other's companion so long as you both shall live, *preserving yourselves for each other and from all others and also throughout eternity, reserving only those rights which have been given to my servant Joseph by revelation and commandment and by legal authority in times passed.* If you both agree to covenant and do this, I then give you, S. A. Whitney, my daughter, to Joseph Smith, to be his wife, to observe all the rights between you both that belong to that condition. I do it in my own name and in the name of my wife, your mother, and in the name of my holy progenitors, by the right of birth which is of priesthood, vested in me by revelation and commandment and promise of the living God, obtained by the Holy Melchisedeck [priest?] Gethrow and others of the Holy Fathers, commanding in the name of the Lord all those powers to concentrate in you and through you to your posterity forever. All these things I do in the name of the Lord Jesus Christ, that through this order he may be glorified and that through the power of anointing David may reign King over Israel, which shall hereafter be revealed. Let immortality and eternal life hereafter be sealed upon your heads forever and ever.[27]

Eight months later, Smith blessed both Sarah Ann and Kingsbury. For Sarah Ann he offered an important addition for her future, something that emphasized the perseverance of sealings in general:

Nauvoo City
March 23d 1843

Oh Lord my God thou that dwellest on high bless I beseach of thee the one into whose hands this may fall and crown her with a diadem of glory in the Eternal worlds Oh let <it>be sealed this day on high that She Shall come forth in the first reserrection to recieve the Same and verily it Shall be so saith the Lord if She remain in the Everlasting covenant to the end as also all her Fathers house Shall be Saved in the Same Eternal glory and if any of them Shall wander from the foald of the Lord they shall not perish but Shall return Saith the Lord and be Saived in and by repentance be crowned with all the

---

27. "Revelation Received 27 July 1842"; emphasis added. The document is apparently a later copy of the original. However, see Smith's acknowledgement of the instruction in Joseph Smith, Letter to Brother and Sister Whitney &c., August 18, 1842.

fullness of the glory of the Everlasting gospel these promises I Seal upon all of their heads in the name of Jesus Christ by the Law of the holy priesthood Even so Amen

Joseph Smith

Sarah Ann Whitney[28]

The promise that "all her Fathers house Shall return" if they go astray, repent, and "be crowned with all the fullness" is represented in verses 19 and 26 as well as Smith's preaching following the plural marriage revelation.

The reference to David and the "power of anointing" combines the Old Testament, possibly the Mormon endowment speech initiated in May 1842, and perhaps a prolegomena to the Council of Fifty's plan to reinstate the Kingdom of God. The ritual language makes clear that the high priesthood "powers" are to concentrate in Sarah Ann and in her posterity, a reference that blossomed in the temple with its own lineage promises. Joseph Smith felt the future David would be a child of his own, the first born following his sealing to Emma. After his death, Emma gave birth to David Hyrum Smith. The name was chosen in deliberate prophetic determination.[29]

The reference to Jethro (Gethrow), father-in-law of Moses, provides a link between the sealing enterprise of polygamy and the high priesthood. According to a September 1832 revelation by Smith, it was Jethro who ordained Moses to the high priesthood (D&C 84:6). This attention to an important figure in the high priesthood line of ascent links the general "sealing to eternal life" of 1831, the patriarchal sealings after 1834, and the familial-community sealings of Nauvoo; it further suggests an evolving vision of what "restoration" meant along with its symbols and icons.[30]

---

28. "Blessing to Sarah Ann Whitney, 23 March 1843."

29. Valeen Tippetts Avery, *From Mission to Madness: Last Son of the Mormon Prophet*, 21–23; D. Michael Quinn, *The Mormon Hierarchy: Origins of Power*, 230–31; and Elizabeth Ann Whitney, "A Leaf from an Autobiography," 105.

30. M. Guy Bishop, "Eternal Marriage in Early Mormon Marital Beliefs," 84; and Bergera, "The Earliest Sealings," 41–66. See also Smith, "Early Mormon Priesthood Revelations," 13–19. The appearance of Jethro may allude to Whitney himself, since Smith figured as Moses from the early days of Mormonism, and Jethro was the father-in-law of Moses (Ex. 4:18; 18:1–27). Acknowledging that the revelation was Joseph Smith's is a letter in his own hand. Joseph Smith, Letter to Newel K. Whitney, Elizabeth Ann Whitney, &c, August 18, 1842. See also B. Carmon Hardy, *Solemn Covenant: The Mormon Polygamous Passage*, 7. Ordained Mormon men often carry a "line of authority" that mimics the concern of the high and patriarchal priesthood found in Doctrine and Covenants 84 and 107, with ascent and descent of authority used as a means of determining the legality

The convergence of the different understanding of sealing is startlingly reflected in Smith's patriarchal blessing of Joseph C. Kingsbury, when the latter agreed to a sham public marriage to Sarah Ann:

> [O]n the 29th of April 1843 I according to President Joseph Smith Couscil & others agreed to Stand by Sarah Ann Whitney as Supposed to be her husband & had a pretended marriage for the purpose of Bringing about the purposes of God. . . . [Joseph said] I Lay My hands upon thy head in the name of Jesus Christ to bestow upon the[e] a Patriarkle Blessing according to the Power and authority of the Holy Priesthood vested in me. I Say unto thee . . . I Seal the[e] up to Come forth in the first reserection unto Eternal Life-And they Companion Caroline who is now dead thou Shalt have in the first Reserection for I Seal thee up for and in her behalf to Come forth in the first Reserection unto Eternal lives (and it Shall be as though She was present her Self) and thou Shalt hail her and She Shall be thine and no one Shall have power to take her from thee, And you both Shall be crowned and enthrowned to dwell together in a Kingdom in the Celestial Glory in the presents of God, And you Shall Enjoy each other Society & Embraces in all the fulness of the Gospell of Jesus Christ Wourls without End And I Seal these blessings upon thee and for thy Companion in the Name of Jesus Christ for thou Shalt receive the holy anointing & Endowment in this Life to prepare you for all these blessings even So Amen"[31]

Kingsbury's blessing included a proxy sealing to his dead wife Caroline, and Kingsbury seems to serve as her proxy in the matter. This was perhaps the earliest proxy sealing in Nauvoo, and its characterization as a patriarchal blessing is important in the high priesthood cycle.

"Whom I have Appointed"

After Joseph Smith's death, the rationale to replace Smith with the Quorum of the Twelve Apostles as the sole dispenser of sealing and polygamy exacted an historical price. Part of that price was to shift the narrative of foundational priesthood authority from the high priest to the office of apostle. This required a new mythos made up of stories of Smith transferring his sealing keys to Young, and eventually (to make the story a continuing one) to all the apostles in some nascent sense. In essence, "apostle" became synonymous with the power to be the "one," the temple priest. Later refinements

---

of priestly actors—much like post-exilic Israel. Indeed, these lines of authority form part of official Church records.

31. Joseph C. Kingsbury, Diary of Joseph C. Kingsbury, April 29, 1843. On the blessing, see "Blessing to Joseph Kingsbury, 23 March 1843," 15.

of the story included the idea that ordination as an apostle and membership to the Twelve Apostles was necessary to possess such keys.[32]

The apostolic story had some drawbacks for Young, and he found it hard to convince some of his fellow apostles that he alone might permit plurality and sealing. However, the recent elevated status of the Twelve made it easier to convince a significant portion of the general membership—particularly among those who had recently converted to Mormonism through the Twelve's missionary efforts. At the time of Smith's death, the perceptions in Nauvoo of the apostles show at least three things: they were accorded a special place among the Saints as gatekeepers of the temple, they were seen as having rights in regard to polygamy that others did not possess, and they were generally revered collectively rather than individually as members of the apostolic quorum. The post-martyrdom apostolic assertions of authority were thus made in the context of preserving Smith's final innovations in worship and praxis.

Once the apostles assumed the role of Church presidency, Young was really the only choice for temple priest, but it took the others time to relinquish their joint claim. Woodruff's July 24, 1846, journal entry tells of one such decision: "Decided in council that no man has a right to Attend to the ordinance of sealing except the President of the Church."[33] Young's ecclesial authority as president of the apostles translated to temple position by virtue of his presence in the other streams of Nauvoo power. Young exercised that position with vigor since he saw it as the key to holding the apostles and the Church together. Wilford Woodruff reported on August 24, 1844, his fellow apostles' testimony of apostolic succession: they were "ordained, anointed and appointed . . . to lead the church," a reference to both their ecclesial and cosmological positioning.[34] The apostles believed they had the power; Young had to make them see that it was his to regulate. That task took time. The narrative had to move away from

---

32. On the high priesthood and the apostles, see Smith, "Early Mormon Priesthood Revelations." See also MacKay et al., eds., *Documents*, 1:245–46. On Young, see John G. Turner, *Brigham Young: Pioneer Prophet*, 160–61; also Terryl L. Givens and Matthew J. Grow, *Parley P. Pratt: The Apostle Paul of Mormonism*, 259, 269–71. Wilford Woodruff journal, August 24, 1844, in Kenney, *Wilford Woodruff's Journal*, 2:455.

33. On Young as the successor to the "one" authorized to seal and engage plurality, see Fillerup, "William Clayton," October 1, 1844. Kenney, ed., *Wilford Woodruff's Journal*, 3:62. Turner, *Brigham Young*, 112, 141.

34. See Kenney, ed., *Wilford Woodruff's Journal*, 2:454–55.

Joseph Smith's singular status that no longer existed. Instead, Young had to construct a narrative that put him in place as "the one," while admitting that he was really not superior to the rest of his colleagues in the Twelve. That narrative developed slowly to the twentieth-century concept that each of the apostles, and they alone, have the power to be the one—to be the superior ecclesial and temple authority—but only in some potential way. That potential could only be realized by Young's death.

The memoir of Boston convert Catherine Lewis is representative of this general view of the apostles by the Nauvoo saints. Lewis came to Nauvoo after Smith's death, convinced by the strong apostolic descriptions of the endowment and its promises of mysteries revealed and blessings conferred. She was immediately recruited as a plural wife. On apostolic preaching, she observed that the apostles saw the Bible and "Book of Covenants" as "dead letters; they went by the Spirit." Lewis's subsequent question was one that would trouble Mormonism through much of the nineteenth century: "Who would be willing to be governed by such a set of men, *without any standard?*"[35] This mirrors Young's own belief that living prophets were of far greater value than any fixed canon. It also reflects the anxiety of Young and the apostles in consolidating their position in an environment that included unpublished revelations such as the plural marriage revelation. Young saw the centrality of Joseph Smith as both a danger and a necessary example, but he was careful to assert his leadership gradually.[36]

At the turn of the twentieth century, Church president Joseph F. Smith (son of Hyrum Smith) broke this paradigm of unique apostolic authority with his movement of Melchizedek Priesthood and Aaronic Priesthood from their 1835 place as mere categorical classes to powers that must be conferred prior to ordination to office. Smith began this move early in his administration, but it did not become Church policy until fifty years after his death, in 1968. An interesting consequence of Smith's idea that was apparently never explored was the impact on the Mormon trope of the "great apostasy." The latter was often styled in terms of the death of the ancient apostles, in which the "keys" died with them, and therefore the ancient Church's ecclesial structures were doomed to die (imaged as they were in terms of a presentist Church policy structure).[37] For Joseph

---

35. Catherine Lewis, *Narrative of Some of the Proceedings of the Mormons*, iv; emphasis added.

36. Wilford Woodruff's journal, August 8, 1844, in Kenney, ed., *Wilford Woodruff's Journal*, 2:436–42. Turner, *Brigham Young*, 114–20.

37. Smith, "Early Mormon Priesthood Revelations," 46.

F. Smith, the category of Melchizedek Priesthood potentially blanketed all offices and actors. Thus, in his words, if the "least elder" happened to be the last Melchizedek Priesthood officer on earth, he could reinitiate all organization, praxis, and sacraments; no angelic visitations would be necessary. Smith believed that all of Joseph Smith's keys and authority were in fact embedded within this vision of the Melchizedek Priesthood—an authority separate from office. Though he did not intend it, this vision essentially moved the theology of priesthood back to the more egalitarian priesthood narrative of 1831 that lacked much of the hierarchical structure that would later arise.[38] For Joseph F. Smith, the conferral of Melchizedek Priesthood allowed the possessor to perform any Church function or sacrament should the circumstance arise. Perhaps to demonstrate the idea, he occasionally allowed patriarchs to organize wards and seventies to ordain high priests and bishops, etc.[39] His phrase, "the priesthood is greater than any of its offices," ultimately stripped particular offices of any real uniqueness, including the apostles. This new way of seeing Church authority did not find strong support among the apostles, and after Joseph F.'s death the new Church presidency tried to nullify its practical aspects.

Joseph F. Smith's policies on priesthood developed over time. In the 1870s, he subscribed to the idea that the high priesthood was superior to the office of seventy, though later he found that seventies could ordain high priests. His idea of a blanket power, Melchizedek Priesthood, behind all authoritative acts and which elders, seventies, high priests, apostles, etc. must first have conferred upon them prior to ordination, obviated any necessary restriction on the acts of such Church officers. However, Smith had no intention of creating chaos in the institutional Church. His rumi-

---

38. That vision has mostly been ignored, perhaps because it smacks of anarchy if promoted too vigorously. Moreover, it provided legitimacy to nearly all the schismata of Nauvoo, not something Joseph F. Smith would have seen as desirable. See Smith, "Early Mormon Priesthood Revelations," 43–6; Joseph F. Smith, *Gospel Doctrine: The Sermons and Writings of President Joseph F. Smith*, ch. 9; Joseph F. Smith, *Conference Report*, October 1902, 87. Some of Smith's associates fronted this idea in council meetings two years before Smith's 1902 address, but when it met with skepticism, Smith dismissed the idea as unimportant. But in fact, he had published his ideas over the signatures of the First Presidency in "The Priesthood and its Offices," 549. See John Henry Smith diary, March 7, 1901, and October 24, 1907, in Jean Bickmore White, ed., *Church, State, and Politics: The Diaries of John Henry Smith*, 477, 591; and Rudger Clawson diary, April 24, 1902, in Stan Larson, ed., *A Ministry of Meetings: The Apostolic Diaries of Rudger Clawson*, 426.

39. Quinn, *Extensions of Power*, 144. This practice never became normative.

nations were derived from his ever-developing interpretations of scripture, and were not intended to turn Mormonism into anarchy. Even so, Smith still saw the high priesthood as a tier above apostle in terms of governance and while Church President, he ordained new apostles as high priests to legitimize their regulation of Church officers.[40]

"A House of Order"

Joseph Smith's preaching and revelations demonstrated the high priesthood cycle. Smith's view of succession joined all the elements of the high priesthood from its initial individual sealings, its power to direct ecclesial affairs, and its housing of the patriarchal power and all the attendant genealogies to its communal and familial sealings exemplified in the plurality of the July 12, 1843, revelation. There is little doubt that Smith intended his brother Hyrum to be his default successor in the high priesthood cycle, and it is clear that the apostles recognized this and the powerful tension resulting from the developing authority of the temple priest and the dynastical role of the Smith family in the high priesthood. As the high priesthood cycle reached its apex in the plural marriage revelation, the apostolic cycle began to take over with the Twelve Apostles being legitimate contenders to head the Church and temple priesthood. The logic of their position grew out of their participation in the four centers of Nauvoo power: polygamy insiders, recipients of the temple endowment, Council of Fifty, and Quorum of the Twelve Apostles. The narratives of apostolic power that surfaced in Utah in later generations were only parts of the succession puzzle.

If there was a weakness in the Young and Kimball narrative of the apostleship beyond its early identification as strictly a mission office, it was that *they* were in fact ordained by high priests. No one thought this unusual in February 1835, since the high priesthood was still the summit of the priesthood in Mormonism at the time, and Young himself claimed that a currently ordained high priest could resurrect Church structure and liturgy from a cataclysmic episode. Young's use of high priest was political, and his eventual views on the high priesthood were quite different from 1830s Mormonism. It was not without purpose that Young omitted the Seventy by name from this kind of emergency, as well as the high council. Both offices had the potential for schism.[41] In a sense, it was the Smith

---

40. Smith, "Early Mormon Priesthood Revelations," 43–46.

41. See Kenney, ed., *Wilford Woodruff's Journal*, 2:439. The apostles had used the April 1835 revelation, now part of Doctrine and Covenants 107, as

family-backed Reorganized Church of Jesus Christ of Latter Day Saints that recognized and held on to the high priesthood cycle. However, the heritage of the Reorganization prevented them from embracing Joseph Smith's final sacraments of the restoration: polygamy and its cousins, the temple rituals.[42]

The apostolic cycle, however, was not without precedent, and it had textual roots in the Articles and Covenants (now essentially Doctrine and Covenants 20). The claim that "[a]n apostle is an elder, and it is his calling . . . to ordain other elders, priests, teachers, and deacons, and to administer the flesh and blood of Christ"[43] was textually linked to the Book of Mormon's instruction that those "who were called the elders . . . ordained priests and teachers" and "administer[ed] the flesh and blood of Christ" (Moro. 3:1, 4:1). These were both connected to Joseph Smith through an April 1830 revelation and expansions of later revelations that called Joseph Smith an apostle (D&C 21:1)—though the meaning was probably interpreted as a commission to evangelize rather than as establishing a position of authority. An earlier revelation (D&C 18) had predicted the calling of twelve apostles in imitation or restoration of New Testament ecclesiastical structure, though the February 1835 fulfillment of that revelation explicitly designated their authority to the evangelizing efforts away from established Church centers. Their power thus worked at the fringe of Church polity. An April 1835 revelation (later a part of Doctrine and Covenants 107) fleshed out the place of the apostolic *quorum* in the Church, giving it ecclesial credentials and judicial powers—though in practice those credentials were restricted again to regions away from the "stakes" of the Church. After the

---

support for their elevation to the First Presidency. The same revelation also had comparable claims about the Seventy and the high council.

42. RLDS Church Historian Heman C. Smith wrote in 1901 that "[w]e do not know whether Joseph Smith taught or practiced polygamy. . . . We do, however, most emphatically repudiate the doctrine, and believe it to be false in theory and corrupt in practice. We take this position without reference to whether Joseph Smith taught or practiced it." Heman C. Smith, *The Truth Defended, or A Reply to Elder D. H. Bays' Doctrines and Dogmas of Mormonism*, 156–57. Smith makes it clear that the plural marriage revelation—even if it could be proven that Joseph practiced it—would not be a valid point of faith, since that requires its acceptance by the RLDS church at large, which by then would have been an extremely unlikely event. LDS leaders deployed a similar logic in relation to a purported revelation to John Taylor in 1886 that commanded its permanent practice. Lyman, *Candid Insights*, 319. James R. Clark, *Messages of the First Presidency*, 5:327–29.

43. Articles and Covenants, circa April 1830 (D&C 20:38–40), earliest known version in "The Mormon Creed," 4.

apostles' successful mission to Europe from 1839 to 1841, Joseph Smith began to enfold many of them into his private circle of trust, sharing concepts such as the temple liturgy and polygamy, while repealing former restrictions on apostolic powers in the center of Zion (not without some resistance and confusion on the part of institutions like the high council).[44]

"As Pertaining to the New and Everlasting Covenant"

Since 1921, introductions to the published revelation described it (with some variation) as "relating to the new and everlasting covenant, including the eternity of the marriage covenant and the principle of plural marriage." This description references the text of the revelation (vv. 6, 19, 26–27, 41–42) and is at the center of an interesting interpretive discussion that, like much of Smith's restorative work, reflects a tradition of evolution and development.

Early Church members saw their baptisms as entry into the new and everlasting covenant. For example, Joseph Knight recorded the following while reminiscing about his early Mormon experiences:

> Joseph said there must Be a Church Biltup. I had Ben there several Days. Old Mr Smith and Martin Harris Come forrod [forward] to Be Babtise[d] for the first. They found a place in a lot a small Stream ran thro and they ware Babtized in the Evening Because of Persecution. They went forward and was Babtized Being the first I saw *Babtized in the new and everlasting Covenant*.[45]

With this in mind, early Mormons would occasionally sign letters with, "yours in the bonds of the new and everlasting covenant." For example, the Presidency of the High Priesthood signed a letter to Edward Partridge on consecration in Missouri: "We conclude our letter by the usual salutation, in token of the new and everlasting covenant."[46]

The plural marriage revelation, however, shifted the new and everlasting covenant from being a reference to a convert's first sacrament to being the penultimate rite of eternal marriage sealing and plurality. This shift had the potential to alter how Smith's other teachings and revelations might be understood.

---

44. Turner, *Brigham Young*, 73–84. Blythe, "William Smith's Patriarchal Blessings," 61–62. John S. Dinger, "'A Mean Conspirator' or 'the Noblest of Men': William Marks's Expulsion from Nauvoo," 12–38.

45. Dean C. Jessee, "Joseph Knight's Recollection of Early Mormon History," 5; emphasis added.

46. Clark, *Messages of the First Presidency*, 1:15.

Consider the current reading of Doctrine and Covenants 131:1–4 (brackets in original):

> In the celestial glory there are three heavens or degrees; And in order to obtain the highest, a man must enter into this order of the priesthood [meaning the new and everlasting covenant of marriage]; And if he does not, he cannot obtain it. He may enter into the other, but that is the end of his kingdom; he cannot have an increase.

Orson Pratt extracted the text of section 131 from a *Millennial Star* installment of the serial printing of the "History of Joseph Smith," which in turn was an edition of the *Deseret News* serial imprint of the manuscript History of the Church.[47]

The entry in the manuscript history is based on the William Clayton journal and differs only slightly in the portions it uses. Below is the Clayton report from his diary for May 16, 1843:

> Went to see Pres. J. who ordered me to prepare for Carthage I returned home & got ready & started about 11 oclock in the New Carriage with prest. J. George Miller, Eliza Partridge, Partridge & J.M. Smith Loran Walker drove. We called at Carthage & saw Styles, Backenstos & others. Tarried about 15 minutes & started again for Ramus where we arrived about 3 ½ oclock. We stayed at W. G. Perkins. Prest. J. & I went to B.F. Johnsons to sleep. Before we retired the Prest. gave bro Johnson & wife some instructions on the priesthood. He put his hand on my knee and says "your life is hid with Christ in God, and so is many others."[48] Addressing Benjamin says he "nothing but the unpardonable sin can prevent him (me) from inheriting eternal glory for he is sealed up by the power of the priesthood unto eternal life having taken the step which is necessary for that purpose."[49]

This statement may speak to the question of whether plural marriages entailed sealing, but it also fits with the nature of the plural marriage revelation: Clayton had taken the step of marrying a second wife. Smith may also have seen this as a test of faith, even a hurdle of death. In any case, no sealings of civil marriages had been performed yet. Thirty-year-old Almera Johnson, one of Joseph's wives, lived in Ramus, Illinois, with her brother Benjamin. Joseph was also married to Almera's older sister, Delcena, who lived in Nauvoo with another of Joseph's wives, Louisa Beaman. On Smith's May visit, Benjamin Johnson reported, "The Prophet again Came and at my house occupied the Same Room & Bed with my

---

47. Historian's Office History of the Church, 5:1551.
48. Colosians 3:3.
49. Fillerup, "William Clayton," May 16, 1843.

Sister that the month previous he had occupied with the Daughter of the Late Bishop Partridge."[50]

Clayton's diary continues,

> He said that except a man and his wife enter into an everlasting covenant and be married for eternity while in this probation by the power and authority of the Holy priesthood they will cease to increase when they die, but those who are married by the power & authority of the priesthood in this life & continue without committing the sin against the Holy Ghost will continue to increase & have children in the celestial glory.[51] The unpardonable sin is to shed innocent blood or be accessory thereto. All other sins will be visited with judgement in the flesh and the spirit being delivered to the buffetings of satan untill the day of the Lord Jesus. I feel desirous to be united in an everlasting covenant to my wife and pray that it may soon be. He also said that in the celestial glory was three heavens or degrees, and in order to obtain the highest a man must enter into this order of the priesthood and if he dont he cant obtain it. He may enter into the other but that is the end of his kingdom he cannot have increase.[52]

An important phrase, "sealed up to eternal life," is borrowed from the early Mormon practice of sealings by high priests and their liturgical branching, the patriarchs. It, however, is used here in a different way. Clayton's recollection makes two points: first, that Clayton had been sealed to Margaret Moon, his first plural wife (the sealing took place on April 27, 1843); and second, that the sealing was apparently unconditional except for committing "the unpardonable sin . . . against the Holy Ghost."[53]

What this all means is further complicated by the also evolving meaning of "eternal life," from an early and simple synonym for a traditional life in heaven to the complex meaning it carried near the end of Smith's life. The Mormon notion of heaven became ever more generously freighted with meaning as Joseph Smith's revelations and sermons continued to expand on Christian eschatology. Hence, a high priest's act of sealing up to eternal life in 1831, a patriarch's similar act in 1834, and the act of the

---

50. Benjamin F. Johnson, Letter to George F. Gibbs, October 1903.

51. Clayton's report shows that sealing, in Joseph Smith's mind, was precisely what it was narrated to be in the plural marriage revelation.

52. Fillerup, "William Clayton," May 16, 1843. This subdivision of the Celestial glory seems to follow from an 1841 sermon by Smith who announced that there were twelve kingdoms within his original four. See Wilford Woodruff, "Book of Revelations," January 30, 1841.

53. For Clayton's note on the sealing, see Fillerup, "William Clayton," April 27, 1843.

temple priest in an 1843 sealing carried different meanings to a recipient. Eternal life in 1831 may have meant enjoying the vision of heaven forever, while in 1843 eternal life meant not just living a godly life joined forever to family and friends but participating in the creative enterprise of God in a very literal fashion.[54] That vision of heaven continued to take shape in various ways after Smith's death.

Additionally, Clayton's diary entry lacks the interpretive phrase that occurs in the current Doctrine and Covenants 131:2: "[meaning the new and everlasting covenant of marriage]." This bracketed explanation was added by Orson Pratt in his 1876 edition of the Doctrine and Covenants, a year after he began using the phrase with some frequency in public addresses.[55] It does not appear in any manuscript or imprint of the revelation previous to 1876.

Pratt's use of the phrase was drawn from the plural marriage revelation (where it appears seven times) and acts as a reference to the sealing sacrament introduced by Smith in full in 1843.[56] Conversely, the phrase also appears in Doctrine and Covenants 22 as a reference to the restored Church and its attendant ordinances.[57] Perhaps the most definite recent preaching here is that of Joseph F. Smith's son, Joseph Fielding Smith:

> Men agree to keep the commandments and the Lord promises to reward them accordingly. The gospel itself is the new and everlasting covenant and embraces all of the agreements, promises, and rewards which the Lord offers to his people.[58]

---

54. Stanley B. Kimball, ed., *On the Potter's Wheel: The Diaries of Heber C. Kimball*, 52.

55. See, for example, Orson Pratt, October 7, 1873, *Journal of Discourses*, 16:251; also John Taylor, November 14, 1877, *Journal of Discourses*, 19:150.

56. See Ehat, "Joseph Smith's Introduction of Temple Ordinances," 37–39. Jacob Scott knew of the plural marriage revelation and wrote to his daughter from Nauvoo: "Several revelations of great utility and common interest have been lately communicated to Joseph and the Church. One is that all marriage contracts or covenants are to be everlasting." Scott's remarks reflect public explanations in the face of the rumored revelation. See Richard P. Howard, "The Changing RLDS Response to Mormon Polygamy: A Preliminary Analysis," 79. George F. Partridge et al., "The Death of a Mormon Dictator: Letters from Massachusetts Mormons, 1843–1848," 583–617.

57. MacKay et al., eds., *Documents*, 1:137.

58. Joseph Fielding Smith, *Conference Report*, October 1970, 26. Smith's statement is perhaps an attempt to harmonize the use of the phrase, since it reflects New Testament language in reference to the ministry and work of Jesus

As one may guess, his father offered a prior reiteration of this generalized reading of "new and everlasting covenant" in the earlier twentieth century.[59]

"Their Covenant and Marriage Are not of Force when They Are Dead"

This revelation introduces another historically important facet of Smith's cosmology: that human earthly relationships—no matter how loyal or loving they may be—cannot become eternal by such a commitment alone.[60] Though marriages may have been performed with a view toward domestic bliss in the afterlife, the imprimatur of an authorized sealing sacrament is necessary, and only Smith had the power to authorize this, or polygamy. While Nauvoo polygamists saw marriage as the way to expand afterlife kingdoms, it was the plural marriage revelation that helped formalize the liturgical aspect and impact. Smith's sermons later in the year may be read as continuations of the revelation, portending the expansion of the 1842 endowment that fall. Notions such as a "grand council in heaven" and the perseverance of child-parent links are illuminated by the revelation only in roundabout ways.[61] In essence, the heaven of Nauvoo was a constructed one, built by forging the divinely efficacious sealing links between the members of one's projected heavenly family.

---

and the apostles. The harmony of all (properly interpreted) scripture was a hallmark of the senior Smith's philosophy, one inherited by his son.

59. Joseph F. Smith, *Conference Report*, October 1902, 3.

60. Samuel Morris Brown, *In Heaven as It Is on Earth: Joseph Smith and the Early Mormon Conquest of Death*, 206–8.

61. See Smith's sermons on August 13, 1843, and October 9, 1843, in Smith et al., "Parallel Joseph." See also his important address delivered on June 11, 1843.

Chapter Five: Verses 16–27

Unconditional Sealing and Eternal Damnation

Marriage sealing and the eventual notion of priesthood adoption appeared at the pinnacle of Mormon liturgy with the plural marriage revelation.[1] Like much of the revelation, this section is laced with warnings concerning a person's eternal state for postponing or failing to comply with its mandates.

16 Therefore, when they are out of the world they neither marry nor are given in marriage; but are appointed angels in heaven, which angels are ministering servants, to minister for those who are worthy of a far more, and an exceeding, and an eternal weight of glory.

17 For these angels did not abide my law; therefore, they cannot be enlarged, but remain separately and singly, without exaltation, in their saved condition, to all eternity; and from henceforth are not gods, but are angels of God forever and ever.

18 And again, verily I say unto you, if a man marry a wife, and make a covenant with her for time and for all eternity, if that covenant is not by me or by my word, which is my law, and is not sealed by the Holy Spirit of promise, through him whom I have anointed and appointed unto this power, then it is not valid neither of force when they are out of the world, because they are not joined by me, saith the Lord, neither by my word; when they are out of the world it cannot be received there, because the angels and the gods are appointed there, by whom they cannot pass; they cannot, therefore, inherit my glory; for my house is a house of order, saith the Lord God.

---

1. Smith's broader vision of sealing, one that crossed natural family lines by sealing friend to friend (these were interpreted later as patriarchal bonds and styled as "father" and "son"), provided a more inclusive narrative of sealing and its meaning in heaven. After 1894, sealing boundaries were more narrowly drawn. During Brigham Young's tenure, he saw these non-biological adoption networks experimented with in Nauvoo as the highest earthly sacrament. Jonathan A. Stapley, "Adoptive Sealing Ritual in Mormonism," 83.

19 And again, verily I say unto you, if a man marry a wife by my word, which is my law, and by the new and everlasting covenant, and it is sealed unto them by the Holy Spirit of promise, by him who is anointed, unto whom I have appointed this power and the keys of this priesthood; and it shall be said unto them—Ye shall come forth in the first resurrection; and if it be after the first resurrection, in the next resurrection; and shall inherit thrones, kingdoms, principalities, and powers, dominions, all heights and depths—then shall it be written in the Lamb's Book of Life, that he shall commit no murder whereby to shed innocent blood, and if ye abide in my covenant, and commit no murder whereby to shed innocent blood, it shall be done unto them in all things whatsoever my servant hath put upon them, in time, and through all eternity; and shall be of full force when they are out of the world; and they shall pass by the angels, and the gods, which are set there, to their exaltation and glory in all things, as hath been sealed upon their heads, which glory shall be a fulness and a continuation of the seeds forever and ever.

20 Then shall they be gods, because they have no end; therefore shall they be from everlasting to everlasting, because they continue; then shall they be above all, because all things are subject unto them. Then shall they be gods, because they have all power, and the angels are subject unto them.

21 Verily, verily, I say unto you, except ye abide my law ye cannot attain to this glory.

22 For strait is the gate, and narrow the way that leadeth unto the exaltation and continuation of the lives, and few there be that find it, because ye receive me not in the world neither do ye know me.

23 But if ye receive me in the world, then shall ye know me, and shall receive your exaltation; that where I am ye shall be also.

24 This is eternal lives—to know the only wise and true God, and Jesus Christ, whom he hath sent. I am he. Receive ye, therefore, my law.

25 Broad is the gate, and wide the way that leadeth to the deaths; and many there are that go in thereat, because they receive me not, neither do they abide in my law.

26 Verily, verily, I say unto you, if a man marry a wife according to my word, and they are sealed by the Holy Spirit of promise, according to mine appointment, and he or she shall commit any sin or transgression of the new and everlasting covenant whatever, and all manner of blasphemies, and if they commit no murder wherein they shed innocent blood, yet they shall come forth in the first resurrection, and enter into their exaltation; but they shall be destroyed in the flesh, and shall be delivered unto the buffetings of Satan unto the day of redemption, saith the Lord God.

27 The blasphemy against the Holy Ghost, which shall not be forgiven in the world nor out of the world, is in that ye commit murder wherein ye shed innocent blood, and assent unto my death, after ye have received my new and everlasting covenant, saith the Lord God; and he that abideth not this law can in nowise enter into my glory, but shall be damned, saith the Lord.

"But Are Appointed Angels in Heaven"

Verse 16 of the plural marriage revelation pulls language from the Gospel of Matthew's account in which Jesus responds to the question of the levirate marriages (a passage that has been a talking point for Mormon missionaries since 1852): "For in the resurrection they neither marry, nor are given in marriage, but are as the angels of God in heaven" (Matt. 22:30). Joseph Smith, in his public comments on the revelation following its divulgement in the Nauvoo Expositor, claimed that it was this passage that provoked him to ask God about marriage and that "he received for answer, men in this life must marry in view of eternity, otherwise they must remain as angels, or be single in heaven."[2] In other sermons, Smith extended the reach of eternal sealings to the children of those marriages, saying that "in order for you to receive your children to yourself, you must have a promise, some ordinance, some blessing in order to ascend above principalities or else it [your child] may be an angel."[3]

"Angel" is a complex term in Smith's cosmology and may have both a pejorative sense (as it does in verse 17) as well as a progressive one.[4] Here, the revelation treats becoming an angel and the accompanying impossibility of progress almost as if it were a punishment: "For these angels did not abide my law; therefore, they cannot be enlarged, but remain separately and singly, without exaltation, in their saved condition, to all eternity" (v. 17). Despite their "saved condition," they are to forever be "ministering servants . . . for those who are worthy of . . . far more" (v. 16).[5]

---

2. "To the Public," 1.

3. See Smith's sermon of May 12, 1844, in William V. Smith et al., "The Parallel Joseph"; also William Victor Smith, *Every Word Seasoned with Grace: A Textual Study of the Funeral Sermons of Joseph Smith*, ch. 9.

4. For example, see reports of Smith's October 9, 1843, funeral sermon for James Adams and his May 12, 1844, continuation of the second King Follett Sermon of April 7, 1844, in Smith et al., "The Parallel Joseph."

5. The potentially troubling permanence of this passage has been softened by some who interpreted it in light of Doctrine and Covenants 19:6–7, with the "forever and ever" clause seen as a motivator "that it might work upon the hearts of the children of men" (v. 7) rather than an absolute description. In the "retrenchment" cycle noted by Armand Mauss, pessimism played a central role. The idea of a purgatory-like state that could ultimately lead to exaltation in the afterlife in Mormonism was seen as dangerous. Armand L. Mauss, *The Angel and the Beehive: The Mormon Struggle with Assimilation*.

"Except Ye Abide My Law Ye Cannot Attain to this Glory"

Whether an eternal angelic state is viewed as a punishment or simply a lack of further blessings, the necessity of marriage sealings in these verses form a foundational text for the modern Mormon narrative of family. Four days following the revelation, Smith spoke to the effect that

> All blessings that were ordained for man by the Council of Heaven were on conditions of . . . Law. . . . No man can obtain an eternal blessing unless the contract . . . be made in view of Eternity. . . . Those who keep no eternal Law in this life or make no eternal contract are . . . alone in the eternal world.[6]

The revelation explicitly states that the blessings of eternal sealings were dependent on reception and obedience to the law "in the world" (vv. 15, 22–23, 30) and that "when they are out of the world it cannot be received there" (v. 18). Because of this, reconciliation between this demand and proxy sealing of the dead was a problem that manifested not only in Smith's sermons, but also in later adoption theology and practice. For a time, the internal logic seemed to be that immediate families could use proxy sealing to obtain the blessings of the sealed state when a spouse died unexpectedly, but waiting might be foolhardy, and the implied fear was weighted with the perseverance of sealing. Smith's startling 1836 vision showing his long deceased brother in the midst of God's glory illustrated the terror many Christians felt over missed sacraments or the failure to hear the Gospel message.[7]

Despite the absence of proxy sealing in the revelation, and its suggested dependence on sealings performed during mortality, several of those who heard of the revelation petitioned to be sealed to their deceased spouses,[8] and later sermons by Smith pointed to the possibility of proxy sealings.[9] Soon after Smith's death in 1844, sealing of the living to the

---

6. Franklin D. Richards, "Scriptural Items."

7. On the fear of incomplete sealing, see Brigham Young's 1847 remarks to his "adopted" family in Scott G. Kenney, ed., *Wilford Woodruff's Journal, 1833–1898 Typescript,* 3:134–37. The vision was later canonized as Doctrine and Covenants 137.

8. Brian C. Hales, *Joseph Smith's Polygamy,* 2:173. See also Joseph Kingsbury's patriarchal blessing quoted in Chapter 4.

9. For example, see Joseph Smith's funeral sermons for Elias Higbee and James Adams on August 13, 1843, and October 9, 1843, in Smith et al., "Parallel Joseph"; and Smith, *Every Word Seasoned with Grace,* ch. 4, 5. Hyrum Smith was sealed to his deceased wife, Jershua Barden, and his living wife, Mary Fielding, in May 1843. After the plural marriage revelation, he was sealed to Mary's widowed

dead began to be performed in the Nauvoo Temple. These sealings would cease when Brigham Young's followers began their trek west, and they were not resumed until the temple in St. George, Utah, was completed in 1877—even though sealings between living persons were being performed in the Salt Lake Endowment House and in Utah homes throughout the intervening time.[10] With the building of the St. George Temple, as well as the pending temples in Salt Lake, Manti, and Logan, LDS leadership felt a need for temple liturgy to be more fully regularized and oversaw the production of the first liturgical texts of some of the temple rites.[11]

In 1894, Wilford Woodruff announced a revelation that would end the practice of sealing (adoption) to church leaders instead of parents who died without accepting Mormonism.[12]

"Sealed by the Holy Spirit of Promise"

The revelation makes it explicit that a loyal and fulfilled commitment between spouses alone is insufficient to attain an eternal marriage:

> And again, verily I say unto you, if a man marry a wife, and make a covenant with her for time and for all eternity, if that covenant is not by me or by my word, which is my law, and is not sealed by the Holy Spirit of promise, through him whom I have anointed[13] and appointed unto this power, then it is not valid neither of force when they are out of the world, because they are not joined by me, saith the Lord, neither by my word; when they are out

---

sister, Mercy Thompson. Mercy Fielding Thompson, Autobiography. See also Joseph Smith's January 21, 1844, sermon in Kenney, ed., *Wilford Woodruff's Journal*, 2:342. For more on Joseph Kingsbury's proxy see Chapter 4.

10. Stapley, "Adoptive Sealing Ritual," 55, 91–92. Sealings for both the living and dead were performed in the Nauvoo Temple. Willard Richards kept a "Book of Proxy" indicating Nauvoo temple sealings for the dead during 1845–46 (copy in possession of the author) where such sealings were recorded. Lisle G. Brown, "'Temple Pro Tempore': The Salt Lake City Endowment House," 54. For some data from Richards's book see Gary J. Bergera, "The Earliest Sealings for Civilly Married Couples Living and Dead"; Lisle G. Brown, *Nauvoo Sealings, Adoptions, and Anointings*; and Lyndon W. Cook, ed., *Nauvoo Marriages: Proxy Sealings 1843–1846*.

11. Stapley, "Adoptive Sealing Ritual," 103.

12. Woodruff announced the revelation in the April 1894 General Conference. Wilford Woodruff, "The Law of Adoption," 145–52. See also the Epilogue.

13. As with verse 7, the use of "anointed" here simply means that Smith is designated for this work. Associating future events with these and similar passages does violence to the text.

of the world it cannot be received there, because the angels and the gods are appointed there, by whom they cannot pass; they cannot, therefore, inherit my glory; for my house is a house of order, saith the Lord God (v. 18).

For a marriage covenant to continue into the afterlife, the angels and gods guarding heaven must be able to recognize the authority by which that covenant was made. This may have referenced the endowment ritual, which was expanded to include women a few months later. Brigham Young seemed to have this understanding when he spoke at the cornerstone ceremony of the Salt Lake Temple and alluded to the language of the revelation:

> Your *endowment* is, to receive all those ordinances in the House of the Lord, which are necessary for you, after you have departed this life, to enable you to walk back to the presence of the Father, passing the angels who stand as sentinels, being enabled to give them the key words, the signs and tokens, pertaining to the Holy Priesthood, and gain your eternal exaltation in spite of earth and hell.[14]

In order to pass by the angels, the covenant must be "sealed by the Holy Spirit of Promise" (v. 18). This language echoes the letter to the Ephesians (1:13) that refers to the promise of the Holy Spirit following baptism. It also appears in earlier revelations with respect to those who enter the highest of heavens (D&C 76:53), receive the second Comforter (88:3), or are blessed by the sealing power of the Church patriarch (124:124). None of these uses points to temple rituals of sealing-as-marriage or the sealing networks that developed in Nauvoo.[15] Instead, all seem connected to the high priesthood tradition of individual salvation or blessings.

Seals and sealing were part of a long tradition in Protestant discourse, and Mormon incarnations of the idea drew from this tradition and were importantly prominent after the June 1831 ordinations of high priests. As discussed in the previous chapter, after that time sealing up to eternal life was a practice of high priests in the Church for the next several years.[16] A late 1832 revelation (now Doctrine and Covenants 88) evoked the lan-

---

14. Brigham Young, April 6, 1853, *Journal of Discourses*, 2:31. See also Orson Hyde, October 6, 1859, *Journal of Discourses*, 7:313.

15. Stapley, "Adoptive Sealing Ritual," 57.

16. See for example, Minute Book 2, October 25, 1831. On seals and sealing language in Protestant discourse, see Emery Battis, *Saints and Sectaries: Anne Hutchinson and the Antinomian Controversy in the Massachusetts Bay Colony*, 105; Samuel M. Brown, "Early Mormon Adoption Theology and the Mechanics of Salvation," 8–9; and Thomas Y. How, *A Vindication of the Protestant Episcopal Church*, 26–27.

guage of "the Holy Spirit of promise" (88:3) as it called for the building of
a temple, but this temple would be more of a holy school than a ritual center (88:117–19). The ideas underlying the anointings and blessings of the
Kirtland temple, together with the forthcoming office of the high priesthood patriarch, overhauled the sealing to eternal life but kept its individual
application and Protestant footing. This picture was radically challenged
by the plural marriage revelation. While sealings before and after the plural
marriage revelation carried a similar antinomian (salvation-assured) feel,[17]
the Holy Spirit of Promise is recast in the revelation as a sealing ritual:

> And again, verily I say unto you, if a man marry a wife by my word, which
> is my law, and by the new and everlasting covenant, and it is sealed unto
> them by the Holy Spirit of promise, by him who is anointed, unto whom
> I have appointed this power and the keys of this priesthood; and it shall
> be said unto them—*Ye shall come forth in the first resurrection; and if it be*
> *after the first resurrection, in the next resurrection;* and shall inherit thrones,
> kingdoms, principalities, and powers, dominions, all heights and depths—
> then shall it be written in the Lamb's Book of Life, that he shall commit no
> murder whereby to shed innocent blood, and if ye abide in my covenant,
> and commit no murder whereby to shed innocent blood, it shall be done
> unto them in all things whatsoever my servant hath put upon them, in time,
> and through all eternity; and shall be of full force when they are out of the
> world; and they shall pass by the angels, and the gods, which are set there, to
> their exaltation and glory in all things, as hath been sealed upon their heads,
> which glory shall be a fulness and a continuation of the seeds forever and
> ever. (132:19; emphasis added)[18]

Here, sealing is nearly unconditional, with the exception being those
who fail to "abide in my covenant" to not "shed innocent blood." Joseph

---

17. Mormon antinomianism was carefully and distinctly countered in the
twentieth century by a pessimism born at least partly in early Utah. For an
example of this early drift, see Heber C. Kimball, October 6, 1855, *Journal of
Discourses*, 3:124; also David John Buerger, "'The Fulness of the Priesthood': The
Second Anointing in Latter-day Saint Theology and Practice," 39, 43–44. The
looming Mormon Reformation pushed the theological pendulum even further
from the picture of salvation assurance. On the reformation movement, see John
G. Turner, *Brigham Young: Pioneer Prophet*, 255–64; and Matthew Bowman, *The
Mormon People: The Making of an American Faith*, ch. 6. Compare Sarah Ann
Whitney's blessing in Chapter 4.

18. The language, "if ye abide in my covenant" is a reference to the provisions
of sealing in the verse. On the effect of sealing for the sinner, see Sarah Ann
Whitney's blessing in Chapter 4.

Smith was aware of the stake that the revelation made in the antinomian debates, and he addressed the topic of assured salvation in the first part of his first King Follett funeral sermon on March 10, 1844.[19] He is reported as saying:

> Now we come to talk about election. A great deal is said about it, one way or another. But they do not know anything about it—the doctrine that the Presbyterians and Methodists have quarreled so much about. The Presbyterians say, "once in grace, always in grace," the Methodist says once in grace, [one] can fall from grace and [be] renewed again. There is some truth in both these statements. Paul says in the sixth chapter of Hebrews that after arriving at a certain knowledge and then fall[ing] away it is impossible to renew them again. Well Paul, the Presbyterian says, once in grace, always in grace. I say it is not so. The Methodist says, once in grace [one] can fall from grace and be renewed again (you can have grace today, fall from it tomorrow, [the] next day have grace again). But the scriptures and the spirit of Elijah would show them both false, and take a road between them both. For according to the scriptures if a man receive the good word of God and tasted of the powers of the world to come, if they shall fall away, it is impossible to renew them again, seeing they crucify the son of God afresh, and put him to an open shame. For those who do these sins it is impossible to renew unto repentance, for they are delivered to the buffetings of Satan until the day of redemption. So there is a possibility of falling away [and] you could not be renewed again, *and the power of Elijah cannot seal against this sin for this is a reserve made in the seals and power of the priesthood.*[20]

Between the time of this sermon and his earlier conferral of the "fullness of the priesthood" (including second anointings) on both men and women in September 1843, Smith apparently contemplated two sealings:

---

19. Generally, the sermon of April 7, 1844, is identified as the "King Follett" sermon, but the earlier March 10 sermon was traditionally considered in honor of Follett, a friend and sometime bodyguard of Smith who had died on March 9. See the "Sermon Book" filed in the Nauvoo City Council Proceedings, 1841 February–1845 February. For some of the available texts, see the March 10, 1844, sermon in Smith et al., "Parallel Joseph." Unconditional sealings had a long tradition but specifically in regard to marriage and parent–child sealings, see Smith's funeral addresses for Elias Higbee and James Adams on August 13, 1843, and October 9, 1843, in Smith et al., "Parallel Joseph." On the March sermon and the second Follett sermon of April 7, 1844, as well as Higbee and Adams, see Smith, *Every Word Seasoned with Grace*, chs. 4–7.

20. Emphasis added. Text is taken from Smith, *Every Word Seasoned with Grace*, ch. 6. Franklin D. Richards's notes of the sermon attest to Smith separating murder and the "sin against the Holy Ghost" as "these" sins. Richards, "Scriptural Items."

one, the sealing of husband and wife; the other, a sealing of their particular mansion in heaven. These would further map the earlier, more Protestant conception of sealing onto the ritualized salvific grace of the new temple sacraments.[21] This antinomian-like assurance through temple sealing would be implemented in those performed in the Nauvoo temple after Smith's death, which carried no faithfulness clause.[22]

Within a few years, Brigham Young and the apostles gained a more nuanced view of couple sealing and added a faithfulness clause by 1853 that is still present in the sealing ceremony. (Sealing rituals have changed since then, but those changes have been comparatively minor.) The included clause may have been a practical realization of the nature of new converts in Utah and Young's belief that Smith's death was a result of the apostasy and betrayal of one who had received the Holy Spirit of Promise: William Law. This study of the temple sacraments continued after Nauvoo, with various innovations contemplated (but not always introduced) as cultural sensitivities and needs, which impacted the Latter-day Saints. An example of a change that was never put in practice: apparently administering only "half" of the temple endowment ritual, then marriage (sealing), then a probationary period before a remaining portion of the endowment, as a

---

21. Fillerup, "William Clayton," October 20, 1843. Neither seal was apparently conditional. The second seal probably referred to the "fulness of the priesthood" itself. Andrew F. Ehat, "Joseph Smith's Introduction of Temple Ordinances and the 1844 Mormon Succession Question," 55–56. Identifying the Holy Spirit of Promise with the latter ignores earlier perseverance language in sealings. However, with the later pessimism in sealings, it was natural to assign the Holy Spirit of Promise to the fullness of the priesthood ritual by reading later developments back into previous texts. In Utah sermons, it is evident that different opinions flourished on the nature of the assurance conferred by sacraments like sealing and anointing. Recent Church handbooks of instruction demonstrate the endpoint of this separation of sealing and Holy Spirit of Promise: "The purpose of a temple marriage, referred to in the scriptures as 'the new and everlasting covenant of marriage' (Doctrine and Covenants 131:2), is to seal a husband and wife for time and eternity, subject to their faithfulness. Only a marriage that has been sealed in the temple and confirmed by the Holy Spirit of Promise can be eternal (see Doctrine and Covenants 132:7). Through this ordinance, a couple's children may also be part of their eternal family." *General Handbook of Instructions, Book 1, 2010,* 16.

22. It is possible that Young exercised some latitude in his Nauvoo sacraments, investing some sealings with pessimistic clauses. Records of the Nauvoo temple period suggest that ritual language was flexible and developing.

hedge against the seeming lack of respect for the seriousness of the obligations of the temple.[23]

"Fulness and Continuation of the Seeds"

Posterity was a vital theme in early Mormonism. It appeared both in
contexts of reproduction and adoption. Common knowledge of human
reproductive biology in nineteenth-century America was essentially based
in biblical notions captured in the Abrahamic narrative of Genesis. Joseph
Smith elaborated that narrative in his revelation of the Book of Abraham.
Manuscripts of the book that date from 1835 demonstrate a revelatory
foundation for both sorts of posterity.

> But I Abram and Lot my brothers son, prayed unto the Lord, and the Lord
> appeared unto me, and said unto me, arise and take Lot with thee, for I have
> purposed to take thee away out of Haran, and to make of the[e] <a> minister
> to bear my name ~~unto a people which I will give~~ in a Strange land which I
> will give unto thy seed after thee, for an ~~eternal me morial~~ everlasting posses-
> sion <when> ~~if~~ they hearken to my voice For I am the Lord thy God, . . . my
> hand shall be over thee, and I will make of thee, a great nation. . . . And thou
> shall be a blessing, unto thy seed after thee, that in their hands they shall bear
> this ministry and priesthood unto all nations. . . . [F]or as many as receive
> this gospel Shall be called after thy name, and shall be accounted thy seed.[24]

Arguments over the relative contributions of males and females in
human reproduction are very old. In the centuries leading up to Joseph
Smith's era—and during his lifetime—widely understood ideas of conception placed women in the role of mere receptacles for male seed (semen
is Latin for seed). Anatomists had known for centuries that female sex
organs were in some ways the internal mirror image of those of a male, but
the notion of a female egg combining with male sperm was only speculation and not well accepted.

Instead, the King James Version of the Bible guided the theology of
conception. "Seed" was all there was in the way of generation. Because of his
righteousness, Abraham's *seed* was a valuable commodity. Seed just needed

---

23. Abraham H. Cannon diary, October 9, 1893, in Edward Leo Lyman, ed.,
*Candid Insights of a Mormon Apostle: The Diaries of Abraham H. Cannon, 1889–
1895*, 428. This was not the first time the idea was expressed. David John Buerger,
"The Development of the Mormon Temple Endowment Ceremony," 51–52.

24. "Book of Abraham Manuscript, circa July–circa November 1835–C
[Abraham 1:1–2:18]," 8.

soil and a receptacle to grow. A woman and her womb might be closed or open to seed, depending on God's curse or blessing. The idea was subtly fundamental to polygamy and the revelation on polygamy. In the following chapter, the ideas of adoptive and literal seed are shown to take shape in a debate arising from the plural marriage revelation and Smith's preaching on human protology. Smith's vision of human ontology played an important role in the evolution of the reception and interpretation of that preaching, the revelation, and Mormon proselytizing in the twentieth century.[25]

Meanwhile, the notion of "seeds" as a synonym for posterity, of whatever sort, was part of Smith's early teaching of polygamy and sealings, perhaps even before the July 12, 1843, plural marriage revelation was composed. In the month preceding the revelation, one of Smith's confidants in plural marriage, Heber C. Kimball, expressed his reverent wish for forgiveness and salvation in a journal entry regarding his first wife, Vilate:

> O that I was such a man as I would desire to be, and Thou O God knowest I wish [to] be pure in hart, that all of my sins may be bloted out . . . [and] ever sepperate me from my dear Vilate or anny of those that are con[ne]cted to me by the ties of Na[t]ure Thou knowest I Love my dear family, and may it increase more and more, that [no] power can sepperate us from Each other, that we may dwell to gether through out all Eternity, and thare be [enthroned] on worlds, to propragate that thare may be no end to us or our Seeds.[26]

"Then Shall They Be Gods"

Brigham Young's uneasiness with accepting the antinomian link between sealing and salvation extended to his apprehension of sealing the living to the dead, where the attitudes and faith of the latter were unknown. Eventually, the perseverance advocated by Joseph Smith gave way to a kind of Arminian or Methodist theology, in which endurance to the end was a clause or expectation in every ordinance, even the remaining, relatively rare, unconditional ordinances.[27] Smith's final restorations of sacraments

---

25. On Rabbinical debates over females and reproduction, see Edward Reichmann, "The Rabbinic Conception of Conception: An Exercise in Fertility," 35–44. For some of the historical range of thought on seed and human reproduction, see Jill Lepore, *The Mansion of Happiness: A History of Life and Death*, ch. 1.

26. Stanley B. Kimball, ed., *On the Potter's Wheel: The Diaries of Heber C. Kimball*, 52.

27. On Nauvoo sealings, see Stapley, "Adoptive Sealing Ritual," 60–62, 73. Some have seen in the language of verses 5 and 19 an image of the forthcoming

offered more than salvific assurance. They deemphasized the hierarchical ecclesiastical structure of Melchizedek priesthood offices and instead had a more equitable distribution of powers that were meted out in a temple setting. The ecclesial priesthood of Smith's revelations regulating Church function was an altogether different functionality from the temple priesthood. The latter not only offered the ability to rise to be kings and priests in Israel but also offered an even greater elevation mentioned in verse 20 of the plural marriage revelation, a point of Mormon theology that would draw criticism long after the practice of polygamy had terminated:

> Then shall they be gods, because they have no end; therefore shall they be from everlasting to everlasting, because they continue; then shall they be above all, because all things are subject unto them. Then shall they be gods, because they have all power, and the angels are subject unto them.

This explicit promotion of deification was not only blasphemous and heretical to Protestantism and Catholicism generally, but also Mormon opponents of the revelation viewed it as heresy from within the faith.[28] As

---

(September 1843) "fullness of the priesthood." The text of the revelation works against that. This was a new form of marriage, and from the July 27, 1842, revelation to Newel K. Whitney (quoted in Chapter 4) through the marriages of May 1843, including Kingsbury's proxy sealing, there is no particular expression of pessimism. See Heber C. Kimball's journal entry for January 1, 1846, kept by William Clayton in George D. Smith, ed., *An Intimate Chronicle: The Journals of William Clayton*, 245–46; and Fillerup, "William Clayton," October 20, 1843. On Smith's expansion of both ideas, see his June 16, 1844, sermon in Smith et al., "Parallel Joseph"; as well as the treatment of that sermon in Smith, *Every Word Seasoned with Grace*. On the "fullness of the priesthood," see Buerger, "Fulness of the Priesthood," 38–39; Richard Lyman Bushman, *Joseph Smith: Rough Stone Rolling*, 490–99; Ehat, "Joseph Smith's Introduction of Temple Ordinances," 56–60; and Andrew H. Hedges et al., eds., *Journals, Volume 3: May 1843–June 1844*, xx–xxii.

28. An important fact about the Mormon audience for the revelation is that earlier converts were drawn nearly universally from groups sympathetic to theological pessimism born outside the established denominations. See Stephen J. Fleming, "'Congenial to Almost Every Shade of Radicalism': The Delaware Valley and the Success of Early Mormonism," 129–64. While the deification language of the plural marriage revelation and Smith's preaching on the subject in 1844 drew the ire of dissenters, nearly identical language appeared in "The Vision" of 1832 (D&C 76). The difference, perhaps, was the association of that late language with polygamy and sealing and its more structured notion of eternal life. Indeed, in Smith's rejoinder to the dissenters (his June 16, 1844, sermon), he

part of its exposé of the revelation, the *Nauvoo Expositor* drew attention to this and other Nauvoo teachings:

> Resolved 2nd, Inasmuch as we have for years borne with the individual follies and iniquities of Joseph Smith, Hyrum Smith, and many other official characters in the Church of Jesus Christ, (conceiving it a duty incumbent upon us so to bear,) and having labored with them repeatedly with all Christian love, meekness and humility, yet to no effect, feel as if forbearance has ceased to be a virtue, and hope of reformation vain; and inasmuch as they have introduced false and damnable doctrines into the Church, such as a plurality of Gods above the God of this universe, and his liability to fall with all his creations; the plurality of wives, for time and eternity, the doctrine of unconditional sealing up to eternal life, against all crimes except that of sheding innocent blood, by a perversion of their priestly authority, and thereby forfeiting the holy priesthood, according to the word of Jesus: "If a man abide not in me, he is cast forth as a branch and is withered, and men gather them and cast them into the fire, and they are burned."[29]

The Mormon dissenters involved with the *Nauvoo Expositor* were not alone in their assessment of Smith's preaching and private practice; their new church, The True Church of Jesus Christ of Latter Day Saints, had some followers—though it was quickly disbanded after Smith's assassination.[30] The *Expositor* gave rise to a new iteration of Mormon criticism in the American and world presses, but these critics generally left Smith's cosmology alone in favor of decrying polygamy.

The cessation of polygamy, however, refocused criticism onto the unorthodox cosmology of Mormonism, particularly beginning with the 1903 election of Apostle and Senator-elect Reed Smoot. The goal of the criticism was to tag Smoot as un-American. For example, that year the Presbyterian Teachers' Association of Utah published an early version of a text of Joseph Smith's "King Follett Discourse" with a short preamble noting its unorthodox teaching.[31] They may have hoped that it would appear outlandish to Protestant readers and taint Smoot by association. For the most part though, Mormon theology sans active polygamy drew little attention for

---

remarks as much. Later Church preaching claimed positions varying from near universalism to a far more exclusive outcome.

29. "Resolutions," 2.

30. Steven L. Shields, *Divergent Paths of the Restoration*, 29–30. The group was an eclectic one, whose personalities ranged from the Laws, who were respected in the community, to Chauncy Higbee and others, who were seen as less desirable citizens. Bushman, *Rough Stone Rolling*, 530–31.

31. See *Joseph Smith's Last Sermon as Issued by Elder John Taylor, Nauvoo, Ill.*

much of the twentieth century.[32] It would not be until the Evangelical countercult ministries of the 1960s (made popular by Walter Martin's 1965 *Kingdom of the Cults*) that Mormon cosmology began to receive more careful public attention.

"This Is Eternal Lives"

Joseph Smith was fond of Jesus's Intercessory Prayer in John 17 and deployed it in a number of ways.[33] The plural marriage revelation pulls from verse 3 of that prayer, replacing the singular "life" with the plural "lives": "This is eternal lives—to know the only wise and true God, and Jesus Christ, whom he hath sent" (D&C 132:24). This pluralization of lives points to notions of kingdom expansion that were in development (a concept that will be considered in more detail later),[34] and the verse in its entirety, continuing into the next, further establishes the authority behind the plural marriage covenant:

> I am he. Receive ye, therefore, my law. Broad is the gate, and wide the way that leadeth to the deaths; and many there are that go in thereat, because they receive me not, neither do they abide in my law. (vv. 24–25)

Verse 25 is fascinating for its duality of language. It simultaneously linked both polygamy to the knowledge of God and the rejection of that knowledge to a hellish fate. In doing so, it made the revelation a natural touchstone for later claims of polygamy being a requirement for the highest of heavenly exaltations and cast Emma Smith in the role of the wicked-

---

32. Six years after Smoot's election and eventual seating in the senate, some Protestant imprints were still circulating with the message that polygamy was the central message and the inner core of Mormonism, and that Smoot represented a kind of subversive corruption of American institutions. For example, see "Popular Idea of Mormonism," *Presbyterian Home Mission Monthly*, 280.

33. See the sermons of May 12, 1844, and June 16, 1844, in Smith et al., "Parallel Joseph."

34. Smith's use of Hebrew and Greek sometimes manifested as unfamiliar terminology, and this may be an example. See William Clayton journal for May 17, 1843: "when the word 'ruach' applies to Eve it should be translated lives." Fillerup, "William Clayton." The word "translated" had a broad meaning in Smith's work; "interpreted" may do more justice to the context. "Ruach" is not used in the Hebrew Bible in reference to Eve, but Smith saw its use as implied by the text. His usage suggests the language of the plural marriage revelation, especially verse 63.

est of women. The resulting demotion of Emma took a variety of forms. For example, in October 1844 one man explained that he

> dreamed that he saw the heavens opened and beheld some of the things of eternity. He saw a personage arise out of the earth, and An Elder informed him it was Joseph Smith. Joseph did not speak to him but droped some slips of paper on the ground from whence he rose. . . . [The dreamer] picked up one of them & read the following words: Emma is not worthy of me.[35]

In his diary entry for May 16, 1843, Clayton recorded Smith teaching:

> [I]n the celestial glory was three heavens or degrees, and in order to obtain the highest a man must enter into this order of the priesthood and if he dont he cant obtain it. He may enter into the other but that is the end of his kingdom he cannot have increase.

Read in isolation, this might suggest that mere sealing, and not necessarily polygamy, is sufficient to gain the highest heaven. However, in the larger context, parts of the revelation text, as well as Clayton's diary, pointed toward plurality being essential.

While Brigham Young conditioned entrance into the endowment in Utah upon an expression of belief in the divinity of Mormon polygamy, its practice was not a test of faith, and his discourses on the topic varied over time. For example, in 1866 he taught,

> The only men who become Gods, even the Sons of God, are those who enter into polygamy. Others attain unto a glory and may even be permitted to come into the presence of the Father and the Son; but they cannot reign as kings in glory.[36]

Some years later Wilford Woodruff recorded that Young

---

35. Wilford Woodruff Journal, October 12, 1844, in Kenney, ed., *Wilford Woodruff's Journal*, 2:473. A visitor to Nauvoo told Brigham that Emma was teaching her children that Young was the cause of their father's death. Young replied, "Joseph would have as hard work to dig her out of Hell in the next world as he did in this." Woodruff later reported, "The Conversation turned upon Josephs Children. Brother Taylor said it was a pity that Emma had such an influence over them. B Young said Bless your heart the Lord watches over them & will take care of them." Another man reported that Smith bought a horse for Emma on condition that she would stop using the words, "spiritual wife." Wilford Woodruff's journal for November 3, 1856, and March 5, 1860, in Kenney, ed., *Wilford Woodruff's Journal*, 4:485, 5:440; Valeen Tippetts Avery and Linda King Newell, "The Lion and the Lady: Brigham Young and Emma Smith," 82; On the horse, see William C. Staines, "Report, circa 1854."

36. See Brigham Young, August 19, 1866, *Journal of Discourses*, 11:268–69.

gave good Council & said those who spoke against A Plurality of wives & in there feelings will not receive it will never inherit the Celestial Kingdom of God, for it has always been practiced there and always will be & thousands of women will be saved there who have been trodden under the feet of men & what will be done with them if men did not have more than one wife?[37]

And a year later in 1870 he instructed that

Men and women will be saved in the celestial kingdom without even being married at all—others with only one wife, and some again with many wives—whoever continues faithful to the end, will have all the exaltation they can possibly enjoy.[38]

Such statements, however, do not always make clear what being "saved" entails, and it may be that Young envisioned different levels of Godhood in the afterlife. In the eyes of alert gentile observers, "men become Gods by practicing polygamy, and the greatest polygamist becomes the greatest God."[39]

Shortly before the passing of Young, the narrative of highest salvation depending on plurality increased in Utah as the federal government began to enforce territorial anti-bigamy laws and Mormon leaders risked their well-being in the defense of polygamy. During this time, there was considerable fiery rhetoric at the expense of those who either avoided plurality or argued that it was merely a sideshow that could and should be left behind—a position some political and Church allies put before John Taylor in the last years of his administration as Church president. Taylor had remained loyal to his commitment to the practice, dictating several revelations on the subject and releasing from service a number of local Church leaders who failed to practice plurality.[40]

---

37. Kenney, ed., *Wilford Woodruff's Journal*, 6:493–4

38. Salt Lake City School of the Prophets Minutes, February 12, 1870.

39. Quoted in Jana K. Riess, "Heathen in Our Fair Land: Anti-polygamy and Protestant Women's Missions to Utah," 24–30.

40. James R. Clark, ed., *Messages of the First Presidency of the Church of Jesus Christ of Latter-day Saints*, 2:348. For Taylor's revelations, see Richard Neitzel Holzapfel and Christopher C. Jones, "'John the Revelator': The Written Revelations of John Taylor." For policies, see for example Abraham H. Cannon diary, April 6–7, 1884; for speeches, see Samuel W. Taylor and Raymond W. Taylor, *The John Taylor Papers: Records of the Last Utah Pioneer*, 2:337, 445. On those wishing to persuade Taylor, Drew Briney, *Silencing Mormon Polygamy: Failed Persecutions, Divided Saints and the Rise of Mormon Fundamentalism*, 82. During Brigham Young's tenure, *The Deseret News* had noted that the plural marriage revelation could not be overturned without abandoning all of Joseph Smith's revelations

While polygamy was in full force in Utah, there was still discussion and debate over its necessity behind the scenes. For example, there were occasional discussions of the idea that a monogamous sealing was sufficient for exaltation if the parties at least acknowledged the rightness of polygamy, and even Taylor privately offered that exaltation was possible without polygamy.[41] Many Latter-day Saints simply saw polygamy as "not for them" and do not appear to have suffered any disadvantage from their own perspectives.[42] Moreover, data suggests that daughters in families who did not engage plurality tended to stay out of polygamous relationships themselves, even though they might be sympathetic to the doctrine of plural marriage.[43]

The death of John Taylor in 1887 opened the way for a divorce of sealing and plurality. Government pressure to abandon plural marriage was such that by 1889, many Saints looked for an end-of-the-world moment to save Mormonism.[44] In a sense this happened, but it took place gradually by re-visioning what it meant to be a Latter-day Saint. The Manifesto

(compare B. Carmon Hardy, *Doing the Works of Abraham, Mormon Polygamy: Its Origin, Practice, and Demise*, 322–23). On the *News*, see Samuel Bowles, *Across the Continent: A Summer's Journey to the Rocky Mountains, the Mormons, and the Pacific States, with Speaker Colfax*, 396. Richard S. Van Wagoner, *Mormon Polygamy: A History*, 122–23. See also Kathryn M. Daynes, *More Wives Than One: Transformation of the Mormon Marriage System, 1840–1910*, 72. Taylor proclaimed his absolute loyalty to plural marriage saying, "Are we going to suffer a surrender of this point? No, never! No, never! No, never!" John Taylor, August 20, 1882, *Journal of Discourses*, 23:240–41.

41. First Presidency Letterpress Copybooks, January 26, 1881.

42. In 1899, Lorenzo Snow quoted statistics that suggested 300 women were in surviving plural marriages, while more than 350,000 Church members at large were not involved in polygamy. Stan Larson, ed., *A Ministry of Meetings: The Apostolic Diaries of Rudger Clawson*, 128.

43. This is based on a special data set, but under similar stable circumstances, it seems a reasonable expectation. Kathryn M. Daynes, "Striving to Live the Principle in Utah's First Temple City: A Snapshot of Polygamy in St. George, Utah, in June 1880," 69–95.

44. Joseph Smith told of an 1832 experience that suggested if he lived to age 85 he would meet Jesus, an experience that proved to have a lasting impression on Latter-day Saints. See Smith's remarks in Minute Book 1, February 14, 1835; Andrew H. Hedges et al., eds., *Journals Volume 2: December 1841–April 1843*, 324–5; Smith et al., "Parallel Joseph," March 10, 1844, February 14, 1835; and Dan Erickson, *"As a Thief in the Night": The Mormon Quest for Millennial Deliverance*, 183–84. The expectation based on Smith's revelation is illustrated in Howard Coray, Letter to Martha Lewis, August 2, 1889.

of 1890 signaled the (public) death of the requirement of plurality for exaltation, though in the years following the Woodruff Manifesto many Church leaders still believed that polygamy would return and was the way of heaven. That faith led to secret plural sealings by Church authorities both among themselves and outside the hierarchy after 1890.[45] Belief in plural marriage gradually ceased to be a test of faith after 1890, but Mormon immigrants to the United States at the beginning of the twentieth century still claimed a belief in polygamy under questioning from government officials. As a result they were returned to their home countries.[46] While eventually the Church both publicly and privately abolished any support for more than one sexual partner for any living man, it never overturned the idea that polygamy exists in heaven.[47] Since the time of the Heber J. Grant administration, the focus has been on mere marital sealing as the *sacramental* hurdle to the highest of heavens.

The transition away from polygamy saw an important shift in Mormon cosmology and eschatology, with the anticipation of an imminent millennium being stretched out to a far off epoch of end times. This extended millennial expectation enabled sealing links to be stretched through lost generations and removed the immediate need to be connected via sealings to one of the faithful leaders of early Mormonism. Liturgical practice was gradually reduced to written formula and scriptural mandate, with rituals not founded on text-supported tradition discarded.[48] The secrecy of the polygamy raids played out in a decades-long series of mixed messages, secret extensions of authority, purposeful circumvention of governing quorums, and misperceived discourse in which various Church leaders denied that secret marriages had taken place but allowed and authorized them well into the Joseph F. Smith administration.[49] The commitment to polygamy was

45. Jonathan H. Moyer, "Dancing with the Devil: The Making of the Republican/ Mormon Pact," 502–3.

46. Missionaries continued to teach converts that a belief in polygamy was a Mormon article of faith. Moyer, "Dancing With the Devil: The Making of the Republican/Mormon Pact," 588.

47. Stephen C. Taysom, "A Uniform and Common Recollection: Joseph Smith's Legacy, Polygamy, and the Creation of Mormon Public Memory," 124–26.

48. On the foundation of praxis see Jonathan A. Stapley and Kristine Wright, "Female Ritual Healing in Mormonism," 32–85.

49. Abraham H. Cannon diary, October 7, 1899, in Lyman, *Candid Insights*, 6; Daymon Mickel Smith, "The Last Shall be First and the First Shall be Last," 340–44; B. Carmon Hardy, *Solemn Covenant: The Mormon Polygamous Passage*, 313–23, 370–80; and Moyer, "Dancing with the Devil," 508–11, 579. Provo judge Alfred

strong, and at least some of the faithful feared for their souls if they failed to live up to the mandates of section 132 and the revelations of Taylor and Woodruff. Even four years after the Manifesto, Woodruff opined,

> If men enter into some practice of this character [concubinage] they will be justified in it. The day is near when there will be no difficulty in the way of good men securing noble wives. There are terrible afflictions at the door of this nation which will take their minds away from this people.[50]

This continued devotion to the practice of plural marriage was balanced against what Church leaders saw as the temporal and political salvation of the Church and Utah. That balancing act had costs in conscience and plural family tranquility. Still smarting over the Smoot hearings and the resulting criticisms of the Church and its leaders, the First Presidency proposed a new collection of "Articles of Faith" in the April 1907 general conference. Article 9 read:

> We declare that from principle and policy, we favor: The absolute separation of church and state; No domination of the state by the church; No church interference with the functions of the state; No state interference with the functions of the church, or with the free exercise of religion: The absolute freedom of the individual from the domination of ecclesiastical authority in political affairs; The equality of all churches before the law.[51]

Separation of denominational Church and state was largely a fact in public fora. In private, however, Church leaders still worked to see that sympathetic parties were elected or appointed to positions of influence. The election and seating of Smoot was a victory for Joseph F. Smith, but it signaled the end of high Church officials in elected public office—although

---

Saxey, a civil war veteran and convert with three wives, was concerned over several issues, including Adam-God, continued cohabitation, and the fading of the plural marriage revelation. Smith's reply is apropos the difficult rhetoric of post-Manifesto polygamy, avoiding direct references. See Joseph F. Smith, Letter to A. Saxey, January 9, 1897. Wilford Woodruff's January 26, 1880, "Wilderness Revelation" read: "again I say unto that Nation or House or people, who seek to hinder my People from obeying the Patriarchal Law of Abraham *which leadeth to Celestial Glory* which has been revealed unto my Saints through the mouth of my servant Joseph for whosoever doeth these things shall be damned Saith the Lord of Hosts and shall be broaken up & washed away." Kenney, *Wilford Woodruff's Journal,* 7:615; emphasis added.

50. Abraham H. Cannon diary, April 5, 1894, in Lyman, *Candid Insights,* 492.

51. "The Address," *Conference Report,* April 1907, 14; also Clark, *Messages of the First Presidency,* 4:143–55. The document was a committee report. Committee minutes are summarized in Moyer, "Dancing with the Devil," 553–54.

they did continue to exercise influence in the corporate world. It was not until Spencer W. Kimball's public withdrawal from such corporate positions that other Church leaders gradually followed suit. The new articles of faith were sustained by the conference as an official declaration but seem to have disappeared from Church discourse almost immediately.[52]

"They Receive Me Not"

The secret spiritual economies of Nauvoo and early twentieth-century Utah naturally distanced insiders from outsiders.[53] But in Utah, the end of apostolic-sanctioned polygamy saw a strange reversal of roles. Joseph F. Smith's second manifesto of 1904 wrote a new history for polygamy. Mormons who returned to Utah from Mormon colonies in Mexico after 1910 found themselves shunned, even despised and excluded, from normative Mormon society. The secret institutional memories were largely dead and therefore unhelpful. In the 1880s, monogamist Saints still played an active role in plural marriage by helping polygamists who were hiding from federal authorities; thus rhetoric from the Church that indicated a move away from polygamy was rightfully seen as fodder for gentiles. After 1890, a different strategy was in place. Young monogamist Saints were no longer involved at all in protecting the practice, and the Church rhetoric against continued polygamy that surrounded the Smoot hearings was taken at face value by those younger Mormons. In a painful reversal of the 1880s, returning colonial polygamists would be labeled lesser Saints.[54]

---

52. See the Epilogue to this volume. On the difficulties leading to the Manifesto and the attitudes of Church leaders and members about it, together with their philosophical, ethical, emotional, and political trials in trying to leverage it with national political parties, see Kathleen Flake, *The Politics of American Religious Identity: The Seating of Senator Reed Smoot, Mormon Apostle*; also Moyer, "Dancing with the Devil." On Church authorities and business, see D. Michael Quinn, *The Mormon Hierarchy: Extensions of Power*, ch. 6. On Gordon B. Hinckley's 1996 ruling that all General Authorities withdraw from corporate life, see "General Authorities to Leave Business Boards."

53. Craig L. Foster, "The Persistence of Plural Marriage within Mainstream Mormonism: The Example of the Barr and Mary Lance Musser Family," 290–314.

54. Barbara Jones Brown, "The 'Second Manifesto,' the Mexican Revolution, and the Demise of Post-Manifesto Polygamy"; Barbara Jones Brown, "The Rise and Demise of Latter-day Saint Polygamy in Mexico"; Nancy Tate Dredge, "Victims of the Conflict"; Smith, "Last Shall be First," 319–21; Hardy, *Solemn Covenant*, 295–96.

The salvific tensions over polygamy and its power in the Mormon soteriological narrative almost guaranteed an underground continuation of the practice, even after the Church finally made it perfectly clear that excommunication lay in wait for those who tried it.[55] By 1935 Church leaders had reached a point where they encouraged law enforcement to break up polygamist families and raid collective compounds where polygamists gathered to practice their way of life. The history of these dissenting groups is complex, but it suffices to say that the Church gradually took a strong adversarial position after 1910 and made great efforts to draw boundaries that marked post-1890-manifesto polygamists as wholly other even if they had been (secretly) authorized by the Church president or his agent. Beginning in the 1930s, extra-Mormon polygamists had, largely thanks to Lorin C. Woolley, a tradition that justified their claim of exclusive plural sealing authority. Woolley's largest group of believers fractured in the 1950s, the most significant branches forming two groups, the Fundamentalist Church of Jesus Christ of Latter Day Saints (FLDS) and the Apostolic United Brethren (AUB).[56]

Near the turn of the twenty-first century, Mormons were struggling to differentiate themselves from polygamist sects like the FLDS Church, who frequently topped national headlines because of leader Warren Jeffs's exploits in polygamy and ironhanded social, political, and economic control. Historically, Jeffs and other fundamentalist polygamists saw themselves following the footsteps of Nauvoo clandestine plural practice and the secret post-1890 polygamy out of which they grew. News outlets spilled little ink over the rather stark theological and ecclesial differences that now existed between these groups and the Salt Lake City-based Latter-day Saints. Such differentiation was fine print for specialists, not sound-bite journalism.[57]

---

55. The idea that participants might suffer excommunication for public cover but then be reinstated existed from Joseph Smith's time. Smith told William Clayton, "Says he just keep her [second wife Margaret Moon] at home and brook it and if they raise trouble about it and bring you before me I will give you an awful scourging & probably cut you off from the church and then I will baptise you & set you ahead as good as ever." Fillerup, "William Clayton," October 19, 1843. See also Smith, "Last Shall be First," 342–47.

56. Brian C. Hales, *Modern Polygamy and Mormon Fundamentalism: The Generations after the Manifesto*, chs. 8, 15, 16.

57. Surveys showed that during the FLDS movement in Texas, most Texans made little or no distinction between FLDS and LDS identities. J. B. Haws, *The Mormon Image in the American Mind: Fifty Years of Public Perception*, 179, 195, 220–21.

The bones of the plural marriage revelation still haunted Mormons in their attempts to appear socially and theologically mainstream.[58]

"Which Shall Not Be Forgiven in the World Nor Out of the World"

The revelation speaks of salvation and damnation in relation to the new and everlasting covenant, both with respect to obedience to the requirement in relation to knowledge of it (v. 4) and later the damnation associated with violating the covenant after receiving it (v. 19). As if to emphasize the latter, the revelation again addresses the consequences of those who participate in the covenant then violate it:

> Verily, verily, I say unto you, if a man marry a wife according to my word, and they are sealed by the Holy Spirit of promise, according to mine appointment, and shall commit[59] any sin or transgression of the new and everlasting covenant whatever, and all manner of blasphemies, and if they commit no murder wherein they shed innocent blood, yet they shall come forth in the first resurrection, and enter into their exaltation; but they shall be destroyed in the flesh, and shall be delivered unto the buffetings of Satan unto the day of redemption, saith the Lord God.
>
> The blasphemy against the Holy Ghost, which shall not be forgiven in the world nor out of the world, is in that ye commit murder wherein ye shed innocent blood, and assent unto my death, after ye have received my new and everlasting covenant, saith the Lord God; and he that abideth not this law can in nowise enter into my glory, but shall be damned, saith the Lord. (vv. 26–27)

The proviso here for being "delivered unto the buffetings of Satan" is inherited from an earlier version of high priesthood sealing that incorporated the sacramental washing of the feet. In an 1833 meeting in Kirtland, Joseph Smith provided some instruction on the ritual after performing it with some of his fellow elders:

> The President said after he had washed the feet of the Elders, as I have done, so do ye wash ye therefore one anothers feet, pronouncing at the same time

---

58. J. Spencer Fluhman, *A Peculiar People: Anti-Mormonism and the Making of Religion in Nineteenth-Century America*, 4–8. Ken Driggs, "Imprisonment, Defiance, and Division: A History of Mormon Fundamentalism in the 1940s and 1950s," 65–95.

59. The Kingsbury manuscript reads "and he *or she* shall commit any sin or transgression" (emphasis added). See the Addendum.

through the power of the Holy Ghost that the Elders were all clean from the blood of this generation but that those ~~who~~ among them who should sin willfully after they were thus cleansed and sealed up unto eternal life should be given over unto the buffettings of Satan until the day of redemption.[60]

This washing of feet formed a continuing strand of high priesthood sealing to eternal life that would eventually merge with other Nauvoo sacraments related to the awaited temple and plural marriage revelation. Foot washing resurfaced in Utah in various ways, but its connection to the high priesthood was never emphasized due to the ecclesial shift away from the high priesthood cycle.[61]

The fusion of two extremes—murder and blasphemy against the Holy Ghost (which is frequently referred to as the "unpardonable sin")—submerged Smith's earlier nuance into one idea. Breaking the unconditional seals (in both broad and narrow senses) was linked to a theme Joseph Smith had been preaching for several years after his 1838 Missouri incarceration until his death. Rhetorically based on his interpretation of Hebrews 6:4–6, the notions and penalties associated with murder and the unpardonable sin were frequent in his preaching during this time when discussing eternal judgment.[62] Smith's experience in Missouri made him wary of dissidents.

---

60. Minute Book 1, January 23, 1833. The meeting was a conference of high priests, meeting as a "school of the prophets" at Kirtland, Ohio.

61. On sacralized foot washing and the temple, see Kenney, ed., *Wilford Woodruff's Journal*, 2:293; and Laurel Thatcher Ulrich, *A House Full of Females: Plural Marriage and Women's Rights in Early Mormonism, 1835–1870*, ch. 5.

62. The unpardonable sin was a common theme in Protestant preaching and exegesis. A century and a half before Smith, Robert Russel warned of the hazard in his 1692 *Russel's Sermon on the Unpardonable Sin*. Proximate to Joseph Smith, it is discussed in *The Doctrine and Discipline of the Methodist Episcopal Church* and in Presbyterian minister James P. Wilson's 1830 *A Free Conversation on The Unpardonable Sin*. While Smith disliked the *Discipline* (and may have included it among the creeds condemned in his First Vision [JS-H 1:19]), much of early Mormon terminology and worship forms were taken from Methodism. See Jan Shipps and John W. Welch, eds., *The Journals of William E. McLellin, 1831–1836*, 152; and Christopher C. Jones, "'We Latter-day Saints are Methodists': The Influence of Methodism on Early Mormon Religiosity." This aspect of Smith's preaching never found purchase in Utah. It did however surface in RLDS literature, but in homage to Smith's claims that Hebrews 6 contained the fundamental principles of the gospel, including those missing from the LDS Articles of Faith: resurrection and eternal judgment. See for example Smith's sermons of June 27, 1839, August 9, 1840, August 16, 1840, August 30, 1840,

These sermons frequently acted as warnings to past and present dissidents due to their occasional threats of violence or the violence that was blamed on dissent. Because of Joseph's experiences, he viewed traitors from within as the most painful and perhaps the most dangerous threat of all. The "sons of Perdition" that appeared early in Mormon revelation (D&C 76:30–49) attained physical realization as the perceived traitors who had "denied the Holy Spirit after having received it" (76:35) and "shall not be redeemed in the due time of the Lord" (76:38).[63] With polygamy undoubtedly adding to his fears for the stability of the Church already under strain by striking expansions of cosmology, secret ritual, criminal elements, and political pressures, it makes sense for such a warning to appear in the revelation. [64] Though they are not mentioned in the revelation by name, Smith's sermons and earlier revelations built a bridge between the sons of Perdition and those in the plural marriage revelation who commit "blasphemy against the Holy Ghost" (76:27).

Given the risk of public knowledge of polygamy, it was critical that those who were privy to the practice maintained strict secrecy about it (132:3). Thus, the revelation made clear that after receiving knowledge of the law of plural marriage, a failure to participate resulted in damnation (v. 4). In Nauvoo, the rumor of marital sealing brought people to ask if they might participate in that blessing. The answer was often yes apparently, and it may or may not have resulted in a companion disclosure of polygamy. In contrast to sealing, polygamy was by invitation only and the price of remaining in fellowship, with reputation intact, was silence whether or not the invitation was refused.[65] Seeing the text as tailored to Emma

---

January 12, 1841, May 16, 1841, October 15, 1843, April 7, 1844, and May 12, 1844, in Smith et al., "Parallel Joseph."

63. The title of son of Perdition comes from the New Testament (John 17:12; 2 Thes. 2:3) and is specifically used by Jesus to reference Judas Iscariot. However, the 1890s apostles disputed this title for Judas in the way that Joseph Smith used the term. For example, see Smith's sermon of May 16, 1841, in Smith et al., "Parallel Joseph." On the 1890s discussion, see Abraham H. Cannon diary, November 29, 1893, in Lyman, ed., *Candid Insights*, 441. See also the apostles' discussion of Judas and on Joseph F. Smith's claims on the issue in Anthon H. Lund diary, September 9, 1919, in John P. Hatch, ed., *Danish Apostle: The Diaries of Anthon H. Lund, 1890–1921*, 749–50.

64. Bushman, *Rough Stone Rolling*, 529, 538.

65. Some of the women who kept silent while rejecting polygamy included Sarah Kimball, Cordelia Cox, and Susan Conrad. Patricia H. Stoker, "'The Lord Has Been My Guide': Cordelia Calista Morley Cox (1823–1915)," 54; and William V.

Smith here, its language echoes an 1829 revelation to Martin Harris (now Doctrine and Covenants 19) where God reveals that ultimatums and dire threats of punishment in revelation are less about permanence and more about motivation: "Nevertheless, it is not written that there shall be no end to this torment, but it is written endless torment . . . that it might work upon the hearts of the children of men."[66]

The text of the plural marriage revelation in verse 26, however, seems to have two important omissions from verse 19: First, it eliminates the provision of missing the first resurrection due to sin; second, it eliminates language of "abid[ing] in my covenant." Had the revelation gone through a careful redaction like most of Smith's other published revelations, these omissions might have been revised in some way.[67]

Verse 27, on the other hand, expands earlier notions by defining blasphemy against the Holy Ghost in very specific and limited terms: receiving the new and everlasting covenant (of marriage) and then committing

---

Smith, "A Documentary Note on a Letter to Joseph Smith. Romance, Death, and Polygamy: The Life and Times of Susan Hough Conrad and Lorenzo Dow Barnes."

66. See Michael Hubbard MacKay et al., eds., *Documents, Volume 1: July 1828–June 1831*, 85–92.

67. By Clayton's estimate, the revelation took three hours to put on paper. His description of writing the revelation in his 1876 affidavit is echoed by Parley Pratt on the general subject of writing Smith's revelations: "There was never any hesitation, reviewing, or reading back, in order to keep the run of the subject; neither did any of these communications undergo revisions, interlinings, or corrections." Parley P. Pratt, *The Autobiography of Parley Parker Pratt, One of the Twelve Apostles of the Church of Jesus Christ of Latter-day Saints, Embracing His Life, Ministry and Travels, With Extracts, in Prose and Verse, From His Miscellaneous Writings*, 65–66. William E. McLellin gave a less extreme report on the delivery of Doctrine and Covenants 1: "Joseph would deliver a few sentences and Sydney would write them down, then read them aloud, and if correct, then Joseph would proceed and deliver more." See "Letter from Elder W. H. Kelley," 67. After initial dictation, Joseph Smith's published revelations underwent considerable redaction. For examples, see Robin Scott Jensen, Robert J. Woodford, and Steven C. Harper, eds., *Revelations and Translations: Manuscript Revelation Books, Facsimile Edition*; and David W. Grua and William V. Smith, "The Tarrying of the Beloved Disciple: Intertextuality and the Textual History of the Account of John (D&C 7)." See also Smith's sermon construction for his October 5, 1840, sermon in Smith et al., "Parallel Joseph." Its production was seen as revelatory (at least by the lights of Howard Coray, a clerk working in the office where the sermon was dictated) and the manuscript evidences various changes. Dean Jessee, "Howard Coray's Recollections of Joseph Smith," 344.

murder, which the revelation defines as "to shed innocent blood."[68] There are, then, several ways to see all these referents: shedding innocent blood, blasphemy (sin) against the Holy Ghost, unpardonable sin, and son of Perdition. Some of Smith's surviving sermon texts can be read as splitting murder and the sin against the Holy Ghost, while others conflate them.[69]

---

68. The revelation was egalitarian in contemplating women as capable of both the highest blessing and lowest condemnation. Other revelations (for example, Doctrine and Covenants 76) implied separate female theology ("sons"). This was debated by Church leaders occasionally, with some seeing "daughters of Perdition" as a foregone conclusion, while others seeing it as unlikely. Abraham H. Cannon diary, November 29, 1893, in Lyman, ed., *Candid Insights*, 441. Rudger Clawson diary, March 26, 1903, in Larson, ed., *A Ministry of Meetings*, 560.

69. In nineteenth-century Utah preaching, when the phrase had the chance to percolate a bit, "innocent blood" ranged from the murder of children to the aborting of a fetus to the murder of fellow Saints and so on. One of the more creative discussions was Heber C. Kimball's, who offered a way back from shedding innocent blood. (It is unclear whether Kimball means to split innocent blood and the sin against the Holy Ghost.)

> Still, I believe the greater part of the inhabitants of the earth will be redeemed; yea, all will be finally redeemed, except those who have sinned against the Holy Ghost or shed innocent blood; and they never can be redeemed until that debt is paid. And I do not know any way for them to pay it, unless they are brought back again to a mortal existence, and pay the debt where they contracted it. (November 22, 1857, *Journal of Discourses*, 6:67.)

This is near universalism or, more properly, universal reconciliation. Universalism in America had elements in the seventeenth century, but began in earnest in the eighteenth century. An important example was Elhanan Winchester's sermon, "The Outcasts Comforted; A Sermon Delivered at the University of Philadelphia, January 4, 1782, to the Members of the Baptist Church, Who Have Been Rejected by Their Brethren, for Holding the Doctrine of the Final Restoration of All Things, Published at the Earnest Desire of the Hearers." See also Janet Moore Lindman, "'Bad Men and Angels from Hell': The Discourse of Universalism in Early National Philadelphia"; and Ann Lee Bressler, *The Universalist Movement in America*. On the separation of innocent blood and the Holy Ghost see Brigham Young's July 20, 1848, remarks recorded in Richard Ballantyne's Journal. Young posited an interesting solution to the riddle of infinity when it came to the sons of Perdition. Those who were thus lost would, in effect, be spiritually recycled: their spirits would be "disorganized" and identities annihilated, the resulting "spiritual matter" would become part of the basic elemental material substance of the spiritual world, which could then be organized into new creations. In a sense, Young's preaching built on Joseph Smith's "anything that has a beginning,

The conflation of these two sins (denying the Holy Ghost and committing murder), though not uniform in time, appears later in Smith's career and may reflect his heightened concern over disloyalty in his inner circle and its possible consequences. This conflation, however, is not consistent: in one of his later sermons, Smith suggests in a discussion of the fate of King David that murder, while it seems to break these nearly unconditional seals, was not enough to become a son of perdition.[70] Franklin Richards reports Joseph Smith teaching in 1844 that David would eventually find salvation:

> there are two sins against which this power [of Christ's Atonement] does not secure or prevail they are "The sin against the Holy Ghost" And "shedding of innocent Blood" which is equivalent to "crucifying the Son of God afresh & putting him to an open shame" Those who do these it is impossible to renew unto repentance for they are delivered to the buffettings of Satan untill the day of redemptions illustrated the case of David said he could not obtain celestial glory and the reason why he had any hope or obtained a Promise that of his seed one should be raised up to reign over Israel forever was because that he had not spoken against the spirit & because he had not done this he ~~was renewed unto repentance and~~ obtained promise that God would not leave his soul in Hell.[71]

Indeed, Smith proclaims that it is the subject and fate of *possible* sons of perdition that precipitated a premortal "war in heaven." One of the fundamental principles of Mormon belief is the notion that all human beings existed as preexistent souls or spirits before birth. In this state, a plan of progression was proposed by God to allow these spirits to become embod-

---

may have an ending" ontology by creatively reversing its original intent. See also Brigham Young, August 31, 1856, *Journal of Discourses*, 4:31–32; Brigham Young, October 9, 1859, *Journal of Discourses*, 7:282.

70. See Smith's sermons on May 16, 1841, January 12, 1841, October 3, 1841, October 15, 1843, April 7, 1844, and May 12, 1844, in Smith et al., "Parallel Joseph." The subject of "eternal judgment" from Hebrews 6:2 was often the springboard for Joseph Smith's discussions of ultimate sins. The 1832 revelation (D&C 76) on nuanced rewards in the afterlife offered considerable discussion of the sons of Perdition. That revelation seems to classify them as a different category from murderers. Smith's sermons also disconnect the two, though both sins break sealings. Smith saw prayer for a murderer's soul (and presumably for one who had sinned "against the Holy Ghost") as a waste of breath—such a prayer indicating a lack of understanding of the dreadful and inevitable consequences involved.

71. See Richards's March 10, 1844, entry in Franklin D. Richards, "Scriptural Items."

ied beings. Smith's version of preexistence contained much of the social politics, charisma, and influence present in human social architectures, yet another way that Nauvoo impressed the earthly topography of human relations onto the landscape of heaven.[72] The conflict in heaven, as Smith saw it, was not whether sin and subsequent penalty would exist for mortals. It was over the proposition that some human mortals could eventually be lost forever in hell (as these sons of perdition). Smith claimed that it was just the *possibility* of a sin that placed humans outside the power of atonement that caused a war in heaven. George Laub summarized Smith's ideas:

> [Jesus] stated he could save all those who did not sin against the Holy Ghost and they would obey the code of laws that were given. But their circumstances were that all who would sin against the Holy Ghost should have no forgiveness neither in this world or in the world to come.[73]

A war of ideologies was fought in heaven, resulting in those who objected to God's proposition being "cast out."[74] There is thus an important irony in Smith's version of the war. Those on the wrong side ended out in the same Hell they had argued against as a possible fate in their future mortal probation.

This war in heaven later became a substantial point in the Mormon theological narrative of human freedom, but its explicit causal dependence on a class of humans damned forever as sons of perdition was left out of that later narrative. Rather than seeing the war through Smith's Nauvoo preaching and the polygamy revelation, the later narrative looked to Smith's early revelation in his revision of the Genesis text. There, Smith dictated that Lucifer/Satan/Devil "sought to destroy the agency of man"

---

72. For a survey of Christian belief in human preexistence, see Terryl L. Givens, *When Souls Had Wings: Pre-Mortal Existence in Western Thought*. For Smith, embodiment brought power and protection to a bare soul. Embodied beings enjoyed a certain protection against the otherwise overwhelming force of powerful unembodied beings. See Smith's sermons on January 5, 1841, and May 14, 1843, in Smith et al., "Parallel Joseph." On Smith's theology of embodiment, the importance of the body for Mormon cosmology, and the intellectual heritage of that system, see Samuel Morris Brown, *In Heaven as It is On Earth: Joseph Smith and the Early Mormon Conquest of Death*, chs. 4, 10. See also Doctrine and Covenants 130:2.

73. See George Laub journal, 16, 17.

74. See Smith's May 16, 1841, and April 7, 1844, sermons in Smith et al., "Parallel Joseph"; and Smith, *Every Word Seasoned with Grace*, ch. 7.

and take the role of Christ, guaranteeing that all souls would be saved.[75] Though it could be argued that Smith's explanation was merely a more detailed version of this early revelation, his story of (future) sons of perdition as the ignition point of the war was left behind.[76]

Many Latter-day Saints viewed the Utah conflicts with the United States government regarding polygamy and the unity of church and state as encroachments on fundamental constitutional freedoms, a theme that has recently returned to center stage in Mormon teaching.[77] The war in heaven became a preexistent proxy for a spiritual war on earth; Satan and his servants were seen in the role of the Federal Government and its agents or perhaps as their ignorant puppets.[78]

---

75. These characters are nearly always identical in Mormon discourse. See Moses 4:1–4 and Abraham 3:22–28.

76. The meaning of the war became focused on Lucifer's desire for power. See, for example, Orson Pratt, November 22, 1873, *Journal of Discourses*, 16:318; Melvin J. Ballard, October 6, 1918, *Conference Reports*, 149; Rulon S. Wells, April 7, 1930, *Conference Reports*, 70; Marion G. Romney, April 7, 1945, *Conference Reports*, 87; and more recently, M. Russell Ballard, "Return and Receive," and Joy D. Jones, "A Sin-Resistant Generation."

77. The theme of constitutional religious freedom has recently returned to Mormon speech and writing, again over marriage issues, but this time in regard to gay marriage and fears of reverse discrimination against entities refusing to acknowledge any internal legitimacy of gay marriages. See, for example, Kaimipono David Wenger, "'The Divine Institution of Marriage': An Overview of LDS Involvement in the Proposition 8 Campaign," 705–51.

78. To understand the logic in this position, see Bruce R. McConkie, "Be Valiant in the Fight of Faith" as well as references in note 77. See also Wilford Woodruff, October 5, 1890, in Brian H. Stuy, *Collected Discourses*, 2:124; and Larson, ed., *A Ministry of Meetings*, 522.

Chapter Six: Verses 28–45

Polygamy and the Afterlife

Joseph Smith generally played the role of chief judge over theological matters, but his approach to the innovations or traditions of others was often gentle. At times he embraced them, while at other times he might disagree but still defend the rights of others to believe differently. He could, however, be critical of those who claimed his ideas as their own.[1] This often-collaborative environment for theologizing presents challenges for fully understanding Smith's theology, as it can be difficult to untangle Smith's views from those of his colleagues. This is especially true with the burgeoning Mormon pamphleteering industry, which would have been impossible for Smith to fully vet. Men like Parley Pratt took Smith's revelations and often made their own superstructures of thought, but frequently presented the whole as representative of authoritative Mormon theology. Sometimes Smith corrected them, other times he left them alone. When Joseph Smith's centering voice was silenced in death, his followers sometimes filled that vacuum with their own speculations and revelations. The apostles in particular, based on their more or less egalitarian structure, felt some freedom to exercise their individual theological voices. For example, Lyman Wight's mission to Texas, while approved by Smith, went against Brigham

---

1. Plagiarism was not unusual in either literature or speech of the day and no systematic ethic existed for citation or credentials. Smith was sometimes incensed over those who claimed his "revelations" as their own. What he meant in this case was his oral teaching, not the canon. Offenders included Parley Pratt. See Smith's remarks to the Nauvoo Relief Society, April 28, 1842, Relief Society Minute Book. On his part, Smith probably borrowed from his coreligionists. For example, the statements in the so-called Articles of Faith found in his letter to John Wentworth and published in the March 15, 1842, issue of the *Times and Seasons*, probably drew on previous attempts at systemizing Mormonism, most proximate by Orson Pratt. David J. Whittaker, "The 'Articles of Faith' in Mormon Literature and Thought." See also Oliver Cowdery's list of eight points in Oliver Cowdery, "Address," 2.

Young's wish to focus on the Nauvoo temple; Parley Pratt's theology of love and marriage contrasted markedly with Young's and Kimball's; and Orson Pratt's beliefs regarding Mormon cosmology diverged from Smith in a number of important ways and violated Young's sensibilities on other counts.[2] This theological tension may have been somewhat healthy, but in extremes it endangered the apostolic goal of creating a cohesive people.

With the failure of the Missouri Zion project, Smith seemed to build in a series of tests to weed out potential dissenters, or at least prevent weak supporters from becoming his confidants and insiders. Those he selected for a preview of the Nauvoo endowment oaths and polygamy should have proven their staying power. The system had its weaknesses, as some insiders like William and Jane Law fell by the wayside and created deep unrest. The secret practice of polygamy was fundamentally unsuitable for a testing ground, largely because it was just too slow a process for discovering the crucially loyal among the Latter-day Saints. These tests are implied in the revelation along with its impressive cosmological visions. With these, the revelation on polygamy added new vistas to the meaning of "being saved," opening up a future of endless fulfillment as God's agents in creation and salvation.

> 28 I am the Lord thy God, and will give unto thee the law of my Holy Priesthood, as was ordained by me and my Father before the world was.
>
> 29 Abraham received all things, whatsoever he received, by revelation and commandment, by my word, saith the Lord, and hath entered into his exaltation and sitteth upon his throne.
>
> 30 Abraham received promises concerning his seed, and of the fruit of his loins—from whose loins ye are, namely, my servant Joseph—which were to continue so long as they were in the world; and as touching Abraham and his seed, out of the world they should continue; both in the world and out of the world should they continue as innumerable as the stars; or, if ye were to count the sand upon the seashore ye could not number them.
>
> 31 This promise is yours also, because ye are of Abraham, and the promise was made unto Abraham; and by this law is the continuation of the works of my Father, wherein he glorifieth himself.

---

2. On Wight, see Michael Scott Van Wagenen, *The Texas Republic and the Kingdom of God*; Melvin C. Johnson, *Polygamy on the Pedernales: Lyman Wight's Mormon Villages in Antebellum Texas, 1845–1858*. On Parley Pratt and Young, see Benjamin E. Park, "Early Mormon Patriarchy and the Paradoxes of Democratic Religiosity in Jacksonian America," 183–208. On Orson Pratt, see William V. Smith, *The King Follett Sermon: A Social History*. See also Gary J. Bergera, *Conflict in the Quorum: Orson Pratt, Brigham Young, Joseph Smith*.

32 Go ye, therefore, and do the works of Abraham; enter ye into my law and ye shall be saved.

33 But if ye enter not into my law ye cannot receive the promise of my Father, which he made unto Abraham.

34 God commanded Abraham, and Sarah gave Hagar to Abraham to wife. And why did she do it? Because this was the law; and from Hagar sprang many people. This, therefore, was fulfilling, among other things, the promises.

35 Was Abraham, therefore, under condemnation? Verily I say unto you, Nay; for I, the Lord, commanded it.

36 Abraham was commanded to offer his son Isaac; nevertheless, it was written: Thou shalt not kill. Abraham, however, did not refuse, and it was accounted unto him for righteousness.

37 Abraham received concubines, and they bore him children; and it was accounted unto him for righteousness, because they were given unto him, and he abode in my law; as Isaac also and Jacob did none other things than that which they were commanded; and because they did none other things than that which they were commanded, they have entered into their exaltation, according to the promises, and sit upon thrones, and are not angels but are gods.

38 David also received many wives and concubines, and also Solomon and Moses my servants, as also many others of my servants, from the beginning of creation until this time; and in nothing did they sin save in those things which they received not of me.

39 David's wives and concubines were given unto him of me, by the hand of Nathan, my servant, and others of the prophets who had the keys of this power; and in none of these things did he sin against me save in the case of Uriah and his wife; and, therefore he hath fallen from his exaltation, and received his portion; and he shall not inherit them out of the world, for I gave them unto another, saith the Lord.

40 I am the Lord thy God, and I gave unto thee, my servant Joseph, an appointment, and restore all things. Ask what ye will, and it shall be given unto you according to my word.

41 And as ye have asked concerning adultery, verily, verily, I say unto you, if a man receiveth a wife in the new and everlasting covenant, and if she be with another man, and I have not appointed unto her by the holy anointing, she hath committed adultery and shall be destroyed.

42 If she be not in the new and everlasting covenant, and she be with another man, she has committed adultery.

43 And if her husband be with another woman, and he was under a vow, he hath broken his vow and hath committed adultery.

44 And if she hath not committed adultery, but is innocent and hath not broken her vow, and she knoweth it, and I reveal it unto you, my servant Joseph, then shall you have power, by the power of my Holy Priesthood, to

take her and give her unto him that hath not committed adultery but hath been faithful; for he shall be made ruler over many.

45 For I have conferred upon you the keys and power of the priesthood, wherein I restore all things, and make known unto you all things in due time.

"As Innumerable as the Stars"

During the 1839–1846 period, two notions of kingdom expansion—expanding one's glory in the hereafter—existed in quiet, logical tension. Both had textual roots from the New York and Kirtland periods, and both captured those roots in terms of two different protologies (origin narratives).[3] They may be briefly outlined as the following:

1. Kingdom expansion for a person in the hereafter was based on having a large earthly progeny. In this way, after death and the exaltation of those children, their own god-like activities of world-peopling and priesthood connection made one a greater "king and priest, queen and priestess."[4] The protological background here was one of human beings as uncreated centers of consciousness. Smith preached the latter idea on numerous occasions and used it as a point of comfort to the bereaved: a loved one's personality and mind never ends *because it never began*. They survive by the inherent logic of eternal existence. Joseph Smith's narrative of preexistence saw eternal spirits being recruited by God to participate in an adoptive process designed to bring them eventual everlasting joy.[5]

2. More wives in mortality meant faster growth of "spirit" progeny in the hereafter, though precisely how or what that meant was not really fleshed out until after Smith's death (by Orson Pratt, W. W. Phelps, Eliza R. Snow, and others). In short, it came to entail heavenly pregnancy and birth of spirit bodies—such that Pratt saw heavenly gestation as comparable to mortal gestation, necessitating

---

3. This kingdom building notion that seemed to become a near obsession, which I later term kingdom "fever," was a feature of, and a rationalization for, the enterprise of plural marriage. (See the discussion of verses 58–63 in Chapter 9.)

4. Parley P. Pratt, *Autobiography of Parley Parker Pratt,* ch. 20.

5. This cosmology/ontology idea was present in Smith's sermons from 1839 to his death. See William Victor Smith, *Every Word Seasoned with Grace: The Funeral Sermons of Joseph Smith,* ch. 7. See also Samuel M. Brown, "Believing Adoption," 45–65. Smith, *The King Follett Sermon.*

the advantage of multiple wives.[6] The protological essence here, however, was divided. For example, Pratt himself found it difficult to escape the Cosmological Argument, because for him there had to be a first ancestor produced by the natural forces of the spiritual universe. What became the more normative mythos, championed by Brigham Young, was eternal ancestry—the *eternal machine of spirit production*—or as the much later James Talmage put it, "parent–derived eternity." One had no beginning in the sense that one's spirit was born in the heavens to parents whose spirits were once born in the heavens, *ad infinitum*.[7] This notion is the mirror image of a popular conception of immortality that says one is immortal if one has a continuing string of descendants (or perhaps adopted intellectual descendants).

Both stories of preexistence shared the same teleological theme: the greater one's posterity, the greater one's glory—and that theme was the outward logic of polygamy.[8]

Smith's frequent discourse on the eternal nature of a human spirit was surrounded by a web of language that made the individual souls of human beings non-contingent. After Smith's death, his language on the eternity of individual persons gradually became speech about the eternity of spirit propagation. Brigham Young and a number of the apostles saw an infinite regression of gods (Orson Pratt was a hold out) where God had a father, who also had a father, and so forth. (Smith's final Nauvoo sermons were

---

6. According to Orson Spencer, heavenly procreation was a natural and intended consequence of the physical and spiritual beauty of celestial persons. Heavenly pregnancy was to be "without pain or sorrow or travail." The existence of carefree gestation was founded in the removal of the Edenic curses. Orson Spencer, *Patriarchal Order, or Plurality of Wives!*, 2.

7. For Talmage's theory, see Smith, *The King Follett Sermon*, ch. 3.; James E. Talmage, Letter to Mary B. Parker, June 22, 1932; James E. Talmage, Letter to Joseph F. Smith, January 5, 1907; James E. Talmage, Letter to Joseph F. Smith, February 13, 1907; James E. Talmage diary, July 22, 1906.

8. Clayton summarized Smith saying: "those who are married by the power & authority of the priesthood in this life & continue without committing the sin against the Holy Ghost will continue to increase & have children in the celestial glory." Unfortunately, the mechanism for such "increase" left inference to fill in the details. But the nature of Nauvoo made sex and gestation in heaven no great leap of logic, though Eliza Snow found the idea an inductive analogical exercise. Fillerup, "William Clayton," May 16, 1843.

and often are read this way, though not presently in public preaching.)[9] In part, this evolution in protological narrative was fueled by a need for unity among the wilderness Saints, with complex underpinnings in the social dynamics of pioneer life. Those dynamics were generated in significant ways by polygamy with its attending spiritual economy—an economy that had developed a robust theological mythos, eloquently expressed by Orson Pratt in his 1852 sermon accompanying the first imprint of the plural marriage revelation.[10]

In the decade leading up to his assignment to the official Joseph Smith history in 1901 (which would eventually be published in a six-volume series at the beginning of the twentieth century), Mormon historian and member of the First Council of the Seventy B. H. Roberts saw the theological discontinuities between Utah and Nauvoo.[11] Smith's Nauvoo preaching resurfaced in some detail both in the history and late nineteenth-century sermon imprints, and Roberts's ready-made cure created a perpetual stir in Mormon theological circles, despite its being the most heroic solution to a genuine practical conundrum. Given Orson Pratt's story of birthing spirits in heaven, Eliza R. Snow's paean to a Heavenly Mother, and Joseph Smith's preaching that human individual consciousness had no beginning, Roberts found a theological seam that accommodated all three themes.[12]

---

9. J. Spencer Fluhman, *A Peculiar People: Anti-Mormonism and the Making of Religion in Nineteenth-Century America*, 5.

10. Brigham Young stated at the 1852 announcement of the polygamy revelation: "When a man commences the work of his exaltation, he begins at the last thing that will be completed. Our spirits, thousands of years ago, were first begotten; and at the consummation of all things, when the Savior has finished his work and presented it to the Father, he will be crowned." "A Special Conference of the Elders of the Church of Jesus Christ of Latter-Day Saints," 26.

11. Roberts was finally tasked with editing and publishing the work of early Church historians and clerks in their production of Joseph Smith's history, probably to help remove him from the public eye for a time. Roberts was sometimes unpredictable in public venues, giving political speeches that inflamed both Church leaders and "gentiles." Nevertheless, some of that work brought criticisms of his theological interpretations by other leaders like Charles Penrose. The move and its result were rather ironic in that Penrose was once given a similar task for the same reason. Jonathan H. Moyer, "Dancing With the Devil: The Making of the Republican/Mormon Pact," 256; Rudger Clawson diary, December 29, 1899, in Stan Larson, ed., *A Ministry of Meetings: The Apostolic Diaries of Rudger Clawson*, 127.

12. The Pratt brothers agreed that whatever the genesis of spirits, they were material, and that material came under Joseph Smith's anti-ex-nihilo theology.

By deploying language from the Book of Abraham, Roberts and fellow thinker Nels Nelson saw the beginnings of human beings as raw "intelligences" (Abr. 3:21–22; D&C 93:29), eternal agents who *chose* to become a part of God's family by being embodied in a material spirit body—a nod to Smith's declaration that spirits are material (D&C 131:7).[13] Such spiritual bodies were procreated, as Brigham Young taught, through heavenly sexual intercourse between God and his Wives (Adam and Eve for Young, the less specific God the Father and Mother for the less radical). From that point, Roberts and Nelson tied in the normative view of spirits becoming embodied as mortals via birth to human parents.

Paralleling the debates over the two eschatologies of Nauvoo and Utah, Roberts's interpretative claim concerning human spirits was seen as either an obvious explanation of various salvation stories within Mormonism, or an unjustified, even dangerous speculation. Protestants, however, were not alone in wishing to maintain a level of epistemic distance between God and human kind, as some Church leaders found Roberts's idea demeaning to God's divinity because it did not make man's existence entirely contingent and dependent of God—even though God was contingent (*as* God at least) irrespective of the rejection of Roberts's or Smith's theology. The story is interesting and complex, and it reveals theological fault lines between prominent voices in historical Mormonism, voices that are still embedded in Mormon discourse.[14]

For those who found Roberts intolerable, this provided a useful—if acontextual—explanation of Smith. On Snow, see Daniel Walker Howe, *What Hath God Wrought: The Transformation of America, 1815–1848*, 726. Snow's poem is her 1845 *My Father in Heaven*, set to music as a hymn, *Oh My Father*. Eliza R. Snow, "My Father in Heaven." See Laurel Thatcher Ulrich, *A House Full of Females: Plural Marriage and Women's Rights in Early Mormonism, 1835–1870*, 134.

13. Roberts narrative was largely based on Smith's April 7, 1844, sermon textually reproduced in 1855–56 Utah as a redaction-fusion of longhand sources. In one source for the sermon Smith stated, "God himself finds himself in the midst of spirits and glory, because he was greater, saw proper to institute laws for those who were in less intelligence, that they might have one glory upon another." William V. Smith et al., "The Parallel Joseph," April 7, 1844.

14. Mormon authors Bruce R. McConkie and Truman G. Madsen are examples. Compare Madsen's *Eternal Man* and Bruce R. McConkie, *Mormon Doctrine*, s.v. "Life." On McConkie, see Matthew Bowman, *The Mormon People: The Making of an American Faith*, 201–5.

"As Touching Abraham and His Seed"

Joseph Smith's early revisions of Genesis (the Book of Moses) were at least echoed in most versions of Utah eschatology, while Nauvoo eschatology was often seen in terms of Smith's translation of the Book of Abraham and his Nauvoo preaching. In the first two decades of the twentieth century within the Church, critics of Roberts attacked the reliability of reports of Joseph Smith's sermons, and they crafted various scripture proof-texts to show that Roberts's exposition was misleading and perhaps even blasphemous.[15]

Whatever the notion of kingdom expansion in the afterlife, this portion of the plural marriage revelation addresses "the law" with more specificity: it was not just about generating eternal contracts; it was about husbands with multiple wives siring children with those wives—whether it be mortal or spirit children in whatever fashion.[16] Admittedly, the terminology is unclear in some respects, and one gets the feeling that had the revelation been intended for the public, it would have gone through edits and revisions (as previous revelations had) to make it more focused and less personal.

This portion of the revelation begins with God making clear the eternal nature of this covenant:

> I am the Lord thy God, and will give unto thee the law of my Holy Priesthood, as was ordained by me and my Father before the world was. (v. 28)

This "law" (polygamy), like the Church sacraments, was planned and approved in heavenly councils before mortal persons began to inhabit the world.[17] In Joseph Smith's sermons, he sees the temple and all other salvif-

---

15. For further details, see Smith, *Every Word Seasoned with Grace*, ch. 7; and Smith, *The King Follet Sermon*. Charles W. Penrose offered a long critique of Roberts in a note to Joseph F. Smith. See Charles W. Penrose, "Immortality of the Spirit and Soul."

16. Heber C. Kimball was an early initiate into plurality. His plan was to marry elderly women with the hope that it would satisfy Smith's command. He was wrong. Smith pointed out (per verse 48 of the plural marriage revelation) a much younger widow as a proper candidate. Daynes, *More Wives Than One*, 29.

17. See, for example, Smith's letter excerpts in Doctrine and Covenants 128 or his sermon of June 11, 1843. In the record reconstruction process of the 1850s, Brigham Young and other leaders reviewed the developed texts of Smith's sermons that they deemed most important. The June 11 sermon was one of those. For the somewhat disappointingly meager reports of the June 11 sermon, see Smith et al., "Parallel Joseph," June 11, 1843.

ic sacraments of Mormonism as a key part of the work of what he termed "the Grand Council of heaven before the world was."[18]

The revelation then proceeds to answer the opening question posed at its very beginning: what of the ancient Patriarchs and polygamy? It answers:

> Abraham received all things, whatsoever he received, by revelation and commandment, by my word, saith the Lord, and hath entered into his exaltation and sitteth upon his throne.
>
> Abraham received promises concerning his seed, and of the fruit of his loins—from whose loins ye are, namely, my servant Joseph—which were to continue so long as they were in the world; and as touching Abraham and his seed, out of the world they should continue; both in the world and out of the world should they continue as innumerable as the stars; or, if ye were to count the sand upon the seashore ye could not number them. This promise is yours also, because ye are of Abraham, and the promise was made unto Abraham; and by this law is the continuation of the works of my Father, wherein he glorifieth himself.
>
> Go ye, therefore, and do the works of Abraham; enter ye into my law and ye shall be saved. But if ye enter not into my law ye cannot receive the promise of my Father, which he made unto Abraham.
>
> God commanded Abraham, and Sarah gave Hagar to Abraham to wife. And why did she do it? Because this was the law; and from Hagar sprang many people. This, therefore, was fulfilling, among other things, the promises. Was Abraham, therefore, under condemnation? Verily I say unto you, Nay; for I, the Lord, commanded it. (vv. 29–35)

The answer is that plural marriage was divinely mandated in the ancient past and is now again. However, the revelation goes beyond this and utilizes the ancient patriarch to again emphasize the importance of obeying the commandment and reiterates the consequences for disobedience. By extending the story to include Sarah and Hagar, the revelation shows its primary nature and purpose. It was directed to Emma Smith: "Sarah gave Hagar to Abraham to wife. And why did she do it? Because this was the law" (v. 34). Emma read (or heard the passage read by Hyrum) and understood the message. Terribly conflicted over the revelation, she reportedly burned the original. However, despite her immediate revulsion, she was apparently deeply impressed by the revelation and felt bound in some respects by its provisions—at least while her husband lived.

---

18. In addition to the June 11, 1843, sermon and Doctrine and Covenants 128:5, see Smith's sermons of January 5, 1841, August 13, 1843, August 27, 1843, and May 12, 1844, in Smith et al., "Parallel Joseph."

The revelation's designation of Joseph Smith's descendancy from Abraham wasn't new; this claim also appears in the Book of Mormon (2 Ne. 3:11–15) as well as early patriarchal blessings, and it was important for Mormons' understanding of Smith's authority in Utah. What it meant for Smith to be a descendant of Abraham was not entirely clear, and there were some seemingly different narratives for it—such as seeing Joseph Smith as a "pure Ephraimite" or even as a descendant of Jesus himself. (The latter explained the tribe of Judah's presence in New Testament genealogies for some Mormons.)[19] Membership in Israelite tribal families was important in early Mormonism, played strongly in Book of Mormon teachings, and continued a theology of an American Zion and Israel that echoed the Puritan narrative of emigration inherited by early Mormon converts. Israelite descendancy was important enough that converts were believed to literally become part of Israel through baptism (and rebaptism) in Zion.[20]

Early patriarchal blessings often, but not always, declared that the blessed one descended from one of the sons of Jacob (Israel), the grandson of Abraham. This familial belonging, like the singular sealings of the high priesthood, presaged and influenced Nauvoo sealing and adoption—an embodiment of previously spiritual frameworks that evoke similar and paradoxically contrary processes in American Protestantism to rationalize religious belief in the face of the epistemology of the Enlightenment.[21]

The concept of adoption into a tribe of Israel, however, signaled a somewhat lesser status of the Church convert in early preaching. For example, in 1839 Smith proclaimed that a natural descendant of Abraham is better gifted in ways than someone made into a descendant:

---

19. Jesus's marital status was important as an archetype for the plural marriage mythos in Utah. For example, see Jedediah M. Grant, August 7, 1853, *Journal of Discourses*, 1:345–46.

20. Jonathan A. Stapley and Kristine Wright, "'They Shall be Made Whole,': A History of Baptism for Health."

21. See Samuel M. Brown, "Early Mormon Adoption Theology and the Mechanics of Salvation"; on Protestants, see Leigh Eric Schmidt, *Hearing Things: Religion, Illusion, and the American Enlightenment*, 201; Mark A. Noll, *America's God: From Jonathan Edwards to Abraham Lincoln*, 362–64. Lorenzo Snow preached that all the Church leaders were literal descendants of Jesus. Claims like these are like spiritual enthusiasm. Less important or even irrelevant as a lasting tradition, they were powerful in the immediate world of the community. See Elizabeth O. Anderson, ed., *Cowboy Apostle: The Diaries of Anthony W. Ivins*, 211.

There is two Comforters spoken of [one] is the Holy Ghost the same as given on the day of Pentecost and that all Saints receive after faith. Repentance & Baptism. This first comforter or Holy Ghost has no other effect than pure intelligence. It is more powerful in expanding the mind enlightening the understanding & storeing the intellect with present knowledge of a man who is of the literal Seed of Abraham than one that is a gentile though it may not have half as much visible effect upon the body for as the Holy Ghost falls upon one of the Literal Seed of Abraham it is calm & serene & his whole soul & body are only exercised by the pure spirit of Intelligence; while the effect of the Holy Ghost upon a Gentile is to purge out the old blood & make him actually of the seed of Abraham. That man that has none of the blood of Abraham (naturally) must have a new creation by the Holy Ghost, in such a case there may be more of a powerful effect upon the body & visible to the eye than upon an Israelite, while the Israelite at first might be far before the Gentile in pure intelligence.[22]

This secondary category of a naturalized or adopted descendancy of Abraham was a forerunner to what was seen for a time as the highest of earthly sacraments: the creation of adopted priesthood descent lines— lines that many saw as replacing biological child-parent connections. Through sealing adoptions, family genealogies were rebuilt in new ways through sealing two biologically unrelated adult men as father and son. Adoptions were complicated by hierarchical conceptions of glory, just as polygamy was, and competition was often a factor in both.[23]

This adoption practice, active in Nauvoo after Joseph Smith's death, did not altogether replace the ideal power of literal blood descent. If one were the natural child of Brigham Young, it was unlikely that one would

---

22. From Willard Richards's copy of a report of Joseph Smith's June 27, 1839, instruction. See Smith et al., "Parallel Joseph," June 27, 1839. Smith's account of the enthusiasm of Mormonism is interesting, and it reflects his moderating sympathy for such spiritual displays. The enthusiasm of Kirtland was largely represented as ritual and interpretation in Nauvoo. Willard Richards, "Pocket Companion written in England," 15–22.

23. Many complex relationships were possible. Adoptive mothers and fathers often thought of these sealings as replacements of both mortal and postmortal relationships, with adopted "children" calling new parents "mother" and "father." See Jonathan A. Stapley, "Adoptive Sealing Ritual in Mormonism." On sealings and competition, see John G. Turner, *Brigham Young: Pioneer Prophet*, 160. See also the Epilogue.

abrogate that in favor of another sealed adoptive father. Others simply felt disloyalty to beloved parents as they contemplated a spiritual adoption.[24]

The "blood of the Prophets" trope was strong in Utah, and it broadened and deepened into both generational Church authorities and the hope of general preservation (or return to the fold) of the posterity of Church leaders. The idea encouraged the close family ties found in the highest Church councils, and in some cases it motivated the selection of Church leaders.[25] While Smith's ancestry may have been the subject of speculation, the idea that his descendants were destined or at least marked for Church leadership was a belief not ignored in Utah, and it became the central claim of authority for the Reorganized Church. The banner of a Smith-line of authority was taken up by Smith himself in some respects before he died—though prior to Nauvoo he saw his own successors in different ways. Moreover, his revelations named some offices as participating in an ancestral mythology, such as bishops as descendants of Aaron and patriarchs as descendants of ancient Joseph. One interesting account of this belief plays out in the pages of Isaac Sheen's short-lived Covington, Kentucky, serial, *Melchisedic and Aaronic Herald.*[26] Sheen welcomed Joseph Smith's brother William as

---

24. Council of Fifty member John Pack wrote, "I want my Children to be sealed to me and I want to be sealed to my Father and my Father to his Father and so on from Son to Father." John Pack, "Autobiography-Reminiscence (1809–1849): Recollections of John," May 16, 1847. See also Stapley, "Adoptive Sealing Ritual," 53–55, 78.

25. One example was Heber J. Grant. Grant related a revelation that his elevation to the apostleship came at the (posthumous) requests of his levirate father, Jedediah M. Grant, and his sealed father, Joseph Smith. Heber J. Grant, *Conference Report* (October 1918): 24. Rudger Clawson, one of the apostles in turn-of-the-century Utah, believed those with "gentile" blood were natural unbelievers. Rudger Clawson diary, October 4, 1904, in Larson, ed., *Ministry of Meetings*, 774–75. At least one Mormon told of his experience being rejected from leadership in favor of a Smith family member during the selection of the original Quorum of the Twelve Apostles. Oliver Cowdery and David Whitmer, two of the selection committee, separately stated the same idea. See Oliver Cowdery, Letter to Brigham Young, February 27, 1848; and Scott G. Kenney, ed., *Wilford Woodruff's Journal, 1833–1898, Typescript,* 3:335, 4:275.

26. Isaac Sheen, *Melchisedic and Aaronic Herald* 1, no. 2 (March 1849): 1–2, no. 9 (April 1850): 3. The title on the masthead varied in spelling and content from issue to issue, from *Aaronic Herald* to the one noted here, to *Melchisedeck and Aaronic Herald,* and finally to *Melchisedek and Aaronic Herald.* One interesting item in issue no. 8 was the appearance of the Book of Abraham, with Sheen

Church president regent for Joseph's children. A half-century later in Utah, Joseph F. Smith (the son of Hyrum Smith) indoctrinated his sons with the same idea of superior, believing blood, and at least to some degree, his daughters as well.[27] Several of his descendants would be called to the leading bodies of the Church, including his sons Hyrum Mack Smith and his name-sake, Joseph Fielding Smith; a grandson by marriage (Elder Bruce R. McConkie); and a great-grandson (Elder M. Russell Ballard).

"It was Accounted unto Him for Righteousness"

In his epistle to the Romans, Paul contrasts Abraham's works and accompanying worldly glory with his loyalty to God and a recognition of righteousness: "For if Abraham were justified by works, he hath whereof to glory; but not before God. For what saith the scripture? Abraham believed God, *and it was counted unto him for righteousness*" (Rom. 4:2–3; emphasis added). In its continued discussion of Abraham, the plural marriage revelation echoes this passage to emphasize faithfulness to God ahead of obedience to recognized law:

> Abraham was commanded to offer his son Isaac; nevertheless, it was written: Thou shalt not kill. Abraham, however, did not refuse, and it was accounted unto him for righteousness. (v. 36)

---

accepting the work as inspired, something the majority of Midwestern Saints who gathered around Joseph Smith III later rejected.

27. See Joseph F. Smith, Letter to Joseph F. Smith Jr., September 14, 1899. On "believing blood," see Armand L. Mauss, *All Abraham's Children: Changing Mormon Conceptions of Race and Lineage*, 22–36. On blood, lineage, and ancestral mythos extended from bishops and patriarchs to general Church leadership, see Stapley, "Adoptive Sealing Ritual," 69, 77. See also William V. Smith, "Early Mormon Priesthood Revelations: Text, Impact, and Evolution"; and Brown, *In Heaven as it is on Earth*, ch. 8. Modern biology suggests that the physical content of such "ancient blood" theories is largely empty and must be seen as spiritual designations of blessing rather than announcements of dominant or even unique chromosomal descent. The study of genomic material shows that all peoples of European descent share a relatively small number of genetic ancestors dating from one to two millennia. Peter Ralph and Graham Coop, "The Geography of Recent Genetic Ancestry across Europe." See also Douglas L. T. Rhodes, Steve Olson and Joseph T. Chang, "Modelling the Recent Common Ancestry of all Living Humans," 562–66. Genetic bottlenecks essentially require that if any living humans descend from Abraham, all do. Smith's Book of Abraham posits a symbolic descent based on conversion (Abr. 2:10).

The language reveals a divine command ethic that recognizes the mutability of law and the reality of conflicting moral and legal obligations in scripture, with righteousness being the mark of those who place contemporary loyalty to God above all other previous obligations. This ethic perhaps most notably appears in an alleged letter by Joseph Smith to Nancy Rigdon, daughter of Smith's counselor, Sidney Rigdon.[28] Nancy had evidently rejected a marriage proposal by Smith, appealing to scriptural and moral reasoning in opposition to it. In response to the rejection, Smith wrote a letter to her that read, "That which is wrong under one circumstance, may be, and often is, right under another. God said, thou shalt not kill, —at another time he said, thou shalt utterly destroy. This is the principle on which the government of heaven is conducted—by revelation adapted to the circumstances in which the children of the kingdom are placed. Whatever God requires is right." Published in Springfield, Illinois, in the *Sangamo Journal* by a disgraced John Cook Bennett, the letter created a stir among the political papers of the state.[29] Statements by the Rigdon family carefully approached the letter as problematic, but the marriage proposal itself probably did occur.[30]

Smith saw divine authority as necessarily superseding any worldly or civil authority, and thus acts performed by priesthood office were superior to any civil acts. When Ohio failed to recognize Mormon officials as clergy, he boldly proceeded to perform a marriage by his office as President of the High Priesthood. In Nauvoo, this ethic circulated in Smith's inner circle, seeing civil marriage and other contracts as fluid in the face of priesthood. In the words of historian Samuel Brown, "in the calculus of the

---

28. The best-known example in Mormon scripture may be the murder of Laban in the Book of Mormon (1 Ne. 4:7–18). However, the Old Testament is replete with such examples, as the letter notes.

29. A provenance for the published letter—along with the original—apparently does not exist beyond Bennett's claims, although it seems it was "owned" by the Utah Mormons. The letter is styled by Bennett as an apology for polygamy, in fact a kind of warning and a proposal to Rigdon. If it is authentic, Nancy's acceptance might have made a large difference in Sidney's future and perhaps the future of Mormonism. Joseph Smith, Letter to Nancy Rigdon; compare with "6th Letter from Gen. Bennett," 2. On Nancy Rigdon and Joseph Smith, see Andrew H. Hedges, Alex D. Smith, and Richard Lloyd Anderson, eds., *Journals, Volume 2: December 1841–April 1843*, xxix; and Gerrit J. Dirkmaat, "Searching for 'Happiness': Joseph Smith's Alleged Authorship of the 1842 Letter to Nancy Rigdon."

30. See Merina Smith, *Revelation, Resistance and Mormon Polygamy,* 85, 111, 114. Brian C. Hales, *Joseph Smith's Polygamy,* 1:476–89.

Mormon heavenly family, civil marriages were as meaningless as unauthorized baptisms."[31] The plural marriage revelation, however, does not wholeheartedly embrace a rejection of civil or non-priesthood authority, and it acknowledges earlier on that at least some of those contracts would be honored by the spiritual world—even if they "have an end when men are dead" (v. 7). Polygamy pushed this contrast to the extreme, as it not only asserted a superseding authority but also contradicted both civil and even canonized Church law, classifying both as irrelevant.[32] This ordering of Joseph Smith's religious authority above that of civil law, religious precedent, and common social mores affirmed a place for Smith as an uncontested leader, a position the Laws, Higbees, and other new dissenters publicized in their *Nauvoo Expositor*.[33] The complaints of the dissenters were rattled off as though they were chaotic manifestations of an ego gone wild.

Joseph Smith's controls of Nauvoo political, civic, and marriage projects were inextricably linked, and that same linkage continued in the Utah manifestation of his revelations and nascent policy. The relative position of Church authority and civil authority in the lives of Latter-day Saints was one issue at the heart of federal intervention in Territorial Utah, Utah's application for statehood, and the seating of Elders B. H. Roberts (in 1898) and Reed Smoot (in 1903)—who were both general authorities of the Church—in the United States Congress.[34] Reversing the explicitly linked

---

31. Brown, *In Heaven as It Is on Earth*, 242. On Smith's early marriage rite, see Kathleen Flake, "The Development of Early Latter-day Saint Marriage Rites, 1831–53," 77–102. The ever-critical *Warsaw Signal* gave its typically somewhat-slanted take on the idea. Its December 31, 1845, issue held that for "those who have received their endowment, all old things are done away and everything has become new. This is taken literally and applied to marriage and all other contracts." Mercy Thompson's recital of the events of 1843 may suggest this. Carol Cornwall Madsen, ed., *In Their Own Words: Women and the Story of Nauvoo*, 195.

32. For a later example in the contest of attitudes on civil and priesthood ranking, see Donald G. Godfrey and Rebecca S. Martineau-McCarty, *An Uncommon Common Pioneer: The Journals of James Henry Martineau, 1828–1918*, 440.

33. If the motives of Nauvoo polygamists were not always pure, the same was true of dissenters who were often irritated with Church leaders over economic, business, and growth issues. The Laws, for example, felt pinched by Joseph Smith's public arguments for immigrants buying Church-owned lands in Nauvoo against their holdings on the bluff where the temple site stood. See Smith's sermon of October 29, 1842, in Hedges et al., *Journals*, 2:164–65.

34. Both were troubled by post-Manifesto polygamy in different ways. Roberts was refused his seat by the House, Smoot underwent years of hearings on

authorities, the Smoot senate hearings settled the issue for the Church, making it clear that disputes between Church authority and civil authority would, in the end, firmly side with the latter.

With Mormon national loyalty established by the Smoot hearings, the twelfth Article of Faith to "believe . . . in obeying, honoring, and sustaining the law" became a standard backed up by an earlier 1831 revelation: "Let no man break the laws of the land, for he that keepeth the laws of God hath no need to break the laws of the land" (D&C 58:21). With some irony, this standard placed the Saints at the heart of patriotic America, and for that matter, as patriots in every nation in the world. In contrast to the willful disobedience to civil law of the previous half century, it made civil disobedience into sin and worked to cast the Church in the image of the ideal American citizen. The move to complete obedience to civil authority was not embraced by all, though, and Church leaders were divided over the issue of continuing polygamy after the Woodruff Manifesto—many of whom had risked their freedom and futures in opposition to the federal government. Some saw it as keeping the law of God in the face of inferior obligation, while others found it subversive and contrary to fundamental principles of honesty and integrity. The tugs and pulls between civil and Church polity were and are complex.[35] J. Golden Kimball, enthused at first over the "second manifesto" of 1904, gradually saw contradictions in behavior impossible to explain.[36] Lorenzo Snow's logic of continuity with the people of America would have put an end to polygamy on the basis of honor; ". . . in order to satisfy the honorable people of the nation [who] . . . look upon the United States as the greatest nation on the earth and feel that its laws are supreme—and that

---

whether he should be ejected from the Senate. See Kathleen Flake, *The Politics of American Religious Identity: The Seating of Senator Reed Smoot, Mormon Apostle.* More recently it was an issue in the Mitt Romney campaign for President of the United States. J. B. Haws, *The Mormon Image in the American Mind: Fifty Years of Public Perception*, 17.

35. See Doctrine and Covenants 58:19–23; Matthew C. Godfrey et al., eds., *Documents: Volume 2: July 1831–January 1833*, 12–21; Moyer, "Dancing with the Devil," 492–96; Stapley, "Adoptive Sealing Ritual," 80–69; Susan L. Warner, "Sharing Time: I Believe in Obeying the Law;" and T. S. Hettinger, "It's the Law." The Smoot admissions, however, hardly settled the debate. See Boyd K. Packer, "Our Moral Environment," 66–8; Karl-Heinz Schnibbe et al., *When Truth was Treason: German Youth Against Hitler: The Story of the Helmuth Hübener Group.*

36. J. Golden Kimball journals, 1883–1887; 1895–1908, 22:144–53.

when it comes to the question of law, the Latter-day Saints should bow" but his fellow apostles were powerfully conflicted on the issue.[37]

"They Have Entered Into Their Exaltation. . . . Therefore He Hath Fallen From His Exaltation"

The plural marriage revelation continued its use of Paul to explain not only Abraham's polygamy, but also that of his son and grandson, Isaac and Jacob:

> Abraham received concubines,[38] and they bore him children; and it was accounted unto him for righteousness, because they were given unto him, and he abode in my law; as Isaac also and Jacob did none other things than that which they were commanded; and because they did none other things than that which they were commanded, they have entered into their exaltation, according to the promises, and sit upon thrones, and are not angels but are gods.[39] (v. 37)

Abraham's being "accounted unto . . . righteousness" is extended from his attempt to sacrifice his own son (in violation of the command to not

---

37. Rudger Clawson diary, December 30, 1899, in Larson, ed., *A Ministry of Meetings*, 128.

38. Although concubines were mentioned in the revelation and were an item of discussion in Utah, it was never clearly defined in a modern context. Christine Talbot, *A Foreign Kingdom: Mormons and Polygamy in American Political Culture, 1852–1890*, ch. 5; B. Carmon Hardy, *Solemn Covenant: The Mormon Polygamous Passage*, ch. 6; and Samuel Taylor and Raymond Taylor, *The John Taylor Papers*, 1:58–59, 86–93. Utah First Presidency member George Q. Cannon thought of concubines as basically post-1890 sealed mistresses. Not legally married per se, they would be sexual partners able to "multiply and replenish" the earth, until the injustices of U.S. law could be righted; thus they would be able to raise children born in the latter day sealing covenant but without the complications implied by bigamy statutes and overt marriage. How this might have skirted the "cohabitation" charge he did not explain. Abraham H. Cannon diary, April 5, 1894, in Edward Leo Lyman, ed., *Candid Insights of a Mormon Apostle: The Diaries of Abraham H. Cannon*, 492.

39. On angels and gods, John D. Lee's recollections of Nauvoo saw plural marriage as the dividing line: eternal marriage only gained one angelic status, while plurality offered divinity. The Nauvoo language of sealing, while not perfectly known and not uniform, is less definite, yet Lee was steeped in temple happenings following Smith's death. John D. Lee, *Mormonism Unveiled; or the Life and Confessions of the Late Mormon Bishop, John D. Lee*, 166.

kill) to his acceptance of concubines who provided him with increased posterity (in violation of antebellum moral sentiment). Further affirming the righteousness of entering into polygamy, deification is this time tied more directly to polygamy: Abraham, Isaac, and Jacob are now gods—not in spite of their polygamy, but because of it. The repeated emphasis that they "did none other things *than that which they were commanded*" seems to allude to and establish a textual prohibition of rogue polygamous relationships not authorized by the "one on the earth [Smith] . . . on whom this power and the keys of this priesthood are conferred" (v. 7), rather than a recognition of them not committing murder or blaspheming against the Holy Ghost.

Paired with the affirmative stories of Abraham, the revelation also approaches the cases of David's and Solomon's own plural marriages. While polygamy was tied to the exaltation of the Patriarchs, polygamy could also be a problem for sinners as evidenced by their descendent, David. David is a complex character in Hebrew histories, yet he was still a figure of pride. In the New Testament, Matthew's Gospel makes David's kingship a signal part of Jesus's status in the Christian story. David's rise from shepherd boy to successor of Saul is packed with dizzying twists and turns, many of which show David's deeply troubling human foibles. The eschatological fate of David was a contested topic in the larger Protestant world and was a recurring topic for Joseph Smith.[40] The Book of Mormon glowered, "Behold, David and Solomon truly had many wives and concubines, *which thing was abominable before me*, saith the Lord" (Jacob 2:24; emphasis added). But Jacob's condemnation of David for his polygamous practice was simultaneously too broad and too narrow in Joseph Smith's theology.

Joseph Smith spent considerable time with David's premeditated murder of Uriah. In his exegesis of Hebrews 6 under the rubric, "eternal judgment"—a phrase he interpreted in terms of unforgivable transgressions (see the previous chapter)—Joseph moved to make this doctrine one of the fundamental articles of the Mormon faith.[41] Smith's discussions of eternal judgment and Uriah's murder serves an important chronological purpose for the plural marriage revelation.

From 1839, Joseph Smith consistently scoured his disciples with sermons drawn out of the dangers of disloyalty. The failure of the Zion enterprise and the departure of the founding New York contingent of church

---

40. For an example of Protestant debate over David, see Jonathan Edwards, "The Justice of God in the Damnation of Sinners," 344.

41. See Smith's sermons of August 9, 1840, August 16, 1840, January 12, 1841, and October 15, 1843, among many others in Smith et al., "Parallel Joseph."

leaders marked him with a fear that inside traitors were the most dangerous of enemies, and the betrayals and apostasies of Missouri and Kirtland motivated a new discursive climate. Insiders who turned on Smith would suffer ultimate punishment in the afterlife. The revelation fit with Smith's double-barreled threat against turncoat behavior.[42]

> David also received many wives and concubines, and also Solomon and Moses my servants, as also many others of my servants, from the beginning of creation until this time; and in nothing did they sin save in those things which they received not of me. David's wives and concubines were given unto him of me, by the hand of Nathan, my servant, and others of the prophets who had the keys of this power; and in none of these things did he sin against me save in the case of Uriah and his wife; and, therefore he hath fallen from his exaltation, and received his portion; and he shall not inherit them out of the world, for I gave them unto another, saith the Lord. (vv. 38–39)

The revelation shares considerable intertexuality with the Book of Mormon while modifying Jacob's flat condemnation of polygamy (and specifically that of David's). That intertextuality makes the revelation a commentary on Jacob's sermon. Specifically, the plural marriage revelation alludes to Jacob's language to teach that "David [and Solomon] also received many wives and concubines, . . . and in nothing did they sin *save in those things which they received not of me*" (v. 38; emphasis added). Rather than polygamy being David's sin, the revelation recasts the Book of Mormon's general condemnation to specifically unauthorized marriages "which they received not of me," which points back to the previous verse's warning to engage in "none other things than that which they were commanded" (v. 37). As it is in the revelation as a whole, the subtler message here is one to Emma Smith—that unlike David and Solomon's unauthorized marriages, Joseph received his wives from God.

The conflict between the Book of Mormon and the plural marriage revelation was not lost on believers, and practitioners of polygamy generally appealed to what seems to be an exception clause following the discussion of David's wives in the Book of Mormon:

> Wherefore, this people shall keep my commandments, saith the Lord of Hosts, or cursed be the land for their sakes. For if I will, saith the Lord of Hosts, raise up seed unto me, I will command my people; otherwise they shall hearken unto these things. (Jacob 2:29–30)

---

42. Brigham Young came to share the same fear, though he saw Joseph Smith's reaction as ineffective. Young was more rigid than Smith in his policies to protect his life and purge dissent. Turner, *Brigham Young*, 151–53, 171–74, 184–88.

An 1883 sermon by Erastus Snow exemplifies such an attempt to bring the Book of Mormon and plural marriage into harmony, and at the same time it reveals that Jacob's sermon appealed to Latter-day Saints who questioned polygamy:

> Now, those who take this other view, and are trying to convince themselves that this is an institution of man and not of God, bring forth the law that was given to the Nephites of old upon the American continent, which was given them by Jacob, the brother of Nephi, and which you can read, as doubtless you have often read, in the Book of Mormon. Jacob arraigned some of the people because the men were giving way to the lusts of the flesh and the pride of life, and whoredoms, and they attempted to justify themselves in their whoredoms by referring to what is written in the Jewish Scriptures concerning David and Solomon and other men having many wives and concubines, which Jacob informed the Nephites was an abomination in the sight of the Lord, and gave unto them a commandment that not any man among them should have save it be one wife, and concubines they should have none, saying that the Lord "delighteth in the chastity of woman." And in the same connection the Lord said: "For if I will, saith the Lord of Hosts, raise up seed unto me, I will command my people; otherwise they shall hearken unto these things." Now, there was a reason why the Lord gave this commandment to the Nephites. But this reason did not exist when the Lord called Abraham and promised that, his seed should be like the sand upon the sea shore for number. He recognized the righteousness of a plurality of wives, and never at any time did he restrict them from the days of Abraham until Christ, so far, as we have any record in the Jewish Scriptures. But there were reasons, as I said before, why he restricted the Nephites, but in this restriction He intimated that when the time should come that He should raise up seed unto himself, He would command His people. [43]

Interestingly, while Snow here attempts to reconcile the Book of Mormon and Mormon polygamy, he does not attempt to harmonize the abomination of David's marriages in the Book of Mormon and the sinlessness of those marriages (besides the betrayal and murder of Uriah) in the plural marriage revelation.

Joseph Smith's recital of David's fate is curious given verses 19 and 26 of the revelation. Indeed, his views regarding the shedding of innocent blood and blasphemy against the Holy Ghost complicate his teaching over time, as does the revelation. At first glance, the revelation seems to suggest that David's assignations with Bathsheba were the issue that damned David. But the mention of Uriah provides context for Smith's preaching

---

43. Erastus Snow, June 24, 1883, *Journal of Discourses*, 24:163.

on David. Early parts of the revelation claimed that only shedding innocent blood could break sealing bonds though other transgressions might
require the life of an offender. (See Chapter 2 and the discussion of Robert
Thompson and Brigham Young.) There are multileveled punishments
here (such as death, destruction, eternal damnation, being barred from
highest glory, and temporary damnation), and whether they were a consistent whole in Joseph Smith's mind is impossible to tell at this distance.
Could polygamous adultery really bring about the fall of David? Did the
revelation imply that David was a *permanent* loss because of his adultery?
Smith's preaching offered another explanation.

As a preacher, Smith could be adventurous in his interpretations of
scripture, and he approached the problem of David on at least two occasions in creative ways and always in the context of eternal judgment. Two
examples in particular preceded and followed the revelation, one from
May 1841 and another from March 1844. Aside from the cultural context
of Zion, the textual context for Smith's remarks in both cases is Peter's
sermon in Acts 2:

> For David speaketh concerning [Jesus], I foresaw the Lord always before my
> face, for he is on my right hand, that I should not be moved: Therefore did
> my heart rejoice, and my tongue was glad; moreover also my flesh shall rest
> in hope: Because thou wilt not leave my soul in hell, neither wilt thou suffer
> thine Holy One to see corruption. Thou hast made known to me the ways of
> life; thou shalt make me full of joy with thy countenance. Men and brethren,
> let me freely speak unto you of the patriarch David, that he is both dead and
> buried, and his sepulchre is with us unto this day. (Acts 2:25–29)

A report of the 1841 sermon reads:

> Even David, must wait for those times of refreshing, before he can come
> forth and his sins be blotted out; for Peter speaking of him says, "David hath
> not yet ascended into Heaven, for his sepulchre is with us to this day:" his
> remains were then in the tomb. Now we read that many bodies of the saints
> arose, at Christ's resurrection, probably all the saints, but it seems that David
> did not. Why? because he had been a murderer. If the ministers of religion
> had a proper understanding of the doctrine of eternal judgment, they would
> not be found attending the man who had forfeited his life to the injured laws
> of his country by shedding innocent blood; for such characters cannot be
> forgiven, *until they have paid the last farthing.* The prayers of all the ministers
> in the world could never close the gates of hell against a Murderer.[44]

---

44. "To those of our readers who reside at remote distances from this place . . . ,"
429–30; emphasis added. See also "Extracts from William Clayton's Private Book,"

For first century Jews and Christian Jews in particular, David would (eventually) be in heaven. To say otherwise would have been dangerous for early Christians. Smith goes beyond anything in the Petrine sermon and well beyond any implied adultery penalty of the revelation. It was murder that damned David and for which he forfeited the highest rewards in the afterlife.

A report of Smith's March 10, 1844, sermon reads:

> [T]here are two sins agains[t] which this power [priesthood sealing] does not secure or prevail they are "The sin against the Holy Ghost" And "shedding of innocent Blood" which is equivalent to "crucifying the Son of God afresh & putting him to an open shame" Those who do these it is impossible to renew unto repentance for they are delivered to the buffettings of Satan untill the day of redemptions illustrated the case of David said he could not obtain celestial glory and the reason why he had any hope or obtained a Promise that of his seed one should be raised up to reign over Israel forever was because that *he had not spoken against the spirit* & because he had not done this he was renewed unto repentance and obtained promise that God would not leave his soul in Hell.[45]

Smith's point was that while murder is a sin so horrific that it results in permanent damnation, the sin against the Holy Ghost was even direr. Both sins were potent enough to dissolve the "Holy Spirit of promise" of verse 19.

Importantly for verse 19, the 1844 sermon reported by Richards suggests the separation of murder and sin against the Holy Spirit. The emphasis on murder is connected to the discussion of the sons of Perdition in the previous chapter as well as Smith's work to erect a bulwark against a repetition of the Missouri disappointments. His reduction of David's status recalls similar criticisms of David by Martin Luther and John Calvin and was prescient of modern readings of the Old Testament.[46] Whatever

---

in George D. Smith, ed., *An Intimate Chronicle: The Journals of William Clayton*, Appendix A.

45. Reported by Franklin D. Richards, "Scriptural Items"; emphasis added. Wilford Woodruff's report of the same sermon adds that a new or replacement David will be born in the end times: "the priesthood that he received & the throne & kingdom of David is to be taken from him & given to another by the name of David in the last days, raised up out of his linage." Wilford Woodruff's journal, March 10, 1844, in Kenney, ed., *Wilford Woodruff's Journal*, 2:364. See also the revelation to Newel K. Whitney discussed in Chapter 4.

46. The idea of a new (or replacement) David is suggested by Old Testament passages and appears in Jewish, Christian, and Mormon literature on the end times. That David was *permanently* consigned to hell was not an unusual

the resolution of Smith's ideas around the complex of ultimate sins and death penalties, their use makes the revelation on polygamy one fraught with threat, awe, and fear—the psychological force of which was largely targeted to and felt by Emma Smith.[47]

"And Restore All Things"

One of the more popular explanations of polygamy in later decades was that it was a necessary part of the divine mandate to gather all "dispensations" into the restored Church of Christ, bringing together all of the doctrines and sacraments revealed at different times throughout humankind's religious history, including innovations never before revealed (D&C 124:41). In the plural marriage revelation, God tells Joseph Smith,

> I am the Lord thy God, and I gave unto thee, my servant Joseph, an appointment, and restore all things. Ask what ye will, and it shall be given unto you according to my word. (132:40)

Smith saw his prophetic office in the high priesthood as not just a return of the ancient Christian church—that was far too narrow—but also a final restoration of every epoch of Godly intervention in the biblical history of man, from Adam and the antediluvian prophets, through Abraham, Moses, the Israelite prophets, and into the times of Jesus and early Christianity. Like Matthew's genealogy of Joseph, Joseph Smith's revelations gave voice to the line of ancient protocols and priesthood, con-

---

Protestant position either (Calvin and Luther both saw David as a terrible king and man). On the "return of David," in various belief communities, see Yuzuru Miura, "David in Luke-Acts: His Portrayal in the Light of Early Judaism." David's story in the Old Testament histories represents the intertwining of texts and stories from different eras, much of it the result of an attempt to rehabilitate David's reputation. The historicity of David's life incidents in the Bible has little actual impact on the text of the revelation, which deploys David as a stock example for the theology of ultimate sins. Meir Sternberg, *The Poetic of Biblical Narrative: Ideological Literature and the Drama of Reading*, 188. For a popular but somewhat sensationalist work, see Joel Baden, *The Historical David: The Real Life of an Invented Hero*, 18–52. For a more scholarly but still accessible biography see Steven L. McKenzie, *King David: A Biography*, ch. 8.

47. "The Mormons in Nauvoo: Three Letters from William Law on Mormonism," 6.

necting the final dispensation of God's work to all that had gone before.[48]
The new latter-day dispensation drew on these in preparation for the return of the Millennial Christ. Mormonism was to be the fulfillment of the Pauline "gather[ing] together of all things in Christ" (Eph. 1:10). In an October 5, 1840, address Smith declared that

> all the ordinances and duties that ever have been required by the priesthood under the direction and commandments of the Almighty ~~in the last dispensation at the end thereof~~ in any of the dispensations, shall all be had in the last dispensation at the end thereof. Therefore all things had under the Authority of the Priesthood at any former period shall be had again—bringing to pass the restoration spoken of by the mouth of all the Holy Prophets.[49]

Smith's restoration narrative turned Protestant notions of dispensation vertically. Protestants in the large saw dispensations as confining periods of God's interaction with mankind. What God did or allowed in one era of His work was not license to humans in another era. Most often deployed with the idea of cessation—that the Spirit's ecstatic workings (tongues, prophecy, healing, etc.) with the Church of the first Christian era had ceased—it answered the discomfort of many preachers with the excesses of revival enthusiasm. The Book of Mormon labeled that sort of dispensationalism as orthogonal to righteousness, a sign that the world was devoid of faith (Morm. 9:7–8). Rather, miracles would only cease "according to the unbelief of the children of men" (Moro. 10:19).

Smith's account of dispensations read all former eras of God's work as coming together in a last dispensation (which began with Smith's commission to restore *all things*). This was the great divide between Smith and most other restorationists who wanted to bring back the principles of the ancient Christian church but not its practices of canonical extension or spiritual exotica. Instead, Smith saw dispensations as stepping-stones to a final joining of all truth—past, present, and future.[50] This was the justification of Smith's fascination with God's ancient peoples and their

---

48. For example, see Doctrine and Covenants 84:6–17 for the high priesthood's ascent, and Doctrine and Covenants 107:41–57 for a descent of the patriarchal priesthood.

49. Joseph Smith, "An Investigation of the Priesthood from the Scriptures." This is perhaps the only sermon Smith dictated before delivery; it was read by Robert Thompson at the Church conference rather than by Joseph Smith.

50. On King James usage in Mormon discourse on dispensations, see Philip L. Barlow, "The BYU New Testament Commentary: 'It Doth Not Yet Appear What It Shall Be,'" 76.

languages: their truth and their practice must return.[51] And because the project of restoration was the appointment "given unto . . . my servant Joseph," it largely explains why his successors did not feel the urge to continue further restorative work. (See the discussion of verse 45 below.)

"Hath Committed Adultery and Shall Be Destroyed"

The extended discussion of adultery in the plural marriage revelation implies that it, in the context of polygamy, was a concern that needed to be addressed. This was almost surely meant to speak to Emma Smith's anxiety over the practice of polygamy, but it may also reflect Hyrum's involvement as interlocutor. The original "Law of the Church" (D&C 42)[52] briefly covered the subject among a list of multiple commandments largely derived from the Sermon on the Mount:

> Thou shalt love thy wife with all thy heart, and shalt cleave unto her and none else. And he that looketh upon a woman to lust after her shall deny the faith, and shall not have the Spirit; and if he repents not he shall be cast out. Thou shalt not commit adultery; and he that committeth adultery, and repenteth not, shall be cast out. But he that has committed adultery and repents with all his heart, and forsaketh it, and doeth it no more, thou shalt forgive; But if he doeth it again, he shall not be forgiven, but shall be cast out. (42:22–26)

The plural marriage revelation offered a somewhat different approach with different rules for men and women in plural relationships, differences echoed both in the patriarchal mythos of polygamy and the cultural patriarchy of the antebellum age.

> And as ye have asked concerning adultery, verily, verily, I say unto you, if a man receiveth a wife in the new and everlasting covenant, and if she be with another man, and I have not appointed unto her by the holy anointing, she hath committed adultery and shall be destroyed. (132:41)

Although a husband and wife might be sealed, the revelation leaves open the possibility of the wife being "appointed" to someone else. Thus, sexual relations with another man would only be adultery if she were not appointed to him. Though the language here is somewhat confusing, it

---

51. Brown, *In Heaven as It Is on Earth*, 129–36, 191–93, 272.

52. See Robin Scott Jensen, Robert J. Woodford, and Steven C. Harper, eds. *Revelations and Translations: Manuscript Revelation Books, Facsimile Edition*, 95–105; and Michael Hubbard MacKay et al., eds., *Documents, Vol. 1: July 1828–June 1831*, 245–56.

may be interpreted (together with verses 42 and 61) in terms of polyandry or "dual wives."[53] Emma Smith was aware of rumors involving her husband and married women and may have seen such an implication.[54] The complex relationship between priesthood hierarchy and civil law further complicated the way this verse was understood in Utah. Regardless of the details of the revelation's meaning, the severity of violation was made clear with the instruction that the guilty "shall be destroyed." In the isolation of Utah, such adultery was called out as a capital offense, with a *Deseret News* editor writing: "[C]lose the door against adultery. . . . Public opinion here pronounces the penalty of death as the fitting punishment for such crimes."[55] Legal statute in the territory, however, lacked this extreme approach and instead mandated that convicted adulterers be imprisoned.

The next verses expand on the notion of sexual impropriety in the new institution of plural marriage and complicate the narrative of David.

> If she be not in the new and everlasting covenant, and she be with another man, she has committed adultery. And if her husband be with another woman, and he was under a vow, he hath broken his vow and hath committed adultery. And if she hath not committed adultery, but is innocent and hath not broken her vow, and she knoweth it, and I reveal it unto you, my servant Joseph, then shall you have power, by the power of my Holy Priesthood, to take her and give her unto him that hath not committed adultery but hath been faithful; for he shall be made ruler over many. (vv. 42–44)[56]

---

53. Perhaps the discussions of concubines among Church leaders after the Woodruff Manifesto alluded to ideas here. See also verse 61 of the plural marriage revelation. Rumors of Smith's involvement with married women were circulating from the time of John C. Bennett. His apparent attempt to marry Sarah Pratt created a deep fissure between her and husband Orson Pratt that had continuing effects to the end of their lives. Samuel Brown coined the term "dual wives" for Joseph Smith's sealed wives who were simultaneously married to other men. Brown, *In Heaven as It Is on Earth*, 242.

54. See Joseph Smith's sermon on May 26, 1844, in Smith et al., "Parallel Joseph"; and Richard Lyman Bushman, *Joseph Smith: Rough Stone Rolling*, 433–66. Smith frequently referred to or even delivered special revelations when he proposed to women. In the case of Nancy Hyde, wife of Apostle Orson Hyde, his proposal to her was augmented by a written revelation. See Hedges et al., *Journals*, 2:xxvi, 37.

55. "Our Southern Settlements," 5. Thirteen years before the *Deseret News* mention, First Presidency member Jedediah Grant instructed departing missionaries to teach "every adulterer should die." Thomas Bullock minutes, September 6, 1855.

56. Language here is pulled from Jesus's parable of the talents (Matt. 25:14–30). Smith used the story during his April 2, 1843, visit to Ramus, Illinois, in reference

This passage speaks to the viability of secular marriage. Although not a part of the *cultus* of Nauvoo sealing and plurality, secular marriages (vows not made in the new and everlasting covenant) are recognized under the rules of eternal marriage. They would not continue past death but were nevertheless binding during mortality—though the rule suggested by the revelation seems to have been more fluid in practice. Dual marriages (women married to husbands of lesser stature, sealed to men of greater stature) in Nauvoo and on the trail west suggest a hierarchy of vows in polygamous Mormonism, at least among elites like Joseph Smith and Brigham Young.[57]

The revelation's rules of adultery do not explicitly call for the destruction of male adulterers as it does with female violators (v. 41), though such men would still be subject to being "destroyed in the flesh" for "any sin or transgression of the new and everlasting covenant" (v. 26).[58] Also, like David (v. 39), the guilty man loses his wife or wives as they are "take[n] . . . and give[n]" to someone worthy (2 Sam. 12:11). This language of taking and giving of wives between men is a clear imitation of Old Testament views of ownership and obedience and reveals an inequality between men and women that echoed the patriarchal structure of antebellum America.[59] The theme of women as chattel is difficult to avoid. Moreover, there is little about love and attraction here. In practice, divorce among polygamists was

---

to multiple wives. See Hedges et al., *Journals*, 2: appendix 2. The "vow" of verses 43 and 44 may be a reference to Joseph Smith's suspicion that William Law was an adulterer. Conflicting stories exist surrounding Smith's relationship to William and Jane Law. Some relate that Smith proposed marriage to Jane and claim William was guilty of adultery, while others work to make the Laws as considering polygamy since Smith made acceptance of polygamy a prerequisite to sealing. Perhaps there were other situations to which the words applied, but they seem narrowly crafted. However, applying the words to the Laws, the timeline means that the revelation is partly prophetic rather than a narration. On the Laws, see Lyndon Cook, "William Law, Nauvoo Dissenter," 64–65; Bushman, *Rough Stone Rolling*, 528–9; and Brian C. Hales, *Joseph Smith's Polygamy*, 2:222.

57. For several examples, see Ulrich, *A House Full of Females*, ch. 5.

58. See the somewhat more egalitarian form in the speculative modern revision in Chapter 11.

59. Benjamin Park has argued for a progressive equality in Smith's theology at the time, and there is no doubt that Joseph Smith was no extremist in his view of woman as submissive to man. However, Park also notes that this potential for female empowerment was largely overturned in the months and years after Smith's death. See Benjamin E. Park, "Early Mormon Patriarchy and the Paradoxes of Democratic Religiosity in Jacksonian America."

often connected to romance and loving presence, or lack thereof, as well as occasional adulteries.[60] The short clause, "and she knoweth it," is oddly redundant if it refers to her own fidelity. The phrase, though awkwardly placed, refers to a wife's knowledge of her husband's infidelity. However, a wife's knowledge of her husband's infidelity was insufficient to sever a sealing; that knowledge had to be revealed by God to Smith as well, who could then "appoint" her to someone else.

The revelation here recreates the unclear relationship of adultery, David, murder, the sin against the Holy Ghost, and the Holy Spirit of promise, and never resolves it. The text moves beyond the monogamous assumptions of church law in terms of adultery (D&C 42:74–77, 80–82) and lacks any repentance clause. The ad hoc nature of these rules suggests the possibility that Smith had a case in mind. What that may have been is unknown. With Emma as the intended recipient of the revelation, were the passages on adultery a warning to her? Was she tempted to retaliate over polygamy? The remaining verses of the revelation highlight the unresolved nature of Joseph and Emma's struggles over plural marriage.

According to Smith's teachings, David's ultimate curse is due to his murder of Uriah. This makes a merely adulterous male like and unlike David. An adulterous though not murderous male may lose his (sealed) wives, just as David lost his wives (2 Sam. 12:11), but is the ultimate salvation of a sealed couple at stake in cases of adultery? In verse 19, the promise of salvation except for those "who shed innocent blood" suggests that is it not. However, the continued eternal sealing as marriage *partners* seems to be at stake. Could the curse of verse 26 (being "delivered unto the buffetings of Satan unto the day of redemption") include the fate of losing a partner? The revelation seems to create a theological antinomy over the status of adultery relative to the sins that "break" the seals of the priesthood. Adultery may result in a man's wives being "given" to another man. Does this imply that such a man has somehow lost the blessing of verse 19? How is this theological impasse to be resolved? An important, related question concerns the effect of excommunication on sealings. As we shall see, the theology of excommunication is somewhat confused historically in Mormon literature and regulation. Looming in the background is the threat that priesthood acts can be dissolved by the same person (v. 7) that authorized them: "loosed on earth and in heaven." Perhaps this is what

---

60. For example, see Turner, *Brigham Young*, 188–95, 236–43; and Paula Kelly Harline, *The Polygamous Wives Writing Club: From the Diaries of Mormon Pioneer Women*, ch. 11.

is implied by the taking and giving of wives for an adulterous male. The absolute nature of verse 19 suggests the need for some further explanation of the fate of men and women who are sealed and then sin. Ultimately, verse 19 was ignored in favor of a pessimistic view of the perseverance of sealing. (See the Epilogue of this volume.)

In 1883 John Taylor reported applying the plural marriage revelation in a case of adultery:

> A certain Bishop wrote to me to know what should be done in the following case: A man had been away from home on a mission, and during his absence his wife had committed adultery. I replied that the woman would have to be severed from the Church; but requested that the aggrieved husband should call upon me. He did so, bringing with him his delinquent wife and three beautiful little boys—three as beautiful little boys as I ever saw. He also brought with him the villain who had done the damage. But I told him to take him away, I would have no communication with such a contemptible wretch. The husband explained that he wished to talk with me in the presence of his wife, if it was agreeable. He wanted to know what was to be done in the case. I told him I should be under the necessity of confirming the Bishop's decision in the case, but I will have read to you what the law says upon the subject.
>
> George Reynolds, who is one of my secretaries, was present, and I asked him to read certain portions of the revelation on celestial marriage; for they had been married according to that order. That revelation states that, "If a man receiveth a wife in the new and everlasting covenant, and if she be with another man, and I have not appointed unto her by the holy anointing, she hath committed adultery and shall be destroyed." And in another place it says, "they shall be destroyed in the flesh, and shall be delivered unto the buffetings of Satan unto the day of redemption, saith the Lord God."
>
> Now, said I, I did not make that law. I find it in the word of God. It is not my province to change it. I cannot make any change. I am sorry for these little children. I am sorry for the shame and infamy that has been brought upon them; but I cannot reverse the law of God. I did not commit this crime; I am not responsible for it; I cannot take upon myself, the responsibility of other peoples' acts. Well, it made my heart ache. The husband wept like a child, so did the woman; but I could not help that. I speak of this for the purpose of bringing up other things, and of presenting them before the people. And the principle I desire to impress upon their minds is, that we have no right, any of us, to violate the laws of God.[61]

---

61. John Taylor, ca. June 1883, *Journal of Discourses*, 24:232.

More than his predecessor Brigham Young, Taylor was motivated and governed by the written canon.[62] Whereas Young saw the scripture as more fluid and adaptable, Taylor here shows a strict and rigid compliance to the canon.[63] This is clearly stated in his drafts of a long 1876 letter to Young, outlining his careful scriptural exegesis of the structure of Church leadership.

"I Have Conferred Upon You the Keys"

Verse 45 begins with a frequent theme in Joseph Smith's preaching on restoration and keys, possibly reflecting the yet unpublished and at the time the largely unknown text of an April 3, 1836, vision (now section 110).[64]

> For I have conferred upon you the keys and power of the priesthood, wherein I restore all things, and make known unto you all things in due time.

The second phrase reaffirms the promise (see verse 40) that Joseph Smith is the restorer, bringing back everything, including Abrahamic polygamy.[65] Every ancient era from Christianity to Israel and their biblical ancestry was a target for restoration. Even animal sacrifice was considered by Smith and original planning for the Salt Lake Temple included an altar for sacrifice—perhaps not the Mosaic version, which the Book of Mormon declared dead, but the pre-Mosaic sacrifices performed by Adam (Moses 5:5) and the Patriarchs. From Joseph Smith's October 5, 1840, sermon:

> These sacrifices as well as every ordinance belonging to the priesthood will when the temple of the Lord shall be built and the Sons Levi be purified be fully restored and attended to then all their powers, ramifications, and bless-

---

62. Catherine Lewis, *Narrative of Some of the Proceedings of the Mormons*, iv; Robin Scott Jensen et al., eds., *Revelations and Translations, Vol. 2: Published Revelations*, xxxv; Brigham Young, sermon, October 8, 1866. Wilford Woodruff journal, January 27, 1860, in Kenney, ed., *Wilford Woodruff's Journal*, 5:429.

63. Young noted that he spent little or no time with scripture after his move into the leadership of the Church. "I never read much scripture. I have not time to read it. I am a perfect Bible myself." Reported in Thomas Bullock, "Booklet (#5), 1845 June 1–July 27," June 29, 1845. See also John G. Turner, *The Mormon Jesus: A Biography*, 107.

64. Smith, "Early Mormon Priesthood Revelations," 53–55.

65. See Joseph Smith's March 10, 1844, sermon in Smith et al., "Parallel Joseph." On Smith's use of Elias as name and title, see Samuel Brown, "The Prophet Elias Puzzle," 1–17. As Brown argues, an important role of Elias, as the doublet of Elijah, was to liberate "Elijah" for what amounted to the mystical work of the high priesthood.

ings–this the Sons of Levi shall be purified. ever was and will exist when the powers of the Melchizedek Priesthood are sufficiently manifest. Else how can the restitution of all things spoken of by all the Holy Prophets be brought to pass. It is not to be understood that, the law of moses will be established again with all it rights and variety of ceremonies, ceremonies, this had never been spoken off by the prophets but those things which existed prior Moses's day viz Sacrifice will be continued –It may be asked by some what necessity for Sacrifice since the great Sacrifice was offered? In answer to which if Repentance Baptism and faith were necessary to Salvation existed prior to the days of Christ what necessity for them since that time.

That Young meant to carry out the instructions in plans for the temple in Salt Lake City was reported by Wilford Woodruff: "Under the pulpit in the west end will be a place to offer sacrifices. There will be an altar prepared for that purpose so that when any sacrifices are to be offered, they should be offered there."[66]

---

66. Kenney, ed., *Wilford Woodruff's Journal*, 5:140.

Joseph Smith and the Keys of the Kingdom

The next several verses affirm Joseph Smith as the one (and only one) authorized to exercise and oversee sealing ordinances, and they reveal Smith's own guaranteed exaltation:

46 And verily, verily, I say unto you, that whatsoever you seal on earth shall be sealed in heaven; and whatsoever you bind on earth, in my name and by my word, saith the Lord, it shall be eternally bound in the heavens; and whosesoever sins you remit on earth shall be remitted eternally in the heavens; and whosesoever sins you retain on earth shall be retained in heaven.

47 And again, verily I say, whomsoever you bless I will bless, and whomsoever you curse I will curse, saith the Lord; for I, the Lord, am thy God.

48 And again, verily I say unto you, my servant Joseph, that whatsoever you give on earth, and to whomsoever you give any one on earth, by my word and according to my law, it shall be visited with blessings and not cursings, and with my power, saith the Lord, and shall be without condemnation on earth and in heaven.

49 For I am the Lord thy God, and will be with thee even unto the end of the world, and through all eternity; for verily I seal upon you your exaltation, and prepare a throne for you in the kingdom of my Father, with Abraham your father.

50 Behold, I have seen your sacrifices, and will forgive all your sins; I have seen your sacrifices in obedience to that which I have told you. Go, therefore, and I make a way for your escape, as I accepted the offering of Abraham of his son Isaac.

By drawing on the language of Jesus giving the keys of the kingdom to Peter to bind and loose in heaven and on earth (Matt. 16:19), these verses bring together the earlier sealing to eternal life and later sealing of relationships into one.

"I Say Unto You, My Servant Joseph"

A January 1841 revelation (now Doctrine and Covenants 124) told of a sealing power associated with the office of patriarch: "I give unto you Hyrum Smith to be a patriarch unto you, to hold the sealing blessings of my church, even the Holy Spirit of promise, whereby ye are sealed up unto the day of redemption, that ye may not fall notwithstanding the hour of temptation that may come upon you" (124:124). Forty years later, after Church President John Taylor sent polygamy underground and disconnected sealings from centralized authority, this 1841 revelation was deployed to allow local patriarchs to perform plural sealings. The secrecy of underground polygamy and especially the secretly authorized post-manifesto marriages laid down shielded lines of communication, such that one Church leader could easily have been ignorant of the provisions made by another. Once authorization was given to one man or another to solemnize marriages, such permission was hard to withdraw, as evidenced by the number of early twentieth-century plural marriages by patriarchs. To be able to honestly deny its continued practice, some Church Presidents asked not to be informed of the results of such authority.[1] Moreover, when such authority was given, it was given with a caution of anonymity, and couples were enjoined not to divulge the name of the person who performed a sealing.[2]

Apostles in Utah were generally authorized to travel in outlying communities and seal couples who, for whatever reason, were constrained from coming to a temple. But those sealings, following the tradition of Nauvoo, were to be ratified in a temple when circumstances allowed—at least prior to the Woodruff Manifesto.[3] In Utah, Brigham Young encouraged the idea

---

1. Daymon Mickel Smith, "The Last Shall be First and the First Shall be Last," 341–49; B. Carmon Hardy, *Solemn Covenant: The Mormon Polygamous Passage,* 313–23. It was not unusual for men who acted as sealing agents in Utah temples to be Church patriarchs. See also John Taylor, October 19, 1884, *Journal of Discourses,* 25:355.

2. The secrecy of polygamy during the raid and beyond makes it difficult to profile actors. This was particularly true after the turn of the century. See for example, Barbara Jones Brown, "The Rise and Demise of Latter-day Saint Polygamy in Mexico"; Hardy, *Solemn Covenant,* 313–19, 322.

3. Rudger Clawson reports Joseph F. Smith advising the apostles to stop the practice out of fear that investigators attached to the Smoot hearings were watching Mormon practices of sealing/marriage in an attempt to out post-Manifesto polygamy. Francis M. Lyman, president of the apostles, called for a vote to cease all sealings outside of temples. While the resulting vote was unanimous in the

that sealing was an authority that traveled with apostolic office. In the twentieth century, "the sealing power" became an established meme, as though it was somehow separate from (or an addition to) priesthood. In its present praxis, the connection between the 1841 revelation and temple sealing authority is apparent in the way the latter mimics the patriarchal office. Like men ordained to the office of patriarch, a man chosen to officiate in sealings carries that authority throughout his lifetime but cannot exercise it outside his assigned jurisdiction.[4] Without explicit regulation, the office of "sealer" has effectively become another branch in the high priesthood cycle.[5]

Although the January 1841 revelation appeared to place both the power to seal and the power to curse in the hands of Hyrum Smith (D&C 124:91–93), there were important differences in meaning between that revelation and the plural marriage revelation. Hyrum Smith's office, as it was announced in 1841, was seen in a context *outside* the sealing praxis of 1843.[6] In other words, the New Testament-based binding and loosing that Mormons had appropriated to the high priesthood and then refined to the patriarchal office was apparently seen by Joseph Smith as having an

---

affirmative, private divisions over the practice of polygamy among the apostles still existed, and those divisions continued to foster plural marriages. Rudger Clawson diary, September 29, 1904, in Stan Larson, ed., *A Ministry of Meetings: The Apostolic Diaries of Rudger Clawson*, 130, 552, 777.

4. Current practice, extending from at least the David O. McKay years, for authorizing men to act as sealers has used the language of *conferral* rather than ordination or setting apart: "I have this date conferred the sealing power upon _____ to be exercised in the _____ Temple in behalf of both the living and the dead." Joseph Smith's sermons and practice suggest that he might appoint any male church member to do a specific sealing, though this did not carry any continuing permission to repeat the ritual elsewhere. It is unlikely that he thought any special authority was needed beyond ordination to elder or high priest, etc. *provided he gave permission*. William Clayton reported that in sealing Lucy Walker to Smith, he acted in the office of "elder." See William Clayton, Affidavit, February 16, 1874, reprinted in Chapter 1.

5. "Sealers" are (now) uniformly high priests. Heber J. Grant, Letter to Lewis R. Anderson, March 5, 1935.

6. Illustrated by the results of Hyrum Smith sealing Parley Pratt and his wife Mary Ann. Hyrum's "keys" were not those of the plural marriage revelation, though the confusion was not just theoretical. Hyrum sealed other couples, and it is not clear in every case whether Joseph gave permission. The summer 1843 sealing of Howard and Martha Coray was one example. Howard Coray, "Autobiography," 25–26.

ecclesial attachment that was not applicable to the communal sealing of husband and wife, child and parent, and, eventually, friend to friend by adoption. Joseph Smith even broached the idea that his brother Hyrum take the position of Church president while Joseph withdrew to dictate the temple priesthood and engage his other seeric offices. Church members within earshot and unaware of Smith's introduction of new sacraments were confused and upset by the suggestion.[7]

"Shall Be Eternally Bound in the Heavens"

While high priests were initially charged with the ability and duty to seal up to eternal life followed by the Church patriarch (an office originating on December 6, 1834), these sealings were not communal in nature—though in early instances, the action was occasionally declared *en masse* in small groups.[8] The plural marriage revelation formalized the sealing of one person to another, a process linked to Joseph Smith's teaching and preaching of the promise of Elijah to restore the sealing of "the children to their fathers" (Mal. 4:6). Once interpreted more in terms of connecting or welding together the dispensations of the past,[9] this new understanding of sealing promoted a more local vision of heaven, one grounded in relationships formed through a complex network of marriages, children, and, eventually, spiritual adoption. While the latter might refer to sealing biological parents to children, its full intent was to create new non-biological families, sealing a man to another man as father and son. Brigham Young saw that process as correcting the chaos of mortality based on a premortal—preordained—structure for the family of man, and he assigned that

---

7. See Smith's sermons given shortly after the plural marriage revelation on July 16, 1843, and July 23, 1843, in William V. Smith et al., eds. "The Parallel Joseph." On adoption, see John G. Turner, *Brigham Young: Pioneer Prophet*, 139.

8. On sealing groups, see, for example, Wilford Woodruff's journal, April 6, 1837, in Scott G. Kenney, ed., *Wilford Woodruff's Journal, 1834–1898, Typescript*, 1:132; and David John Buerger, "Salvation in the Theology of Joseph Smith," 159–69. Early Zion-centric Mormonism saw salvation as a community enterprise, but as noted elsewhere, that very early spiritual and economic vision of a "collective rapture" became embodied in the Nauvoo endowment and sealings, while an Enochian Zion was postponed to the Millennium. See Mark Ashurst-McGee, "Zion Rising: Joseph Smith's Early Social and Political Thought," 199–202.

9. See Joseph Smith diary, August 27, 1843, in Andrew H. Hedges et al., eds., *Journals, Volume 3: May 1843–June 1844*, 85–87.

vision to Joseph Smith.[10] Exemplifying the eternal familial relationships they were creating, these sealing adoptions were manifested in real parent-child language and loyalties.[11]

This vision of heaven encouraged by the plural marriage revelation was more than a mild rereading of early high priesthood power, based on a theology modeled more on a Puritan heaven; in Nauvoo, proto-heavens were *created* by forming networks of sealing in and between families.[12] The distinction is evident in Smith's August 27, 1843, sermon, if read without modern distinctions of priesthood. Smith often used the word "priest-hood" to refer to ordained offices or the performance of some particular sacrament, rather than the categories of authority introduced in his April 1835 revelation (now Doctrine and Covenants 107:1–57).[13] In his August 27, 1843, sermon, Smith lingered on the notion of three priesthoods in the ascending order of Aaronic (or Levitical), Abrahamic (or Patriarchal), and Melchizedek (not the Melchizedek priesthood of modern Mormon discourse): "Abraham's preisthood was of greater power than Levi's and Melchizedeck's was of greater power than that of Abraham."[14] Of these priesthoods, "Abrahams Patriarchal power [was] the greatest yet experienced in this church."[15] However, that priesthood pales in comparison to that of Melchizedek in James Burgess's notes on the sermon:

> Abraham's was a more exalted power or preisthood he could talk and walk with God and yet consider how great this man was when even this patriarch

---

10. In a dream, Young "told [Joseph Smith] that the Latter Day Saints was very anxious to know about the law of adoption and the sealing powers . . . . [Young] saw how we were organized before we took tabernacles and every man will be restored to that . . . ." Hosea Stout diary, in Juanita Brooks, ed., *On the Mormon Frontier: The Diary of Hosea Stout, 1844–1889*, 1:238. Thomas Bullock reported that Young asked Smith in the dream what the Saints should do about sealing. The response was that they should get "the Spirit of the Lord" and it would lead them right. See Willard Richards journal (entry by Thomas Bullock), February 28, 1847.

11. For example, Eliza R. Snow, Letter to Sister East, April 23, 1883.

12. These Nauvoo networks became oddly complex, and in later practice the rare marriages between uncles and nieces, and brothers to half-sisters, afforded strange titles. Kathryn A. Daynes, *More Wives Than One: Transformation of the Mormon Marriage System, 1840–1910*, 26, 69, 205. John D. Lee, *Mormonism Unveiled, or the Life and Confessions of the Late Mormon Bishop, John D. Lee*, 167.

13. See William V. Smith, "Early Mormon Priesthood Revelations: Text, Impact, and Evolution."

14. James Burgess journal, August 27, 1843, in Smith et al., "Parallel Joseph."

15. Franklin D. Richards, "Scriptural Items."

Abraham gave a tenth part of all his spoils and then received a blessing under the hands of Melchesideck even the last law or a fulness of the law or preisthood which constituted him a king and preist after the order of Melchesideck or an endless life.[16]

This superior priesthood that would make someone a king or priest after the order of Melchizedek would be revealed in the sealing and anointing of the temple. Such a priesthood was epitomized by Jesus, a "high priest for ever after the order of Melchisedec" (Heb. 6:20) and was "a priesthood which holds the priesthood by right from the Eternal Gods.—and not by descent."[17] The plural marriage revelation seems to hover over this sermon, with its references to endless lives, sealing,[18] Abraham, the epistle to the Hebrews, and Smith's assurance of his own salvation.[19] Not requiring a genealogy, the Melchizedek high priesthood is the final earthly endowment of authority. It confers the power to make a new genealogy, this time a descending one not dependent on ancestry but on priestly status. Ultimately, the sermon pointed to Smith's final addition to temple ritual, the "second anointing" or fullness of the priesthood initiated in September 1843.

The thread tying these themes together is the figure of Elijah, the messenger who delivers the final branching of the high priesthood—a concept that went back to the first ordinations of high priests in 1831.[20] Wilford Woodruff's audit of Smith's language in January 1844 shows the depth of this image:

The Bible says "I will send you Elijah before the great & dredful day of the Lord Come that he shall turn the hearts of the fathers to the Children & the hearts of the Children to their fathers lest I Come & smite the whole earth

16. James Burgess journal, August 27, 1843, in Smith et al., "Parallel Joseph."

17. Joseph Smith diary, August 27, 1843, in Hedges et al., *Journals*, 3:85–87.

18. "[H]e shall send Elijah law revealed to Moses in Horeb—never was revealed to the C. of Israel and he shall reveal the covenants to seal the hearts of the fathers to the children and the children to the fathers.—anointing & sealing—called elected and made sure without father &c. a priesthood which holds the priesthood by right from the Eternal Gods.—and not by descent from father and mother." Ibid., 3:86.

19. "I Prophecy that all the powers of Earth & Hell shall never be able to overthrow this Boy for I have obtained it by promise." August 27, 1843, entry in Richards, "Scriptural Items."

20. Michael Hubbard MacKay et al., eds., *Documents, Volume 1: July 1828–June 1831*, 321–23. Smith revised the Malachi text in a number of different ways. For example, see Kenney, ed., *Wilford Woodruff's Journal*, 2:341. See also Smith's April 7, 1844, sermon in Smith et al., "Parallel Joseph."

with a Curse," Now the word turn here should be translated (bind or seal)
But what is the object of this important mission or how is it to be fulfilled,
The keys are to be delivered the spirit of Elijah is to Come, The gospel to
be esstablished the saints of God gatherd Zion built up, & the Saints to
Come up as Saviors on mount Zion but how are they to become Saviors on
Mount Zion by building their temples erecting their Baptismal fonts & going forth & receiving all the ordinances, Baptisms, Confirmations, washings,
anointings ordinations & sealing powers upon our heads in behalf of all our
Progenitors who are dead & redeem them that they may Come forth in the
first resurrection & be exalted to thrones of glory with us, & here in is the
chain that binds the hearts of the fathers to the Children, & the Children to
the Fathers which fulfills the mission of Elijah[21] & I would to God that this
temple was now done that we might go into it & go to work & improve our
time & make use of the seals while they are on the earth & the Saints have
none to much time to save & redeem their dead, & gather together their
living relatives . . . that they may be sealed & saved.[22]

Here it is easy to see that the high priesthood practice of sealing individuals to eternal life (that continued to exist within the practice of Church
patriarchs) had extended to saving and exalting the human family collectively through a network of sealed familial relationships. This would
eventually, if temporarily, extend more broadly in linkages to friends and
Church officials whose salvation was not in doubt.

"Whosesoever Sins You Remit"

An unusual aspect in this section of the plural marriage revelation is the
power given to Joseph Smith to remit or retain sins: "and whosesoever sins
you remit on earth shall be remitted eternally in the heavens; and whosesoever sins you retain on earth shall be retained in heaven" (v. 46). The paral-
lels to Catholicism are evident and symbolize much of what Protestants

---

21. The Malachi passage's first appearance in a written revelation was the one
delivered after the Saints were ordered by vigilantes to leave Jackson County,
Missouri. Its context and form suggest political and missionary action: "Therefore,
renounce war and proclaim peace, and seek diligently to turn the hearts of the
children to their fathers, and the hearts of the fathers to the children; And again,
the hearts of the Jews unto the prophets, and the prophets unto the Jews; lest I
come and smite the whole earth with a curse, and all flesh be consumed before
me" (D&C 98:12–13).

22. Wilford Woodruff journal, January 21, 1844, in Kenney, ed., *Wilford
Woodruff's Journal*, 2:341–42.

despised about Rome. While there was some discussion of this idea in later Church administrations, it received little mention beyond the eventual practice of the restoration of blessings for those rebaptized after excommunication.[23] Parallel to this, however, was the power to both refuse forgiveness and curse with damnation—something already suggested in verse 19 and which Smith had these "keys" to exercise.[24]

The ability to retain or remit sins in the context of the revelation highlights the importance of plural marriage in Joseph Smith's broader narrative of salvation and exaltation at this point, and these verses suggest an unconditional nature of sealing, with an emphasis that recipients "*shall be* sealed in heaven; . . . *shall be* eternally bound in the heavens; and whosesoever sins . . . *shall be* remitted eternally in the heavens" (v. 46; emphasis added). This relationship between sealing and assured salvation works to establish the point that authorized plural marriages were without condemnation—a message, again, probably primarily directed at Emma Smith. Using the language of a bride being given to her husband (see verses 16, 37, 39, 44, 51–53, 61–63, 65), the Lord tells Joseph Smith:

> And again, verily I say unto you, my servant Joseph, that *whatsoever you give* on earth, and *to whomsoever you give any one* on earth, by my word and

---

23. More than half a century later, George Q. Cannon preached that the Church president had power, in the sense that Jesus demonstrated with the paralytic, to forgive sin. George Q. Cannon, April 6, 1900, *Conference Report*, 10–14. John Taylor held a softer position, allowing that no forgiveness of sins was possible other than that granted by faith, repentance, and baptism. John Taylor, February 1, 1874, *Journal of Discourses*, 16:373. Contrast this with Orson Hyde, April 8, 1853, *Journal of Discourses*, 6:312.

24. In early Christian thought, Peter's commission to "retain" sins meant simply the refusal to baptize. For a generation in early Mormonism, missionaries had cursed unreceptive villages, towns, and persons, who refused to hear their warning voices. Legends followed the great itinerant Lorenzo Dow (1777–1834) in similar practices. Stories circulated that Dow had cursed this or that town, and the village failed to prosper and eventually disappeared (or caught fire and burned down). On one of Dow's curses, see "Death at 105 Draws Curtain on Cursed Town." The Mormon practice was usually thought of as a testimony to be exacted at the divine judgment in the afterlife. On mentions of curses in Smith's revelations, see Doctrine and Covenants 60:15; 78:12; 82:20–21; 104:9–10. Matthew W. Godfrey et al., eds., *Documents*, 2:198–99, 235–37. On missionary practice, see, for example, Jan Shipps and John W. Welch, eds., *Journals of William E. McLellin: 1831–1836*, 47. For a twentieth-century opinion on the Mormon practice of cursing or retaining sins in the twentieth century, see J. Reuben Clark, *On the Way to Immortality and Eternal Life*, 372.

according to my law, it shall be visited with blessings and not cursings, and with my power, saith the Lord, and *shall be without condemnation on earth and in heaven* (v. 48; emphasis added).

This verse does a few things: First, it makes clear that not only is plural marriage "without condemnation," but it also is deserving of blessings for those who participate in it—making polygamy a higher state than monogamy. Second, it again reaffirms Smith as authorized to select (or at least approve) partners among those who married in plurality, a role he filled with rigor.

While there is no contemporary record of Smith confirming the transfer of his sole authority to sanction sealing and polygamy in case of his death, he constructed at least three ways by which a claim to the singular sealing authority could be made. First, the Smith family, in the person of Hyrum the Patriarch, became the obvious successor by virtue of both his blood and ecclesiastical relationships to Joseph Smith. Secondly, by initiating some of his trusted colleagues into the Nauvoo "fullness of the priesthood" or second anointing, a ritual that may have included a kind of dormant permission to perform sealings,[25] Joseph enfolded select groups into corps having special knowledge or responsibility. Finally, he began to elevate the status and responsibilities of the Twelve Apostles—many of whom were involved in the Nauvoo endowment (anointed quorum), polygamy, and the Council of Fifty. This increased status eventually culminated in a purported "final charge" or "last charge" assigning the apostles the duty to carry on the work of the Church.[26] Unfortunately, there is no immediate contemporary evidence for such a charge.[27] Regardless of

---

25. Brigham Young, December 26, 1845, Heber C. Kimball diary, as quoted in David John Buerger, "The Fulness of the Priesthood: The Second Anointing in Latter-day Saint Theology and Practice," 24.

26. Wilford Woodruff, December 12, 1869, *Journal of Discourses*, 13:164. Early records suggest the alternate interpretation that the charge meant the Twelve was charged to continue the Council's work. Christopher James Blythe, "The Church and Kingdom of God: Ecclesiastical Interpretations of the Council of Fifty," 100–130. Later, Brigham Young occasionally used the Fifty as a kind of appeals court when he felt some Church council failed to rule properly.

27. Many hoped that the recently opened minutes of the Nauvoo Council of Fifty might reveal such an incident. But apparently no such episode was recorded. Alexander L. Baugh and Richard Neitzel Holzapfel, "I Roll the Burthen and Responsibility of Leading This Church Off from My Shoulders on to Yours: The 1844/1845 Declaration of the Quorum of the Twelve Regarding Apostolic Succession," 4–19. A proposed explanation by Orson Hyde was never printed, although Hyde probably intended to do so. Given the possible confusion with the apostles and the Fifty, it

what Smith may or may not have made explicit in private, Young held authority that he regarded as superior to any other claim of succession. By being both initiated into the fullness of the priesthood and chief apostle, he felt enough standing to preserve and protect those who had engaged in the part of Joseph Smith's innovations in Nauvoo that required the most profound social capital—polygamy.[28]

Brigham Young's most important problem after Smith's death and his subsequent resolve that the Church could carry on ("the keys of the kingdom are right here with the church") was convincing his fellow quorum members that he was now the *sole* source of permission for plurality and sealing (see Chapter 2). Some, like Parley Pratt, John Taylor, Orson Pratt, and Lyman Wight, saw the commissioned equality of members of their quorum as delivering the same permits to all, and convincing them otherwise required a long and careful process, an unsuccessful one in Wight's case. By January 1845, Parley Pratt wrote that Young had authority to determine sealing. However, he wrote that the same power belonged to the First Presidency as well, and in August 1844 the apostles had been sustained as the First Presidency of the Church. Pratt had serious reservations about giving up that position in the winter of 1847 and he and Taylor sealed plural wives without Young's knowledge. The apostles finally voted Young as Church president when Pratt and Taylor were away from headquarters.[29] Later Church presidents would exercise varying degrees of control over sealings carried out by the apostles and their legatees.

---

may have been seen as tainted in the sense that many members of the Fifty probably interpreted the experience somewhat differently. Some at least saw the entire Fifty as authoritative. The Fifty were fundamentally unwieldy, both too large to make quick decisions and fiercely loyal to Smith. Thus, Smith's death placed a question mark over that body. The apostles knew their ecclesiastical leader. It was vital for Brigham Young to assert leadership without dependence on the Council of Fifty in ecclesial matters but that action was not obvious to all. On Hyde's statement: "Orson Hyde, Certificate About the Twelve, circa 1845 March," Brigham Young Office Files. For minutes of the Fifty, see Matthew J. Grow et al., eds., *Administrative Records: Council of Fifty, Minutes, March 1844–January 1846*, 62.

28. Turner, *Brigham Young*, 114.

29. Parley P. Pratt, "Proclamation to the Church of Jesus Christ of Latter-Day Saints: Greetings," 151. Wilford Woodruff's journal, December 1847, Turner, *Brigham Young*, 171–74. Terryl L. Givens and Matthew J. Grow, *Parley P. Pratt: The Apostle Paul of Mormonism*, 169–74. Melvin C. Johnson, *Polygamy on the Pedernales: Lyman Wight's Mormon Villages in Antebellum Texas, 1845–1858*, 91–92.

"With Abraham Your Father"

Polygamy and sealing became the final additions in Smith's expanding story of Abraham that began with the Bible and grew with his translations and revelations. The next verses of the revelation were probably meant to impress the reader (Emma) with Joseph Smith's status before God. The revelation implied that Joseph had standing to call Emma to repentance along with other critics of the marriage project:

> For I am the Lord thy God, and will be with thee even unto the end of the world, and through all eternity; *for verily I seal upon you your exaltation*, and prepare a throne for you in the kingdom of my Father, with Abraham your father. Behold, I have seen your sacrifices, and will forgive all your sins; I have seen your sacrifices in obedience to that which I have told you. Go, therefore, and I make a way for your escape, as I accepted the offering of Abraham of his son Isaac. (vv. 49–50; emphasis added)

By rhetorically paralleling Joseph Smith to the polygamous Abraham (the textual impetus for the revelation), it not only authorized polygamy in general but also presented Joseph Smith as a concrete example of someone exalted because of plural marriage and not in spite of it. This was important for those who believed that Joseph was acting on personal impulse with polygamy, perhaps particularly Emma. It further brought together the past and present, making Smith and the revelation crucial links in the great chain of God's word from the beginning.[30]

For Orson Pratt's still prickly feelings over Young's move, see George Q. Cannon journal, October 6, 1880, *The Journal of George Q. Cannon.*

30. The myth of pristine scripture as uniform in message is a strong one in Mormonism, reinforced by Smith's treatment of the Hebrew Bible as a redacted text, once preaching Christian doctrine in its original state, a position present in some degree in the Book of Mormon. Eighteenth- and nineteenth-century German scholars had developed what was sometimes called a scientific approach to scripture. These textual theories were sometimes used to diminish the role and meaning of Lutheran theology, but the tools made valuable contributions to the study of the Bible. Protestants became split over the results in general, and Latter-day Saints followed suit in some respects, with the fundamentalist reaction eventually exercising considerable influence in Mormonism. Catholics took a somewhat more centrist approach and as a result avoided some of the conflicts that divided Protestants. Philip L. Barlow, *Mormons and the Bible: The Place of Latter-day Saints in American Religion.* Many Latter-day Saints subscribe to more fundamentalist methodology. The idea is described in Protestant literature under the rubric of "plenary inspiration." For a succinct description, see Joseph Fielding McConkie, "A Historical Examination of

Perhaps further addressing Emma (or other confidantes who had felt a strong aversion to the practice), the revelation suggests that Smith's taking of wives was an Abrahamic test for him—an undesirable necessity to prove one's faith in God. In essence, it enabled Smith to imply his own displeasure with the practice while defending his obedience to it. This meshes well with the reminiscent tales of an angel with a drawn sword threatening him with death or worse if he did not comply with the polygamy imperative.[31] God's telling Smith, "I make a way for your escape, as I accepted the offering of Abraham of his son Isaac," alludes to the sparing of Isaac and may have meant that Joseph was no longer required to seek more wives (or at least practice plurality as he had been). His attempts to contract new marriages seemed to slow after the revelation, though it did not cease entirely.

"I Seal Upon You Your Exaltation"

Smith's role as a key piece in God's plan for humanity was even more important in the networking chain of the exalted human family. Smith's assurance of exaltation had a power to bring all those sealed to him to the same exaltation. He announced this to a number of potential plural wives in his proposals (and the idea appears in the sealing language of his 1842 marriage to Sarah Whitney). Though not mentioning polygamy, Smith as the foundational link in the latter-day work of exaltation is easily seen in his March 10, 1844, sermon reported by Wilford Woodruff:

> Again the doctrin or sealing power of Elijah is as follows if you have power to seal on earth & in heaven then we should be Crafty, the first thing you do go & seal on earth your sons & daughters unto yourself, & yourself unto your fathers in eternal glory, & go ahead and not go back, but use a little Craftiness & seal all you can; & when you get to heaven tell your father that what you seal on earth should be sealed in heaven I will walk through the gate of heaven and Claim what I seal & those that follow me & my Council.[32]

---

the Views of the Church of Jesus Christ of Latter-Day Saints and the Reorganized Church of Jesus Christ of Latter-Day Saints on Four Distinctive Aspects of the Doctrine of Deity Taught by the Prophet Joseph Smith," 31–32. See also Joseph F. Smith's letters to his missionary son Joseph Richards Smith in Great Britain in 1899, especially his letter of September 13, 1899.

31. Reminiscent accounts of angelic threats are cataloged in Brian C. Hales, "Encouraging Joseph Smith to Practice Plural Marriage: The Accounts of the Angel with a Drawn Sword," 55–71.

32. Wilford Woodruff's journal, March 10, 1844, in Kenney, ed., *Wilford Woodruff's Journal*, 2:359–66. While "crafty" may have been a buzz-word for

In this sermon, Smith outlines what may have been his primary purpose in polygamy: the establishment of sealing networks, in which families were joined to each other through sealing bonds that guaranteed salvation to those sealed to him. In that light, one can somewhat understand why some women—or their families through them, like fourteen-year-old Helen Mar Kimball, daughter of Heber and Vilate Kimball—might desire to be joined to Smith. Heber Kimball placed considerable pressure on Helen to be sealed to Smith, and the motivation was likely to cement a connection to Smith. The (virtually unbreakable) sealing link to Smith, whose exaltation was assured, meant that Kimball's family had staked a claim in the glory of the hereafter.[33]

This is not the only revelation where Joseph Smith received assurance of salvation. But in this case, the revelation speaks to the idea of perseverance as mediated by liturgy in the context of the most mature version of heaven in Mormonism: exaltation. As observed already, it seems Smith's liturgical innovation in Nauvoo is directed toward an embodiment or reification of the spiritual claims in his earlier revelations. For example, his and Sidney Rigdon's February 16, 1832, vision of heaven (D&C 76) proclaims that "the Holy Spirit of Promise . . . sheds forth upon . . . priest and kings . . . after the order of Melchizedek" who "are gods" (76:53–58). These promises were eventually pronounced on recipients of the Nauvoo endowment.[34] His May 6, 1833, revelation (D&C 93) promised that the faithful "shall see [God's] face" (93:1), and the Nauvoo endowment concluded with the faithful symbolically admitted to God's presence.[35]

Masons in the audience—particularly in a sermon proximate to a deceased Mason—it hinted back to the plural marriage revelation's notion of sealing. In his (plural) marriage proposal to Mary Lightner, Smith referenced an assurance of salvation that suggests the text of the July 12 revelation: "I know that I shall be saved in the Kingdom of God. I have the oath of God upon it . . . All that he gives me I shall take with me for I have that authority and power conferred upon me." Todd M. Compton, *In Sacred Loneliness: The Plural Wives of Joseph Smith*, 210–26.

33. Smith was sealed to another girl of fourteen, Nancy Winchester. Compton, *In Sacred Loneliness*, 498, 605–8. Stanley B. Kimball, *Heber C. Kimball: Mormon Patriarch and Pioneer*, 307–16.

34. Brigham Young, August 6, 1843, in Kenney, ed., *Wilford Woodruff's Journal*, 2:270–71.

35. See also Doctrine and Covenants 88:3–4, etc., a revelation that studies metaphysical echoes of section 76 and then takes some initial steps in their empirical consequence.

The plural marriage revelation and Nauvoo practice and teaching identified this sealing with the Holy Spirit of Promise mentioned earlier in the revelation (vv. 7, 18, 26). When Benjamin Johnson recalled his sealing to first wife, Melissa, in 1843, he characterized it as being "sealed by the Holy Spirit of Promise."[36] William Clayton reported Smith saying on the occasion, "there was two seals in the Priesthood. The first was that which was placed upon a man and woman when they made the covenant and the other was the seal which allotted to them their particular mansion."[37] Much speculative speech about the fullness of the priesthood sacraments—anointing men and women as priests and priestesses, first delivered in September 1843—led to a belief that verses 19, 26, and 49 looked forward to that. However, as sealing became increasingly conditional after leaving Nauvoo, the phrase gradually became disassociated from the sealing sacrament itself and began to instead refer to private spiritual assurances by the Holy Ghost of one's own salvation. Perhaps experience taught Church leaders in Utah that a narrative of endurance to the end was a safer theme for the great majority of Saints who were largely new to the faith, a teaching nearly uniform in the twentieth century.[38]

Combined with the 1840 restoration of baptism for the dead, proxy sealing meant that a deceased spouse might be sealed to a living one. This gave rise to the question of whether plural sealings through sequential wives were sufficient to place one in the highest heaven. That is, if a man's first wife died, and he remarried, assuming both were sealed to him, did he and his first spouse fulfill the imperative of the plural marriage revelation? Joseph F. Smith and George Q. Cannon responded in the negative. There was simply too much effort and sacrifice among participants for Hyrum's son to exchange that sacrifice for safety. For him, that was the coward's way.[39]

---

36. Benjamin Franklin Johnson, *My Life's Review*, 85–86.

37. Fillerup, "William Clayton," October 20, 1843.

38. James Talmage was an exception to this drift in interpretation. He judged the Holy Spirit of Promise in the revelation to mean the authority exercised by the authorized administrator of the ordinance. James E. Talmage, Letter to Elder Charles R. Brashear, November 27, 1922.

39. Wilford Woodruff journal, March 9, 1884, in Kenney, ed., *Wilford Woodruff's Journal*, 8:235–36. On Cannon, see *The Journal of George Q. Cannon*, August 28–29, 1875. On Joseph F. Smith's philosophy of life that led him to this stance, see Stephen C. Taysom's forthcoming biography of Joseph F. Smith, University of Utah Press, 2018.

Modern observers may find it hard to appreciate the cachet a new written revelation from Joseph Smith had among Latter-day Saints. The first few years of the Church had seen a steady and heavy flow of newly-dictated revelations; by the time of the plural marriage revelation it had been over two years since the previous one (D&C 124). Dictating the July 12, 1843, plural marriage revelation was necessary to the preservation of polygamy (and sealing) beyond Smith's lifetime and those of his immediate colleagues, whatever the effect on its immediate and intended target (Emma). Though much of its context might be lost to history, the written word was far more powerful and egalitarian than purported recollections, tradition, and private accounts. Strange, threatening, intensely personal, and spiritually profound, the revelation was a powerful symbol to those who knew of it, and it created a bright line in the sand for Mormonism's inner circle and then later for the entire Mormon-conscious world.[40] For many years, those who rejected the idea of polygamy found themselves barred from temple Mormonism, and missionaries tutored new converts in its heavenly origins, if not its practice, even into the twentieth century.[41]

Polygamy in the material presence of the plural marriage revelation marked one more step in a transition from a charismatic religion of angels and golden plates to a reification of that charisma in physical rite and praxis. Early Latter-day Saint men and women who claimed heavenly visions, healings, glossolalia (speaking in an unknown tongue), seer stones, and other manifestations as articles of faith, gradually reimagined salvation as a material sacramental adventure, a material salvation written most profoundly within the practice of plural marriage in which salvation was not fated, but still capable of a material antinomian-like certainty.

---

40. The revelation was known and perhaps published among the Texas followers of Lyman Wight, a second-generation apostle who ultimately rejected Brigham Young, and it influenced the practice of polygamy among other parts of the Nauvoo diaspora. James Strang's followers reject the present form of section 132 as a Utah forgery, but in essence the "law of Sarah" (vv. 61–66) existed in Strangite practice. On Wight publishing the revelation, see B. H. Roberts interview with Gideon Carter in B. H. Roberts, *Succession in the Presidency of the Church of Jesus Christ of Latter-day Saints* 2nd ed., 122–25.

41. Reed Smoot diary, December 29, 1910, January 3, 1911, December 31, 1914, July 27, 1915, Harvard S. Heath, ed., *In the World: the Diaries of Reed Smoot*, 254–55; Jonathan H. Moyer, "Dancing with the Devil: The Making of the Republican/Mormon Pact," 588.

The Secret of Emma

While earlier parts of the revelation seemed to implicitly address her, the next portion of the revelation is, without question, explicitly directed to Emma Smith. Providing an uncomfortable peek into the tension that polygamy put on her relationship with Joseph Smith, the revelation commands Emma to join in and receive the doctrine of polygamy, with eternal consequences for failing to do so; it also commands her to properly respond to a few unspecified but related issues that Emma most certainly understood.

51 Verily, I say unto you: A commandment I give unto mine handmaid, Emma Smith, your wife, whom I have given unto you, that she stay herself and partake not of that which I commanded you to offer unto her; for I did it, saith the Lord, to prove you all, as I did Abraham, and that I might require an offering at your hand, by covenant and sacrifice.

52 And let mine handmaid, Emma Smith, receive all those that have been given unto my servant Joseph, and who are virtuous and pure before me; and those who are not pure, and have said they were pure, shall be destroyed, saith the Lord God.

53 For I am the Lord thy God, and ye shall obey my voice; and I give unto my servant Joseph that he shall be made ruler over many things; for he hath been faithful over a few things, and from henceforth I will strengthen him.

54 And I command mine handmaid, Emma Smith, to abide and cleave unto my servant Joseph, and to none else. But if she will not abide this commandment she shall be destroyed, saith the Lord; for I am the Lord thy God, and will destroy her if she abide not in my law.

55 But if she will not abide this commandment, then shall my servant Joseph do all things for her, even as he hath said; and I will bless him and multiply him and give unto him an hundred-fold in this world, of fathers and mothers, brothers and sisters, houses and lands, wives and children, and crowns of eternal lives in the eternal worlds.

56 And again, verily I say, let mine handmaid forgive my servant Joseph his trespasses; and then shall she be forgiven her trespasses, wherein she has

trespassed against me; and I, the Lord thy God, will bless her, and multiply her, and make her heart to rejoice.

57 And again, I say, let not my servant Joseph put his property out of his hands, lest an enemy come and destroy him; for Satan seeketh to destroy; for I am the Lord thy God, and he is my servant; and behold, and lo, I am with him, as I was with Abraham, thy father, even unto his exaltation and glory.

The intent of this passage seems to sharply jump around, reading like bits of revelation hastily fused together. In contrast to Smith's earlier published revelations, the plural marriage revelation is a reminder that many of his previous revelations had undergone significant redaction and revision before publication. The unpolished nature of the text of this revelation suggests that if Joseph Smith had intended it to be published, it might have taken a different final form.[1]

Here, the revelation seems to acknowledge Joseph Smith's careful struggle to deliver— from portions of past revelations, scripture, and experience—a text that served Hyrum Smith's hope for a document he might use to convince Emma of polygamy's divine origin. While the text did not have the immediate effect he hoped for, Hyrum seems to have found it impressive to the point that it rendered obvious to him the virtues of plurality and its sealing subtext.

"That Which I Commanded You to Offer Unto Her"

Since it was first dictated in 1843, verse 51 has been puzzling to readers outside the original core group of recipients, and there is no definitive information about its meaning.

Verily, I say unto you: A commandment I give unto mine handmaid, Emma Smith, your wife, whom I have given unto you, that she stay herself and partake not of that which I commanded you to offer unto her; for I did it,

---

1. As noted previously, strong evidence for this, aside from the revelation itself, is found in the redactions of Smith's other revelations. See Robin Scott Jensen et al., *Manuscript Revelation Books*. Other evidence is presented below. It may be argued that Joseph Smith held a higher status in 1843 than when the 1833 Book of Commandments or the 1835 Doctrine and Covenants were in production. It is not clear whether a committee of editors might have functioned with the seeming freedom that editors had a decade before this revelation. Grant Underwood, "Revelation, Text, and Revision: Insights from the Book of Commandments and Revelations," 67–84.

saith the Lord, to prove you all, as I did Abraham, and that I might require an offering at your hand, by covenant and sacrifice. (D&C 132:51)

Central to this verse is the possibility of some sort of offer from Joseph Smith to Emma—perhaps to counter her discomfort and anger over his secret marriages to other women. That the revelation itself failed to do so is shown by her stark pronouncement that she "did not believe a word of it." Her relationship with the revelation was complicated by Joseph's past claims of prophethood. Her actions over the previous decades had shown her to be an ardent believer in those claims. Among the several suggested meanings of this verse the most likely may be an economic one. Emma had four living children, and the welfare of her children had been in jeopardy on many occasions. An Ohio mob whose actions with tar and feathers may have contributed to the death of an adopted son, the near freezing death of her family on a forced march in the winter of January 1838, the four month incarceration of her husband in Liberty, Missouri, and the deaths of children at Hawn's Mill all must have weighed on her as she contemplated the contents of the revelation.

The next day William Clayton recorded: "This A.M. J[oseph]. sent for me. & when I arrived he called me up into his private room with E[mma]. and there stated an agreement they had mutually entered into they both stated their feelings on many subjects & wept considerable O may the Lord soften her heart that she may be willing to keep and abide by his Holy Law."[2] Joseph expressed the fear that Emma might divorce him over his participation in polygamy, and he told Clayton to turn over half of his interest in the small steamboat *Maid of Iowa* to Emma as well as sixty city lots owned by the Church in Joseph Smith's name—something that seems to run counter to the instructions in verse 57 to "let not my servant Joseph put his property out of his hands." There, the revelation called for Emma to refuse the offering of verse 51 claiming that it was actually a test in the spirit of Abraham's requirement to sacrifice his own son. It does not seem that his interest in the steamboat was ever turned over, as it was still claimed by Church trustees after Joseph's death and the boat was sold at the direction of Brigham Young on June 15, 1845.

There is another possibility for what that offer entailed. According to William Law, a friend of Emma even after Law's falling out with Joseph, the offer was actually the choice of another partner for Emma—a poly-

---

2. Robert Fillerup, ed., "William Clayton's Nauvoo Diaries and Personal Writings," July 13, 1843.

amorous relationship (perhaps also hinted at in verse 54). In a series of letters Law claimed that Emma told him that she and Joseph had come to a resolution involving "equal rights":

> Well, I told you that she [Emma] used to complain to me about Joseph's escapades whenever she met me on the street. <u>She spoke repeatedly about that pretended revelation.</u> She said once: "The revelation says I must submit or be destroyed. Well, I guess I have to submit." On another day she said: "Joe and I have settled our troubles on the basis of equal rights."[3]

Law claimed that Joseph had offered Emma another husband as compensation if she would cease opposition to polygamy.[4] Given the strange relationships and secret practices of Nauvoo, Law's accusation can't be dismissed completely, but the more likely meaning of "equal rights" seems to be the economic security for Emma and her children. The reference in verse 57 to Joseph not letting property out of his hands seems connected to the deal worked out between the Smiths. The entire segment requires some insider knowledge to decode, knowledge that seems to have died with the two principals.

"Receive. . . . [or] Be Destroyed"

After alluding to and rescinding whatever offer or penalty she may have previously been given, Emma was commanded to receive Joseph's other wives—at least the ones "who are virtuous and pure before [God]" (v. 52)—as well as Joseph himself—"and to none else" (v. 54). She is further told that if "she will not abide this commandment she shall be destroyed" (v. 54). The immediate interpretation of this might be to assume that such destruction refers to death; however, the next verses acknowledge the possibility that Emma might still take up the original offer: "But if she will not abide this commandment, then shall my servant Joseph do all things for her, even as he hath said" (v. 55). The logic here works against "destroyed" as "death"; rather, as in previous verses (vv. 26, 41), the penalty of being destroyed was a spiritual curse. In succeeding Church administrations it was interpreted as excommunication.[5] Thus, the revelation suggested that if Emma rejected her husband's polygamous marriages, she would yet live on, but without the

---

3. "The Mormons in Nauvoo: Three Letters from William Law on Mormonism," 6. See also Lyndon Cook, "William Law, Nauvoo Dissenter," 47–72.

4. "The Mormons in Nauvoo," 6.

5. The usage alludes to 1 Corinthians 5:1–5 and probably its context. Barth Campbell, "Flesh and Spirit in 1 Cor. 5:5: An Exercise in Rhetorical Criticism of

benefits associated with being sealed to Joseph.[6] In summary, Joseph Smith is promised that he will be blessed and "give[n] unto him an hundred-fold in this world, of fathers and mothers, brothers and sisters, houses and lands, wives and children, and crowns of eternal lives in the eternal worlds" (v. 55) with or without Emma. She can either accept polygamy and participate in her husband's rewards or she can refuse and be left to make an afterlife without him. As in verse 44, the revelation in the context of verse 19 may imply that Emma would not be blocked from heaven, but only that it would be without Joseph—as she had not shed innocent blood. If so, she would still be turned over to the "buffetings of Satan" (v. 26) but eventually saved in the future kingdom (with *some* partner apparently). Alternatively, the revelation could imply that her sealing would be dissolved, a possibility in the binding–loosing speech incorporated from Matthew 16:19, perhaps negating any promises associated with it.

Even with the threat of destruction for rejecting polygamy, Clayton's account suggests that Emma had already chosen that alternative. If so, her apparent reconciliation with Joseph over polygamy later that year suggests that she did not hold to her immediate decision. After Joseph's death, however, she would carefully deny knowledge of the revelation or Joseph's investment in polygamy.

As noted already, Emma's reputation in Utah suffered over her reluctance to embrace plurality and the migration to Utah (while necessarily objecting to the leadership of the apostles), and Brigham-led saints worked to cement that reputation through public statements and affidavits. For example, in 1854 William Thompson made a statement about a purported visit to the Nauvoo Mansion House a decade earlier on July 9, 1843:

> I had some business with him [Joseph Smith]; he and his family was eating dinner, Sister Emma, Mother Smith & Young Joseph was present & some others that I did not know. Brother Joseph and Emma was talking about the Mornings Sermon. Emma said that he had made some statements that the Brethren & Sisters thought aplied to her that was not very complimentary she said she wanted him to apologise or explain in the afternoon after some talk backwards & forwards Between Joseph Emma & others at the Table, Bro Joseph Looked at me where I was sitting In the south part of the house

---

the NT," 331–42. See Smith's sermon of March 1, 1835, in William V. Smith et al., "The Parallel Joseph," and Fillerup, ed., "William Clayton," May 16, 1843.

6. This is congruent with Joseph's apparent policy that eternal marriage was contingent on accepting the "principle," in cases where an invitation to participate in plurality was involved.

he said Looking at me at the same time pointing his finger at Emma & said that there woman was the greatest Enimy I ever had in my Life. yes said he again that there woman was the greatest Enemy I ever had in all my Life & my Bro Hyrum was always my best friend.[7]

Thompson was incorrect in his dating. The sermon alluded to was given on July 16, 1843, four days following the revelation. In a letter to Brigham Young on July 18, 1843, Willard Richards reported the sermon saying "a mans foes being they of his own house" and speculated that the foe was possibly Nauvoo stake president William Marks, or Marks's counselor "Bro. Coles" [Cowles] or Parley Pratt.[8]

"For He Hath Been Faithful Over A Few Things"

It is made clear in the revelation that Joseph's eternal blessings would continue, with or without Emma Smith. Joseph's family was to extend far beyond what mortal biology could afford. Foreshadowing the priesthood adoptions that later Church leaders pursued, with Smith as the center of a latter day divine network of souls in heaven and on earth, the revelation made Emma's part in the Prophet's life seem important but not necessary for his ultimate glory in the afterlife. Verse 53 echoes what Joseph said during a visit to Benjamin Johnson's home in Ramus, Illinois, on April 2, 1843. Joseph told Johnson that he would preach the next day and that only Johnson would understand the meaning. Johnson recalled,

> the Prophet . . . . and others came to Macedonia to hold a meeting, which was to convene in a large cabinet shop owned by Brother Joseph E. and myself, and as usual he put up at my house. Early on Sunday morning he said, "Come Brother Bennie, let us have a walk." I took his arm and he led the way into a by-place in the edge of the woods surrounded by tall brush and trees. Here, as we sat down upon a log he began to tell me that the Lord had revealed to him that plural or patriarchal marriage was according to His law; and that the Lord had not only revealed it to him but had commanded him to obey it; that he was required to take other wives; and that he wanted my Sister Almira for one of them, and wished me to see and talk to her upon the subject. If a thunderbolt had fallen at my feet I could hardly have been more shocked or amazed. He saw the struggle in my mind and went on to explain. But the shock was

---

7. William Thompson, Affidavit, August 23, 1854.

8. Willard Richards, Letter to Brigham Young, July 18, 1843. Parley Pratt's name was crossed out in the letter, suggesting that Pratt had joined the inner sanctum of polygamy around the time of the letter's composition. On the sermon, see Smith et al., "Parallel Joseph," July 18, 1843.

too great for me to comprehend anything, and in almost an agony of feeling I looked him squarely in the eye, and said, while my heart gushed up before him, "Brother Joseph, this is all new to me; it may all be true—you know, but I do not. To my education it is all wrong, but I am going, with the help of the Lord to do just what you say, with this promise to you—that if ever I know you do this to degrade my sister I will kill you, as the Lord lives." He looked at me, oh, so calmly, and said, "Brother Benjamin, you will never see that day, but you shall see the day you will know it is true, and you will fulfill the law and greatly rejoice in it." And he said, "At this morning's meeting, I will preach you a sermon that no one but you will understand. And furthermore, I will promise you that when you open your mouth to your sister, it shall be filled."

The sermon was on the parable of the talents:

> What is the meaning of the scriptures. he that is faithful over a few things shall be made ruler over Many? & he that is faithful over Many shall be made ruler over many more? What is the meaning of the Parable of the 10 talents? Also conversation with Nicodemus. except a man be born of water & of the spirit.—I shall not tell you?[9]

The parable's instruction "thou hast been faithful over a few things, I will make thee ruler over many things. . . .Take therefore the talent from him, and give it unto him which hath ten talents . . . and he shall have abundance" (Matt. 25:28–29) is a clear rhetorical source for the plural marriage revelation's instruction concerning adultery: "take her and give her unto him that hath not committed adultery but hath been faithful; for he shall be made ruler over many" (D&C 132:44). The reference made acquiring wives a feature of mortal duty and reward in heaven, an important part of polygamy's justification. Moreover, the parable seen through this lens suggests that one wife was simply not enough.

"Let Not My Servant Joseph Put His Property Out Of His Hands"

This section of the revelation ends with the mention of a property sale or exchange as though it were a prior topic of discussion—perhaps referring to the offer to Emma that was alluded to in verse 51. Whatever

---

9. Andrew H. Hedges et al., *Journals, Volume 2: December 1841–April 1843*, 323–26. For Johnson's reminiscence, see E. Dale LeBaron, *Benjamin Franklin Johnson: Friend to the Prophets*, 227. Smith married two of Johnson's sisters. On the sisters, see Todd M. Compton, *In Sacred Loneliness: The Plural Wives of Joseph Smith*, 288–305.

the intended exchange might have been, it is unclear what its retraction was meant to accomplish. How the disposition of property would ease the way for an "enemy" is not evident from the text, but it might imply that property afforded Joseph Smith some security for possible legal action and accompanying expenses.

Joseph Smith's financial arrangements and Emma's potential divorce speak to issues of marriage and divorce law in antebellum America. Divorce required men to prove adultery and required women to prove desertion and lack of support. Smith's transferring a steamboat and land to his wife may have complicated any divorce case. Divorce in early nineteenth–century America nearly always entailed children being placed in the custody of the estranged husband. Divorce proceedings also required the principals to completely divulge the details of conflict. All of these points were fraught concepts for Joseph and Emma.[10]

The conveyance of property from Joseph (most of which was purchased with some form of credit), as trustee for the Church, to Emma would also have been problematic. American law was only beginning to consider the separation of a wife's property from her husband's holdings, with New York only recently (1840) moving to protect a wife's property from her husband's creditors. Congress had also passed a bankruptcy law in 1841 (effective February 1, 1842), and the LDS First Presidency took advantage of the law to try to expunge their crippling debts incurred in Ohio and Missouri in behalf of the Church.[11] Joseph's position as trustee-in-trust for the Church became a liability for Emma, since Illinois law placed harsh limitations on the holdings of any trustee. Any lots Clayton may have made over to Emma were still considered by the courts as inheritance and were subject to debt collection. By law, Emma's share of Joseph Smith's estate amounted to one sixth of the proceeds of what became a complicated and fraud-plagued estate sale and in the end Emma received only a small amount compared to Smith's interest in the *Maid* (valued at about $1,300 at the time) and the property value of the city lots.[12]

---

10. Naomi R. Cahn, "Faithless Wives and Lazy Husbands: Gender Norms in Nineteenth-Century Divorce Law."

11. See *The Wasp* (Nauvoo, IL) (May 7, 1842): 3. Mark Lyman Staker, *Hearken, O Ye People: The Historical Setting of Joseph Smith's Ohio Revelations*, chs. 32–35.

12. On the *Maid of Iowa*, see Donald L. Enders, "The Steamboat *Maid of Iowa*: Mormon Mistress of the Mississippi," 321–35. On Smith's estate, the bankruptcy act, and Emma Smith's inheritance, see Dallin H. Oaks and Joseph L. Bentley, "Joseph Smith and the Legal Process: In the Wake of the Steamboat

The tangled legal proceedings over Smith's estate were also causally linked to polygamy and the revelation via the Bennett scandal in Nauvoo and his subsequent publicity campaign. Bennett's claims regarding Smith's wrongdoings were a connecting thread through official charges and allegations that drew out the settlement of Emma Smith's inheritance for a decade.[13]

The financial arrangements, however, did not lay Emma's discomfort to rest. By mid-August, her opposition was further hardened. Clayton reported Joseph telling him:

> that since E[mma] came back from St Louis she had resisted the P[riesthood] in toto & he had to tell her he would relinquish all for her sake. She said she would [have?] given him E[mily] and E[liza] P[artridge] but he knew if he took them She would pitch on him & obtain a divorce & leave him. He however told me he should not relinquish any thing.[14]

Her tentative offer of the Patridge sisters was probably due to her suspicion that Joseph had already considered Eliza for marriage. A few months earlier, prior to the revelation, Clayton reported that when Emma found Joseph with Eliza behind a locked door in their home, she became furious and "tried to force open the door"—though Joseph claimed he was only questioning the girl about Joseph Jackson, a man who had threatened him.[15]

Over time, the financial and human impact of the plural marriage revelation was huge. The separation of personal property and Church property was never fully worked through until after the death of the third Church president, John Taylor. The difficulties over Brigham Young's estate were manifold, especially due to the congressional response to polygamy and in particular the Morrill Anti-Bigamy Act of 1862. This placed severe limits on holdings of the trustee, capping real estate at a value of $50,000. To safeguard Church interests, Brigham Young housed many Church operations under his personal financial umbrella and personal estate. Thus, Church holdings became inextricably linked to him. Untangling that weave was a years-long process, and it never worked to everyone's satisfaction.[16] When Heber J. Grant became President of the

---

Nauvoo," 735–82. On the precipitation of the national financial difficulties, see Daniel Walker Howe, *What Hath God Wrought: The Transformation of America, 1815–1848*, 373–86, 573, 593.

13. Oaks and Bentley, "Steamboat Nauvoo," 781.

14. Fillerup, ed., "William Clayton's Nauvoo Diaries," August 16, 1843.

15. Ibid., May 23, 1843.

16. Leonard J. Arrington, "The Settlement of the Brigham Young Estate, 1877–1879," 1–20.

Church in 1918, he gradually moved to have Church property held not by the Church as a legal entity (something it never recovered after its disincorporation by the Morill Anti-Bigamy Act), but by the use of a legal innovation borrowed from antique Catholic practice—the corporation sole—in the name of the Church president.[17]

When the plural marriage revelation was acknowledged publicly in 1852, the financial impact was significant both in terms of new converts, loss of existing members, and a required missionary effort to seek an acceptable public rationalization for polygamy.[18] Significant financial expenditures occurred in the lobbying of congress over proposed hostile legislation, particularly during the raid. The costs were immense in terms of Church recovery time and the diversion of funds from Church growth, Church schools, and physical plant. Economic disasters were doubly impactful since they not only infected Church investments, but also Church member donation profiles. After the end of polygamy, and as the Church became more integrated in American society, the revelation had a more subtle but positive effect. Its principle of sealing was the (usually unreported) foundation for Church proselytization with the "families are forever" slogan, an idea attributed to elaborations of the visitation of Elijah (D&C 110). Only with the attacks of conservative Protestant forces, Church dissenters, and the countercult warriors in the latter half of the twentieth century did the revelation once again become a liability in conversion and retention, and the associated financial costs in donations and public relations efforts.[19]

At the October 1890 Church conference following the announcement of the Manifesto, George Q. Cannon rationalized the plural marriage revelation as a testing ground, a sacrificial offering, designed to create conflict with the World. If so, it was a success.[20]

> Think of how many doctrines have been taught that have been new to the world, but that God has revealed in our day! How could we understand them unless the Spirit of God bore testimony to them? Who on the earth believed them? They were not sanctioned by tradition.

---

17. Matthew Bowman, *The Mormon People: The Making of an American Faith*, 171.

18. Richard S. Van Wagoner, *Mormon Polygamy: A History*, 86. Polly Aird, *Mormon Convert, Mormon Defector: A Scottish Immigrant in the American West, 1848–1861*, 88–90.

19. J. B. Haws, *The Mormon Image in the American Mind: Fifty Years of Public Perception*, 201–3, ch. 5.

20. Bowman, *The Mormon People*, 125.

They were not upheld by the common belief of man. They were new to this generation. Yet, though they shocked the prejudices of mankind, and perhaps startled us as Latter-day Saints, when we sought God for a testimony concerning them, He never failed to give unto us His Holy Spirit, which witnessed unto our spirits that they were from God, and not of man. . . . All that we can do is to seek the mind and will of God, and when that comes to us, though it may come in contact with every feeling that we have previously entertained, we have no option but to take the step that God points out, and to trust to Him, as we were often told by President Young, for the results. That is the way this Church is led. There is no being, save the Lord himself, who knows the end from the beginning. Who of us would be tested if we were in that condition?[21]

21. George Q. Cannon, "Enduring to the End."

Chapter 9: Verses 58–63

The Mechanics of Plurality and Kingdoms of Heaven

Much of the plural marriage revelation up to this point can be simplistically divided into two kinds of content: 1) Joseph was right in his practice of plural marriage; and 2) Emma was wrong in her rejection of the practice. The present portion of the revelation (verses 58 through 63), however, shifts away from these topics and instead focuses on the actual practice of entering into plural marriages.

58 Now, as touching the law of the priesthood, there are many things pertaining thereunto.

59 Verily, if a man be called of my Father, as was Aaron, by mine own voice, and by the voice of him that sent me, and I have endowed him with the keys of the power of this priesthood,[1] if he do anything in my name, and according to my law and by my word, he will not commit sin, and I will justify him.

60 Let no one, therefore, set on my servant Joseph; for I will justify him; for he shall do the sacrifice which I require at his hands for his transgressions, saith the Lord your God.

61 And again, as pertaining to the law of the priesthood—if any man espouse a virgin, and desire to espouse another, and the first give her consent, and if he espouse the second, and they are virgins, and have vowed to no other man, then is he justified; he cannot commit adultery for they are given unto him; for he cannot commit adultery with that that belongeth unto him and to no one else.

62 And if he have ten virgins given unto him by this law, he cannot commit adultery, for they belong to him, and they are given unto him; therefore is he justified.

63 But if one or either of the ten virgins, after she is espoused, shall be with another man, she has committed adultery, and shall be destroyed; for they

---

1. As noted above, "the keys of this priesthood" might be read as "the keys of this ministry of sealing and plural marriage." The subject of the verse is Joseph Smith.

are given unto him to multiply and replenish the earth, according to my commandment, and to fulfil the promise which was given by my Father before the foundation of the world, and for their exaltation in the eternal worlds, that they may bear the souls of men; for herein is the work of my Father continued, that he may be glorified.

The difference in purpose here, along with the structure of the Kingsbury manuscript, leads to the possibility that a portion of the revelation was added in response to Emma Smith's rejection and burning of the original dictation. (See the discussion of verse 61 below and the Addendum at the end of this volume.)

"I Will Justify Him"

If there is any doubt what the "law" really refers to in the revelation, these passages make it clear. This section opens up in verse 59 by pulling language from one of Mormonism's favorite proselytizing passages on priesthood, Hebrew 5:4 ("And no man taketh this honour unto himself, but he that is called of God, as was Aaron").[2] With the basis of divine authority, it then seems to give amazing carte blanche to Smith:

> I have endowed him with the keys of the power of this priesthood, if he do anything in my name, and according to my law and by my word, he will not commit sin, and I will justify him. (v. 59)

Joseph had been secretly (even to Emma) practicing polygamy for years, and the passage is probably meant to justify those relationships to her. It also echoes a long conflicted theme in Mormonism that obligated Latter-day Saints to obey Church leaders without criticism.[3] However, whatever

---

2. Hebrew 5:4. The passage became doubly encoded in Mormon scripture because its Mormon interpretation (perhaps via Orson Pratt) appears in Articles of Faith 5. David J. Whittaker, "The 'Articles of Faith' in Mormon Literature and Thought," 77.

3. A well-known example appears in a speech by Elder Ezra Taft Benson in 1980: "The prophet is the only man who speaks for the Lord in everything. . . . Follow . . . and be blessed, reject . . . and suffer." Ezra Taft Benson, "Fourteen Fundamentals in Following the Prophet." In 1869, Abraham O. Smoot pronounced, "the first step to greatness is obedience without questioning our superiors." Luke William Gallup journal, April 4, 1869. See also Turner, *Brigham Young*, 250–54; "Elder Decries Criticism of LDS Leaders"; Steven L. Peck, "When Our Leaders Speak, The Thinking Has Been Done"; and Henry B. Eyring, "The Lord Leads His Church."

potential sins Joseph is protected from or absolved of, the next verse makes it clear that Joseph had his own transgressions that would necessitate God to "justify him; for he shall do the sacrifice which I [God] require at his hands" (v. 60). Unlike the discussion of sacrifice in verses 50 and 51, the required sacrifice here is not textually connected to Abraham and is yet to be made. The passage offers no suggestion of what this sacrifice may be.

"If Any Man Espouse a Virgin"

On the surface, verse 61 appears to be a prohibition of polyandry, barring a plural marriage of one man to another man's wife by requiring that additional prospective wives "have vowed to no other man." However, in the broader context of the revelation, "vow" seems to specifically refer to marriage sealings that are done "by my [God's] word" (vv. 18–19) and not a simple civil marriage that is "not bound by any law when they are out of the world" (v. 15). In practice, Joseph Smith's own marriage sealings to women who were already civilly married suggest such an interpretation.[4]

In the earliest manuscript copy of the revelation (the original dictation being destroyed by Emma Smith), the Kingsbury manuscript reveals a possible delay between the writing of verse 60 and the rest of the revelation beginning with verse 61. (See the Addendum.) It is impossible to know precisely how long this delay was, but some bounds are possible. While the other verses were still transcribed by Kingsbury, the break between the verses is made evident by the use of a different quill and shade of ink. Furthermore, Kingsbury altered his style somewhat after the break, including the nearly exclusive use of the ampersand in the later text—as opposed to its complete absence prior to the break—indicating that some time may have passed between his resuming the transcription.

Kingsbury himself may have given another explanation for the different script in 1892, nearly 50 years after the revelation was penned. When Kingsbury was called as a witness in the "Temple Lot" case, he stated that while copying the revelation, Hyrum Smith came to retrieve the original. Kingsbury testified under direct examination that,

> I went off . . . and copied it . . . I copied the revelation on plural marriage
> that he [Newel K. Whitney] handed me and just as I got through the copy-

---

4. On these "dual wives," as well as some controversies surrounding them, see Samuel Morris Brown, *In Heaven as it is on Earth: Joseph Smith and the Early Mormon Conquest of Death*, 241–47. Andrew H. Hedges et al., *Journals*, 2, xxiv–xxx. See also Chapter 6.

ing of it, Hyrum Smith came in and wanted the revelation.—the original revelation, was what he wanted. He came in to see how I got along with it,—That is Bishop Whitney did, and then he went out and told Hyrum Smith that he would hand him the revelation in a few minutes, for I was not quite through the copying of it. Well when I got through making the copy, I took the one I had made myself and read it and he took the original and read it as the same time to see if I had made any mistakes, and that it was correct, and when he found that it was all correct he took the one that the one that I had made and went out to the door and handed it to Hyrum Smith who was outside of the door ready to take it.[5]

Kingsbury's testimony may offer a reason for the more abbreviated format of verses 61 through 66. While the testimony is not completely clear, it suggests that Kingsbury was under some pressure to finish his copying work near its end when he was interrupted and that this may account for the use of the somewhat less careful form in the final part of the text of the revelation.[6]

The last six verses of the revelation undoubtedly predate Joseph Smith's death for a number of reasons, including the *Nauvoo Expositor*'s mention of "marrying virgins"—a term that does not occur in the revelation until verse 61. If the later text was a response to Emma Smith's rejection of the revelation, then it was not included in Clayton's original dictation. If so, the additional text may have responded to Emma's reluctance over at least two of the young wives she seemed familiar with, Eliza and Emily Partridge.

Given Joseph Smith's marriages to women who had been or were still married, the use of the word "virgins" in the revelation does not seem to refer to women who have never experienced sexual intercourse.[7] Virgin might mean virtuous, an exemplary person perhaps, but the revelation certainly emphasizes sex (verse 63, for example, and the passages on adultery). Indeed, reproduction seems to be the primary purpose behind polygamy. The knowledgeable 1843 reader may have seen this condition as

---

5. Joseph C. Kingsbury testimony in United States testimony 1892, United States Court of Appeals (8th circuit).

6. See the Addendum.

7. Examples of Smith's wives who were married to him and simultaneously to other men include Zina Huntington Jacobs, Sylvia Lyon, and Patty Sessions. Bushman, *Rough Stone Rolling,* 438–41; Richard S. Van Wagoner, *Mormon Polygamy,* 41–49. Todd M. Compton, *In Sacred Loneliness: The Plural Wives of Joseph Smith,* 639–41. Brigham Young carried out a similar program and it is evident that on at least some of those occasions, deep romantic feelings were generated. See John G. Turner, *Brigham Young: Pioneer Prophet,* 134–36.

"free of fornication/adultery," a possible meaning of virgin. In that sense it represented a continued emphasis in Mormon scripture that began in the Book of Mormon and was confirmed by the Law of the Church (Doctrine and Covenants 42 and its various extensions). The passage was likely one for Emma's benefit. Emma was only directly involved in some of Smith's marriages to women who had no history of sexual experience (the Partridge and Lawrence sisters).

The revelation's use of virgins shares text with Paul's letter to the Corinthians: "if a virgin marry, she hath not sinned" (1 Cor. 7:28). But Paul's concept of virgin seems to clash with the context of the revelation's use of the term. Paul clearly intended virgin to mean a woman who had no sexual experience. That was too broad a category for the revelation if, as noted above, it was actually meant to apply to all of Joseph Smith's marriages. Part of the puzzle of plurality, throughout its existence in Nauvoo and then under the shelter of Utah Mormon mainstream practice, was its evolving conceptual position in the salvific narrative. Paul's addressing the questions of marriage and celibacy in the letter to the Corinthians is an important example. His admission that Jesus had never addressed the questions he was faced with meant that his apostolic office must suffice. So it was with Smith and the resolution of a bitter challenge to reconcile a revelation and the mental and moral abrasion in his followers. His successors that continued the embrace of plurality dealt with the same stress, a stress that manifested in continuing theological, moral, and social strains.

The practical picture of plurality is clearly seen in the family of Utah polygamist John D. T. McAllister who married nine living women (and in his temple enthusiasm, many more single deceased women) and was adopted as the son of Brigham Young and his own biological mother. He lived sporadically with most of his wives, and jealousy or perceived neglect resulted in two divorces (that is, the sealings were cancelled). Two other wives were never sexual partners and never shared the same roof with McAllister. Some of his wives apparently had strong romantic feelings for him, while others did not. Plurality was typically complex and its inherent male-female imbalances leave its imprint on Mormons still.[8]

---

8. Wayne Hinton, "John D. T. McAllister: The Southern Utah Years, 1876–1910," 106–36.

"To Multiply and Replenish the Earth"

While the creation of an interconnected network of sealed—and thus saved—persons was a significant result and evident purpose of plural marriage, the revelation makes it clear that it also had a purpose in mortality. Speaking of wives in a polygamous marriage, the revelation states:

> [T]hey are given unto him to multiply and replenish the earth, according to my commandment, and to fulfil the promise which was given by my Father before the foundation of the world, and for their exaltation in the eternal worlds, that they may bear the souls of men; for herein is the work of my Father continued, that he may be glorified. (v. 63)

The revelation makes it clear that plurality was not some otherworldly connection. It had the vital, present, and human purpose of filling the earth with the posterity of its participants. Coupled with the Book of Mormon's exception clause of polygamy being commanded by God to "raise up seed unto me" (Jacob 2:30), the revelation seems to promote the notion that some "seed" are more valuable than other seed—though, ironically, polygamy apparently failed to produce any offspring for Joseph Smith.[9] Contemporary testimony and later affidavits in Utah make it clear that the small cadre of Nauvoo polygamists—including Smith—were sexually active. However, because polygamous relationships had to remain secretive in Nauvoo, sex in plurality was most likely limited while Smith lived. It would have been especially limited for individual wives when considering its distribution among polygamous partners.[10]

The revelation theologized sex and gave it divine utility in plurality: children. But as noted, sex in early Nauvoo polygamy was rather unproductive.[11] The rules for sex were probably driven by the propensities of the

---

9. See the discussion of "believing blood" and the "blood of the prophets" in Chapter 6.

10. Parley Pratt's 1843 letters to plural wife Elizabeth Brotherton (older sister to the Martha Brotherton mentioned above) demonstrate a similar strategy: "Perhaps I may not See you to night because of other matters. If not I will see you tomorrow night at the same place at Six O Clock or between that and nine." Parley P. Pratt, Letter to Elizabeth Brotherton, October 7, 1843. Terryl L. Givens and Matthew J. Grow, *Parley P. Pratt: The Apostle Paul of Mormonism*, 205–6; Bushman, *Rough Stone Rolling*, 490–95. A "blessing meeting" in early Utah shows that children were born to plural wives in Nauvoo. See "Bishops' Blessing Meeting," Historian's Office General Church Minutes, 1837–1877, Salt Lake City, January 6, 1850.

11. There were stories of abortion for plural wives in Nauvoo, mediated by John Bennett. Given attitudes about abortion in other contexts, such a practice

parties, their cultural upbringing, and their religious scruples. But with the isolation of Utah, Church leaders—men and women—spoke out on the topic. The logic of these later verses in the revelation helped fuel a drive to build one's kingdom—a drive that was present in much of Nauvoo and early Utah polygamy, helping to encourage marriages between older men and youthful women. "Kingdom fever" was a feature of the early incarnation of the system, a "get all you can" philosophy drenched in a picture of an afterlife where glory and family enlargement were one.[12]

A connection between ethical behavior toward unborn preexistent spirits and the personal glory found in God-like activity was at work in the theological framework of polygamy and procreation. This connection naturally extended from Smith's earlier 1829 revelation on the eternal joy that would result from helping others attain salvation:

> Wherefore, you are called to cry repentance unto this people. And if it so be that you should labor all your days in crying repentance unto this people, and bring, save it be one soul unto me, how great shall be your joy with him in the kingdom of my Father! And now, if your joy will be great with one soul that you have brought unto me into the kingdom of my Father, how great will be your joy if you should bring many souls unto me! (D&C 18:14–16)

---

among Nauvoo polygamists seems extremely far-fetched. One of Mormon Apostle George A. Smith's plural wives gave a reminiscent eyewitness report for Emma at the delivery of a plural baby. See Linda King Newell and Valeen Tippetts Avery, *Mormon Enigma: Emma Hale Smith*, 211–12; Lucy Meserve Smith statement, May 18, 1892. Abortion claims appear in the testimony of Sarah Pratt, widow of Orson Pratt. See Newell and Avery, *Mormon Enigma*, 111; one of Bennett's circle, Gustavus Hills, seduced and impregnated Mary Clift (1815–1850) suggesting that she would become his spiritual wife (ca. January 1842). In an 1842 deposition Clift testified that Hills offered her an abortion and that he had sexual congress with another woman in addition to his legal wife. Clift became a plural wife of Theodore Turley in 1844. Nauvoo Stake High Council Court Papers, September 4, 1842; Journal History of the Church, 1896–2001, August 29, 1847; also John S. Dinger, *The Nauvoo City and High Council Minutes*, 424–26; Michael Hicks, *Mormonism and Music: A History*, 42. George D. Smith, *Nauvoo Polygamy: "... But We Called It Celestial Marriage,"* 348–50.

12. Robert Fillerup, ed., "William Clayton's Nauvoo Diaries and Personal Writings," August 11, 1843. Joseph Fielding journals, 1837–1859, 5:57. Andrew F. Ehat, "'They Might Have Known That He Was Not a Fallen Prophet'—The Nauvoo Journal of Joseph Fielding," 145. Jonathan A. Stapley, "Adoptive Sealing Ritual in Mormonism," 63, 85–86. Brigham Young, April 6, 1862, *Journal of Discourses*, 9:269–70.

Assuming that children raised in righteous homes were more likely to be brought into the kingdom of God, it became imperative that unborn spirits be given the increased possibility of being reared in righteous Mormon households.[13] Polygamy was understood as increasing those chances. Adoption had an altruistic angle too.[14] Wilford Woodruff observed: "It may be a correct doctrine that a man's Kingdom will consist of only the fruit of his own loins. Yet Jesus Christ died to save the whole world, and if we as Apostles and Elders, do nothing for the human family only for the fruit of our own loins, we shall not do much towards . . . saving the souls of men."[15] Through the combination of evangelizing, procreating, and adopting, a person could exponentially increase their eternal joy and glory as the salvific fruits of these efforts multiplied through generations. This hearkened back to the promise made to Abraham and extended to Smith earlier in the revelation:

> Abraham received promises concerning his seed, and of the fruit of his loins—from whose loins ye are, namely, my servant Joseph—which were to continue so long as they were in the world; and as touching Abraham and his seed, out of the world they should continue; both in the world and out of the world should they continue as innumerable as the stars; or, if ye were to count the sand upon the seashore ye could not number them. This promise is yours also, because ye are of Abraham, and the promise was made unto Abraham; and by this law is the continuation of the works of my Father, wherein he glorifieth himself. (D&C 132:30–31)

Connected to Woodruff's vision of salvific power was the important notion that sealing or adoption to a man with assured salvation (usually perceived in terms of Church standing) carried with it a promise of one's own inherited glory. Women who saw themselves in plurality had important motives for seeking the most desirable companion in view of an associated standing in the afterlife.[16] Smith made this a part of his own marriage proposals—that through sealing all of his kin would be drawn into heaven with him. The revelation thus declared that Smith's own salvation was guaranteed.

---

13. William C. Staines, "Statement." Brigham Young, July 14, 1855, *Journal of Discourses*, 3:264. Paula Kelly Harline, *The Polygamous Wives Writing Club: From the Diaries of Mormon Pioneer Women*, 109.

14. See the discussion of the salvific nature of adoption in Chapter 6.

15. Wilford Woodruff, Letter to Samuel Roskelley, June 8, 1887. Stapley, "Adoptive Sealing Ritual in Mormonism," 103.

16. On the resulting aspirational search for the most desirable men, see the Epilogue.

Though kingdom fever was an important force in the early years of polygamy, it was logistically and socially defective in terms of community survival and expansion in Utah. While the old guard maintained very large families, Brigham Young saw the folly of teaching that older men, even if important in the Church hierarchy and of sufficient wealth, should gather large groups of young wives. It caused community tensions and worked against ambition and growth in a hard country in need of the civilizing effects youthful marriages brought. Young steered young women to marry young single men. His popular apocryphal meme about the dangers of single young men was based on experience. Kingdom fever remained to some degree, and it formed part of the message that anti-Mormonism used to characterize the religion of the Latter-day Saints.[17] In 1846, Willard Richards observed that kingdom expansion was also an obvious consequence of sealing between parent and child (and hence an argument for plurality):

> [If a man] had 12 Daughters he would give them to 12 good men allowing it should be their choice. Then if these men should become 12 Kings he would have connection with 12 Kingdoms and they would be under obligations to Sostain him. Said that those who were so over ancious to have their family all piled in one little corner together would by & by find themselves the lesser number.[18]

Daughters were as utilitarian as sons in kingdom growth.

Joseph Smith's own polygamy was only a passing interpretation of the institution in the large, at least for the rank and file.[19] Hence, emphasis on plurality remained, but the Nauvoo urgency to "seal all you can" largely

---

17. John Cradlebaugh, *Mormonism: A Doctrine That Embraces Polygamy, Adultery, Incest, Perjury, Robbery and Murder*, 4.

18. Maurine Carr Ward, ed., *Winter Quarters: The 1846–1848 Life Writings of Mary Haskin Parker Richards*, 83–84. On age disparity, see Kathryn M. Daynes, *More Wives Than One: Transformation of the Mormon Marriage System, 1840–1910*, 107–8.

19. Daynes, *More Wives Than One*, 106–53. Heber C. Kimball had 45 wives and 65 children, Orson F. Whitney, *The Life of Heber C. Kimball, an Apostle: The Father and Founder of the British Mission*. Even Eliza Snow's advice to young women on marriage to older men (see Chapter 10 and the Epilogue) was not really tinged with kingdom fever; it was about her concern over salvation safety. On young marriage and society, see Heber C. Kimball, October 6, 1855, *Journal of Discourses*, 3:125; Brigham Young, April 1, 1863, *Journal of Discourses*, 10:224; On damping Nauvoo kingdom fever, see Turner, *Brigham Young*, 157. For Brigham Young's somewhat flexible boundaries on wife-taking when ages were

died a practical death among most Latter-day Saints.[20] The hard facts of frontier life largely overcame the drive of kingdom fever, though aspects of the latter still continued. For example, men sometimes married widows or divorced women and their young daughters at the same time, both before and after Young's death. The pressures of the Mormon Reformation and, much later, continuing polygamy during the federal raid helped keep some of these breaches of Victorian taboos in place.[21]

Later polygamous marriages were relatively modest in size, counting both the living and dead. There were, however, exceptions. John McAllister, a member of the St. George temple presidency and later president of that temple, was sealed to a remarkable number of deceased women.[22] In an April 1894 meeting of the presidency and apostles, Wilford Woodruff announced that he was sealed to nearly 400 deceased women in his own family tree:

> In searching out my genealogy I found about four hundred of my female kindred who were never married. I asked Pres. Young what I should do with them. He said for me to have them sealed to me unless there were more than 999 of them. The doctrine startled me, but I had it done.

His counselor, George Q. Cannon, privately observed, "There has been a disposition since the days of Nauvoo for men to seek to add to their future kingdoms by having dead persons sealed and adopted to them."[23] Adding to one's kingdom was an important aspect and motivation for nineteenth-century polygamy and proxy sealing.[24] It was Woodruff's 1894 revelation ending the practice of adoption that ultimately led to the end of this practice of sealing living men to many of their deceased female rela-

---

widely mismatched, see Wilford Woodruff journal, June 14, 1857, in Scott G. Kenney, *Wilford Woodruff's Journal, 1834–1898, Typescript,* 5:58.

20. For Smith's instructions on the urgency to seal, see Chapter 7.

21. Harline, *The Polygamous Wives Writing Club,* 185.

22. One thousand wives was the theoretical upper limit apparently. Abraham H. Cannon diary, April 5, 1894, in Edward Leo Lyman, ed., *Candid Insights of a Mormon Apostle: The Diaries of Abraham H. Cannon, 1889–1895,* 489. For others who had large numbers of such wives, see, for example, A. Karl Larson and Katherine Miles Larson, eds., *The Diary of Charles Lowell Walker,* 1:464–65; Donald G. Godfrey and Rebecca S. Martineau-McCarty, eds., *An Uncommon Common Pioneer: The Journals of James Henry Martineau, 1828–1918,* 296, 321–22.

23. Lyman, ed., *Candid Insights of a Mormon Apostle,* 490.

24. Amasa Lyman: "When it comes to the game of kingdoms, I can hold my own with any of them." See Lyman, ed., *Candid Insights of a Mormon Apostle,* 490.

tions. The revelation mitigated the reasons for such sealings—a practice based in the theory that not only were women more likely to be accepting in the afterlife, but that their refusal of sacraments in the afterlife would not damage links in the heavenly chain from the present back to Adam.[25]

"For They Belong To Him"

For Mormon polygamy, as with almost all patriarchal cultures, the ground rules for sex were mostly dictated by men—though, oddly enough, the ground rules generally promoted the view that sex was for reproduction and not for pleasure. Combined with the plural marriage revelation, it was commonly taught that if a man engaged in sex for pleasure with his wives then he risked becoming subservient to those women and generating destructive jealousy among them, both of which could result in him losing the power to lead his families to exaltation by failing at the God-given role of presiding over wives and children. Furthermore, it was believed by some that sex for pleasure during pregnancy could cause children to be born with lesser ability, beauty, or stature.[26] Apostle Orson Hyde, 1857:

> Now when the proper intercourse which is necessary for the propagation of our species takes place between a man and a woman, and no more than that—the balance of his power of muscle—goes to strengthen other parts of his system, and thus gives him power over disease and enables him to prolong his life. But when the contrary is the case the man becomes prostrated, by this overindulgence and having given his strength to women, he becomes prostrated and is rendered liable to disease—not only this . . . [he] becomes weak in mind, and debilitated in intellect and . . . why is it some are born Idiots? It is because . . . they were not let alone in their Mother's womb. . . . I will venture to say, that in a Majority of cases, out of one hundred times, one has gone to propagate our species and ninety nine to the gratification of our baser passions. . . I say . . . where there is no intercourse of this kind, only with the prospect of children being born—That family can be governed.[27]

---

25. Lorenzo Snow, "St. George Sermon," 3. Jonathan A. Stapley, *The Power of Godliness: Mormon Liturgy and Cosmology*, ch. 2. However, Woodruff still felt some hesitancy over the prospect of living women being sealed to the unproven dead. Lyman, ed., *Candid Insights of a Mormon Apostle*, 489.

26. Anti-Mormon literature described the children of polygamy in just such ways. Blair Dee Hodges, "Intellectual Disability in Mormon Thought and History, 1830–1900," ch. 4.

27. Luke William Gallup journal, February 11, 1857, in B. Carmon Hardy, *Doing the Works of Abraham, Mormon Polygamy: Its Origin, Practice, and Demise*, 133–35.

There was yet considerable variation in attitudes about sexual desire in nineteenth-century Mormons, unsurprisingly similar in many ways to attitudes in the larger world—some men bragging about their self-mastery in avoiding desire altogether, others recounting the dangers of doing so. Women entered the discussion in several ways, some seeing physical affection as key in making sexual experiences into love-building episodes rather than soul-diminishing exercises. Hyde's prescription was not universally accepted by his own estimation (though it was echoed by Brigham Young and others) and, as Hannah King observed, this rather mechanical version of sex without love and mutual desire had its dehumanizing aspects in an institution seemingly founded on the sacrifice and obedience of women.[28]

Hyde's sort of folk physiology and psychology mirrored the primitive understanding of human nature of the time; but plurality was especially subject to such claims, given its isolated clientele and their perception of reliable sources. Speculations on social structure in the larger world, such as the incorrect belief that the U.S. population was made up of considerably more women than men, were held as fact in Utah even among the more educated Saints.[29] As late as 1947, LDS authors were penning books

---

28. See Hannah King, "Procreation," 51. Belinda Pratt, perhaps the earliest public Mormon female voice on sexual matters (1854), reiterated a no-sex rule during pregnancy or menstruation. This was "nature's law" and polygamy afforded obedience by allowing a man to leave one wife alone when in those states. See below, and Peter Crawley, *A Descriptive Bibliography of the Mormon Church*, 3:131.

29. On claims of population imbalance in America, see Orson Pratt in the compilation *Discourses on Celestial Marriage*. On Hyde, see Hardy, *Doing the Works of Abraham*, 132, 138–40. On sexual issues, Ruth C. Engs, *Clean Living Movements: American Cycles of Health Reform*. See Engs's treatment of Sylvester Graham in particular. On male dominance in Mormon discourse about polygamy, see Bradley Kramer, "Keeping the Sacred: Structured Silence in the Enactment of Priesthood Authority, Gendered Worship, and Sacramental Kinship in Mormonism," 125. Some Mormons may have seen (mortal) sex desire as a necessary evil, but they were not ignorant of worldly practice. Oliver B. Huntington, "History and Life of Oliver B. Huntington, Also His Travels & Troubles, written by himself," June 12, 1842, (page 5). The variety of attitudes among Mormons here is displayed in the complaint of one of John D. Lee's plural wives; Lee's libido was far beyond Hyde's ideal. See Turner, *Brigham Young*, 159. On romantic love often being a part of plurality, even "polyandrous" unions or dual wives, see Turner, *Brigham Young*, 134–35; also Hinton, "John D. T. McAllister." On American myths of procreation and the nature and foundation

with suspect claims in this direction. Elder John A. Widtsoe wrote to one author, "In reading the manuscript [of your book] . . . are you saying that eligible men were scarce in Utah at the time Jacob Hamblin married his second wife? We have tried to discover the truth with regard to the male and female population of the state at that time . . . . Ever since statistics have been kept, male members have been in preponderance."[30] Kathryn Daynes notes that in sample populations in St. George and Manti, Utah, Latter-day Saint men married widows and divorced women with significant frequency in plurality and statistics suggest previously married women were an important pool of females for potential plural mates. However, few argued that this marriage pattern was the main reason for polygamy.[31]

"That They May Bear the Souls of Men"

While historically there are different ways to understand the child-bearing utility of polygamy in the plural marriage revelation, its obvious social work was to increase the number of children born to polygamous patriarchs ("they are given unto him to multiply and replenish the earth" [v. 61]). This would have followed the Book of Mormon's exception for polygamy to "raise up [mortal] seed unto me [the Lord]" (Jacob 2:30). However, in post-Nauvoo theology it gained a dual meaning that included eternal fecundity in heaven. This reading extended the meaning of "bear the souls of men" in verse 63 away from the Book of Mormon's exception to raise righteous children, and instead reads it as referring to the procreation of future premortal spirits. In doing so, the nature of the human spirit itself was shifted through the notion of celestial procreation.

From 1839 to his death, Joseph Smith frequently taught the eternal nature of the human spirit (that is, spirits having no beginning and no end). This suggested that family expansion in heaven is the result of divinized persons replicating God's cosmological creative acts and salvific works with new worlds, where the mortal inhabitants of such worlds become

---

of modern American marital theories, see Jill Lepore, *The Mansion of Happiness: A History of Life and Death*, chs. 1, 5.

30. John A. Widtsoe, correspondence. My thanks to Ardis E. Parshall for bringing this to my attention. Compare Widtsoe's similar response in his book, *Evidences and Reconciliations: Aids to Faith in a Modern Day*, 390.

31. Daynes, *More Wives Than One*, 101, 127, 168–69. See also Orson Pratt, *The Seer*, 110. But see Lyman, *Candid Insights of a Mormon Apostle*, 492.

the adoptive family of the corporate heaven. A report of an April 7, 1844, sermon by Smith has him teaching:

> God himself finds himself in the midst of Sp[irits] & bec[ause] he saw proper to institute laws for those who were in less intelligence that they mit [might]. have one glory upon another in all that knowledge power & glory & so took in hand to save the world of Sp[irits].[32]

If the image of Heaven as a Heavenly Earth captured much of Smith's later speech and many of his revelations,[33] the understanding of the souls or spirits of men as products rather than beneficiaries of that creative act contradicted their advertised eternal nature—a point of contradiction that later Mormon thinkers like B. H. Roberts tried to reconcile, not without considerable controversy.[34]

While celestial procreation as a sexual analogue of mortal reproduction does not seem to be an intended part of Smith's cosmology, his public remarks, like the marriage revelation itself, could be interpreted in ways that allowed for procreated souls in heaven. Following a July 16, 1843, sermon, just four days after the dictation of the plural marriage revelation, polygamy insider Franklin Richards interpreted Smith's teaching as, "The earthly is the image of the Heavenly shows that [it] is by the multiplication of Lives that the eternal worlds are created and occupied that which is born of the flesh is flesh that which is born of the Spirit is Spirit."[35]

It is important to remember that human souls, in Mormon cosmology, chose to come to the mortal state as preexistent spirits. They did not fall

---

32. Thomas Bullock minutes, April 7, 1844.

33. See Stanley B. Kimball, ed., *On the Potter's Wheel: The Diaries of Heber C. Kimball*, 52. Parley Pratt produced one of the earliest rationalizations of a Mormon domestic heaven. It appeared during the time when polygamy was still secret, so it is a paean to monogamy in heaven. Importantly, while Pratt tells of a reuniting in heaven, and the internal logic of the piece is sealing, there is no mention of gaining *more* children in heaven. Parley P. Pratt, "Celestial Family Organization," 1–2.

34. See the discussion of spirits in Chapter 6. Roberts's ideas in speech and print were closely tied to his work with Smith's sermon of April 7, 1844, often called the King Follett Sermon. See William V. Smith, "The King Follett Sermon: A Social History." See also, William Victor Smith, *Every Word Seasoned with Grace: A Textual Study of the Funeral Sermons of Joseph Smith*, ch. 7, appendices.

35. Multiplication of "Lives" is linked to the revelation's words, "continuation of the seeds." For Franklin Richards's excerpt, see "Scriptural Items." See also Smith et al., "Parallel Joseph," July 16, 1843.

from heaven out of boredom or sin in a Platonic drama.[36] Smith's instructions in his April 7, 1844, sermon that "you have got to learn how to be gods yourselfs" was a clear allusion to the plural marriage revelation and its relative incarnation in proto-temple rituals he introduced between the spring of 1842 and the fall of 1843. It would suggest that the revelation's "continuation of the seeds forever and ever" (v. 9) referred to carrying on God's work by adopting souls into the divine family.[37] The lack of explicit clarification by Smith, however, opened the door to many extrapolations in future generations: Mormons had the key of knowledge that showed them that their families made bodies for the souls procreated by the Parents in Heaven and that human biology and heavenly biology were one.

Others who heard the revelation or earlier instruction in polygamy perhaps dimly saw the implications that would fully flower in Utah: peopling worlds by an analogue of human sex.[38] In 1845, Mormon theologian and poet Eliza Snow took the idea of preexistent souls, combined it with Smith's revelation on polygamy, and wrote her interpretation in poetic form. Her text seems to rule out any figurative interpretation of the revelation. Published as "My Father in Heaven," Snow's answer to the conundrum of female inclusion within a theology that was already drifting from Smith's mysterious pluralism read,

> O my Father, thou that dwellest
> In the high and glorious place;
> When shall I regain thy presence,
> And again behold thy face?
>
> In thy holy habitation
> Did my spirit once reside?

---

36. Terryl L. Givens, *When Souls Had Wings: Pre-Mortal Existence in Western Thought*, 77.

37. For an elaboration of this adoption see Samuel M. Brown, "Believing Adoption," 45–65.

38. Perhaps Heber C. Kimball's reverent wish for forgiveness and salvation may be read this way: "O that I was such a man as I would desire to be, and Thou O God knowest I wish [to] be pure in hart, that all of my sins may be bloted out . . . . [and] ever sepperate me from my dear Vilate or anny of those that are con[ne]cted to me by the ties of Na[t]ure Thou knowest I Love my dear family, and may it increase more and more, that [no] power can sepperate us from Each other, that we may dwell to gether through out all Eternity, and thare be [enthroned] on worlds, to propragate that thare may be no end to us or our Seeds." Kimball, ed., *On the Potter's Wheel*, 52.

> In my *first* primeval childhood
> Was I nurtur'd near thy side?
>
> . . . .
>
> I had learn'd to call thee father
> Through thy spirit from on high;
> But until the key of knowledge
> Was restor'd, I knew not why.
>
> In the heav'ns are parents single?
> No, the thought makes reason stare;
> Truth is reason-truth eternal
> Tells me I've a mother there.[39]

Snow's text reads the plural marriage revelation onto God's life and implies that the Heavenly Parents procreate children, a theme of *imitatio parenti* that developed in succeeding decades to make Mormon marriage praxis an earthly duty that imitated and engaged the heavenly world in a very literal way. The poem's logic thus sees a Mother as a necessity, given the Fatherhood of God.[40]

A decade after Smith's death, Orson Pratt framed Snow's idea in a way that became largely normative over the next century and a half of Mormonism, taking the image of human beings as the children of God to its most concrete anthropomorphic endpoint.[41] As part of his lengthy serialized defense of polygamy, Pratt wrote:

> Fallen beings beget children whose bodies are constituted of flesh and bones, being formed out of the blood circulating in the veins of the parents. Celestial beings beget children composed of the fluid which circulates in their veins, which is spiritual, therefore their children must be spirits, and not flesh and bones. This is the origin of our spiritual organization in Heaven. The spirits of all mankind, destined for this earth, were begotten by a father, and born of a mother in Heaven. . . .
>
> If we suppose, as an average, that only one year intervened between each birth, then it would have required over on hundred thousand million of years for the same Mother to have given birth to this vast family. . . . If

---

39. Eliza R. Snow, "My Father in Heaven." See also Edward William Tullidge, *The Women of Mormondom*, ch. 19.

40. Susanna Morrill, *White Roses on the Floor of Heaven: Mormon Women's Popular Theology, 1880–1920*, 55. Linda P. Wilcox, "Mormon Motherhood: Official Images," 211–12.

41. One of a large number of examples is Boyd K. Packer, "The Pattern of Our Parentage," 66–69.

the Father of these spirits, prior to his redemption, had secured to himself, through the everlasting covenant of marriage, many wives, as the prophet David did in our world, the period required to people a world would be shorter, within certain limits, in proportion to the number of wives.[42]

Pratt suggested that Celestial partners are so mentally, spiritually, and physically perfected that sexual relations is the inevitable end point, indeed only such beings are permitted to reproduce in the afterlife.[43] His admission of sexual desire in heaven seems to conflict with much of the ascetic picture of Mormon sex attitudes in Utah. But, as observed already, there was built-in dissonance. Furthermore, the celebration of sexuality was viewed by Pratt as a mark of the restoration away from the traditions of fallen Christianity:

> The pure and virtuous daughters of Zion will consider it a great reproach to remain single and have no posterity: hence, their exceedingly great anxiety for husbands, that their reproach may be taken away. . . . Oh, how different will be their feelings from those now manifested by females traditioned under papist and protestant superstitions![44]

Sex in heaven may seem like a validation of the patterns of mortality, but to see it as a necessary component of spirit generation lets the wonderful complexity of human biology invade heavenly precincts with hormone-driven psychology, resulting in a complex theological fruit that still awaits some careful and consistent explanation.[45]

"For Herein Is the Work of My Father Continued"

Pratt's computations and ideas may seem like near blasphemous oddities today, but his theological propositions growing from the plural marriage revelation underlie much of the language heard in modern Mormon preaching. In recent years, Mormon women have sometimes not been as sanguine about eternally producing children on a galactic scale. Smith's ontology and cosmology of eternal spirits may be more comforting on

---

42. Orson Pratt, "The Preexistence of Man," 37–39.

43. Orson Pratt, "Celestial Marriage," 155–57.

44. Orson Pratt, "Christian Polygamy in the Sixteenth Century," 183.

45. Blair Hodges observes that nascent Mormon ideas over sex in heaven were connected to its ardent pre-Millennialism of the 1830s in which sexual activity was assigned, not to the resurrected, but to Millennial mortals. Blair Dee Hodges, "'My Principality on Earth Began': Millennialism and the Celestial Kingdom in the Development of Mormon Doctrine," 44–46.

that score, but even that raises its own theological problems—such as the position of a Mother in Heaven.[46]

The practice of polygamy served to elevate the text of the revelation in several ways. One was the reading of the revelation's deification of humans ("they shall be gods") into the history of God. While Smith himself seemed to do this in his 1844 sermons in some ways—God *became* God in some way—the synergistic elevation took place after Smith's death, when the narrative of a female partner of God became a part of the shift from eternal individuals to the everlasting engine of spirit *production*.[47] It was then that kingdom fever gradually reinterpreted much of Mormon revelation as support for a grand cosmology of generational deification and spirit propagation that *required* polygamy,[48] a polygamy that registered a gradually entrenched pedestal theology that found a surplus of exalted women in heaven, just as it found a more *powerless* spiritual woman on earth.[49]

A heaven that mirrored earthly process and form required God to have a heavenly female partner to procreate the offspring of God.[50] But polygamy rewrote God as a polygamist, who required multiple partners (thence the meme of Mothers in Heaven) to create his human family. Young enriched the story considerably with his teaching that the biblical Adam was in fact the God of humanity (amongst a host of gods). In

---

46. On attempts to reconcile the theological tensions between Nauvoo and Salt Lake City, see Smith, *Every Word Seasoned with Grace,* ch. 7, appendix 1. On mother theology, see Morrill, *White Roses,* 118.

47. See Smith, *Funeral Sermons,* ch. 7.

48. Bowman, *The Mormon People,* 126–30.

49. It was pedestal theology that, at the opening of the nineteenth century, wrote women out of the role of minister and preacher of religion in America. See the Epilogue. See also Christine L. Krueger, *The Reader's Repentance: Women Preachers, Women Writers, and Nineteenth-Century Social Discourse,* 26–27.

50. Smith's early explanation of Revelation (now Doctrine and Covenants 77) and his Bible revision project made human souls preexistent, hinted that those souls were of a kind in Christ and Lucifer, and that those souls were material, enjoying a form that matched their earthly biological embodiment. This at least became a normative version of Mormon cosmology. Smith's material world of souls almost seems to undermine his position that souls need embodiment. They are in fact already material bodies. On the human form of human souls, see Ether 3 in the Book of Mormon and Moses's interview with Satan in Moses 1 of Joseph Smith's translation of the Bible. Smith's declaration of material souls is in Doctrine and Covenants 130:7–8. See Fillerup, "William Clayton," May 16, 17, 1843.

Young's narrative, the Mother was none other than Eve, who doubled, like Adam, as parent of the spirits and bodies of humanity (the latter by sexual relations after eating earthy food).[51]

With the end of polygamy, any theology of Heavenly Mothers, never as popular as the singular Mother, largely disappeared from official discourse. Representing the inheritance of the plural marriage revelation filtered through Utah, Adam-God, the Woodruff Manifesto, and the transitional first quarter of the twentieth century, the teaching of a Mother in Heaven continued. Mother theology, while historically dependent in some sense on the plural marriage revelation and the subsequent projection of its path of deification onto the history of God, is never actually mentioned in the revelation. With the text-based theology of the twentieth century, initiated by Joseph F. Smith and accelerated in the Heber J. Grant era, institutional support for the Mother dwindled, with the exception of Eliza R. Snow's 1845 poem (which would be transformed as the hymn, "O, My Father") and the recognition of "heavenly parents" in the 1995 "The Family: A Proclamation to the World," neither of which are canon but are yet widely appealed to as authoritative.[52]

In 1991, Church President Gordon B. Hinckley, responding to rank and file engagement with the idea of a female deity, framed the Mother as existent but unapproachable. Hinckley traced the idea to Eliza Snow and remarked, "It has been said that the Prophet Joseph Smith made no correction to what Sister Snow had written. Therefore, we have a Mother in Heaven." Smith, however, was dead well before Snow's poem appeared. Locating the imprimatur of Smith for a Mother in Heaven took time and distance. Hinckley continued, "[N]one of us can add to or diminish the glory of her of whom we have no revealed knowledge."[53]

---

51. "Some have thought it strange what I have said Concerning Adam But the period will Come when this people of faithful will be willing to adopt Joseph Smith as their Prophet Seer Revelator & God But not the father of their spirits for that was our Father Adam." See Kenney, ed., *Wilford Woodruff's Journal*, 6:508. For Young, Genesis 3:20 looked backward as much as forward.

52. See Dallin H. Oaks, "The Plan and the Proclamation."

53. On memory theory and Mormon culture, see Stephen C. Taysom, "The Last Memory: Joseph F. Smith and *Lieux de Memoire* in Late Nineteenth-Century Mormonism." See also Taysom, "A Uniform and Common Recollection: Joseph Smith's Legacy, Polygamy, and the Creation of Mormon Public Memory," 121–52. On African-Americans and the temple, see W. Paul Reeve, *Religion of a Different Color: Race and the Mormon Struggle for Whiteness*, 194–98, 202–9. For a memory of memory with Joseph Smith and the Mother, see Susa Young

Despite its lack of textual and elaborating institutional support, the idea of a Mother in Heaven maintained importance as a figure of example for Latter-day Saints and a representation of the ultimate in salvation for both men and women. Beginning as an icon for the nature of the Celestial life, She also stood for the earthly picture of preexistence, framing spirits as children, male and female, imprinted with the images of parents who sired them in precisely the way of earthly parents. While there is a natural modern reluctance to engage the remarkable frankness of the nineteenth century, the legacy of that frankness undergirds the Mormon heaven discourse of the present day—as does, in some respects, the reconciliation between Utah and Nauvoo offered by B. H. Roberts, though that is rarely attached to his name.[54]

Gates, *History of the Young Ladies' Mutual Improvement Association of the Church of Jesus Christ of Latter-Day Saints*, 16. Gordon B. Hinckley, "Daughters of God," 97. For a collection of Mormon references to a Heavenly Mother, see David L. Paulsen and Martin Pulido, "'A Mother There': A Survey of Historical Teachings about Mother in Heaven," 70–126.

54. See Chapter 5. The most recent acknowledgement of Mother in Heaven appears in a Church approved anonymous essay on the LDS Church's website. See "Mother in Heaven."

The Law of Sarah

The final verses again speak to the painful dynamic between Joseph and Emma Smith, with Joseph being the one "who holds the keys of this power" and Emma being threatened to "be destroyed" for failing to accept plural marriage. If this portion of the revelation was written sometime after the first sixty verses (see Chapter 9 and the Addendum), then this final portion seems to speak to Emma's rejection of the revelation and essentially tells her that her objections do not curtail her husband's ability to take new wives. Those objections merely place her spiritual standing in jeopardy.

64 And again, verily, verily, I say unto you, if any man have a wife, who holds the keys of this power,[1] and he teaches unto her the *law of my priesthood*,[2] as pertaining to these things, then shall she believe and administer unto him, or she shall be destroyed, saith the Lord your God; for I will destroy her; for I will magnify my name upon all those who receive and abide in my law.

65 Therefore, it shall be lawful in me, if she receive not this law, for him to receive all things whatsoever I, the Lord his God, will give unto him, because she did not believe and administer unto him according to my word; and

---

1. Here, "power" completely assumes the place of "priesthood" earlier in the revelation (vv. 19, 61). This not only shows Smith's fluid use of terminology but also the possible later dictation of this portion of the revelation. The word also clearly maps out the male-dominated nature of polygamy.

2. Emphasis added. The "law of my priesthood" specifically refers to polygamy and not mere eternal marriage. According to Wilford Woodruff, Joseph Smith said that Parley Pratt's "glory would be clipped" in the afterlife if he did not have an eternal spouse, even though Pratt had received the fullness of the priesthood (or second anointing). It's possible that Smith was arguing that both seals were necessary; it is also possible that Smith feigned ignorance of Pratt's sealing to Elizabeth Brotherton in order to protect them. Smith gave an important sermon the same day linking Elijah, the temple, and the necessity of receiving all ordinances. Wilford Woodruff's journal, January 21, 1844, in Scott G. Kenney, *Wilford Woodruff's Journal, 1833–1898, Typescript*, 2:340–41.

she then becomes the transgressor; and he is exempt from the law of Sarah, who administered unto Abraham according to the law when I commanded Abraham to take Hagar to wife.

66 And now, as pertaining to this law, verily, verily, I say unto you, I will reveal more unto you, hereafter; therefore, let this suffice for the present. Behold, I am Alpha and Omega. Amen.

Emma has been taught the "law" and is required to "administer unto him" or "be destroyed" (v. 64). The revelation calls this the law of Sarah. There is an obvious difference between what Emma is required to do and Sarah's giving of Hagar to Abraham in the Genesis account. The latter acts as a remedy for Sarah's infertility, while neither Joseph nor Emma Smith suffered from infertility. However, the revelation adds a statement that better connects the Abraham–Sarah story with that of the Smiths. The revelation indicates that God "commanded Abraham to take Hagar to wife" (v. 65). Sarah's part was simply to hand her servant over, the implication being that Sarah did not initiate the transaction. Likewise, Emma was to do the same.

"If She Receive Not This Law"

The revelation makes it explicit that Emma's acceptance or approval is not required for Joseph to continue taking more wives if commanded to do so: "it shall be lawful in me, if she receive not this law, for him to receive all things whatsoever I, the Lord his God, will give unto him, because she did not believe and administer unto him according to my word" (v. 65). The "law of Sarah" thus only applies if "Sarah" (the wife, particularly Emma) is willing. If not, "she becomes the transgressor" and the husband is exempted from requiring her permission. Hence, the law of Sarah is in fact, a law *for* Sarah. It does not give rights: it demands cooperation.

In other words, the plural marriage revelation does not require that the husband ask his first wife for permission to take on more wives, with the new marriages being contingent on her assent or dissent. Rather, it utilized the Old Testament narrative to *require* the wife to give assent to her husband's taking new wives to spread his seed (theoretically, at least). Simply put, under the law of Sarah the wife can either grant permission for her husband to marry additional wives or she can be damned.

By 1843 Joseph Smith had already married most of his wives without consulting Emma, which was perhaps the context for the revelation's earlier discussion of the sinless plurality of David, Solomon, and others who "had received many wives and concubines" (v. 38). This may have been a new regulation for Joseph—that he could no longer marry additional wives without Emma's knowledge.

With this new provision, Joseph's act of taking more wives seemed to have been significantly curtailed after the revelation. However, it did not end completely. Joseph still made other proposals of marriage, apparently without Emma's knowledge. If the law of Sarah was a later circumstantial addition as a response to Emma's rejection story related by William Clayton, then it may have been added to ensure that Joseph could bypass Emma completely if he felt she would never give permission to be sealed to more wives.[3]

"I Will Reveal More unto You, Hereafter"

The importance of a textual authority for polygamy cannot be overestimated, even if that text remained essentially hidden for nine years. After 1852, anyone could appeal to the revelation, though its canonical status was perhaps not firm until 1880. Later nineteenth-century Utah practice does not mention the "law of Sarah" explicitly, though consultations between a man and first wife were generally a given—perhaps because in Utah, at least until the raid, plural wives were more or less in the open. First wives often discouraged their husbands from entering polygamy with some frequency, either by direct action or demonstrable sorrow over the prospect. In some cases at least, men simply proceeded secretly, but keeping a new union a secret was a burden that made little sense in most cases.[4]

The federal prohibition of polygamy in territorial Utah sometimes complicated relationships between first wives and husbands, adding to the tension over hiding marriages from the marshals. One southern Utah couple, unable to have children, was also unable to come to agreement over plurality. The bishop wrote to President John Taylor over the issue, revealing that the woman threatened to turn the husband into federal authorities if she found he engaged another woman. Taylor replied to the bishop by referencing the plural marriage revelation: "If it weren't for the

---

3. One example was Susan Conrad (an unsuccessful proposal). Proposals that resulted in marriage were Melissa Lott (September 1843) and Fanny Young (November 1843). On Conrad, see William V. Smith, "A Documentary Note on a Letter to Joseph Smith."

4. John G. Turner, *Brigham Young: Pioneer Prophet*, 240. Stephanie Smith Goodson, "Plural Wives," 89–111.

law of man, he could do this without her consent, after having given her the privilege of exercising the right of the law of Sarah. As we are now situated he cannot do this without endangering his liberty."[5]

With the end of plurality in the twentieth century, social and religious understandings of infertility shifted. Plural marriage had always been coupled with reproduction, so when a family was not blessed with children a new wife offered a legitimate cure. The common perception that women were merely uterine repositories for male seed manufactured blame for women when children were not forthcoming. The Church ending the possibility of remedying infertility through plural marriage marked a new discursive emphasis. The issue was, however, two-sided in that some single women felt that the end of polygamy limited the opportunity for a proven righteous husband—one they could trust to be an eternal partner and give them children. (Eliza Snow's earlier counsel to young women had been to marry an older man in plurality rather than risk a fraught relationship with an unproven young man.)[6] The impulse for assurance found in the power of sealing (v. 19) was as strong as any romantic tie for many.

The plural marriage revelation's warning that the sealing ritual had to be done in mortal life when opportunity existed played into Joseph Smith's theological narrative of an eternal grace through liturgy that was established in the premortal life. Women who felt closed off in a narrowed field of worthy males could and did feel a crisis of being. The theological salve for the frustration and worry was the appeal to a just God, but that could feel strange in a world where earthly sacraments were the answer to salvific yearning. The end of plurality saw the reemphasis of alternate narratives. God would not betray those who, in their hearts, wanted to do his will but were prevented by the chances of life. The awaited Millennium and proxy work for the dead now became the time and means to remedy the fate of those who were not able to participate in all of the necessary sacraments for exaltation. Moving away from the belief that the highest form of exaltation was limited to those who accepted polygamy in mortality, the expectation would change to nearly all accepting the message of salvation in the afterlife. If a woman (or man) had to wait until then for

---

5. Taylor recommended a possible course: divorce. John Taylor, Letter to A. Kimball, November 19, 1886, First Presidency letterpress copybooks (typescript). In another letter from John Taylor, it shows that Taylor had made a careful study of the 1843 revelation and in particular this effect of the "law of Sarah." John Taylor, Letter to John Rogerson of Parowan, January 20, 1884.

6. Eliza R. Snow, "A Synopsis," *Woman's Exponent* 3, no. 23 (1875): 178–79.

an open opportunity to receive all of the necessary sacraments, that opportunity would eventually come.[7] Lorenzo Snow typified this comforting discourse: "no Latter-day Saint who dies after . . . a faithful life will lose anything . . . when opportunities were not furnished to him or her." Snow pointed to his famous sister Eliza, now dead, who had no children in life. She would find resolution in the afterlife, not merely reconciliation, and a restoration of missing blessings.[8]

7. Abraham H. Cannon diary, April 5, 1894, in Edward Leo Lyman, ed., *Candid Insights of a Mormon Apostle: The Diaries of Abraham H. Cannon, 1889–1895,* 491.

8. Lorenzo Snow, "St. George sermon," 10. Jonathan A. Stapley, *The Power of Godliness: Mormon Liturgy and Cosmology*, ch. 2. See also Marybeth Raynes and Erin Parsons, "Single Cursedness: An Overview of LDS Authorities' Statements about Unmarried People," 217–27.

Chapter 11

A Speculative Modern Revision

As discussed through the volume, the plural marriage revelation seems to have been dictated for a limited audience—particularly Emma Smith—and was never meant for public consumption. Depending on one's perspective, it is embarrassing for Joseph Smith, for Emma, and perhaps for both. It deploys language that, in appropriating biblical voices and figures, applies a message of moral authority. This message, placed over and against the modern message of Mormonism, reveals a work of specific private purpose. I doubt that Joseph ever wanted to invite the public to critique Emma's behavior over these intimate matters, or for that matter, his own. As another example, the language of "ten virgins," an obvious echo if not allusion to Jesus's parable in Matthew 25, may elicit abhorrence from a modern audience. Of course, scripture is a product of its time and circumstance, meant to be reinterpreted as circumstances change. This raises the question of what such a revelation might have looked like if it were meant from the beginning to be public, out-in-the-open, Divine Counsel. Joseph Smith himself understood his revelations to have fluidity, and he and others revised, amended, and cropped them within his lifetime to address contemporary needs and align with newer revelations. Shortly before his death he offered some hints, given his remarks before the Nauvoo City Council in June 1844, on how he might have revised the revelation for the public. There, he argued that the revelation concerned eternal marriage and that polygamy was only included as historical commentary.[1]

In the time between Brigham Young's death and John Taylor's selection as Church President, Apostle Joseph F. Smith spoke of the revelation's private intent:

> When the [plural marriage] revelation was written, in 1843, it was for a special purpose, by the request of the Patriarch Hyrum Smith, and was not then designed to go forth to the church or to the world. It is most probable that

---

1. See Chapter 1.

had it been written with a view to its going out as a doctrine of the church, it would have been presented in a somewhat different form. There are personalities contained in a part of it which are not relevant to the endeavor.[2]

One alternative in dealing with the revelation, given that it focuses on a practice that is forbidden in the present LDS Church, is to simply delete it from the Doctrine and Covenants. In 1930, James E. Talmage edited an abbreviated version of the Doctrine and Covenants, perhaps partly with the intent of removing section 132 from view. Church President Heber J. Grant signed off on the attempt, but public complaints by polygamists outside the Church made Grant withdraw the imprint.[3] There is precedent for both modification of written revelations and deletion of elements from the Mormon canon by Smith himself (important examples were revelations that now appear as sections 68, 78, and 107 in the Doctrine and Covenants, and the article on marriage that appeared in the 1835 Doctrine and Covenants).[4] Joseph Smith's spiritual anthropology made room for such changes, improvements, and redactions. He distrusted human language as deeply flawed in its ability to convey the range of meaning and truth that existed in the Divine Mind.[5]

---

2. Joseph F. Smith, June 23, 1878, *Journal of Discourses*, 20:29.

3. Polygamist rumors about Grant and the Loren Woolley mythology of authoritative continuance of plural marriage outside the LDS Church had made Grant very sensitive to any interaction with post-manifesto polygamists through the media. On the Talmage effort, see *Latter-day Revelations: Selections from the Book of Doctrine and Covenants of the Church of Jesus Christ of Latter-day Saints*. On Woolley, see Matthew Bowman, *The Mormon People: The Making of an American Faith*, 178–79.

4. On section 78, see Christopher C. Smith, "The Inspired Fictionalization of the 1835 United Firm Revelations." On sections 68 and 107, see William V. Smith, "Early Mormon Priesthood Revelations: Text, Impact, and Evolution." During Smith's project to revise the Bible, he sometimes went back to previous revisions, adding or deleting text. Later, in sermons, he sometimes addressed further revisions. One of the texts he returned to most frequently was the prophecy in Malachi regarding the fathers and the children, substituting or changing words as suited his purpose. For example, see the March 10, 1844, sermon in William V. Smith et al., "The Parallel Joseph."

5. Frustrated with the difficulties of the written language to clearly portray meaning and intent, Smith described it as "crooked," "broken," "scattered," "imperfect," and almost a "total darkness." Joseph Smith, Letter to William W. Phelps, November 27, 1832, in Matthew C. Godfrey et al., *Documents, Volume 2, July 1831–January 1833*, 318–19.

On the other hand, in the spirit of Smith's modifications to his previous revelations, one could speculate how the revelation might have been adapted today if the text of the revelation was modified to eliminate the imperative to practice plural marriage but preserve important details about sealing, including the salvific pessimism (or unguaranteed salvation) that was introduced after Nauvoo. Such a revision may have taken a form like the following (bold type in the text indicates added words not present in the original, but reflecting later praxis or teaching; omitted passages are indicated in footnotes):

Section 132

Revelation given through Joseph Smith the Prophet, at Nauvoo, Illinois, recorded July 12, 1843. See Official Declaration 1. Historically the revelation contained text on the practice of plural marriage. As that practice was terminated in the Church many years ago, the text pertaining specifically to Joseph Smith's family and plural marriage has been removed from the revelation. Full texts of Joseph Smith's revelations are available as a part of the Joseph Smith Papers, Documents Series.

Verily, thus saith the Lord unto you my servant Joseph, that inasmuch as you have inquired of my hand to know and understand wherein I, the Lord, justified my servants Abraham, Isaac, and Jacob, as also Moses, David and Solomon, my servants, as touching the principle and doctrine of their having many wives and concubines. Behold, and lo, I am the Lord thy God, and will answer thee as touching this matter. Therefore, prepare thy heart to receive and obey the instructions which I am about to give unto you.[6] For behold, I reveal unto you a new and an everlasting covenant.[7]

For all who will have a blessing at my hands shall abide the law which was appointed for that blessing, and the conditions thereof, as were instituted from before the foundation of the world. And as pertaining to the new and everlasting covenant of marriage, it was instituted for the fulness

---

6. Omitted: "for all those who have this law revealed unto them must obey the same."

7. Omitted: "and if ye abide not that covenant, then are ye damned; for no one can reject this covenant and be permitted to enter into my glory."

of my glory.[8] And verily I say unto you, that the conditions of this law are these: All covenants, contracts, bonds, obligations, oaths, vows, performances, connections, associations, or expectations, that are not made and entered into and sealed by the Holy Spirit of promise, of him who is anointed, both as well for time and for all eternity, and that too most holy, by revelation and commandment through the medium of mine anointed, whom I have appointed on the earth to hold this power (and I have appointed unto my servant Joseph to hold this power in the last days, and there is never but one on the earth at a time on whom this power and the keys of this priesthood are conferred), are of no efficacy, virtue, or force in and after the resurrection from the dead; for all contracts that are not made unto this end have an end when men are dead.

Behold, mine house is a house of order, saith the Lord God, and not a house of confusion. Will I accept of an offering, saith the Lord, that is not made in my name? Or will I receive at your hands that which I have not appointed? And will I appoint unto you, saith the Lord, except it be by law, even as I and my Father ordained unto you, before the world was?

I am the Lord thy God; and I give unto you this commandment— that no man shall come unto the Father but by me or by my word, which is my law, saith the Lord. And everything that is in the world, whether it be ordained of men, by thrones, or principalities, or powers, or things of name, whatsoever they may be, that are not by me or by my word, saith the Lord, shall be thrown down, and shall not remain after men are dead, neither in nor after the resurrection, saith the Lord your God. For whatsoever things remain are by me; and whatsoever things are not by me shall be shaken and destroyed.

Therefore, if a man marry him a wife in the world, and he marry her not by me nor by my word, and he covenant with her so long as he is in the world and she with him, their covenant and marriage are not of force when they are dead, and when they are out of the world; therefore, they are not bound by any law when they are out of the world. Therefore, when they are out of the world they neither marry nor are given in marriage; but are appointed angels in heaven, which angels are ministering servants, to minister for those who are worthy of a far more, and an exceeding, and an eternal weight of glory. For these angels did not abide my law; therefore, they cannot be enlarged, but remain separately and singly, without exalta-

---

8. Omitted: "and he that receiveth a fulness thereof must and shall abide the law, or he shall be damned, saith the Lord God."

tion, in their saved condition, to all eternity; and from henceforth are not gods, but are angels of God forever and ever.

And again, verily I say unto you, if a man marry a wife, and make a covenant with her for time and for all eternity, if that covenant is not by me or by my word, which is my law, and is not sealed by the Holy Spirit of promise, through him whom I have anointed and appointed unto this power, then it is not valid neither of force when they are out of the world, because they are not joined by me, saith the Lord, neither by my word; when they are out of the world it cannot be received there, because the angels and the gods are appointed there, by whom they cannot pass; they cannot, therefore, inherit my glory; for my house is a house of order, saith the Lord God.

And again, verily I say unto you, if a man marry a wife by my word, which is my law, and by the new and everlasting covenant of marriage, and it is sealed unto them by the Holy Spirit of promise, by him who is anointed, unto whom I have appointed this power and the keys of this priesthood; and it shall be said unto them—Ye shall come forth in the first resurrection; and if it be after the first resurrection, in the next resurrection; and shall inherit thrones, kingdoms, principalities, and powers, dominions, all heights and depths—then shall it be written in the Lamb's Book of Life, that he shall commit no murder whereby to shed innocent blood, it shall be done unto them in all things whatsoever my servant hath put upon them, in time, and through all eternity **inasmuch as they are faithful**; and shall be of full force when they are out of the world; and they shall pass by the angels, and the gods, which are set there, to their exaltation and glory in all things, as hath been sealed upon their heads, which glory shall be a fulness and a continuation of the seeds forever and ever.

Then shall they be gods, because they have no end; therefore shall they be from everlasting to everlasting, because they continue; then shall they be above all, because all things are subject unto them. Then shall they be gods, because they have all power, and the angels are subject unto them.

For strait is the gate, and narrow the way that leadeth unto the exaltation and continuation of the lives, and few there be that find it, because ye receive me not in the world neither do ye know me. But if ye receive me in the world, then shall ye know me, and shall receive your exaltation; that where I am ye shall be also. This is eternal lives—to know the only wise and true God, and Jesus Christ, whom he hath sent. I am he. Receive ye, therefore, my law. Broad is the gate, and wide the way that leadeth to the deaths; and many there are that go in thereat, because they receive me not, neither do they abide in my law.

Abraham received all things, whatsoever he received, by revelation and commandment, by my word, saith the Lord, and hath entered into his exaltation and sitteth upon his throne. Abraham received promises concerning his seed, and of the fruit of his loins—from whose loins ye are, namely, my servant Joseph—which were to continue so long as they were in the world; and as touching Abraham and his seed, out of the world they should continue; both in the world and out of the world should they continue as innumerable as the stars; or, if ye were to count the sand upon the seashore ye could not number them.

This promise is yours also, because ye are of Abraham, and the promise was made unto Abraham; and by this law is the continuation of the works of my Father, wherein he glorifieth himself. Abraham was commanded to offer his son Isaac; nevertheless, it was written: Thou shalt not kill. Abraham, however, did not refuse, and it was accounted unto him for righteousness, as Isaac also and Jacob did none other things than that which they were commanded; and because they did none other things than that which they were commanded, they have entered into their exaltation, according to the promises, and sit upon thrones, and are not angels but are gods.[9]

I am the Lord thy God, and I gave unto thee, my servant Joseph, an appointment, and restore all things. Ask what ye will, and it shall be given unto you according to my word.[10] For I have conferred upon you the

---

9. Omitted: "David also received many wives and concubines, and also Solomon and Moses my servants, as also many others of my servants, from the beginning of creation until this time; and in nothing did they sin save in those things which they received not of me. David's wives and concubines were given unto him of me, by the hand of Nathan, my servant, and others of the prophets who had the keys of this power; and in none of these things did he sin against me save in the case of Uriah and his wife; and, therefore he hath fallen from his exaltation, and received his portion; and he shall not inherit them out of the world, for I gave them unto another, saith the Lord."

10. Omitted: "And as ye have asked concerning adultery, verily, verily I say unto you, if a man receiveth a wife in the new and everlasting covenant, and if she be with another man, and I have not appointed unto her by the holy anointing, she hath committed adultery and shall be destroyed. And if her husband be with another woman, and he was under a vow, he hath broken his vow and hath committee adultery. And if she hath not committed adultery, but is innocent and hath not broken her vow, and she knoweth it, and I reveal it unto you, my

keys and power of the priesthood, wherein I restore all things, and make known unto you all things in due time.

And verily, verily, I say unto you, that whatsoever you seal on earth shall be sealed in heaven; and whatsoever you bind on earth, in my name and by my word, saith the Lord, it shall be eternally bound in the heavens; and whosoever sins you remit on earth shall be remitted eternally in the heavens; and whosoever sins you retain on earth shall be retained in heaven. And again, verily I say, whomsoever you bless I will bless, and whomsoever you curse I will curse, saith the Lord; for I, the Lord, am thy God. And again, verily I say unto you, my servant Joseph, that whatsoever you give on earth, and to whomsoever you give any one on earth, by my word and according to my law, it shall be visited with blessings and not cursings, and with my power, saith the Lord, and shall be without condemnation on earth and in heaven. For I am the Lord thy God, and will be with thee even unto the end of the world, and through all eternity; for verily I seal upon you your exaltation, and prepare a throne for you in the kingdom of my Father, with Abraham your father. Behold, I have seen your sacrifices, and will forgive all your sins; I have seen your sacrifices in obedience to that which I have told you. Go, therefore, and I make a way for your escape, as I accepted the offering of Abraham of his son Isaac.[11]

Verily, if a man be called of my Father, as was Aaron, by mine own voice, and by the voice of him that sent me, and I have endowed him with the keys of the power of this priesthood, if he do anything in my name, and according to my law and by my word, he will not commit sin, and I will justify him. Let no one, therefore, set on my servant Joseph; for I will justify him; for he shall do the sacrifice which I require at his hands for his transgressions, saith the Lord your God.[12] And now, as pertaining to this law, verily, verily, I say unto you, I will reveal more unto you, hereafter; therefore, let this suffice for the present. Behold, I am Alpha and Omega. Amen.

---

servant Joseph, then shall you have power, by the power of my Holy Priesthood, to take her and give her unto him that hath not committed adultery but had been faithful; for he shall be made ruler over many."

11. Omitted: verses 51 through 58.

12. Omitted: verses 61–65.

Chapter 12

Epilogue: The Legacy of the Plural Marriage Revelation

The plural marriage revelation is not often referenced today. The twentieth-century Church of Jesus Christ of Latter-day Saints was anxious to distance itself from polygamy; when the revelation was mentioned, it was usually referred to for its statements regarding sealing.[1] The distancing was also reflected in Church publications and manuals of the twentieth century. As historian Stephen Taysom observed,

> the church decided in the late 1990s to publish a volume of teachings from church presidents to be used in church classes . . . and went directly to Brigham Young. In the chronology of Young's life, the manual lists his first marriage, but no others. Several selections in the manual [were] altered from 'wives' to 'wife' in an effort to remove references to polygamy . . . one could read . . . and never know [Young] was a polygamist.[2]

The plural marriage revelation left a lasting legacy in Mormonism, one that hit its peak in the latter-half of the nineteenth century; and despite the LDS Church's distancing from the practice itself, its accumulated theological superstructure is widely and deeply entrenched in LDS theology and practice. Moreover, the revelation's historical wake still has considerable influence on the way the Latter-day Saints and their institutions see the outside world and their relationship to it.

---

1. See, for example, J. M. Sjodahl, "Temple Marriage an Antidote Against Divorce," 1099.

2. Stephen C. Taysom, "A Uniform and Common Recollection: Joseph Smith's Legacy, Polygamy, and the Creation of Mormon Public Memory," 140. As Taysom observes, Joseph Smith's polygamous relationships received very little mention in Church imprints after 1950. The recent creation of essays on polygamy at the Church's official website, lds.org, was meant to counter claims that the Church covers up the truth about its founder.

The Severity and Consequences of Adultery

Nauvoo seethed with rumors about secret, authorized sexual freedoms. The counterbalancing speech grew rather extreme, with Joseph Smith publicly disclaiming any association with such things. These statements were carefully worded to avoid alarming polygamists, and at the same time they attempted to reassure the ignorant. An important example, and one that became decontextualized to the point that it fostered unjustified apologetics over the fate of (repentant) adulterers, came in a Nauvoo High Council trial on September 25, 1843. Wilford Woodruff reported in his journal:

> I was called in the evening to a Council with the Twelve. When I arived at Joseph Smith's Store I found the High Council sitting on a case of Harrison Sagers for some improper Conduct or offer towards some female. At the close President Joseph Smith made an address upon the subject which was highly interesting & *its tendency was to do away with evry evil & practice virtue & Holiness before the Lord.* That the Church had not received any license from him to commit adultery fornication or any such thing but to the contrary *if any man Commit adultery He Could not receive the Ceslestial kingdom of God.* Even if he was saved in any kingdom it could not be the Celestial kingdom.
>
> He said he thought the many examples that had been manifest John C Bennet & others was sufficient to show the fallacy of such a course of conduct. He condemned the principle in toto & warned those present against going into those evils, for they would shurely bring a Curse upon their heads.[3]

Sagers was acquitted on the adultery charge and when his wife Lucinda filed a complaint with the First Presidency for abandonment, the high council again acquitted Sagers.[4] Hyrum Smith had read the plural marriage revelation to the high council only a short time before the Sagers trial. Not only is the idea that adulterers are permanently barred from celestial glory a new one, it also violates the revelation's text (v. 19). The hoped-for effect of the speech appears to be three-fold at least: warn off imitators of polygamy, show non-participating insiders Smith's position regarding polygamy and adultery (as it did for Woodruff), and cast John C. Bennett as a son of Perdition.

---

3. Scott G. Kenney, ed., *Wilford Woodruff's Journal, 1833–1898, Typescript,* 2:327–28; emphasis added. See also Nauvoo Stake High Council minutes, November 21, 1843, April 13, 1844.

4. Whether Sagers was a practicing polygamist at this point is unknown. Rumors circulated that Sagers and his sister-in-law were man and wife. George D. Smith, *Nauvoo Polygamy: ". . . But We Called It Celestial Marriage,"* 346–47, 617–18.

While the speech was undoubtedly for effect, it was unfortunately propagated in print for later generations. A decade later, Woodruff's account was combined with Smith's journal entry for eventual publication in the *History of the Church*. The shock value of Smith's words is hard to underestimate for the repentant adulterer in Mormonism. The 1843 marriage revelation displayed some inconsistency in language, marking adultery as a somehow Davidic-level sin (vv. 44),[5] but even John Taylor (despite his and other's sometimes florid rhetoric) could be flexible. According to counselor George Q. Cannon, John Taylor ruled that endowed adulterers must be excommunicated and never be readmitted to the Church.[6] This policy may not have been uniform as illustrated by one couple in particular: they were sealed in Nauvoo but later split in Utah after the wife became attracted to another man, and her husband, angry over her behavior, left for Montana. When the husband returned, his wife had been sealed as the third wife to the attractive man.[7]

Other Church authorities could be even more extreme and advocated the death penalty for adultery; however, it was one thing to express such ideas and another thing to act on them. For example, although Lorenzo Snow taught that adultery was punishable by death,[8] when a sixteen-year-old plural wife of his (married in Nauvoo) fell in love with another man while Snow was absent on a three-year mission, he never broached the subject of extreme penalties in that case. However, even after decades had passed, the apostle refused to give permission for his sealing to be cancelled to his still plural wife. The drama played out in correspondence between the Church presidency and the couple in the early 1880s. Eventually, Snow relented.[9]

---

5. See Chapter 6. On later use of the notion that adultery barred somone from Celestial glory, see Melissa Lambert Milewski, ed., *Before the Manifesto: The Life Writings of Mary Lois Walker Morris*, 360, diary entry for Wednesday January 24, 1883.

6. Cannon's remarks may have been for effect as in Smith's case. George Q. Cannon, October 5, 1884, *Journal of Discourses*, 25:328.

7. Anthon H. Lund diary, May 10, 1920, in John P. Hatch, ed., *Danish Apostle: The Diaries of Anthon H. Lund*, 766.

8. See Abraham H. Cannon diary, December 2, 1890, in Edward Leo Lyman, ed., *Candid Insights of a Mormon Apostle: The Diaries of Abraham H. Cannon, 1889–1895*, 162.

9. Abraham H. Cannon diary, April 5, 1894, in Lyman, ed., *Candid Insights*, 493. See also First Presidency letterpress copybooks, June 9, 1880.

Utah Politics and the Revelation

When the Mexican War concluded in 1848, the United States territorial expansion had extended from the Mississippi to the Pacific Ocean. Latter-day Saints were already beginning to occupy the valley of the Great Salt Lake, creating a nominal presence of Americans near the center of the ceded territory.[10] This played into the complex political landscape of the era, dominated by questions over the expansion of black slavery and the balance of sectional power in Washington. Stephen A. Douglas offered a bill that created the territories of California, Utah, and New Mexico in the context of the ominous Compromise of 1850. When President Millard Fillmore sent political appointees to Utah to staff territorial offices, they were generally frustrated by Mormon resistance to outside regulation of courts and territorial administration. The appointees were shocked by polygamy, abruptly departed the territory, and claimed that the Mormons were the cultural equivalents of the Indian "savages."[11]

Attempting to counter the claims of these officials, a remarkable and trusting friend to the Mormons, Thomas L. Kane, wrote an influential pamphlet that was circulated in Washington. Kane's work to defuse the charges of polygamy and despotism in Utah finally drew Church leaders to share the facts of polygamy with him. Kane had dismissed the allegations of polygamy as the frustrations of men who had their hopes of influence and power dashed by discerning Mormons. Disappointed that he had been misled by the Saints, he saw the news as a violation of his trust and compared it to a "wife's infidelity." Kane, however, returned to his defense of the Saints and advised them to go public with polygamy.

After polygamy and the revelation were made public in August 1852, the sympathy that Kane had garnered in Washington dissipated, and his voice on how to handle the Mormons became muted. The polygamy revelation, in both senses of the word, brought delay to what Brigham Young and others saw as security in statehood. It would be a long postponement. After an interval of peace, a costly state of war ensued between Utah and

---

10. On the military district that became Utah territory, see David M. Potter (with Don E. Fehrenbacher), *The Impending Crisis: America Before the Civil War, 1848–1861*, 199–225. See also Brent M. Rogers, *Unpopular Sovereignty: Mormons and the Federal Management of Early Utah Territory*, ch. 2.

11. One appointee sermonized the Mormons on such moral failures to their faces. Matthew J. Grow and Ronald W. Walker, ed., *The Prophet and the Reformer: The Letters of Brigham Young and Thomas L. Kane*, 124–25.

the United States Army leading up to the 1878 *Reynolds v. United States* decision and the 1890 Woodruff Manifesto—both of which would significantly affect how the Church interpreted the plural marriage revelation and how the US government interpreted religious freedom. Utah would not gain statehood until six years after the Manifesto.[12]

Polygamy not only affected Utah politics, but it also had important effects on American concepts of state and federal powers. Between the 1852 announcement and the Civil War, Washington political mechanisms shifted inexorably away from a party politics that sought balance among sectional forces. Parties had worked as stabilizing forces between slave and free states since a party could only be effective at controlling congress and the presidency if it gathered adherents from both sections, resulting in parties that sublimated extremes within their ranks. However, Polk's Mexican cession and the population boom in the northern states drove the fears of southern Democrats and Whigs. They became more sensitive to even moderate positions like those held by Douglas who fought, successfully, to see Kansas and Nebraska enter territorial status under the Compromise of 1850, which allowed territories to decide by popular vote whether they would allow slavery or not. Geographically, Kansas, Nebraska, Utah, and New Mexico were all ill-suited to agriculture that made slavery economically advantageous.

Whigs failed to take advantage of the sectional heat, and southern Democrats became more and more isolated as their northern component became increasingly opposed to slavery. From the ashes of the dying Whigs came the Republican Party. Largely a northern institution, Republicans held up a banner that saw both slavery and polygamy as barbaric. However, the building conflict with the South over slavery gave Mormons some breathing space until the Civil War, leaving polygamy as the remaining barbaric practice to put an end to. While the Morrill Anti-Bigamy Act failed to affect the status of polygamy in Utah, it did pave the way for successive measures that eroded the powers of states and territories against the national government, culminating in the Immigration

---

12. On Douglas, see Potter, *Impending Crisis*, 112, 157, 272; see also Norman F. Furniss, *Mormon Conflict: 1850–1859*, 30–38; John G. Turner, *Brigham Young: Pioneer Prophet*, 198–99. On Kane, see Grow and Walker, *The Prophet and the Reformer*, 11–12, 120, 138, 144. On polygamy and the lead up to the Utah War, see William P. MacKinnon, *At Sword's Point, Part 1: A Documentary History of the Utah War to 1858*, ch. 1. See also Rogers, *Unpopular Sovereignty*, ch. 5.

Act of 1891 that included a provision barring polygamists from entering the United States.

The failure of statehood is perhaps less appreciated than it could be. The relationship between the federal government and state governments before the war was more one of separation than unity. Joseph Smith's denigration of state rights in Nauvoo was a two-edged sword. If the Saints had managed to make the military district of Utah into a state, it would have given them important and almost impenetrable protections against an interventionist federal authority. Already, the Compromise of 1850 swung on issues of what a state might or might not allow within its borders. If Utah had become a state, it is doubtful that many of the other states would have supported James Buchanan's authorization to send a large military force to subdue the Mormons. The bulwark of state rights was only breached with the Civil War and the South's reconstruction. However, by 1852 Mormon polygamy was too popular of an issue to be dismissed, and the Mormon influence on politics in Utah seemed too repugnant upon close investigation. The brilliant in-fighting of Congress, so valued by its members as a manifestation of constitutional protections, could never happen in a territorial legislature controlled by men who owed nearly unquestioning allegiance to Brigham Young.[13]

During the interim years between 1852 and 1890, the government in Washington reacted again and again to polygamy and the Mormon claim that they engaged in it by God's commandment. This contest of opinion was one that pitted the power of government against the acts of believers. For Latter-day Saints, the first amendment seemed to be the correct stage for the drama to play out on, but as it turned out, it was far less a political-religious controversy and more of an issue of conflicting moralities between minority and majority populations. Protestant morality largely articulated the nation's standing, whatever internal inconsistencies that standing entailed (such as African slavery and the subjugation of women). That morality was impervious to Mormon arguments over freedom of religion. In a Supreme Court decision preceding the Manifesto, the US government declared:

> [T]he property of the said corporation [the Church] . . . [is to be used to promote] the practice of polygamy—a crime against the laws, and abhorrent to the sentiments and feelings of the civilized world. . . . The organization of a community for the spread and practice of polygamy is, in a measure,

---

13. Turner, *Brigham Young*, 197–99.

a return to barbarism. It is contrary to the spirit of Christianity and of the civilization which Christianity had produced in the Western world.[14]

The courts consistently ruled that polygamy, whatever its foundation in belief, would not be tolerated in the United States. The contest resulted in Mormons continuing Joseph Smith's quest to find a place where the Saints could practice their commandments in freedom, expressed by colonies in Canada and Mexico. Inevitably, all those stratagems failed.[15]

Polygamous Praxis in Utah

From 1852 until the early twentieth century, expressed belief in polygamy was a requirement for baptism and receiving temple rituals.[16] At various points, its practice was tied to leadership in the Church, but many Saints simply lived without it. An example was Newman Bulkley. Converted as a teen (ca. 1837), Bulkey was forced from Missouri, married in Nauvoo, and drafted into the Mormon Battalion. He wrote later in life: "Now the tide towards Mormonism was growing stronger, this time because of their belief in poligamy. I was content with one wife." Bulkley was no dissident, and a well-known pioneer and visionary of Springville, Utah.[17] According to historian Kathryn Daynes, "Whatever the Church doctrine . . . there remained a view popular among some Mormons, par-

---

14. *The Late Corporation of the Church of Jesus Christ of Latter-Day Saints v. United States*, 48–49.

15. For the best account of the legal questions surrounding polygamy and the Mormons, see Sarah Barringer Gordon, *The Mormon Question: Polygamy and the Constitutional Conflict in Nineteenth-Century America*. For Latter-day Saints in Mexico, see Barbara Jones Brown, "The Rise and Demise of Latter-day Saint Polygamy in Mexico." For Canada, see John C. Lehr, "Polygamy, Patrimony, and Prophecy: The Mormon Colonization of Cardston," 114–21.

16. For an example of Young's requirement of belief, see First Presidency to stake presidents and bishops of Iron and Washington Counties, March 2, 1856, in Devery S. Anderson, *The Development of LDS Temple Worship, 1846–2000: A Documentary History*. Belief in plural marriage gradually ceased to be a test of faith after 1890, but Mormon immigrants to the United States at the beginning of the twentieth century were still acknowledging a belief in polygamy under questioning from government officials. As a result they were returned to their home countries. Jonathan H. Moyer, "Dancing With the Devil: The Making of the Republican/Mormon Pact," 588. Heath, ed., *In the World*, 205.

17. Newman Bulkley autobiography [unpaginated].

ticularly monogamous ones, that shunned plurality for themselves and their own families, even if they might condone it for others."[18]

In the ideal polygamist relationship (which sometimes existed at moments in time), first wives might approach and coach new candidate wives. During plurality, wives in general commiserated and supported sister wives, shared mothering and sorrows, exercised spiritual power in healing and blessing, and eventually offered potent community influence through unofficial means. Wives in large plural households operated as essentially single mother networks in many cases. That social complexity could generate a lexical complexity that helped children feel connected and valued in a system far removed from the Victorian ideal. Children affectionately called other wives "aunt" and might have had close relationships with wives who served as school teachers, catechistic mentors, and caretakers.[19] That ideal, however, was rarely achieved; with some frequency, hard feelings existed between wives (and between their respective children). Often, wives were planted in communities distant from their husbands and other wives, and that isolated the components of polygamous families. This was particularly true during the federal raid in the 1880s.

The multiple roles wives played in these marriages bolstered the perception that women were, on the whole, far more likely to be spiritually inclined than males—and at the same time, far more spiritually powerless. Polygamy was viewed as a means to link the many spiritually inclined women with the few spiritually powerful or authoritative men. Eliza Roxcy Snow thus advised young women:

> [T]here are few young men now-a-days who will prove saviors, you will have to go in groups, to the few who are worthy. Joseph Smith said (and he knew by revelation) that there were more good women than men on earth; that proves the wisdom of plurality. Girls, marry good noble men. I don't care if they are old men if they are men of God.[20]

---

18. Kathryn M. Daynes, "Striving to Live the Principle in Utah's First Temple City: A Snapshot of Polygamy in St. George, Utah, in June 1880," 73.

19. Sarah and Amanda Mousley married Angus M. Cannon the same day and spent much of their married life under the same roof or next door. See Madelyn Stewart Silver Palmer, "'Joyful Were My Feelings,' Sarah Maria Mousley Cannon (1828–1912)," ch. 2.

20. Eliza R. Snow, "A Synopsis," 178–79. Snow's advice was not singular. "Knew by revelation" is probably a reference to the 1843 revelation itself.

Finding salvation through marriage was a commonplace idea in polygamous Utah. Ironically, the failure of such marriages was not rare.[21]

While rhetorically placing women on a pedestal of spiritual superiority, this view also worked to place women in inferior positions, such as by encouraging the desire to be married to one of the Mormon elites. Marriage to a high Church authority gave significant social standing to a woman. This worked to create a kind of patriarchal hegemony. Competition among females for a place in a highly regarded male's family was real.[22] While early Utah saw considerable freedom for women to move on from an unsatisfactory marriage, their choices could be limited in the marriage marketplace, and marriage was often the only real alternative to an even more difficult hardscrabble existence. Eliza Snow's advice shows the Utah marriage ethic as one that placed the larger emphasis on the next life, not mortality, and that left a woman concerned for her salvation a limited field of action as she experienced the echoes of Joseph Smith's words: *I claim what I seal.*

When the federal raid on polygamy came, the pressures on polygamous families redoubled, and men were often absent for much longer periods. As a rule, wives of the same husband rarely lived under the same roof for long. Combined, there could be significant isolation between such plural households.[23]

One Mormon woman who spoke out on behalf of polygamy in early Utah was Belinda Pratt, a wife of Parley Pratt. She noted the mutual affection between Parley's wives as a mark of divine sanction.[24] But Belinda's experience eluded many, and as the younger generation of women became more educated, they began to choose romance over Eliza Snow's advice.

---

21. Paula Kelly Harline, *The Polygamous Wives Writing Club: From the Diaries of Mormon Pioneer Women,* 176, 179.

22. For instance, Brigham Young fielded numerous requests from women, and in a post-mortal version, many women desired to be sealed to Joseph Smith. Turner, *Brigham Young,* 375–77; Jonathan A. Stapley, "Adoptive Sealing Ritual in Mormonism," 106. Latter-day Saint polygamy shared aspects of polygamous unions in general around such points. Exploitation of position is a feature of polygamy in many cultures. L. L. Betzig, "Despotism and Differential Reproduction: A Cross-Cultural Correlation of Conflict Asymmetry, Hierarchy, and Degree of Polygny," 209–221. Miriam Koktvedgaard Zeitzen, *Polygamy: A Cross-Cultural Analysis,* 99, 107, 126.

23. Jessie L. Embry, *Mormon Polygamous Families: Life in the Principle,* 108.

24. See Belinda Pratt, *Defence of Polygamy, By a Lady of Utah, in a Letter to Her Sister in New Hampshire,* 6.

To counter the trend, Church publications sought to paint a picture of polygamy as though the ideal was the norm. But observation was more powerful than literature.[25] After the Woodruff Manifesto of 1890, there were obvious mixed feelings regarding the announcement and its meaning.[26] Divided loyalties over the issue were displayed in Church public media. For example, the *Young Woman's Journal* editor candidly discussed lived polygamy and the response of many women to the Manifesto.[27] In private settings, the discussion was more intense, with the apostles wondering which course the Church was going to take. The revelations of John Taylor and Wilford Woodruff troubled some, since they seemed to allow little leeway in jettisoning polygamy. Woodruff had declared in an 1888 meeting of the apostles where a proposition to abandon polygamy was heard that if they had entertained the idea the Lord would reject them, that "celestial marriage had come to stay for all time."[28] Then after the surprise of the Manifesto, the Church presidency's testimony before government officials surprised the apostles with a declaration of monogamy for current polygamists.[29] Others saw the death of (mortal) polygamy as a "grave problem" for young women in the Church, believing that there just weren't enough young men of worth to marry them. "Mary Howe" wrote in 1891:

> Years ago, such a thing as an old maid was almost an unknown person. . . . [N]ow this order of things (polygamy) has vanished, owing to the determined efforts of our parental government. The question now arises, what is to become of our surplus girls? . . . [M]others in this city of Salt Lake are already discussing the future and its gloomy outlook, and many are saying that it is preferable to allow girls to marry outside the Church than not to marry at all.[30]

---

25. Sherry Baker, "Creating a Shared History: Serial Narratives in the *Young Woman's Journal*, 1880–1894," 180–81.

26. Kathleen Flake, *The Politics of American Religious Identity: The Seating of Senator Reed Smoot, Mormon Apostle*, 30–31, 71, 74.

27. "Why was the Manifesto Issued?" 275–78.

28. John Henry Smith diary, December 20, 1888, in Jean Bickmore White, ed., *Church, State, and Politics: The Diaries of John Henry Smith*, 214.

29. Woodruff took it back in private, but for many plural wives the damage was done. On the internal discussions, see for example, Abraham H. Cannon diary, Sept. 30, 1890; Oct. 1, 1890; Oct. 7, 1890; Oct. 15, 1890; Jan. 30, 1891; April 2, 1891; Jan. 15, 1892; April 1, 1892, in Lyman, ed., *Candid Insights*, 135–41, 145–48, 151–52, 179, 195, 292–93, 316–19.

30. Mary Howe, "Professional and Business Opportunities for Women," 24. Mary Howe was a pen name used by *Young Woman's Journal* editor, Susa Young

Mary's solution was that it was better for girls to become independent professionals and remain single than marry outside Mormonism. She wrote a series of articles about entering various disciplines like dentistry, law, retail, stenography, medicine, and photography. Abraham Cannon noted an April 27, 1891, conversation with a woman in Brigham City, Utah: "there were over 25 unmarried ladies of her age in Brigham City alone, who would now most likely be left as old maids." The revelation's verdict on unmarried status was powerful.[31] The nature of the historical record finds official sources deficient in the voices of women who entered plurality. They neither preached in broad venues nor operated in Church government in the early decades of Utah. Common local Church "callings" beyond bishoprics, their clerks, and "teachers" (and the occasional ward Relief Society), were largely nonexistent in Utah until the 1870s. Church meetings were usually sparsely attended unless an authority visited, and church meeting halls were often far too small. Female preaching was important in early Utah, but it was limited to ad hoc prayer meetings until church auxiliaries were established; its nature and content is generally lost to us.[32]

In reviewing nineteenth-century Mormon literature on polygamy it is difficult not to notice a change of emphasis over the messages of the plural marriage revelation. The duality of the message—that polygamy was needed for salvation *and* to produce more offspring—remained, but

---

Gates. See Lisa Olsen Tait, "Between Two Economies: The Business Development of the *Young Woman's Journal,* 1889–1900," 13n36.

31. B. Carmon Hardy, *Doing the Works of Abraham, Mormon Polygamy: Its Origin, Practice, and Demise,* 353.

32. On the functional Church in early Utah, see William G. Hartley, "Common People: Church Activity During the Brigham Young Era," 255, 262–65. On Mormon women in Utah, see Jill Mulvay Derr, Janath Russell Cannon, and Maureen Ursenbach Beecher, *Women of Covenant: The Story of Relief Society;* Richard L. Jensen, "Forgotten Relief Societies, 1844–67," 105–25; "Record of the Female Relief Society Organized the 9th of Feby in the City of Great Salt Lake 1854." On women and the politics of the Manifesto, see Carol Cornwall Madsen, "Schism in the Sisterhood: Mormon Women and Partisan Politics, 1890–1900," 212–41. On women and Mormon ritual, Jonathan A. Stapley and Kristine Wright, "Female Ritual Healing in Mormonism," and Jonathan A. Stapley, "Last Rites and the Dynamics of Mormon Liturgy," 96–128. On the documentary record of female preaching in Utah, see Jill Mulvay Derr, Carol Cornwall Madsen, Kate Holbrook, and Matthew J. Grow, eds., *The First Fifty Years of Relief Society: Key Documents in Latter-day Saint Women's History.*

the two horns of the individual's dilemma traded places of importance for men and women. Should a woman engage polygamy because it is a gateway to the highest heaven, or should she engage polygamy because her ultimate reward depends on the size of her kingdom in heaven? The questions may be thought naïve, since they seem connected in obvious ways. But Mary Howe's lament suggests that it is the first question that was important at that point in history. And, it is the question that survived the end of polygamy in (nearly) its original form. The second question survived too, but its meaning was recast in terms of birth control in monogamy and found support in certain odd tentacles of the Progressive Movement, such as the rise of marriage counseling and a reinforcement of sexual roles in marriage.[33]

The federal raid had the makings of a Mormon Underground Railroad very like the abolitionist myth of the 1840s–50s. That mythology elaborated a vast and detailed network, a well-organized system operated by various agents, conductors, and station keepers with standard techniques of disguise, evasion, and blending into the environment. This romance, that nevertheless reflected a heroic reality, became exalted in the public's imagination because it served the narratives of abolitionist and slave owner alike, because the Union triumphed, and because it represented a war against a great social evil.[34] The raid never found its heroes in detailed and repeated exploits of polygamist fugitives because polygamy had to disappear in a post-Manifesto world. Only Protestants wanted to publicly remember the Mormon polygamist past and the story of men and women who jumped bail, hid behind false walls, leaped from moving trains, and wore disguises through enemy territory to gain at last their place in the sun of northern Mexico. An enforced quieting and then a generational forgetfulness meant that the raid was seen, if at all, as a tiny blip of civil disobedience in an otherwise uniform picture of twentieth-century clean living patriots. That same forgetfulness came to apply equally to the revelation.[35] Polygamy and slavery occupied a strange inversion, where the "heroes" stood on opposites sides of a social justice equation.

---

33. Jill Lepore, *The Mansion of Happiness: A History of Life and Death*, 81–94, 118–24.

34. Potter, *The Impending Crisis*, 132–39; Jean M. Humez, *Harriet Tubman: The Life and the Life Stories*. On forgetting the Raid, see Taysom, "Uniform and Common Recollection."

35. For examples of evading federal marshals hunting polygamists and related matters, see First Presidency Letterpress Copybooks, June 25, 1885 (two women

After the 1890 Manifesto, the revelation was mentioned less and less often in public. A short list of examples appeared in *The Deseret News* in 1903 when Joseph F. Smith declared that rejecting the revelation was "equivalent to rejecting God himself."[36] Some Church leader's attitudes demonstrated that since the Church as a public institution no longer advocated polygamy, they had kept their pledges with the federal government, even though privately, they continued to approve plural marriages on a case by case basis. Other leaders felt the strain of saying one thing and doing another. Charles Penrose wrote, "We should either stand firmly by that which we have announced, or come out boldly and recede from it candidly."[37] Penrose echoed the earlier thought of Lorenzo Snow. In a meeting of the First Presidency and Quorum of the Twelve, Snow said,

> [we should obey the law] in order to satisfy the honorable people of the nation, who are willing to send their sons into battle for the defense of our country, and when they fall in battle it is looked upon as an honor. They are willing to make this sacrifice for their country. They look upon the United States as the greatest nation on the earth and feel that its laws are supreme— *and that when it comes to a question of law, the Latter-day Saints should bow.* It is necessary sometimes for the saints to make sacrifices for the good of their fellowmen, that the honorable ones of the earth perchance may be saved. This is one of those times. There are, he said, about 300 plural wives among the saints who are bearing children, as against the body of the church—say 350,000—who are not in polygamy. These 300 women for the good of the nation and of the church should be willing for a time to refrain from having

---

sent to prison, new techniques by marshals); July 27, 1885 (Lorenzo Snow on the run in San Francisco); August 5, 1885 (purchasing land in Mexico), August 14, 1885 (location of various apostles in hiding); September 5, 1885 (land in Mexico); September 10, 1885 (land problems in Mexico, capture of polygamists, hiring of attorneys); September 17, 1885 (Grover Cleveland and pressure on the Church); September 21, 1885 (strategies to deed Church properties to avoid confiscation by the government); September 23, 1885 (Lorenzo Snow proselytizing under an assumed name among Indian tribes in the Northwest not approved). Scott G. Kenney papers, Marriot Library, University of Utah.

36. Joseph F. Smith, "President Smith Speaks Again," 12. Smith stated to the Smoot senate committee, however, that mentions of the revelation were curtailed. "President Smith's Testimony," 26.

37. Charles W. Penrose, Letter to Heber J. Grant, February 14, 1906, in Moyer, "Dancing with the Devil," 510–11. See also Moyer, "Dancing with the Devil," 361–62.

children. They would lose nothing by it, for the Lord would reward them abundantly.[38]

Abandoning polygamy was still a difficult proposition. Plural marriage represented such a deep bargain in the psyches of those who promoted, allowed, and practiced it, that they could not simply brush it aside.

Church leaders were reluctant to shut the door completely on a return of the practice and kept it going on a small scale in the first decade of the twentieth century. The Smoot hearings forced Church leaders, particularly Joseph F. Smith and Francis M. Lyman, into uncomfortable admissions regarding their own beliefs and practices, as well as a public theology that failed to match their private views.[39] Smoot urged Joseph F. Smith to issue a second confirming manifesto pressing for the removal of two apostles as proof of Mormon sincerity in its promises that polygamy was dead. In doing so, Smoot led the way into a new view of the nature of revelation as well as the balance between loyalty to nation and loyalty to religion.[40] Smoot tried, on a number of occasions, to commit his fellow apostles and President Joseph F. Smith to discipline any surviving post-1890 polygamists. The response was mixed, but eventually they agreed to have any men in that group released from important Church positions. Smoot felt that by requiring any Saints to sustain such men meant that they sustained their acts in relation to polygamy; more importantly for him, it was harmful publicity for the political freedom from Church leaders that he was hoping to convince Congress that he possessed. He considered the *Salt Lake Tribune*'s continued emphasis on post-Manifesto marriages a danger, given that such stories were redistributed in Eastern newspapers.[41]

A Legacy of Sealing

The end of public and then privately authorized polygamy came, but there was a silent theological corollary of the plural marriage revelation: widowers and divorced men may marry again and be sealed to that new

---

38. Larson, ed., *Ministry of Meetings*, 128. Emphasis added.

39. Some of those included statements to the effect that Smith was not subject to visions or new written revelations and therefore could not possibly veto Woodruff's Manifesto. "President Smith's Testimony," 26.

40. Flake, *The Politics of American Religious Identity*, 56–81; Moyer, "Dancing with the Devil," 477.

41. Richard S. Van Wagoner, *Mormon Polygamy: A History*, 177–83. Heath, ed., *In the World*, 69–71, 72, 78–79, 99, 108.

partner without dissolving the sealings to their previous spouses. While not polygamous in mortality, their relationship in the afterlife would be one of plurality. Hyrum Smith's words were still a potent background to Mormon marriage:

> I married me a wife & was the only one who had any write to her – till we had 5 chi'l the cov.t was made for our lives - she fell into the grave bef God shewed us this order God has shewn me that the Cov.t is dead, & had no more force neither could I have her in the res.n, but we sho.d be as the angels- it troubled me. Bro J s.d you can be sealed to her upon the same prin as you can be bap for the dead what can I do for my 2.nd wife - you can make a cov. with her for etern & sealed to her & she [Mary Fielding–his second wife] s.d I will act as proxy for the one that is dead- and I will be sealed to you for eternity-[42]

After Joseph Smith's death, a relatively robust practice developed of sealing men to other men as father and son, without a biological relationship.[43] Called "adoption," it served two salvific purposes with a background based in Malachi 4:6: "And he shall turn the heart of the fathers to the children, and the heart of the children to their fathers, lest I come and smite the earth with a curse." Smith had redefined "turn" as "seal" in sermons, and the curse of an impending second coming of Jesus and the "smite the earth with a curse" combined to place a sense of urgency in the binding together of the Saints. Real anxiety existed, and continued to exist in Utah, over the proposition of sealing a chain of ancestors to one's self. How could one know if those dead relatives would fully accept the rituals performed in their behalf? Was that the real meaning of the passage? Or could it mean that only sure links must exist in the chain to avoid the curse? What if one's dead ancestor was disqualified from glory over a presently unknown sin, even murder? The necessity of an unimpeachable chain of sealings and the limited time to accomplish that led to the idea that those who were sure links in the salvific chain, like Smith himself, were the only certain anchors. Hence many men were sealed to other men

---

42. Hyrum Smith, sermon, Thomas Bullock minutes, April 8, 1844.

43. John M. Bernhisel, a New York City doctor and a confirmed bachelor, came to Nauvoo in 1843. In October 1843, Bernhisel was sealed to a number of his deceased relatives, including his own sister. In February 1846 as the Saints were departing the city, Bernhisel was adopted to Joseph Smith, and thus "inheriting the eternal godhead" indicating Smith's cosmological status. Samuel Morris Brown, *In Heaven as it is on Earth: Joseph Smith and the Early Mormon Conquest of Death*, 203–4.

at the top of the priesthood chain, to the apostles after Smith's death, and then to Smith himself. These lesser men in the chain would, together with those sealed to them, be assured safety at the imminent end of the world. This was the practice of adoption. It effected real relationships in the here and now, with men and women using titles of mother and father with such adopted parents and assuming rights to inheritances. These relationships became so complex that Brigham Young halted adoption after the Latter-day Saints left Nauvoo, stating that, unlike marriage sealings, they must be confined to a temple.[44]

After the dedication of the temple in Salt Lake City, President Wilford Woodruff began to feel that the Second Coming was not in the near future and that sealings to biological lines (barring known problems with persons in those lines) should be the practice. Woodruff announced his determination to the apostles on April 5, 1894. Apostle John Henry Smith reported,

> The Presidency and members of the Quorum of 12 met at 10 a.m. Prest. W. Woodruff announced the Doctrine of adoption to be that the members of famalies should connect their line just as far as possible and then join the whole to the Prophet. Wives in the church can have ordinances performed for their dead husband who were not in the church and be sealed to such husband. We had a most happy day, all present endorsing this Doctrine. We partook of the sacrament. It was a most joyous day.[45]

President Woodruff made these notations in his journal:

> [April] 5 I met with the Presidency & Twelve Apostles Upon the Subject of Endowments & Adoption And the following is a Revelation to Wilford Woodruff upon that Subject.

> April 6 1894 The Presidency & Twelve Apostles met in Conference in the ~~Tabernacle~~ /Temple/ in S L City at 10 oclok. Prest W Woodruff a Revelation concerning the Endowments & Adoptions which was received by my Councillors & Ten of the Twelve Apostls. All of the Apostles present. Br Lund in England & M Thatcher at home. We opened the Conference.[46]

Woodruff and his first counselor, George Cannon, occupied the entire general conference Sunday meetings on April 8 in preaching on the change.

---

44. See Stapley, "Adoptive Sealing Ritual in Mormonism," 55.

45. John Henry Smith diary, April 5, 1894, in White, ed., *Church, State, and Politics*, 307.

46. Woodruff left space in the journal to record a revelation text, but it was never inserted. Kenney, ed., *Wilford Woodruff's Journal*, 9:296–98.

The complexity that proxy sacraments and the 1894 Woodruff revelation induces on the 1843 plural marriage revelation is illustrated by the way Church leaders now address the emotional investment of descendants of divorced and widowed couples. For example, although neither the 1894 revelation nor the 1843 revelation sets a precedent for it, at the present time a dead woman who was married to different (now deceased) husbands in life may be sealed by proxy to those men. Woodruff saw these relationships as being sorted out in the afterlife. During Joseph F. Smith's administration, a number of cases came before Smith involving widows who wished to be sealed to new husbands. In one case, Smith wrote: "if you desire in your heart to be sealed to the young man referred to . . . we know of no reason why this may not be done. . . . [T]he record of your sealing to your first husband need not be disturbed." No such option exists for a living woman at present. Even so, it seems understood that this is merely a temporary measure. In present theology, while men could be simultaneously sealed to multiple women in the eternities, such women would have to choose one or the other relationship while in the afterlife.[47]

The separation of church and state in Utah and the end of polygamy made some unusual conditions with sealing more common. Sealings now generally continue to be in force between legally divorced couples, and currently married couples could, in theory, have their sealings cancelled and remain legally married.[48] The cancellation of sealing is contained in the plural marriage revelation where sealed wives can be taken from one man and given to another (v. 44). The liturgical aspect of cancellation has never been elaborated by ritual: it simply amounts to a stamp or signature by the appropriate person, the Church president or assignee in the seat of Joseph Smith. In nineteenth-century Utah, where church and state were often one, women might approach the Church president directly when requesting a divorce (cancellation). These were usually granted forthwith and without expectations of remarriage.[49] Brigham Young may have varied

---

47. *General Handbook of Instructions, Book I 2010*, 19–21. Joseph F. Smith, Letter to _____, May 25, 1912. Joseph F. Smith, Letter to _____, May 29, 1912. Stapley, *Power of Godliness*, ch. 2.

48. Other terms similar to cancellation were used. For example, Joseph F. Smith diary, August 30, 1912, uses the phrase: "Granted a church divorce." "Temple divorce" was also common.

49. Turner, *Brigham Young*, 241–43. Eugene E. Campbell and Bruce L. Campbell, "Divorce among Mormon Polygamists: Extent and Explanations," 4–23. Kathryn M. Daynes, "Breaking the Seal: Analysis of Cancellations of

in his opinion on whether such acts were in fact effective, but he was probably the exception. In December 1869, Young was reported as saying, "A Bill of Divorce that is given to many is no Better than a peace of Blank paper. A woman who is sealed to a good man who bears the Priesthood if that man honors that Priesthood if that woman leaves him of her own accord & she is sealed to a dozen other men *the first man will hold her in the resurrection if he wants her unless she should be sealed to a Man of a Higher Priesthood.*"[50] By higher priesthood, Young probably meant higher ecclesial office—though the statement might refer to the priesthood cosmology induced by adoptive positioning. The privilege of office was reflected in the adoption and marriage culture of Nauvoo and Utah, where a woman might be appropriated from one husband to another—as happened with Zina Diantha Huntington and husband Henry Jacobs. Zina, sealed to Joseph Smith for eternity, was "elevated" to Brigham Young's household for time.[51] During the Taylor and Woodruff administrations, these divorces were clearly meant as sealing cancelations.[52]

The status of widows and divorcees has always been distinct in twentieth-century Church culture, often sharing many of the consequences of separation—though the former at least enjoys a clear scriptural mandate to be nurtured. The latter may carry a related burden of sorrow, but it would also carry a kind of stigma.[53] It seems clear that though the difficulties incurred by requesting or receiving cancellation are similar for both a divorced woman and a widowed woman, individual cases could vary dramatically. Under current practice, cancellation is usually not considered without a remarriage present or on the horizon, and even then may fail to be secured. These women must petition for a cancellation of their first sealing and clear the hurdle of family discomfort over what is often perceived to be a massive challenge to family loyalty. And women of what-

---

Sealing by Brigham Young." While in modern times a sealing cancelation is not generally granted among the divorced without another impending marriage (especially when children are involved), exceptions exist. Circumstances can still trump general rules.

50. Kenney ed.,, *Wilford Woodruff's Journal*, 6:507; emphasis added.

51. See Marilyn Higbee, ed., "'A Weary Traveler,': The 1848–50 Diary of Zina D. H. Young," 86–125.

52. John D. T. McAllister journal as noted in Wayne Hinton, "John D. T. McAllister: The Southern Utah Years, 1876–1910," 120–22.

53. The traditional stigma is partly an inheritance of nineteenth-century divorce law. For example, a woman could only be divorced for adultery in America at large.

ever status who seek a sealed marriage with an LDS male whose previous marriage ended in death or divorce but is still sealed to his past wife, must contemplate a possible shared relationship in the afterlife.[54]

Of course, not all women despised having or potentially having a sister-wife, and it is important in both religious and sociological senses that many who have married in the footsteps of a deceased sealed wife have announced spiritual confirmation of the commitment.[55] Modern Mormon women and men generally see marriage sealing in a temple as the ideal, and if that aspiration is not present in a potential partner, love often takes second place. During the days of open polygamy, many Saints saw polygamy in the same make-or-break light. For many nineteenth-century Mormons, polygamy led to the highest heaven, and both men *and* women could signal that their availability hinged on the commitment to engage in future plural relationships.[56] When polygamy discourse ceased, those attitudes created social and theological distance between younger and older Saints.

With the cosmology that developed after the death of Joseph Smith, plural eternal marriage sealings may be seen to include continuing sexual relations between the resurrected husband and each of his glorified wives. And while no one normally dwells on the thought of a future divorce, the contemplation of a former partner's remarriage is rendered all the more complex if this involves deconstructing a sealing. Children can also make such issues even more intense. For a time at least, Church policy parsed children to different husbands of the same wife, even if no living sealing existed. A husband and wife who were never sealed but had children while the husband lived seemed to present a problem if the widow remarried (and was sealed to her living husband) and had children in the second marriage. Church leaders saw Woodruff's 1894 change of practice as dictating that the children of the deceased husband be sealed to him, and

---

54. Bradley H. Kramer, "Keeping the Sacred: Structured Silence in the Enactment of Priesthood Authority, Gendered Worship, and Sacramental Kinship in Mormonism," 123.

55. Anne Osborn Poelman, *The Simeon Solution: One Woman's Spiritual Odyssey*. On Heavenly Mothers, see Kramer, "Keeping the Sacred," ch. 5.

56. For example, in 1885, a young Theresa Thompson only gave her consent to her beau provided he bore solemn witness that he intended to live the "principle." Polygamy was the higher law, the celestial way, the only sure way to exaltation. Barbara Jones Brown, "The 'Second Manifesto,' the Mexican Revolution, and the Demise of Post-Manifesto Polygamy."

not adopted to the second husband, even though no sealing bond existed between the wife and her first husband.[57]

A Theological Legacy

An Eternal Restoration of Polygamy

Despite the cessation of the practice and the distancing of its past implementation, there is a considerable cloud of traditions that has circulated in Mormonism on the return of polygamy before the final judgment of mankind, a tradition inherited from both the transitional feelings of Church leaders after 1890 and, of course, the canonization of the plural marriage revelation. One of these traditions stems from the pedestal theology mentioned above, styling women as fundamentally more spiritual than men. If the population of righteous women significantly outnumber that of righteous men, then every faithful Mormon man (in the end times) will be besieged by women desiring eternal companionship.[58] Isaiah 4:1 ("in that day seven women shall take hold of one man, saying, We will eat our own bread, and wear our own apparel: only let us be called by thy name, to take away our reproach") is frequently invoked to support such a view.[59] That said, it seems naïve to believe that there are not many

---

57. "It was decided today that in cases where women had been sealed to men who were not their first husbands, and children who were not united to their natural fathers, these ordinances might now be performed for the dead husbands and fathers . . . " Abraham H. Cannon diary, June 14, 1894, in Lyman, ed., *Candid Insights of a Mormon Apostle*, 520. Ten years before, Church President John Taylor ruled in the case of a woman with a deceased husband who had since been sealed to another man. Taylor told the woman that her children by the first husband (to whom she was not sealed) had their choice in being sealed to their biological father or their stepfather. If the former, the biological father had to receive a proxy endowment and be sealed to a "suitable" woman by proxy. L. John Nuttall papers, MSS 790, Box 4, book 3, letter 245.

58. In practical terms the early Utah years contained an image of this. There were several single women who made the trek to Utah on their own. They were generally looked after by "captains" in the train, and with some frequency developed feelings for those men, who in turn invited them to join their families in Utah.

59. While the idea has not been celebrated in print recently, it was in early Utah. See, for example, Heber C. Kimball, "Remarks," 4. The current position still bears some marks of the heyday of polygamy. See the footnotes for Isaiah 4:1 in the latest (2013) LDS edition of the Bible. During the administration of

Latter-day Saint women who perceive a future polygamous state as anxiety inducing, undesirable, or perhaps even evil. One anthropologist who recently studied Mormon discourse recounts interviews with Mormon women over the question of post-mortal polygamy. One response seems to characterize the bulk of that aspect of the study: "Every night I pray that my husband will die before I do."[60]

The Eternal Woman

Seeing God in the image of Man is one of the historically frank heresies of Mormonism, a heresy multiplied by the largely embraced logic of Eliza Snow's "My Father in Heaven":

> I had learned to call thee Father,
> Through thy Spirit from on high,
> But until the key of knowledge
> Was restored, I knew not why.
>
> In the heavens are parents single?
> No, the thought makes reason stare!
> Truth is reason, truth eternal
> Tells me I've a mother there.[61]

Coupled with the fact that post-mortal polygamy continues embedded in Mormon praxis and thought, this offers some circumstantial liturgical foundation for the position that God and a plurality of Goddesses rule in Heaven. The singular Goddess, Priestess, Queen, Mother, is partly a modern work in the image of public modern Mormonism that selectively reads

---

George Albert Smith (1945–51) church leaders privately took up the question of Emma Smith and the eventual return of polygamy. Being part of the restoration, they felt it must return eventually. See "Council of the Twelve Meeting Minutes."

60. Kramer, "Keeping the Sacred," 123. See also Daniela Johnson-Bennion, "Comparing Themes of Polygamy in Mormon Women's Public and Personal Writings as Found in the Woman's Exponent and Their Diaries During the Edmunds Act, the Edmunds-Tucker Act, and the Manifesto." Johnson-Bennion observes that while public statements by Utah-era plural wives generally defended the practice, private reports almost wholly communicated feelings of heartache, jealousy, and loneliness attributed to causes incident to polygamy.

61. Eliza R. Snow, "My Father in Heaven." See William V. Smith, *The King Follett Sermon: A Social History.*

(and forgets) the record of the past.[62] Whether monogamous or plural, the projection of the mortal family onto the heavenly necessarily involved the contemporary and cultural views of the latter.

In a carefully selective way, Mormon discourse on women and men has largely echoed Victorian modalities. Victorian mores were ostensibly driven by New Testament passages like 1 Peter 3:1–6 that began with instructing "ye wives, be in subjection to your own husbands" (1 Pet. 3:1). As one handbook for the sexes in Joseph Smith's day stated, women were in their proper place and able to exercise their natural gift as more spiritually influential when quietly and domestically obedient to their husbands.[63] Historian's Carroll and Charles Rosenberg summarized: [W]oman "was more spiritual than man, yet less intellectual, closer to the divine, yet prisoner of her most animal characteristics, more moral than man, yet less in control of her very morality."[64] This pedestal theology was (relatively) new in Protestant thought at the time, and it continues in some Evangelical thought-threads as well as Mormonism. This language became one of styling women as gate-keepers of male sexual morality in Mormonism, partly as a legacy of polygamy whose narrative saw women's bodies as a means of banking the otherwise uncontrollable male sexual drive, and at the same time passively policing male sexual behaviors in several ways—such as telling girls and women to avoid "immodest" clothing to prevent boys and

---

62. This kind of forgetfulness is not a reality somehow limited to Mormonism or any group with a significant history. Taysom, "A Uniform and Common Recollection," 115–16.

63. Marshall Hall, *Commentaries on some of the more important of the Diseases of Females*, 2.

64. Carroll Smith-Rosenberg and Charles E. Rosenberg, "The Female Animal: Medical and Biological Views of Woman and Her Role in Nineteenth-Century America," 338. An 1855 revision of an 1842 Joseph Smith sermon suggested similar mid-century Mormon thought. See the comparative records of Smith's sermon to the Nauvoo Relief Society on April 28, 1842, in William V. Smith et al., "The Parallel Joseph." However, this "isolation by elevation" of women was not the only theological position. Brigham Young occasionally saw women as inferior to men in nearly every respect. Turner, *Brigham Young*, 158. Compare Joseph F. Smith's unpublished article, ca. 1915, "Unchastity, The Dominant Evil of the Age." On roots of female theology in the nineteenth century, see Krueger, *Reader's Repentance*, 26–27. The nineteenth-century trend to infantilize white women extended across the culture. For example in the loss of their limited suffrage that came in concert with the same trend for free black males. Daniel Walker Howe, *What Hath God Wrought: The Transformation of America, 1815–1848*, 497.

men from having sexual thoughts. Polygamy was the solution to male desire and Brigham Young taught that men should enjoy their wives as much as they wished, within certain boundaries. Doing so meant the end of the brothel by both enabling men to fulfill their natural sexual desires and opening marriage opportunities to women who would otherwise turn to prostitution out of desperation.[65]

In 1875, prominent Latter-day Saint Emily Spencer painted a caricature of the wife who is "strong minded" and socially guns down her husband over his weaknesses. Her reaction to this decomplexified straw woman illustrates the accepted vision of domestic life:

> To me it is always a painful sight to see a woman stepping into a man's place as head of the family, oftentimes treating her husband as though he were a child, turning innocent words into ridicule, smiling and winking at her own smartness, or chiding him for some slight carelessness that really was no harm. I have wondered if the feelings of the husband were sensitive enough to be wounded; or if blunted by continued repititions of the same character? Man is ahead of us, God has placed him there, and we need not fight against it. If you have husbands living their religion . . . let them lead and you follow. Let them dictate and you obey. Then you will be happy and in your proper place.[66]

Polygamy had the tendency to emphasize that wives were property by partner arithmetic if nothing else, and the plural marriage revelation contributed to such a view. (For example, see verse 61 of the revelation: "for they are given unto him; for he cannot commit adultery with that that belongeth unto him and to no one else.") Even in monogamy, except in unusual circumstances, a nineteenth-century woman was effectively the property of her father, and then husband if she married. For much of American history, a woman's life was bound by the common law heritage of the colonials. A married woman was a dependent of her husband, a status similar to an underage child. When a husband died, his wife could not be the guardian of the minor children. Any property she brought to the marriage belonged to her husband and she was only entitled to one third of the estate. By the time of Joseph Smith's death, state laws had only begun to moderate this patriarchal prejudice. The property theme of the

---

65. On Young, see Brigham Young, Remarks, December 9, 1847. On brothels, see Orson Pratt, "Celestial Marriage," 124. Pratt was arguing with Millard Fillmore's first batch of appointees who brought back shocking tales of polygamy.

66. Emily Spencer, "Strong Minded Women," 179.

revelation may not have fallen on deaf ears, but it was not terribly far from societal norms in monogamy.[67]

In Eliza Snow's advice to women (discussed above), she characterizes men as "saviors," an idea that echoed Joseph Smith's own sealing narrative and the nature of Mormon sacramental faith in the nineteenth century. For Smith, polygamy was justified by kingdom expansion. That expansion took the form of broad familial connections and consequent progeny. However, Smith was unsuccessful as the sire of many children and may have had none by his plural wives. Despite this, the Book of Mormon justification for polygamy was pointed: to increase the population of God's people. Utah polygamy fostered both ideas, and it used the idea of spirit children in heaven, blessed by an interpretation of the plural marriage revelation (particularly verse 63), as a justification for heavenly polygamy. The Utah experience suggests, however, that if polygamy was a superior way to achieve the goal of increasing the population of Mormons, it largely failed in that task (compared to what could have been achieved through monogamy). Instead, it illustrated a somewhat different story—one that replaced the total number of children born into the faith with the number of children born into spiritually elite households. Polygamy could succeed in the task of building the Mormon kingdom if that task was interpreted in terms of elite males who possessed relative wealth and Church status, which afforded them the ability to produce more children by a larger group of wives—even if any given wife had fewer children compared to monogamous wives.[68] Polygamy in that environment might provide a large posterity to those men even though on the average it did not provide

---

67. Nineteenth-century women made social gains first in property ownership, then the ability to retain their income, and finally the legal ability to engage in business enterprise. But this came well after Emma Smith's marriage to Joseph. Melissa J. Homestead, *American Women Authors and Literary Property, 1822–1869.* Linda E. Speth, "The Married Women's Property Acts, 1839–1865: Reform, Reaction, or Revolution?," 12–15. Linda K. Kerber, *Women of the Republic: Intellect and Ideology in Revolutionary America,* 137–42, 157–84.

68. Population studies on polygamy in nineteenth-century Utah suggest a fertility advantage for men who took a second wife, but fertility with third and later wives generally decreased markedly per wife. Stanley Ivins, "Notes on Mormon Polygamy," 229–39; James E. Smith and Phillip R. Kunz, "Polygyny and Fertility in Nineteenth-Century America," 465–80. See Kathryn M. Daynes, *More Wives Than One: Transformation of the Mormon Marriage System, 1840–1910,* 7–10, 100–102.

a significant advantage over the entire population. In that sense, polygamy both encouraged and fulfilled the notion of the "blood of the prophets."[69]

Eternal Gender

The potential of more children being fathered by spiritual elite males was not limited to mortality. In Utah elaborations of the afterlife, spirit children had sex identity, since their creation was considered to be essentially identical to conception and gestation in human procreation. That facet of polygamy endures as a tradition in the modern LDS Church, exemplified by the 1995 "The Family: A Proclamation to the World," which states:

> All human beings—male and female—are created in the image of God. Each is a beloved spirit son or daughter of heavenly parents, and, as such, each has a divine nature and destiny. Gender is an essential characteristic of individual premortal, mortal, and eternal identity and purpose.[70]

The Proclamation continues this theme, with Mormon cultural values concerning the eternal sex and gender of nurturer versus provider being impressed onto premortal society—in much the same way that nineteenth-century Mormons saw their polygamous relationships reflected in their views of the heavenly premortal and postmortal societies among the gods.

It seems unclear what gender might mean for spirit beings. In animals, gender corresponds to physical structure, hormone manifestation, and statistical means in growth patterns as well as chromosome endowment. None of this seems easily assignable to spirit beings, whatever the ontological assumptions might be. But in Mormonism's traditional analogical theology, it most easily fits a heaven where God has a wife, or wives, who birth spirit children. The category discontinuity in this scheme (spirit children from physical parents) was explained by Orson Pratt as a manifestation of the seeming Pauline proscription against *blood* in the veins of the resurrected (1 Cor. 15:50).[71] Instead of blood, the super-ma-

---

69. Jean Tchuenche has shown that, in theory, polygamy can make a significant difference in population gene distribution. Jean M. Tchuenche, "An Age-Physiology Dependent Population Dynamics Model with Polygamy," 42–55.

70. Gordon B. Hinckley, "Stand Strong Against the Wiles of the World," 98–107.

71. Joseph Smith probably developed his "flesh and bones" (D&C 130:22) (rather than flesh and blood) preaching paradigm out of these passages, while Pratt merely saw the logical contours of such a system. It is not clear, for example, whether Smith saw all the physiological consequents Pratt read into blood and spirit dualities. In Smith's sermon of May 12, 1844, for example, Thomas Bullock

terial spirit (D&C 131:7–8) flowed in their bodily circulatory systems; in Pratt's thinking, this made it possible for physical beings to procreate spirit children.[72] This spiritual biology, hanging on an analogical mixture of reason and scripture, saw that discontinuity as one of degree, not of kind. Spirit was a material thing, not an immaterial ideal, and Joseph Smith's early dialogic exposition of the Book of Revelation (D&C 77:2) seemed to give human spirits a material *form*, the same form shared by their future physicality.[73]

Young took this a step further, saying that by the heavenly parents (Adam and Eve) eating the fruit of the physical earth, their systems were "charged" with the physical, whence they could reproduce children of physical flesh. This feature of Brigham Young's Adam-God anthropology was not shared by Pratt, who saw too many contradictions with scripture. Though Pratt was an opponent of Young's Adam mythos, they shared a background cosmology of spirit creation, one that supported polygamy as the most efficient production scheme of the heavenly posterity of God and offered exalted status to the theorized large surplus of saved women. Thus a foundation for gendered spirits came to exist in Utah theological circles that was broader than either Young's or Pratt's alone. The important idea that founded either world-view was this: men were fundamentally less likely to be saved than women. That meant that kingdom expansion depended on relatively few men and a larger number of women.

Spirits with sexual identity implied spirits with human sexual characteristics. This analogical theology naturally leaned against the question of purpose. Spirits cannot procreate in any version of speculative Mormonism. The earlier cosmology that involved eternal uncreated spirit persons might also feature gendered spirits, but then the notion of gender becomes even less clear. The question of purpose has obscure meaning in that context. It becomes part of the self-existent nature of spirits. It is here that the B. H. Roberts's theology rescued the essentials without sacrificing the major points of both eras, even if it inherited many of the same cosmological puzzles. Roberts took Joseph Smith's theology of uncreated spirits and introduced it into the Utah theology of spirits born of the sexual union of divine beings. He did this by positing two stages of hu-

---

reported him saying, "When our flesh is quickened by the Spirit, there will be no blood in the tabernacles." Smith et al., "Parallel Joseph," May 12, 1844.

72. Orson Pratt, "The Preexistence of Man," 37.

73. Perhaps this exposition was founded on the Book of Mormon text of Ether 3.

man preexistence: an uncreated mind, born into a divinely sired body of "spirit" material. The idea became normative to some extent.[74]

The heaven of Nauvoo Mormonism, driven in part by the plural marriage revelation, was one that existed as a divinely supported lattice of beings, held together by everlasting sealing links. Failure to be part of that system meant exclusion from the fullness of God's presence. Therefore the security of those links became primary. Being sealed to dead persons of questionable or unknown faith was a terrible prospect in this world. Wilford Woodruff's 1894 revelation eased the anxiety over having perfect links. The grace of God would be exercised in such cases, allowing for the Saints to be sealed to their deepest known ancestry, and then finally to Joseph Smith himself.[75] In practice, that final sealing was rarely, and then never, performed, since one could never tell when genealogical discovery was complete.[76] The delayed Millennium became a space and time where any challenges involving the faithfulness of the dead could be adjusted according to divine wisdom.

The federal raid of the 1880s made many Saints believe that the end of the world had to be near, and Joseph Smith's revelation that "if thou [Smith] livest until thou art eighty-five years old, thou shalt see the face of the Son of Man" (D&C 130:15)—which he would have been in 1890–1891—helped to support the wish for an end to opposition.[77] Gradually, the ending of polygamy and the unfulfilled expectation of Christ's return allowed Latter-day Saints to further rethink the Millennium as that pro-

---

74. See Chapter 6. See also Smith, *The King Follett Sermon*. On Young's Adam theology, see David John Buerger, "The Adam-God Doctrine," 14–58. The meaning of these ontological/cosmological prescriptions in Mormonism has always been supplied by a ubiquitous analogical vision.

75. Woodruff's 1894 revelation on sealing to ancestors saw development in Woodruff's own life. In 1892, he had his father and grandfather sealed to Joseph Smith, after sealing himself and his wife to his biological father. Stapley, "Adoptive Sealing Ritual in Mormonism," 92n110. Abraham H. Cannon diary, April 5, 1894, in Lyman, ed., *Candid Insights*, 488–94. On the fears of broken or incorrect links, see Orson Pratt's 1876 insertion into the canon, Doctrine and Covenants 128:18.

76. Some found that by linking to European royalty, they could follow (unfortunately fictive) royal genealogies "back to Adam," a popular meme in some parts of twentieth-century Mormonism, inherited from various movements like British Israelism. Robert C. Gunderson, "I Have a Question," 31. Stapley, "Adoptive Sealing Ritual in Mormonism," 113–14.

77. For such rumors and hopes, see Chapter 5.

bationary time to, among many things, solve the difficulty of missing genealogical links going back to the first man and woman, Adam and Eve.[78]

The goal of sealing the human family however continues to draw unanswered challenges from both ends of the genealogical tree. The primacy
of Adam and Eve in Mormon sealing theology, whether or not Young's
anthropology was taken seriously, makes some Mormons nervous about
Darwinian evolution and the potential lack of clear genealogical roots.
The complexities of marriage sealings in the contexts of death, divorce,
and traditional adoption may cause worry over the entangled genealogical
branches. Just as the Millennium became the solution to restoring missing
genealogical links, it also became the solution for these anxieties—a time
when "all will be sorted out in the end." While this may alleviate some
anxiety, it is still evident that the family politics in modern multiple sealings can be difficult, and the troubled relationship between evolution and
Mormon thought has never been suitably resolved.[79]

The Unmarried or Unsealed

A theology surrounding marriage relationships makes necessary implications about the status and position of single, unmarried persons. The
plural marriage revelation is perfectly clear about their status being eternally defined as servants "for those who are worthy of a far more, and an
exceeding, and an eternal weight of glory" (D&C 132:16). Joseph Smith
touched on it in sermons, and extra-canonical material has continued
from that time.[80] Utah Mormonism eventually bricked up the boundary

---

78. Stapley, "Adoptive Sealing Ritual in Mormonism," 116.

79. On the struggle to assimilate Darwin with the Mormon chain of sealings
and the connected theological literalism see William E. Evenson and Duane E.
Jeffrey, *Mormonism and Evolution: The Authoritative LDS Statements*. Richard
Sherlock, "'We Can See no Advantage to a Continuation of the Discussion':
The Roberts/Smith/Talmage Affair," 63–78. Duane E. Jeffrey, "Seers, Savants
and Evolution: The Uncomfortable Interface," 41–75. Steven L. Peck, "Crawling
Out of the Primordial Soup: A Step Toward the Emergence of an LDS Theology
Compatible with Organic Evolution," 1–36. On the theological issues, see Smith,
The King Follett Sermon.

80. A current conception is that the faithful Mormon dead are busy evangelizing
in the world of spirits. Joseph Smith brought the book of Hebrews to bear.
Smith spoke importantly about the "spirits of just men made perfect" as the
spirits of men who had various sacerdotal missions, including preaching to the
dead and delivering the sealing keys/information to mortals. For examples, see

between sermon and canon as *prima scriptura* became the rule. Whatever canonical force those early sermons once had is no longer efficient, powerful though they may be for many. The twentieth century saw to that.[81]

The centrality of marriage sealing in Mormon theology, practice, and culture may act as a difficult and sometimes painful boundary marker for Church members who are not in a sealed husband-wife relationship for whatever reason, as it might not only exacerbate their own internal struggles, but could leave them feeling left out of the mainstream of Church teaching, activity, service, or even salvation when they are in most need of support. The comfort offered by words from Church leaders may seem incomplete or even hurtful compared to the assurance and authority of scripture texts.[82] And so, one cannot but feel the rootlessness of many single Church members who have tried but failed in the Mormon marriage project. They have sermon assurance of their eventual opportunities, but it may be difficult to bridge the chasm of doctrine without a canonized text. And of course there is the nagging question of what post-mortal marriage really means. What is missing, if anything, from the mortal experience? Gordon B. Hinckley, in a sermon titled, "To Single Adults," said,

> You are just as important as any others in the scheme of our Father in Heaven, and under His mercy no blessing to which you otherwise might be entitled will forever be withheld from you.[83]

Smith's sermons on February 9, 1843, August 13, 1843, October 9, 1843, and May 12, 1844, in Smith et al., "Parallel Joseph." Andrew H. Hedges et al., eds., *Journals, Volume 2: December 1841–April 1843*, 257. Vilate Kimball wrote to her missionary husband, "[Joseph] says [the dead] will have the gospel preached to them in prison," Vilate M. Kimball, Letter to Heber C. Kimball, October 11, 1840. Smith's language and imagery were undoubtedly borrowed from 1 Pet. 3:19.

81. The issue is treated in Philip L. Barlow, *Mormons and the Bible: The Place of Latter-day Saints in American Religion*. The speculative theology of nineteenth-century Mormonism was part of the motivation for creating a true canon in Mormonism. While the living prophets were certainly authoritative, their post-Brigham Young speech was to be judged by the written canon, a resolution that was historically Protestant in pattern, if not content. See Kent R. Trembath, *Evangelical Theories of Inspiration: A Review and Proposal*.

82. On assurances to singles that faithfulness will somehow bring all possible blessings, see, for example, Ezra Taft Benson, "To the Single Adult Sisters of the Church," 96–99. On historical remarks by LDS leaders on singles, see Marybeth Raynes and Erin Parsons, "Single Cursedness: An Overview of LDS Authorities' Statements about Unmarried People," 40–45.

83. Gordon B. Hinckley, "To Single Adults," 98.

One of Joseph Smith's sons, Alexander Hale Smith (1838–1909), put some of the anxiety in succinct terms: "Time is a slow coach when one is waiting anxiously the solution of so all important a problem as ones eternal salvations in the celestial kingdom of God."[84]

Salvation for the Dead

Joseph F. Smith, sixth president of the LDS Church, spent decades considering the nature of life after death in Mormon theology. During a long season of prayer near the end of his life, he produced several revelations, one of which refers to itself as "the vision of the redemption of the dead" (D&C 138:60). While not immediately added to the printed canon, it was submitted to and sustained by fellow Church leaders at the next General Conference. Some sixty years later, it was added to the books of LDS scripture (first in the Pearl of Great Price, and then later as Doctrine and Covenants 138), giving a greater canonical foundation for the nature of life between death and resurrection. As important as this was, it may fail to offer much optimism to the unsealed as the plural marriage revelation still waits in the background.

In Eliza R. Snow's marriage advice to young women, she described polygamy as means to ensure that worthy women were able to achieve ultimate salvation in a world of few stalwart men. Perhaps to help solidify the optimistic logic of Woodruff's 1894 revelation and dampen the mortal prerogative supported in the plural marriage revelation, a narration of one of Joseph Smith's experiences during the Kirtland era was added to the Doctrine and Covenants at the same time as Joseph F. Smith's vision of the spirit world. Designated section 137 of the Doctrine and Covenants, the text narrates a vision of Joseph Smith's deceased brother Alvin in the Celestial glory. Smith was apparently shocked by this vision, where a man is admitted to God's presence based not on a faithful sacramental pattern, but on a contra factual: if the opportunity had presented itself, Alvin would have faithfully followed Mormonism (137:6–9). The principle is generalized to all humanity, and a related part of the text embraces deceased children as saved (137:10). Later in Nauvoo, this idea seems forgotten in some respects, though Joseph Smith emphasized on several occasions that children who die prior to the age when the sacraments of salvation may be administered enter Celestial glory. However, their fate within the refined

---

84. Alexander's statement was in the context of the validity of polygamy. Alexander H. Smith, Letter to Samuel H. B. Smith, November 19, 1866.

Celestial architecture of Doctrine and Covenants 131:1–3 that requires participation in the highest order of the priesthood is left unexplained in the canon. Hinted at within the Alvin contra factual is the suggestion that the responses of any person to any circumstance are already known, and hence predetermined by some factor or factors completely knowable by God. A host of logical questions (generally unexplored by Mormons at large beyond simple assertion) linger about the nature of freedom, accountability, transcendence, etc.

Sealing to Eternal Life

While the 1836 vision of Elijah delivering the "keys of this dispensation" (D&C 110:16) did not become public knowledge until 1852, by then Joseph Smith had already established a narrative of visits by John the Baptist and Peter, James, and John to restore sacramental authority and the keys of the kingdom.[85] It would be hard to convince early Mormons that their baptisms or confirmations in the name of Jesus were effectively false gateways to heaven, or that their sealings by the high priesthood were empty; however, in multiple sermons Smith had already tied Elijah to the restoration of the keys of salvific acts and ritual. (See the discussion of D&C 132:46–48 in Chapter 7.) Another understanding of these keys was necessary. By asserting that Elijah was the foundation of sacramental legitimacy and permanence, Smith still drew a sharp boundary between authoritative familial sealing acts and authoritative administration of the Lord's Supper or baptism, or even the work of his brother, the patriarch. The plural marriage revelation supports that distinction in a number of ways, and its more formal and specific sealing helped to define the nature of Nauvoo as the embodiment of the spirit of Mormonism—the sealing *together* of the human family to not just eternal life but a specific architecture of that life.[86] The older sealing, wielded by the high priests and then

---

85. Doctrine and Covenants 27:13–14 suggests this. The timing of that portion of the revelation is in question, but it is clear that the early 1830s saw Smith preaching about the visitations. Michael Hubbard MacKay et al., *Documents, Volume 1: July 1828–June 1831*, 164–66; Nathan Baldwin, "Testimony of an Old Latter-Day Saint," 15.

86. The high priesthood sealing and the sealing of plural marriage may have had a transition period, or perhaps the ritual changed over time. William Clayton reported that when he was sealed to plural wife Margaret Moon, she was "sealed up by the priesthood, by the president---and [then] M[argaret] [was sealed]

their branching office, the patriarchs, needed textual flesh, and that was provided in part by the plural marriage revelation in vv. 19–26.[87]

In his 1839 instruction to the apostles prior to their departure to missionary service in Britain, Joseph Smith heavily emphasized the restoration of the keys of the kingdom, particularly the keys of the patriarchal sealing to eternal life.[88] From this point, the theme of such sealing reached a climax in the January 1841 revelation (now Doctrine and Covenants 124) that called Hyrum Smith to "the office of Priesthood and Patriarch" with the keys "that whatsoever he shall bind on earth shall be bound in heaven; and whatsoever he shall loose on earth shall be loosed in heaven" (124:91, 93). The newer familial sealing evolved in his first plural marriages a few months later (particularly his marriage to Sarah Ann Whitney in early 1842) to the July 1843 plural marriage revelation. These two threads of sealing revealed two distinct sealing heads: Hyrum the Patriarch and Joseph the Priest. This understanding of distinct sealings with distinct authority heavily influenced successors John Taylor and Joseph F. Smith, who both attempted to reinstate the separate functions. Following Joseph F. Smith, the patriarchal office declined in importance.[89]

Together, the Patriarch and Priest placed each individual within a sacral genealogy by blending the plural marriage revelation with parts of the ancient priesthood mythos in Smith's early revelations, as found now mostly in Doctrine and Covenants 107. The ecclesial priesthood of 1830 to 1835 saw a unification of the 1832 ascending narrative of the high priesthood line from the sons of Moses to Adam (D&C 84:6–16) with the 1835 line of

---

to me." Robert Fillerup, ed., "William Clayton's Nauvoo Diaries and Personal Writings," April 27, 1843.

87. The plural marriage revelation was powerful enough that it eventually worked to strip patriarchs in the high priesthood of any kind of sealing in some twentieth-century interpretations (see "Outline of Instructions to Patriarchs"). See Brown, *In Heaven as it is on Earth,* 236 on the two seals.

88. Joseph Smith's June 27, 1839, instruction to the apostles circulated widely during the apostles' 1840 mission to England. Three manuscript copies exist. Willard Richards's "Pocket Companion Written in England"; James Burgess, Journal 1, 89; Wilford Woodruff Book of Revelations, 1841–1842, 27–35.

89. See Joseph Smith's discourse of March 10, 1844. Taylor revived the President of the High Priesthood title and Joseph F. Smith elevated the Church Patriarch above the apostolate. After Joseph F. Smith's death, his son, Hyrum G. Smith, renewed his father's claims over the patriarch's office as superior. The apostles again rejected the idea based on their commission to ordain patriarchs generally. Anthon H. Lund diary, January 2, 1919, Hatch, ed., *Danish Apostle,* 723.

descending patriarchal priesthood that "was instituted in the days of Adam and came down by lineage" (D&C 107:41), the intersection of which was the ancient patriarch, Abraham. The link between Mormonism and Abraham helped frame every Mormon priesthood narrative after 1832.[90]

The unfulfilled promises of the city of Zion and its eschatological placement led to the folding of salvation into the power of the high priesthood, its branches, and its liturgy in Nauvoo.[91] At virtually the same time, the high priesthood and its accompanying sealing power was extracted from the salvific narrative and placed within the sealing liturgy itself. After Smith's death, it was brought under the umbrella of an apostolic reading of priesthood authority.[92] Just as important, the rising position of Elijah as enabler of the linkage of living and dead, together with an expanded freedom of sealing and its meaning, eventually became the engine of the Mormon genealogical juggernaut following Wilford Woodruff's 1894 revelation that blessed the sealing of biological familial lines as far back as research would allow.[93]

The Celestial Family

Latter-day Saint life in nineteenth-century Utah was in many ways constructed around the idea of a polygamy founded on the kingdom theology elaborated from the plural marriage revelation. Small communities,

---

90. See William V. Smith, "Early Mormon Priesthood Revelations: Text, Impact, and Evolution," 54.

91. Mormonism of 1830–31 found its purpose in the relocation of the Saints to the safety of modern Israel's prophesied home: joining the Indians in the west promised reclamation of an Enochian Zion. Mark Ashurst-McGee, "Zion Rising: Joseph Smith's Early Social and Political Thought," 205.

92. One of the most succinct summaries of the end myth that naturalizes and legitimizes apostolic power is James E. Faust, "The Keys that Never Rust," 72–74.

93. Genealogy was an idea mentioned in a sermon delivered October 3, 1841. There, Joseph Smith emphasized that the Saints must search their genealogy for names to perform baptisms for the dead. The word did not appear in the published version of the sermon—*Times and Seasons* 2 (October 15, 1841): 577–78. A manuscript audit for the sermon contains this in Church Historian's Office General Church Minutes, October 3, 1841. With the theology of adoption that appeared after Smith's death, genealogical research still held interest for reaching out and providing the sacraments to the dead by proxy but circumstances and facilities limited motivation. Sealings among ancestors were possible, but the danger of *connecting oneself* to those ancestors of unknown faith was a guiding principle.

each centered on a number of family groups, dominated the picture of Utah population. Historian Matthew Bowman describes them as a "dynastic, vaguely medieval" vision of "heaven as a constellation of kingdoms of kin all orbiting a righteous patriarch." But these kinship kingdoms were not just patriarchal harems. They possessed in many cases "a strong female sisterhood, created from the same networks of sister-wives."[94]

The end of polygamy coupled with Woodruff's revelation was earth-shaking for this worldview and shifted the entire Mormon picture of the end of the world. It was, somewhat ironically perhaps, the plural marriage revelation that gave new motivation and meaning to the work of Joseph Smith in the twentieth century. In spite of the death of polygamy, section 132 became one of the thickest (though simultaneously distant) sources for the master narrative of Mormonism in the new century.

Sealing and Excommunication

The effect of excommunication on sealings is made somewhat problematic by the plural marriage revelation. This is a hangover from its doctrine of unconditional sealings taught in verses 19 and 26. To understand the tension here, we must delve into the Mormon theology of excommunication. Very briefly, excommunication in Mormonism involves having one's name removed from the Church membership records, to be taken out of communion with the Church. The terms "blotted out," "cut off," or "cast out" are sometimes cited or derived from scripture as alternative ways to discuss their removal.[95] The spiritual consequence of excommunication is damnation by being placed outside the ritual ladder of salvation.[96] An excommunicated person may not take communion (Lord's Supper)

---

94. Matthew Bowman, *The Mormon People: The Making of an American Faith*, 258.

95. The latter terminology was typical in Protestant exhortations. For example, see the Virginia Baptist *Religious Herald*, May 4, 1832. On Mormon excommunication during the first eight decades of the twentieth century, see Lester E. Bush, Jr., "Excommunication and Church Courts: A Note from the *General Handbook of Instructions*," 74–98.

96. For example, see Smith's revelation explaining the fate of Methodist preacher James Covel: Doctrine and Covenants section 40. Though Covel was never a Church member, his fate is similar to the excommunicated: outside the canon, in the hands of a Providential God. On Covel, see Christopher C. Jones, "Mormonism in the Methodist Marketplace: James Covel and the Historical Background of Doctrine and Covenants 39–40," 67–98.

with the Church, may not address the congregation from the pulpit, may not serve in the Church in any capacity, may not pray in Church meetings, may not participate in Church teaching situations, and may not contribute financially to the Church. An excommunicated member may not enter Church temples or participate any salvific ordinances. An excommunicated member is no longer a member of the Church but the boundary between Church and non-Church is enforced with a strictness not present with other non-members. An excommunicated member has been silenced inside the Church and no local congregation has a record of their previous association with the Church.

However, being removed from local congregation records is not the same as never being there at all.[97] The excommunicated person's identity is still there in records kept at Church headquarters—but a kind of anathema is attached. Something similar is true with regard to having their own name voluntarily removed from Church records. If a person who voluntarily withdrew from the Church were to later have a change of heart and make the steps to return to membership in the Church, he or she will not get a fresh start as if the previous removal had never occurred. The reasons for exiting or excommunication must be discussed with local congregation leaders first. Then there is a procedure that may bring the prodigal back into the fold.

The process of returning from excommunication may be complicated by the circumstances of the original decision for excommunication. These circumstances are defined by the sin that resulted in excommunication, the setting of the sin, and the level of trust the sinner held in the Church: Was he or she an important officer in the Church? Did he or she recruit others to engage in sin of a serious nature, such as a teacher recruiting Sunday School students for sex acts? Was the sin serious and of public knowledge?

When a Church member confesses a serious sin like adultery, for example, there are more than two persons whose lives are affected. The local leaders of the congregation, such as a bishop or stake president, must determine whether the sinner is truly penitent or not. For most sins, excommunication is only applied to a member when many people are affected by the sinner's act or the sinner is unrepentant.

Some sins fall into the category of required excommunication, assuming there are no extenuating circumstances (diminished capacity for example), such as child sex abuse, incest, unrepentant apostasy, and de-

---

97. For current Church policy, see *General Handbook of Instructions Book I, 2010*, 23, 70.

liberate unjustified murder of another human being. This last sin bars the sinner from ever returning to the Church.

If a sinner was a trusted figure such as a bishop, stake president, or other very public ecclesiastical authority, excommunication becomes more likely whether the sinner is penitent or not. If a member had previously received the temple endowment, then excommunication is a more likely possibility than otherwise.

How does excommunication interface with sealing? Today, bishoprics and high councils, the main local Mormon judicial bodies, may both excommunicate and reinstate, but they cannot seal or unseal. The temple priesthood function of sealing is walled off from such ecclesial function. (Presently, no local officer may function on both sides of this wall simultaneously.) The plural marriage revelation suggests this in a sense, as does Joseph Smith's preaching the same year where he expressed the desire to turn over ecclesial functions to his brother, Hyrum;[98] however it becomes clearer in Utah, when Young had secured exclusive authority over sealing acts.

Final approval of "unsealing" or cancellation is now strictly limited to the First Presidency. With conditional sealings, one might suppose that the pessimistic clause ("through your faithfulness") implies dissolution of sealing upon excommunication. But this is difficult, partly because conditional sealings are not scriptural—even though ritual changes began a liturgical pessimism after Nauvoo. The text of verse 26 of the plural marriage revelation implies that excommunication cannot dissolve a sealing.

The separation of ecclesial and sealing authority, coupled with the implicit permanence of sealings, led to the idea of a "restoration of blessings." In effect, excommunication began to be seen as placing the force of temple sacraments in a sort of limbo. They are there, but not. While unable to perform or break sealings, stake presidents may be assigned by the First Presidency to perform a restoration of blessings—a ritual performed by the laying on of hands—and return the member to his or her former status. This includes the state of being endowed in the temple, and any sealing that existed at the time of excommunication.[99] (While stake

---

98. See Smith's sermons of July 16 and July 23, 1843, Smith et al., "Parallel Joseph." Brigham Young once expressed a similar desire for an exclusive devotion to this temple priest role, apparently hoping to leave ecclesial duties to others. See Young's February 16, 1847, remarks in Kenney, ed., *Wilford Woodruff's Journal*, 3:132.

99. For men, the procedure involves restoring the former conferral of Melchizedek Priesthood, then the office held in that priesthood (though not appendage offices like patriarch or bishop). For a recent narrative of the

presidents were permitted to do so historically, for most of the twentieth century the practice was restricted to general authorities.) Such restoration of blessings is prohibited for blessings dissolved by the Church President or entailed by special office or assignment. (For example, an excommunicated patriarch would not generally be restored to the patriarchal office.) Like other sacraments, this one may be declared posthumously.

The restoration of blessings implies that a sealing is still, in some sense, in effect during excommunication. This may even suggest a category of dormant sacraments. The 2010 Church Handbook of Instructions (now titled *Handbook 1: Stake Presidents and Bishops*) says that sealings are "revoked" by excommunication—although the protocol of restoration suggests that since the revoked sacraments may not be repeated, only *restored*, the sacraments are in some way held in escrow and are not erased or fully nullified. In comparison, the 1989 *General Handbook of Instructions* of the Church labels sealings of excommunicated persons as "suspended." The idea evokes the early Mormon practice of removing or simply inactivating the priesthood office of a transgressor.

While sealings may be canceled, this requires a separate action. During the Spencer W. Kimball and Ezra Taft Benson administrations, sealings of children to parents came to be seen as a birthright of the child and not necessarily retained by the parent (as opposed to policies of the nineteenth century, for example). Thus, when a couple had a sealing canceled, the sealing of child to parent remained in effect, in some abstract way. While such sealing is certainly subject to dissolution, the method for such dissolution was seen as independent of the bond that once existed between their parents. The 2010 *Handbook* extended this idea to sealings of couples. If one sealing partner is excommunicated, this must, in the language of the handbook, "revoke" the sealing of the sinner, while the status of being "sealed" remains in effect for the other partner.[100] This is reminiscent of D&C 132:44, which effectively states that a wife whose husband sins deeply enough is "given" to another partner. This is represented in another aspect of the current policy: if a woman finds herself in this situation (having an excommunicated husband whom she has divorced), and wishes to be sealed to another partner, she *must have her prior sealing canceled*—implying that the previous sealing was still in effect.

---

procedure, see M. Russell Ballard, "A Chance to Start Over: Church Disciplinary Councils and the Restoration of Blessings."

100. See *General Handbook of Instructions, I, 2010*, 21.

The tension of sealing and excommunication arises partly out of the nature of Mormon priesthood. Divided most naturally as ecclesial priesthood and temple priesthood,[101] the acts of sealing or reversing sealings lie within the purview of one man's office: that of the temple priest. The power to baptize or excommunicate is by nature a local one, in the hands of mission or local leaders for baptism, and lower and upper courts of judgment in local Mormon congregations for excommunication. Both offices represent bifurcations of the high priesthood, splits that are only unified historically and textually in the president of the high priesthood—in the apostolic cycle, the President of the Church.[102]

Mormonism Today

Following the death of Joseph Smith's last adult contemporary in Church leadership, Lorenzo Snow, Church discourse gradually focused around the modern nuclear family and its sealing centerpiece.[103] For Latter-day Saints after Wilford Woodruff's 1894 revelation, the salvation afforded by sealing became, in some important respects, a new doctrine. And the associated social forces tended to move the answers to pressing questions like those surrounding the inability to marry or have children into a distant future. The arguments for political stability, societal integra-

---

101. Stapley, "Adoptive Sealing Ritual in Mormonism," 57–61.

102. For the origin of such courts, see Smith, "Early Mormon Priesthood Revelations." There is an appeals process from the judgments of lower and upper local councils, but in the present day, it rarely results in an original jurisdiction or rehearing. During the later years of the Joseph F. Smith administration, ca. 1910, the apostles functioned in the role of high council in trying to discipline Mormons who were still marrying in plurality. See Smith, "The Last Shall be First," 326; John Henry Smith diary, July 14, 1909, in White, ed., *Church, State, and Politics*, 625. Reed Smoot diary, September 1, 1909, in Heath, ed., *In the World*, 27. Moyer, "Dancing with the Devil," 578–79, 583.

103. Dan Erickson, *"As a Thief in the Night": The Mormon Quest for Millennial Deliverance*, ch. 9; Thomas G. Alexander, *Mormonism in Transition: A History of the Latter-day Saints, 1890–1930*. To be sure, there were many branches to Church discourse, as there had always been. Mormon preaching from early Utah on was as peppered with practicality as it was theology. As polygamy receded into the background, other boundary revealing narratives took its place: the Word of Wisdom, Law of Tithing, and in general, the importance of self discipline and clean living. Bowman, *The Mormon People*, 151. J. B. Haws, *The Mormon Image in the American Mind: Fifty Years of Public Perception*, 10.

tion, and a new generation of leadership joined to become the engine that brought unanimity to the end of polygamy and a final realization that it would not and could not return—at least not in mortality.[104]

Mormonism was historically classified in much of American public discourse as extra-denominational—that is, something other than religion—a category used to make it exempt from constitutional protections afforded to legitimate religions. It was often polygamy that bolstered such arguments. Conservative American Protestant leaders of the latter half of the twentieth century saw Mormonism as a damning threat to their congregations. In an about-face from the nineteenth century, that threat was partly due to Mormonism's clean-cut media presence.

The late twentieth-century media made Mormons seem like normal upstanding Christian believers, but the construction of temples in heavily evangelical populations such as Atlanta, Dallas, and Denver brought home the dangers to evangelical leaders. The political goal of the Religious Right was to reclaim America for Christianity, and the robust growth of Mormonism, a group who rejected both the traditional Trinitarian understanding of God and the Protestant doctrine of *sola scriptura*, worked against that goal—no matter how many other values the two groups shared.

Fundamentalist Christians teamed with newly formed groups of ex-Mormons to produce and distribute media like the infamous *The God Makers,* whose title was a direct challenge to the deification taught in the

---

104. That the Church president had lost the power to authorize new polygamy without special revelation was a trope that began with Joseph F. Smith's uncomfortable testimony in the Reed Smoot hearings of 1904 and, in essence, confirmed by Smith in his April 1911 General Conference speech. Mormon theological expression in the last half of the twentieth century claimed plural marriage as part of a calculus of final things, like the restitution of Zion in Jackson County, Missouri. For example, Bruce R. McConkie, *Mormon Doctrine,* 578. McConkie wrote, "Obviously the holy practice [polygamy] will commence again after the Second Coming." Joseph F. Smith maintained an underground support for polygamy well after 1904, but he did it outside Church governing councils. D. Michael Quinn, "LDS Church Authority and New Plural Marriages, 1890–1904," 9–105. B. Carmon Hardy, *Solemn Covenant: The Mormon Polygamous Passage,* 319. Nancy Tate Dredge, "Victims of the Conflict." When Salt Lake Temple recorder and author Lycurgus Wilson married Julia Glines in plurality in 1907, he was sent on missions abroad in 1908, and two years later the *Salt Lake Tribune* published the infraction. "Not So Very Former," 4. See also the *Tribune's* reaction to the Church's April 1907 repeated declaration that polygamy was at an end, "Resisted to the Last Ditch," 4. For a list of polygamous marriages following 1904, see Hardy, *Solemn Covenant,* 394–429.

plural marriage revelation. The film, book, and a pool of surrounding literature from the rising counter-cult movement served up a new wave of anti-Mormonism. This time, there was no fixed adversary for Church leaders to defend against. Moreover, this modern movement did not just point its finger at Joseph Smith, it targeted church-going Mormons at large, suggesting they were knowingly part of a sinister cohesive organization with ties to the occult. This new anti-Mormonism had unexpected and real effects on conversion rates and public perception of the Church in the 1980s.[105]

The elevation of Gordon B. Hinckley to Church President helped to dispel negative publicity. His easy interaction with media giants of the time like Mike Wallace and Larry King, his "open for questions" speeches in forums like the National Press Club, and his general respect for the press helped heal some of the difficulties of the 80s and 90s. But looming on the horizon in the United States were issues like gay marriage and a wave of feminist speech about the roles of men and women in the Church. All these issues were again impacted by the plural marriage revelation and its heritage. It remains a living document in the sense that its interpretive history has profoundly affected the Church's response to these and many other social, political, and religious issues.[106]

Section 132 of the Doctrine and Covenants supports a theology that allows Latter-day Saints to bind their loved ones together forever, becoming god-like in their joy, power, and service to a never-ending posterity. It also links that theology to the practice of polygamy. That duality has been at issue from the time the revelation was dictated by Joseph Smith. With the reluctant struggle to end Church-sanctioned polygamy in the decades surrounding 1900, the 1843 plural marriage revelation has gradually become an antique orphan text in some respects, while still serving as the largely silent foundation for much of the modern message of Mormonism: God is real, is closely concerned in present life, and endorses familial love with the promise that all that is good in relationships with those closest to us can continue forever.

---

105. See Haws, *The Mormon Image in the American Mind*, 112–25, ch. 6.
106. The 1995 *The Family: A Proclamation to the World* tested the waters of interpretation for section 132, fixing much of the language that earlier characterized the Utah protology of Mormonism, including the subtext of gendered spirits.

Addendum

The Kingsbury Manuscript

Several early manuscripts of the plural marriage revelation exist. The earliest of these is one written by Joseph C. Kingsbury. Three others were written later as copies of the Kingsbury manuscript. These are the Willard Richards manuscript and two manuscripts written by Horace K. Whitney. In the annotated version of Kingsbury's manuscript below, I note differences between it and the Richards manuscript. The bibliographic data for the Whitney manuscripts appears at the end of this addendum.

To write his copy of the July 12, 1843, revelation, Kingsbury used two 12.5 x 14 inch unlined cream-colored sheets of paper, each folded in half, with the fold parallel to the short dimension of the sheet, and he wrote with quill and ink on both sides of each sheet. (Sometime after writing, the bifolia were folded in fourths for filing.)

The first sheet was inscribed so that page 1 was to the right of the fold on the recto (front) side of the sheet. Page 2 was written on the verso side of the sheet, on the back of page 1. (Page 2 was then on the left side or the verso of sheet one.) Page 3 was to the right of page 2, over the fold line. Finally, the sheet was turned back to the recto, and page 4 was written to the left of page 1. This worked to make the pages like those of a book, and the pattern was repeated with pages 5, 6, 7, and 8 inscribed on the second sheet. Kingsbury numbered the sheets by writing "No. 1" at the top of page 1, and "No. 2" at the top of page 5 (indicating the beginning of the second sheet). Pagination was penciled in later by another hand—probably Willard Richards or possibly someone in the *Deseret News* print shop—beginning with page 2. Thomas Bullock numbered pages 3, 5, and 7 with small inked numerals, probably prior to Richards's graphite numbering.

Richards followed the same pattern in writing his copy of the Kingsbury manuscript, folding two originally unlined cream-colored sheets of paper. Richards was more or less faithful in copying the Kingsbury manuscript. Pilcrow markings were inserted just as in the redacted version of Kingsbury.

Richards made some changes in spelling, such as "entered" for "enterd," and he shortened some sentences by dividing them. Richards overlooked one or two phrases or words, and may have purposely made changes, the differences noted by a later redactor in pencil. For example, Richards wrote the phrase, "a commandment **to** restore all things" rather than the construction in Kingsbury, "**and** restore all things." Richards initially wrote one curious thing in the phrase "let mine handmaid, Emma Smith, receive all those that have . . ." Richards copied "Emma" over another word. The canceled word appears to be part of "mine handmaid" and was probably the result of a homeoteleuton (eye slip), since the phrase "mine handmaid" occurs in several places in the source. Kingsbury's handwriting partially reflects his own idiosyncrasies rather that Clayton's, but a comparison with other writings by Kingsbury shows that he almost certainly had the Clayton manuscript before him, rather than having it read to him—something he recalls in his Temple Lot testimony five decades later (see Chapter 9).

Capitalization at this point in history was still uneven in common handwriting, with writers sometimes forming personal habits that might be nearly self-identifying. Kingsbury forms the letter S in an upper case fashion when it leads a word, but he sometimes does it even when it is the last letter in a word. Such behavior was not unusual among American longhand writers of the period. Kingsbury's school training may be evident in his use of the deprecated double s convention of writing the first s in "ss" in the old elongated form, approximated by *fs*. (Kingsbury's copy shows a reversal of this in the word "transgression.") This characteristic is not reproduced in the transcription below. Newel K. Whitney's son, Horace K. Whitney (1823–1884), made two copies of the Kingsbury manuscript, probably at Winter Quarters in 1847. Brigham Young requested the Kingsbury manuscript in March 1847, and Horace likely made copies for his father who kept a significant collection of manuscripts of Joseph Smith revelations. Copy one is faithful to the Kingsbury manuscript to the point that the "*fs*" construction is duplicated, lines end at the same word, and page content is very nearly the same (these characteristics fade somewhat toward the end of the manuscript). The second Whitney copy is less facsimile-like, and, in its present state, is missing the last paragraph of the revelation.[1]

---

1. Copy one is cataloged as MS 3497, LDS Church Library, and was docketed by Horace Whitney's son, Orson F. Whitney. Orson Whitney wrote at the top of page one, "2nd copy of original mss- this is copy of first copy- made by Horace K. Whitney from the Kingsbury mss, surrendered by Bishop Newel K. Whitney to

The transcription of Kingsbury given below is a diplomatic one. Interlinear insertions by Kingsbury himself are noted by enclosing them < like this >. Cancellations, whether by Kingsbury or later redactors (chronologically identified in notes if possible), are written ~~like this~~. Punctuation and sometimes words were added later to the Kingsbury manuscript appearing usually in a darker ink and different quill. In the transcription, these additions are indicated by enclosure in square [brackets]. At times this added punctuation merely modified Kingsbury's hand, such as a "," being replaced by a ";". The original form in this case is not noted, only the modified form in brackets. Kingsbury interrupted his copying of Clayton's manuscript after what is now verse 60. He then resumed copying with what may be a different ink and quill, possibly at a later time, though perhaps not much later. See the notes below and Chapter 9.[2]

Pres. Brigham Young at Winter Quarters. [O.F.W.]" The second Whitney copy is cataloged as MS 7876. Horace Whitney set type in the first newspaper in Salt Lake City, the *Deseret News*. Orson F. Whitney was a popular Mormon figure (and later, apostle) in early twentieth-century Utah.

2. William Clayton claimed Kingsbury's manuscript was an accurate copy on several occasions. Compare Clayton's affidavit in Chapter 1 with William Clayton, Letter to Madison M. Scott, November 11, 1871. See also Kingsbury's Supreme Court testimony noted in Chapter 9.

The Kingsbury Manuscript

revelation given to Joseph Smith,[3]

Nauvoo, July 12th, 1843.[4]

Verily thus Saith the Lord, unto you my Servant | Joseph, that inasmuch as you have enquired of my | hand to know and understand wherein I the Lord | justified my Servants[,] Abraham, Isaac and Jacob; as | also, Moses, David and Solomon[,] | my Servants[,] as touching | the principle and doctrin of their having many wives | and concubines[:] Behold,[!] and lo, I am the Lord thy God, and | will answer thee as tuching this matter[:] Therefore[,] prepare | thy heart to receive and obay the instructions which I | am about to give unto you, for all those, who have this | law revealed unto them, must obey the Same[;] for behold[!] | I reveal unto you a new and an everlasting covenant, and | if ye abide not that covenant, then are ye damned; for no | one can reject the covenant, and be permitted to enter | into my glory[;] for all who will have a blessing at my | hands, Shall abide the law which was appointed for | that blessing and the conditions thereof, as was instituted | from before the foundation of the world[::] and as pertaining | to the new and everlasting covenant, it was instituted for the | fulneSS of my glory; and he that receiveth a fulness thereof[,] | must and

---

3. Page one of the manuscript was annotated in ink by Thomas Bullock at the top left side with the words, "revelation given to Joseph Smith." Near the right side of page 1 the word "Inside" was written and circled in graphite pencil by Willard Richards. Bullock's annotation was underlined (the word "revelation" was underlined four times) in pencil and an "S" curve drawn from the end of that annotation down to the word "Nauvoo" in the first line of the manuscript. At the top of the page is the notation "No. 1" in apparently the same faded ink as the manuscript and written by Kingsbury. Richards did not copy Bullock's notation "revelation . . ." but rather an unidentified hand added this in graphite on the Richards manuscript. The present condition of the Kingsbury manuscript demonstrates considerable handling. Inked fingerprints dot the pages, possible evidence that it was used in creating an imprint.

4. Kingsbury's script could be somewhat flowery, and the "2" in "12" is easily misinterpreted as a "0." This may account for the initially incorrect date on the Richards manuscript which appears as "Nauvoo July 10th <12th> 1843." There was a double correction of the date, first by Richards or George A. Smith in graphite pencil, then the same correction but in ink by another hand, probably Bullock's.

Shall abide the law, or he Shall be damned, Saith | the Lord God. [¶][5] And verily I Say unto you, that the conditi= | =ons of this law are these[:] all covenants, contracts, bonds, obliga= | =tions, oaths, vows, performances[,] connexions[,] associations or | expectations, that are not made and enter'd into and Sealed | by the Holy Spirit of promise of him who is anointed | both as well for time and for all eternity[,] and that too | most holy[;] by Revelation and commandment[,] through the | medium of mine anointed whom I have appointed on | the earth to hold this power[,] (and I have appointed unto | my Servant Joseph to hold this power in the last days[,] | and there is never but one on the earth at a time on whom | this power and the Keys of this priesthood is confered) are of no | efficacy, virtue or force[,] in and after the resurrection from the | dead[;] for all contracts that are not made unto this end, have an | end when men are dead. [¶] Behold[!] mine house is a house of [6] | order[,] Saith the Lord God, and not a house of confusion. | Will I accept of an offering, Saith the Lord[,] that is not made | in my name[?] or[,] will I receive at your hands, that which | I have not appointed[?] and will I appoint unto you[,] Saith | the Lord, except it be by law, even as I and my Father | ordained unto you, before the world was[?] I am the Lord thy | God[,] and I Give unto you this commandment[,] that no man | Shall come unto the Father but by me[,] or by my word, | which is my law[,] Saith the Lord[:] and every thing that | is in the world, whether it be ordained of men[,] by thrones, | or principalities[,] or powers[,] or things of name whatsoever | they may be that are not by me or by my word[,] Saith the | Lord, Shall be thrown down, and Shall not remain after | men are dead, neither in nor after the resurrection, | Saith the Lord your God: For whatsoever things remaineth | are by me; and whatsoever things are not by me, Shall be | shaken and destroyed. [¶] Therefore[,] if a man marry him a wife, | in the world, and he marry her not by me, nor by <my> word; and | he covenant with her So long as he is in the world, and She | with him, their covenant and marriage is not of force when | they are dead, and when they are out of the world[;] therefore[,] | they are not bound by any law when they are out of the | world[;] therefore, when they are out of the world, they neither | marry nor are given in marriage, but are appointed angels | in heaven, which angels are ministering Servants[7] to minister | for those, who are worthy

---

5. Pilcrows, or paragraph markings, were inserted to show typesetters where to break the text. Unless otherwise noted, similar marks below are dated to ca. 1852.

6. Page one of the Kingsbury manuscript ends here.

7. The text of the Richards manuscript originally read "ministering spirits."

of a far more[,] and an exceding[,] and | an eternal weight of Glory; for these angels did not abide | my law, therefore they cannot be enlarged, but remain | separately and singly without exaltation in their Saved condition | to all eternity[,] and from henceforth are not Gods, but are | angels of God for ever and ever.

And again, verily I Say unto you if a man marry a wife[,] | and make a covenant with her for time and for all Eternity, if | that covenant is not by me[,] or by my word[,] which is my law[,] | and is not Sealed by the Holy Spirit of promise, through him | whom I have anointed and appointed unto this power[,] then it | is not valid, neither of force when they are out of the world[,][8] | because they are not joined by me, Saith the Lord, neither | by my word[,] when they are out of the world[,] it cannot | be received ~~their~~ [there,] because the angels and the Gods are appointed | there, by whom they cannot pass, they cannot[,] therefore[,] | inherit my glory[,] for my house is a house of order Saith the | Lord God. [¶] And again[,] verily I say unto you, if a man marry | a wife by my word[,] which is my law, and by the new and | everlasting covenant[,] and it is Sealed unto them by the Holy Spirit | of promise[,] by him who is anointed[,] unto whom I have | appointed this power[,] and the keys of this priesthood[,] and it | Shall be Said unto them ye Shall come forth in the first resurrection[;] | and if it be after the first resurrection[,] in the next resurrection[,] | and Shall inherit thrones[,] Kingdoms[,] principalites[,] and powers[,] | dominions[,] all heighth[s][9] and depths[,] then Shall it be written in the | Lambs book of life[,] that he Shall commit no murder[,] whereby | to shed innocent blood[;] and if ye abide in my Covenant[10] and commit | no murder whereby to Shed innocent blood[,] it shall be done unto | them in all things whatsoever my servant hath put upon them, | in time and through all Eternity[;] and Shall be of full force | when they are out of the world[,] and they shall pass by the angels | and the Gods which are Set there, to their exaltation and glory in | all things[,] as hath been Sealed upon their heads[,] which glory | Shall be a fullness and a continuation of the Seeds for ever and | ever. [¶] Then Shall they be Gods, because they have no End. | Therefore[11] Shall they be from everlasting to everlasting[,] because | they continue[,] Then Shall they be above all[,] because all things

---

8. Page 2 of the Kingsbury manuscript ends here.
9. Comma scrape erased.
10. Comma wipe erased.
11. Comma wipe erased.

| are subject unto them. Then Shall they be Gods because | they have all power[,] and the angels are Subject unto them. | [¶] Verily, verily[,][12] I say unto you[,] except ye abide my Law[,] ye | cannot attain to this glory[,] for Strait is the Gate[,] and narrow | the way, that leadeth unto the exaltation and continuation of | the lives[,] and few there be that find it[,] because ye | receive me not in the world[,] neither do ye know me. But | if ye Receive me in the world, then ~~Shalt~~ [Shall] ye know me, and | Shall receive your exaltation, that where I am, ye Shall be also. | This is Eternal lives[,][13] to <know> the only wise and true God, and Jesus | Christ whom he hath Sent[.] I am ~~he~~ [He]. Receive ye[,] therefore[,] my[14] | law. Broad is the gate, and wide the way that leadeth | to the deaths[,] and many there are that go in thereat[,] | because they receive me not, neither do they abide my law; — | [¶] Verily[,] verily I Say unto you, if <a> man marry a wife according | to my word, and they are Sealed by the Holy Spirit of promise[15] | according to mine appointment, and he or She Shall commit | any Sin or transgression of the new and everlasting covenant | whatever[,] and all manner of blasphemies[,] and if they commit | no murder wherein they Shed innocent blood, yet they Shall come | forth in the first resurrection[,] and enter into their—exaltation[;] but | they Shall be destroyed in ~~in~~ the flesh[,] and Shall be deliverd unto | the buffetin[gs] of Satan unto the day of redemption[,] Saith the | Lord God. [¶] The blasphemy against the Holy Ghost, which Shall | not be forgiven in the world[,] nor out of the world, is in that ye | commit murder, wherein ye Shed innocent blood[,] and assent | unto my death, after ye have received my new and Everlasting | covenant[,] saith the Lord God[;] and he that abideth not this law[,] | can in nowise enter into my glory[,] but Shall be damned[,] Saith | the Lord[.] [¶] I am the Lord thy God, and will give unto thee the | Law of my Holy priesthood[,] as was ordained by me and my Father | before the world was, Abraham ~~receiveth~~ [received] all things, whatsoever he | received[,] by Revelation and Commandment[,] by my word[,] Saith the | Lord[,] and hath entered ~~in to~~ [into] his exaltation[,] and Setteth upon his | throne. [¶] Abraham received promises concerning his Seed, and of the | fruit of his loins[,] from whose loins ye are[,] viz; my Servant | Joseph[,] which were to continue So long as they were in the | world; and as touching

---

12. Comma scrape erased and then reinserted.

13. Richards originally wrote "life" here in his manuscript instead of "lives." A penciled correction was made by a redactor.

14. Page 3 of the Kingsbury manuscript ends here.

15. Punctuation scrape erased here.

Abraham and his Seed out of the | world[,] they Should continue[,] both in the world and out of | the world should they continue as innumerable as the Stars[;] | or if ye ware to count the Sand upon the Sea Shore[,] ye could | not number them. This promis[e] is yours also[,] because ye are | of Abraham, and the promise was made unto Abraham[,] | and by this law are the continuation of the works of my | Father where in he gloryfieth himself. Go ye[,] therefore[,] | and do the works of Abraham[;] enter ye into my law[,] and ye | shall be Saved, But if ye enter not into my law[,] ye cannot | receive the promises of my Father[;] which he made unto[16] | Abraham[.][¶] God commanded Abraham, and Sarah gave Hagar | to Abraham to wife, and why did she do it? Because this | was the law, and from Hagar Sprang many people.[17] This Therefore[,] was fulfilling among other things, the promises. | Was Abraham[,] therefore[,] under condemnation? Verily[,] I Say unto | you[,] ~~nay~~ [Nay,] for I the Lorde commanded it. Abraham was commanded | to offer his son Isaac; nevertheless[,] it was written thou Shalt not | kill[;] Abraham however[,] did not refuse[,] and it was accounted unto | him for righteousness[.][¶] Abraham received concubines[,] and they bare | him children, and it was accounted unto him for righteousness[,] | because they ware Given unto him, and he abode in my law[:] | as Isaac also[,] and Jacob did none other things[18] than that which they | were commanded[;] and because they did none other things than that | which they were commanded[,] they have enterd into ~~there~~ [their] exalta= | =tion according to the promises, and Sit upon thrones; and are not | angels[,] but are Gods[.] David also ~~receiveth~~ [received] many wives and | concubines[,] ~~and~~ [as] also Solomon[,] and Moses my Servant[;] as also | many others of my Servants from the beginning of creation | untill this time[;] and in nothing did they Sin[,] Save in those | things which they received not of me[.][¶] David[s] wives and | Concubines were given unto him[,] of me[,] by the hand of Nathan | my servant[,] and others of the prophets who had the Keys of this | power[;] and in none of these things did he Sin against me[,] | save in the case of Uriah and his wife[,] and[,] therefore[,] he hath | fallen from his exaltation[,] and received his portion[;] and he Shall | not inherit them out of the world[;] for I gave them unto | another[,] Saith the Lord[.][¶] I am the Lord, thy God[,] and I Gave | unto thee[,] my Servant Joseph[,] an ap-

---

16. Page 4 of the Kingsbury manuscript (and hence the first sheet) ends here.

17. Kingsbury may have sharpened or changed his quill here, but the ink source appears to be unchanged.

18. Comma scrape erased.

pointment[,] and restore all | things[;] ask what ye will and it Shall be given unto you[,] | according to my word[;] and as ye have asked concerning adultery[,] | Verily[,] verily I Say unto you[,] if a man receiveth a wife in the | new and Everlasting covenant[,] and if She be with another man[,] | and I have not appointed unto her by the holy anointing, She | hath committed adultery[,] and Shall be destroyed. If She be not | in the new and Everlasting covenant[,] and She be with another | <man>[,] she has committed adultery; and if her husband be with another | woman[,] and was under a vow, he hath broken his vow[,] and[19] | hath committed adultery[;] and if she hath not committed adultery[,] | but <is> is innocent[,] and hath not broken her vow[,] and She knoweth | it[,] and I reveal in unto you[,] my servant Joseph[,] then Shall | you have power by the power of my Holy Priesthood to | take her[,] and give her unto him that hath not committed | adultery[,] but hath been faithful[;] for he Shall be made | ruler over many[;] for I have conferred upon you the keys | and power of the priesthood[,] wherein I restore all things[,] | and make known unto you all things in due time[.]

[¶] And Verily[,] verily I say unto you, ~~as~~ [that] whatsoever you Seal | on Earth shall[20] be sealed in heaven, and whatsoever | you bind on earth in my name[,] and by my word[,] Saith the | Lord[,] it Shall be eternally bound in the heavens; and | ~~whos<o>ever~~ whosesoever Sins you remit on earth[,] Shall be remitted | eternally in the heavens[;] and whosesoever Sins you retain on earth[,] Shall be retained in heaven. ———

And again[,] verily I say, whomsoever you bless[,] I will | bless[;] and whomsoever you curse[,] I will curse[,] Saith the | Lord, for I the Lord am thy God.

[¶] And again[,] verily I Say unto you[,] my servant Joseph[,] that | whatsoever you give on earth[,] and to whomsoever you give | any one on earth[,] by my word[,] and according to my law, it | Shall be visited with blessings[,] and not cursings[,] and with | my power saith the Lord, and shall be without condemna= | =tion on earth and in heaven; for I am the Lord thy God[,] | and will be with thee even unto the end of the world, and | through all Eternity. For Verily[,] I seal upon you[,] your | exaltation[,] and prepare a throne for you in the Kingdom of | my Father[,] with Abraham your Father. Behold[,] I have | seen your sacrifices[,] and will forgive all your Sins[;] I | have seen your sacrifices in obedience to that

---

19. Page 5 of the Kingsbury manuscript ends here.
20. The word "shall" may modify another undecipherable word.

which I | have told you[:] Go[,] therefore[,] and I make a way for your | escape[,] as I accepted the offering of Abraham[,] of his | son Isaac. [¶] Verily I say unto you[,] a commandment I | give unto mine handmaid[,] Emma Smith[,] your wife[,] whom | I have given unto you, that she stay herself and partake | not of that which I commanded you to offer unto her[21] | For I did it[,] saith the Lord[,] to prove you all[,] as I did | Abraham[;] and that I might require an offering at your hand | by covenant and sacrifice[:] and let mine handmaid[,] Emma | Smith[,] receive all those that have been given unto my | servant Joseph, and who are virtuous and pure before me; | and those who are not pure[,] <and have Said they ware pure[,]> shall be destroyed[,] saith the Lord | God. For I am the Lord thy God[;] and ye shall obey my | voice; and I give unto my Servant Joseph[,] that he | Shall be made ruler over many things[,] for he hath | been faithfull over a few things, and from hencefo= | =rth I will strengthen him[.][¶] and I command mine hand= | =maid[,] Emma Smith[,] to abide and cleave unto my Servant | Joseph; and to none else; But if she will not abide this | commandment[,] she shall be destroyed[,] saith the Lord[;] | for I am the Lord they God, and will distroy her[,] if she abide | not in my law; but if she will not abide this comma= | =ndment, then Shall my servant[,] Joseph[,] do all things for her[,] | even as he had Said, and I will bless him[,] and multiply him[,] | and give unto him an hundred fold in this world[,] of ~~fath=~~ | ~~=ers, and~~ fathers and mothers[,] brothers and Sisters[,] houses and lands[,] | wives and children, and crowns of eternal ~~lifeS~~ [lives] in the | eternal worlds. And again[,] verily I say[,] ~~unto you~~ let | mine handmaid forgive my Servant Joseph his trespases[,] | and then[22] Shall She be forgiven her trespasses[,] wherein | she hath ~~trespased~~ trespaseth against me[,] and I the Lord thy God | will bless her[,] and multiply her, and make her heart to | rejoice. [¶] and again I Say let not my Servant Joseph | put his property out of his hands[,] list an enemy come | and distroy him[,] for Satan seeketh to distroy[;] For I am | the Lord thy God, and he is my servant[;] and behold[!] and lo, | I am with him as I was with Abraham[,] thy Father, | even unto his exaltation and glory. [¶] Now as tuching the | law of the priesthood[,] there are many things perta<n>ing | thereunto. Verily[,] if a man be called of my Father[,] as was | aaron[,] by mine own Voice[,] and by the voice of him | that Sent me, and I have endowed him with the Keys of the | power of this priesthood[,] if he do any thing in my name[,][23] | and

---

21. Page 6 of the Kingsbury manuscript ends here.
22. The word "then" overwrites another partially composed word.
23. Page 7 of the Kingsbury manuscript ends here.

according to my law[,] and by my word[,] he will | not commit sin[,] and I will justify him. Let no one[,] | therefore[,] set on my servant Joseph[,] for I will justify | him[,] for he shall do the sacrifices which I require | at his hands, for his transgressions[,] Saith the Lord[,] your | God. [¶] &[24] again, as pertaining to the Law of the priesthood[;-] if any man espouse a | Virgin, & desire to espouse another[,] & the first give her consent[;] & if he espouse espouse the second, | & they are virgins[,] & have vowed to no other man, then is he justified[;] he cannot commit | adultery[,] for they are given unto him[;] for he cannot commit adultery with that, that | belongeth unto him[,] & to none else[;] & if he have ten virgins given <unto> him by ~~this~~ this | Law, he cannot commit adultery[,] for they belong to him, & they are given unto him[,] | therefore <is he justfied.> But if one[,] or either of the ten virgins, after She is espoused[,] Shall be with |

---

24. Kingsbury switches to a different quill or modifies his quill, making the script thinner. The ink appears darker here, suggesting a change of venue. The ink does not appear to be the same as that used for redactions in the earlier portion of the manuscript. Indeed, the writing with the new quill must predate the folding the manuscript underwent for storage. The new quill and ink effort faded due to friction along the fold. Redaction marks are fresh in this folded area and appear in the same ink as those in the rest of the manuscript. Hence, Kingsbury may have shifted to a different ink and pen, but this happened prior to any editing of the manuscript for publication.

In the rest of the manuscript, Kingsbury shifts to using ampersands for "and," a practice he avoids in the earlier text. This suggests either that he is hurrying to complete the copying, or that the writing in this final section took place at a later date. Perhaps this portion of the revelation was a later addition by Smith (or much less likely, someone else). However, since this portion contains the "ten virgins" language, and this reference is attested in documents from the Nauvoo era during Smith's lifetime, it is unlikely that this language was dictated by any other person than Joseph Smith. The content of this portion of Kingsbury seems to be known in Nauvoo, prior to Joseph Smith's death. See Sarah Scott, Letter to Abigale and Calvin Hall, June 16, 1844, in George F. Partridge, "The Death of a Mormon Dictator, Letters of Massachusetts Mormons, 1843–1848," *The New England Quarterly* 9, no. 12 (1936): 594.

The last section demonstrates another characteristic that suggests it may have been written at least somewhat later than the preceding text. As Kingsbury wrote, his handwriting indicates some increase in fatigue with some letters becoming contracted. In particular, Kingsbury tended to make nearly every "S" in upper case form. As he continued writing, the S contracts to what appears as a lower case letter. In the last section, this process is reversed and the style appears like that of the beginning of the manuscript.

another man[,] She has committed adultery[,] & Shall be distroyed[;] for they are given unto | him to multiply & replenish the Earth[,] according to my commandment[,] & to fulfill the | promise which was given by my father before the foundation of the world[,] & for thine | exaltation in the eternal worlds[,] that they may ~~have~~ [bear] the Souls of men, for herein is | the work of my father continued[,] that he may be Glorified- [¶] And again[,] verily, verily I | Say unto you[,] if any man have a wife who holds the keys of this power[,] & he teaches | unto her the law of my priest-hood as pertaining to these things[,] then Shall She believe | & administer unto him[,] or She Shall be distroyed[,] Saith the Lord your God[;] for I will | distroy her[;] for I will magnify my name[,] upon all those who receive & abide in | my law. Therefore[,] it Shall be lawful in me[,] if She receive not this law[,] for | him to receive all things[,] whatsoever. I the lord[,] his God[,] will give unto him, | because She did not believe & administer unto him according to my word[;] & | She then becomes the transgresser[,] & he is exempt from the law of Sarah[,] who | administered unto Abraham according to the law, when I commanded Abraham | to take Hagar to wife. ~~&~~ [And] now[,] as pertaing to this law[,] verily, verily I Say unto | you, I will reveal more unto you hereafter[;] therefore[,] let this suffice for | the present. Behold[,] I am Alpha & Omega:- <u>Amen</u>.[25]

Notes on Horace K. Whitney Manuscripts of the Plural Marriage Revelation

Prior to giving up the Kingsbury manuscript, Newell K. Whitney's son Horace K. Whitney produced a near facsimile. The manuscript is cataloged as MS 3497 LDS Church Library. The manuscript is written on two bifolia consisting of cream sheets. The sheets measure 12.5 x 16 inches. Each sheet is folded in half to give eight pages in total, each measuring 12.5 x 8 inches. Handwriting is that of Horace K. Whitney and appears to be based on the Kingsbury manuscript, MS 4583, LDS Church Library. Whitney copies MS 4583 very closely, even following Kingsbury's letterforms (such as making upper case a-frame **A** after Kingsbury, rather than Whitney's apparent normal form, *a*). However, Whitney does not slavishly follow Kingsbury's capitalization patterns.

---

25. Below the manuscript text of the last page, the letters WR appear in a large flowing script, probably Willard Richards's.

A second Horace Whitney manuscript is cataloged as MS 7876 LDS Church Library. Written on three bifolia, it is probably based on MS 3497 though a later note suggests it is based on MS 4583. The first and third leaves are blue tint, 9 ¾ x 7 ¾ inches; the second leaf is cream and measures 15 ¾ x 12 ½ unfolded. Folded, it measures 12 ½ x 7 7/8 inches. The first bifold, page 1, has an oval watermark bearing the signature D & J Ames Springfield. Thus the first sheet and almost certainly the third are products of the Ames paper company in Springfield, Massachusetts.[26] The extant manuscript is incomplete, ending in the middle of verse 54. MS 7876 has no paragraphing, and punctuation does not match either the original or redacted settings of MS 4583 (Kingsbury).

---

26. On the Ames brothers, see *The Annual Report of the Library Company of Philadelphia for the Year 2004* (Philadelphia, 2004), 70–71.

Bibliography

1991 Supplement to the 1989 General Handbook of Instructions. Salt Lake City: Church of Jesus Christ of Latter-day Saints, 1991.

"6th Letter from Gen. Bennett." *Sangamo Journal* 10, no. 52 (August 19, 1842): 2.

40 Affidavits on Celestial Marriage, Book number 1, 1869, MS 3423, box 1, fd. 44. LDS Church History Library.

"A Special Conference of the Elders of the Church of Jesus Christ of Latter-Day Saints." *Deseret News—Extra* (September 14, 1852): 1–48.

Aird, Polly. *Mormon Convert, Mormon Defector: A Scottish Immigrant in the American West, 1848–1861.* Norman, OK: University of Oklahoma Press, 2009.

Alexander, Thomas G. *Mormonism in Transition: A History of the Latter-day Saints, 1890–1930.* 3rd ed. Salt Lake City: Greg Kofford Books, 2012.

Allen, James B. "William Clayton and the Records of Church History." In *Preserving the History of the Latter-day Saints,* edited by Richard E. Turley Jr. and Steven C. Harper, 83–114. Provo, UT: Religious Studies Center, 2010.

Allen, James B., and George D. Smith. "Editing William Clayton and the Politics of Mormon History." *Dialogue: A Journal of Mormon Thought* 30, no. 2 (Summer 1997): 129–56.

Allred, James. "Statement." October 15, 1854. CR 100 396, Box 1, fd. 58. LDS Church History Library.

Anderson, Devery S., ed. *The Development of LDS Temple Worship, 1846–2000: A Documentary History.* Salt Lake City: Signature Books, 2011.

Anderson, Elizabeth O., ed. *Cowboy Apostle: The Diaries of Anthony W. Ivins.* Salt Lake City: Signature Books, 2013.

Anderson, Lavina Fielding, ed. *Lucy's Book: A Critical Edition of Lucy Mack Smith's Family Memoir.* Salt Lake City: Signature Books, 2001.

Arrington, Leonard J. "The Settlement of the Brigham Young Estate, 1877–1879." *Pacific Historical Review* 21, no. 1 (Feb. 1952): 1–20.

Ashurst-McGee, Mark. "A Pathway to Prophethood: Joseph Smith as Rodsman, Village Seer, and Judeo-Christian Prophet." MA thesis, Utah State University, 2000.

———. "Zion Rising: Joseph Smith's Early Social and Political Thought." PhD diss., Arizona State University, 2008.

Avery, Valeen Tippetts. *From Mission to Madness: Last Son of the Mormon Prophet.* Chicago: University of Illinois Press, 1998.

Avery, Valeen Tippetts, and Linda King Newell. "The Lion and the Lady: Brigham

Young and Emma Smith." *Utah Historical Quarterly* 48, no. 1 (Winter 1980): 81–97.

Bachman, Danel W. "The Authorship of the Manuscript of Doctrine and Covenants Section 132." In *Eighth Annual Sidney B. Sperry Symposium Brigham Young University*, 27–44. Provo, UT: BYU Press, 1980.

———. "New Light on an Old Hypothesis: The Ohio Origins of the Revelation on Eternal Marriage." *Journal of Mormon History* 5 (1978): 19–32.

Baden, Joel. *The Historical David: The Real Life of an Invented Hero.* New York: HarperCollins Publishers, 2013.

Baggette, S. Patrick, II. "The Temple Lot Case: Fraud in God's Vineyard." *John Whitmer Historical Association Journal* 23 (2003): 121–36.

Baker, Sherry. "Creating a Shared History: Serial Narratives in *Young Woman's Journal*, 1880–1894." MA thesis, University of Utah, Salt Lake City, 1988.

Baldwin, Nathan. "Testimony of an Old Latter-Day Saint." *Deseret News* 34, no. 6 (February 25, 1885): 15.

Ballantyne, Richard. Journal 1848 May–August, MS 7151, LDS Church History Library.

Ballard, M. Russell. "A Chance to Start Over: Church Disciplinary Councils and the Restoration of Blessings." *Ensign*, September 1990, https://www.lds.org/ensign/1990/09/a-chance-to-start-over-church-disciplinary-councils-and-the-restoration-of-blessings.

———. "Return and Receive." *Ensign*, May 2017, https://www.lds.org/ensign/2017/05/saturday-afternoon-session/return-and-receive.

Bancroft, Hubert H. *History of Utah, 1540–1886.* San Francisco: The History Company, 1889.

Barlow, Philip L. "The BYU New Testament Commentary: 'It Doth Not Yet Appear What It Shall Be.'" *Studies in the Bible and Antiquity* 6 (2014): 67–86.

———. *Mormons and the Bible: The Place of Latter-day Saints in American Religion.* 2nd ed. New York: Oxford University Press, 2013.

Bates, Irene M. "William Smith, 1811–93: Problematic Patriarch." *Dialogue: A Journal of Mormon Thought* 16, no. 2 (Summer 1983): 11–23.

Battis, Emery. *Saints and Sectaries: Anne Hutchinson and the Antinomian Controversy in the Massachusetts Bay Colony.* Chapel Hill, NC: University of North Carolina Press, 2011.

Baugh, Alexander L., and Richard Neitzel Holzapfel. "'I Roll the Burthen and Responsibility of Leading This Church Off from My Shoulders on to Yours': The 1844/1845 Declaration of the Quorum of the Twelve Regarding Apostolic Succession." *BYU Studies* 49, no. 3 (2010): 4–19.

Bennett, John C. *Sangamo Journal.* (1842): 1.

Benson, Ezra Taft. "Fourteen Fundamentals in Following the Prophet." *Liahona*, June 1981, https://www.lds.org/liahona/1981/06/fourteen-fundamentals-in-following-the-prophet.

Bergera, Gary James. *Conflict in the Quorum: Orson Pratt, Brigham Young, Joseph Smith.* Salt Lake City: Signature Books, 2002.

————. "The Earliest Sealings for Civilly Married Couples Living and Dead." *Dialogue: A Journal of Mormon Thought* 35, no. 3 (Fall 2002): 49–74.

————. "Identifying the Earliest Mormon Polygamists 1841–44." *Dialogue: A Journal of Mormon Thought* 38, no. 3 (Fall 2005): 1–74.

Betzig, L. L. "Despotism and Differential Reproduction: A Cross-Cultural Correlation of Conflict Asymmetry, Hierarchy, and Degree of Polygyny." *Ethnology and Sociobiology* 3 (1982): 209–221.

Bishop, M. Guy. "Eternal Marriage in Early Mormon Marital Beliefs." *Historian* 53, no. 1 (1990): 77–88.

"Bishops' Blessing Meeting." Historian's Office General Church Minutes, 1839–1877, Salt Lake City, 1850 January 6, CR 100 318, Box 2, fd. 26, LDS Church History Library.

"Blessing to Sarah Ann Whitney, 23 March 1843." Joseph Smith Papers. Accessed December 15, 2017. http://www.josephsmithpapers.org/paper-summary/blessing-to-sarah-ann-whitney-23-march-1843/1.

Blythe, Christine Elyse. "William Smith's Patriarchal Blessings and Contested Authority in the Post-Martyrdom Church." *Journal of Mormon History* 39, no. 3 (Summer 2013): 60–95.

Blythe, Christopher James. "The Church and Kingdom of God: Ecclesiastical Interpretations of the Council of Fifty." *Journal of Mormon History* 43, no. 2 (2017): 100–130.

"Book of Abraham Manuscript, circa July–circa November 1835–C [Abraham 1:1–2:18]." Joseph Smith Papers. Accessed December 12, 2017. http://www.josephsmithpapers.org/paper-summary/book-of-abraham-manuscript-circa-july-circa-november-1835-c-abraham-11-218.

Booth, Ezra. "Mormonism—Nos. VIII–IX." *Ohio Star* 2, no. 49 (December 8, 1831): 1.

Bowles, Samuel. *Across the Continent: A Summer's Journey to the Rocky Mountains, the Mormons, and the Pacific States, with Speaker Colfax.* New York: Hurd and Houghton, 1865.

Bowman, Matthew. *The Mormon People: The Making of an American Faith.* New York: Random House Trade Paperbacks, 2012.

Bradley, Don. "Mormon Polygamy Before Nauvoo? The Relationship of Joseph Smith and Fanny Alger." In *The Persistence of Polygamy: Joseph Smith and the Origins of Mormon Polygamy*, edited by Newell G. Bringhurst and Craig L. Foster, 14–58. Independence: John Whitmer Books, 2010:

Bressler, Ann Lee. *The Universalist Movement in America, 1770–1880.* New York: Oxford University Press, 2001.

Briney, Drew. *Silencing Mormon Polygamy: Failed Persecutions, Divided Saints and the Rise of Mormon Fundamentalism.* N.p.: Hindsight Publications, 2008.

Bringhurst, Newell G. "RLDS Church Reaction to the LDS Doctrine and Covenants' Section 132: Conflicting Responses and Changing Perceptions." In *The Persistence of Polygamy: Joseph Smith and the Origins of Mormon Polygamy*, edited by Newel G. Bringhurst and Craig L. Foster. 257–83. Independence: John Whitmer Books, 2010.

————. "Section 132 of the Doctrine and Covenants: Its Complex Contents and

Controversial Legacy." In *The Persistence of Polygamy: Joseph Smith and the Origins of Mormon Polygamy*, edited by Newel G. Bringhurst and Craig L. Foster. 59–86. Independence: John Whitmer Books, 2010.

Bringhurst, Newell G., and Craig L. Foster, *The Mormon Quest for the Presidency.* Lamoni, IA: John Whitmer Books, 2008.

Brooks, Juanita, ed. *On the Mormon Frontier: The Diary of Hosea Stout, 1844–1861.* 2 vols. Salt Lake City: University of Utah Press—Utah State Historical Society, 1964.

Brotherton, Martha H. "St. Louis, July 13th, A. D. 1842." *American Bulletin* (St. Louis) 1, no. 145 (July 16, 1842): 1.

Brotherton, Elizabeth. "Autobiography of Elizabeth B. Pratt." *Woman's Exponent* 19, no. 12 (1890): 94–95.

Brown, Barbara Jones. "The Rise and Demise of Latter-day Saint Polygamy in Mexico." In *Just South of Zion: The Mormons in Mexico and Its Borderlands*, edited by Jason Dormady and Jared Tamez. Albuquerque: University of New Mexico Press, 2015.

———. "The 'Second Manifesto,' the Mexican Revolution, and the Demise of Post-Manifesto Polygamy." Paper presented at the Mormon History Association Conference, San Antonio, Texas, June 2014.

Brown, Lisle G. *Nauvoo Sealings, Adoptions, and Anointings.* Salt Lake City: Smith-Pettit Foundation, 2006.

———. "'Temple Pro Tempore': The Salt Lake City Endowment House." *Journal of Mormon History* 34, no. 4 (2008): 1–68.

Brown, Samuel M. "Believing Adoption." *BYU Studies Quarterly* 52, no. 2 (2013): 45–65.

———. "Early Mormon Adoption Theology and the Mechanics of Salvation." *Journal of Mormon History* 37, no. 2 (Summer 2011): 3–52.

———. *In Heaven as It Is on Earth: Joseph Smith and the Early Mormon Conquest of Death.* New York: Oxford University Press, 2012.

———. "The Prophet Elias Puzzle." *Dialogue: A Journal of Mormon Thought* 39, no. 3 (Fall 2006): 1–17.

———. "The Translator and the Ghostwriter: Joseph Smith and William Phelps." *Journal of Mormon* History 34, no. 1 (Winter 2008): 26–62.

Buck, Charles. *A Theological Dictionary Containing Definitions of All Religious Terms.* University of Michigan Library, 2009.

Buerger, David John. "The Adam-God Doctrine." *Dialogue: A Journal of Mormon Thought* 15, no. 1 (Spring 1982): 14–58.

———. "The Development of the Mormon Temple Endowment Ceremony." *Dialogue: A Journal of Mormon Thought* 20, no. 4 (Winter 1987): 33–76.

———. "'The Fulness of the Priesthood': The Second Anointing in Latter-day Saint Theology and Practice." *Dialogue: A Journal of Mormon Thought* 16, no. 1 (Spring 1983): 10–44.

———. *The Mysteries of Godliness: A History of Mormon Temple Worship.* Salt Lake City: Signature Books, 2002.

———. "Salvation in the Theology of Joseph Smith." In *Line Upon Line: Essays on*

Mormon Doctrine, edited by Gary James Bergera. Salt Lake City: Signature Books, 1989.

Bulkley, Newman. Autobiography, MS 18706, LDS Church History Library.

Bullock, Thomas. Booklet (#10), 1850 December 29–1851 March 9. Historian's Office General Church Minutes 1839–1877, CR 100 318, box 2, fd. 26, LDS Church History Library.

———. Minutes. Historian's Office General Church Minutes, 1839–1877, CR 100 318, box 1, fd. 20, LDS Church History Library.

Burgess, James. Journal MS 1858, LDS Church History Library.

Bush Jr., Lester E. "Excommunication and Church Courts: A Note from the *General Handbook of Instructions*." *Dialogue: A Journal of Mormon Thought* 14, no. 2 (Summer 1981): 74–98.

Bushman, Richard Lyman. *Joseph Smith: Rough Stone Rolling.* New York: Alfred A. Knopf, 2005.

Cahn, Naomi R. "Faithless Wives and Lazy Husbands: Gender Norms in Nineteenth-Century Divorce Law." *University of Illinois Law Review* (2002). Available online at http://scholarship.law.gwu.edu/cgi/viewcontent.cgi?article=1371 &context=faculty_publications, accessed December 15, 2017.

Campbell, Barth. "Flesh and Spirit in 1 Cor 5:5: An Exercise in Rhetorical Criticism of the NT." *Journal of the Evangelical Theological Society* 36, no. 3 (September 1993): 331–42.

Campbell, Eugene E. and Bruce L. Campbell. "Divorce among Mormon Polygamists: Extent and Explanations." *Utah Historical Quarterly* 46, no. 1 (Winter 1978): 4–23.

Cannon, Abraham H. Journal. L. Tom Perry Special Collections and Manuscripts, Brigham Young University, Provo, Utah.

Cannon, George Q. "Enduring to the End." *Collected Discourses* 2 (October 5, 1890): 115–16.

———. *The Journal of George Q. Cannon.* Salt Lake City: Church Historian's Press, 2016. https://www.churchhistorianspress.org/george-q-cannon.

Carvalho, S. N. *Incidents of Travel and Adventure in the Far West with Col. Fremont's Last Expedition Across the Rocky Mountains: Including Three Months' Residence in Utah, and a Perilous Trip Across the Great American Desert, to the Pacific.* New York: Derby & Jackson, 1857.

Church Historian's Office General Church Minutes, CR 100 318, Box 3, fd. 3. LDS Church History Library.

Church Historian's Office Journal. CR 100 1. LDS Church History Library.

Clark, J. Reuben. *On the Way to Immortality and Eternal Life.* Salt Lake City: Deseret Book, 1950.

Clark, James R., ed. *Messages of the First Presidency of the Church of Jesus Christ of Latterday Saints,* 6 vols. Salt Lake City: Bookcraft, 1965–75.

Clayton, William. Affidavit, February 16, 1874. MS 3423, box 1, fd. 6. LDS Church History Library.

———. Letter to Madison M. Scott, November 11, 1871. MS 4681, fd. 1. LDS Church History Library.

Compton, Todd M. *In Sacred Loneliness: The Plural Wives of Joseph Smith.* Salt Lake City: Signature Books, 1997.

The Conference Minutes and Record Book of Christ's Church of Latter Day Saints, 1838–1839, 1844. CR 100 403, LDS Church History Library.

Conference Report. (Report of the Semi-Annual Conference of the Church of Jesus Christ of Latter-day Saints.) Salt Lake City: Church of Jesus Christ of Latter-day Saints, semiannual.

Cook, Lyndon W., ed. *Nauvoo Marriages: Proxy Sealings 1843–1846.* Provo, UT: Grandin, 2004.

———. *The Revelations of the Prophet Joseph Smith: A Historical and Biographical Commentary of the Doctrine and Covenants.* Salt Lake City: Deseret Book, 1985.

———. *William Law.* Orem, UT: Grandin, 1994.

———. "William Law, Nauvoo Dissenter." *BYU Studies* 22, no. 1 (1982): 47–72.

Coray, Howard. "Autobiography." L. Tom Perry Special Collections and Manuscripts Library, Brigham Young University, Provo, UT.

———. Letter to Martha Lewis, August 2, 1889, holograph, MS 3047, LDS Church History Library.

Costa, M. D. et. al. "A Substantial Prehistoric European Ancestry Amongst Ashkenazi Maternal Lineages." *Nature Communications* 4 (October 2013).

"Council of the Twelve Meeting Minutes." Linda King Newel papers, MS 447, Box 18, fd. 12, Special Collections, Mariott Library, University of Utah.

Cowdery, Oliver. "Address." *Latter Day Saints' Messenger and Advocate* 1, no. 1. (October 1834): 1–2.

———. "Dear Brother." *Latter Day Saints' Messenger and Advocate* 1 (October 1834): 14–16.

———. Letter to Brigham Young, February 27, 1848. Brigham Young office files, CR 1234 1, Box 39, fd. 11, LDS Church History Library.

Cradlebaugh, John. *Mormonism: A Doctrine That Embraces Polygamy, Adultery, Incest, Perjury, Robbery and Murder.* Salt Lake City: n.p., 1877.

Crawley, Peter. *A Descriptive Bibliography of the Mormon Church*, 3 vols. Provo, UT: Religious Studies Center, 1997–2012.

Daynes, Kathryn M. "Breaking the Seal: Analysis of Cancellations of Sealing by Brigham Young." Mormon History Association Conference. May 26–29, 2005.

———. *More Wives Than One: Transformation of the Mormon Marriage System, 1840–1910.* Urbana, IL: University of Illinois Press, 2008.

———. "Striving to Live the Principle in Utah's First Temple City: A Snapshot of Polygamy in St. George, Utah, in June 1880." *BYU Studies Quarterly* 51, no. 4 (2012): 69–95.

"Death at 105 Draws Curtain on Cursed Town." *Chicago Daily Tribune*, November 1, 1949, 17.

Derr, Jill Mulvay, Carol Cornwall Madsen, Kate Holbrook, and Matthew J. Grow, eds. *The First Fifty Years of Relief Society: Key Documents in Latter-day Saint Women's History.* Salt Lake City: The Church Historian's Press, 2016.

Derr, Jill Mulvay, Janath Russell Cannon, and Maureen Ursenbach Beecher. *Women of Covenant: The Story of Relief Society.* Salt Lake City: Deseret Book, 1992.

Deseret News Extra (September 14, 1852).

Dinger, John S. "'A Mean Conspirator,' or 'The Noblest of Men': William Marks's Expulsion from Nauvoo." *The John Whitmer Historical Association Journal* 34, no. 2 (Fall/Winter 2014): 12–38.

———, ed. *The Nauvoo City and High Council Minutes*. Salt Lake City: Signature Books, 2011.

Dirkmaat, Gerrit J. "Searching for 'Happiness': Joseph Smith's Alleged Authorship of the 1842 Letter to Nancy Rigdon." *Journal of Mormon History* 42, no. 3 (July 2016): 94–119.

Discourses on Celestial Marriage. Salt Lake City: Deseret News, 1869.

Doctrine and Discipline of the Methodist Episcopal Church, 10th ed. Philadelphia: Henry Tuckniss, 1978.

Dredge, Nancy Tate. "Victims of the Conflict." In *Mormon Sisters: Women in Early Utah*, edited by Claudia L. Bushman. 133–55. Logan, UT: Utah State University Press, 1997.

Driggs, Ken. "Imprisonment, Defiance, and Division: A History of Mormon Fundamentalism in the 1940s and 1950s." *Dialogue: A Journal of Mormon Thought* 38, no. 1 (Spring 2005): 65–95.

Edwards, Jonathan. "The Justice of God in the Damnation of Sinners." In *The Works of Jonathan Edwards, vol. 19: Sermons and Discourses, 1734–1738*, edited by M. X. Lesser, New Haven: Yale University Press, 2001, 344.

Ehat, Andrew F. "'It Seems Like Heaven Began on Earth': Joseph Smith and the Constitution of the Kingdom of God." *BYU Studies* 20, no. 3 (Spring 1980): 253–80.

———. "Joseph Smith's Introduction of Temple Ordinances and the 1844 Mormon Succession Question." MA thesis, Brigham Young University, 1982.

———. "'They Might Have Known That He Was Not a Fallen Prophet'—The Nauvoo Journal of Joseph Fielding." *BYU Studies* 19, no. 2 (1979): 133–66.

Ehat, Andrew F., and Lyndon W. Cook. *The Words of Joseph Smith*, 2nd ed. Orem, UT: Grandin Book Co., 1991.

"Elder Decries Criticism of LDS Leaders." *Salt Lake Tribune* (August 18, 1985): Section B, page 2.

Enders, Donald L. "The Steamboat *Maid of Iowa*: Mormon Mistress of the Mississippi." *BYU Studies* 19, no. 3 (1979): 321–35.

Engs, Ruth C. *Clean Living Movements: American Cycles of Health Reform*. New York: Praeger, 2001.

Erickson, Dan. "*As a Thief in the Night*": The Mormon Quest for Millennial Deliverance. Salt Lake City: Signature Books, 1998.

Evenson, William E. and Duane E. Jeffrey. *Mormonism and Evolution: The Authoritative LDS Statements*. Salt Lake City: Greg Kofford Books, 2005.

Eyring, Henry B. "The Lord Leads His Church." *Ensign*, November 2017, https://www.lds.org/ensign/2017/11/general-priesthood-session/the-lord-leads-his-church.

Fielding, Joseph. Journals, 1837–1859. MS 1567, LDS Church History Library.

Faust, James E. "The Keys that Never Rust." *Ensign*, November 1994, 72–74.

"Fiftieth Semi-Annual Conference: Fifth Day." *Millennial Star* 42, no. 46 (November 15, 1880): 721–25.

Fillerup, Robert, ed. "William Clayton's Nauvoo Diaries and Personal Writings." Accessed June 13, 2014. http://www.boap.org/LDS/Early-Saints/clayton-diaries.

Flake, Chad J., and Larry W. Draper. *A Mormon Bibliography, 1830–1930: Books, Pamphlets, Periodicals, and Broadsides Relating to the First Century of Mormonism.* Rev. and Enl. Edition. Provo, UT: Brigham Young University Press, 2004.

Flake, Kathleen. "The Development of Early Latter-day Saint Marriage Rites." *Journal of Mormon History* 41, no. 1 (January 2015): 77–102.

———. *The Politics of American Religious Identity: The Seating of Senator Reed Smoot, Mormon Apostle.* Chapel Hill, NC: University of North Carolina Press, 2004.

Flanders, Robert Bruce. *Nauvoo: Kingdom on the Mississippi.* Urbana, IL: University of Illinois Press, 1975.

Fleming, Stephen J. "'Congenial to Almost Every Shade of Radicalism': The Delaware Valley and the Success of Early Mormonism." *Religion and American Culture: A Journal of Interpretation* 17, no. 2 (Summer 2007): 129–164.

Fluhman, J. Spencer. *A Peculiar People: Anti-Mormonism and the Making of Religion in Nineteenth-Century America.* Chapel Hill, NC: University of North Carolina Press, 2012.

Foster, Craig L. "The Persistence of Plural Marriage within Mainstream Mormonism: The Example of the Barr and Mary Lance Musser Family." In *Scattering of the Saints: Schism within Mormonism,* edited by Newell G. Bringhurst and John Hamer. 290–314. Independence: John Whitmer Books, 2007.

Foster, Lawrence. *Religion and Sexuality: The Shakers, the Mormons, and the Oneida Community.* Urbana, IL: University of Illinois Press, 1984.

Furniss, Norman F. *Mormon Conflict: 1850–1859.* New Haven: Yale University Press, 2005.

Gallup, Luke William. Journal, Luke William Gallup papers, 1840–1890, Accn2786, Box 1, fd. 1. Special Collections, University of Utah Libraries, University of Utah, Salt Lake City, Utah.

Gates, Susa Young. *History of the Young Ladies' Mutual Improvement Association of the Church of Jesus Christ of Latter-Day Saints.* Salt Lake City: Deseret News, 1911.

"General Authorities to Leave Business Boards." *Ensign,* April 1996. https://www.lds.org/ensign/1996/04/news-of-the-church/general-authorities-to-leave-business-boards.

General Handbook of Instructions 24. Salt Lake City: Church of Jesus Christ of Latter-day Saints, 1989.

General Handbook of Instructions, Book 1, 2010. Salt Lake City: The Church of Jesus Christ of Latter-day Saints, 2010.

Givens, Terryl L. *By the Hand of Mormon: The American Scripture That Launched a New World Religion.* New York: Oxford University Press, 2002.

———. *When Souls Had Wings: Pre-Mortal Existence in Western Thought.* New York: Oxford University Press, 2010.

Givens, Terryl L. and Matthew J. Grow. *Parley P. Pratt: The Apostle Paul of Mormonism.* New York: Oxford University Press, 2011.

Godfrey, Donald G., and Rebecca S. Martineau-McCarty, *An Uncommon Common*

Pioneer: The Journals of James Henry Martineau, 1828–1918. Provo, UT: Religious Studies Center, 2008.

Godfrey, Matthew C., Mark Ashurst-McGee, Grant Underwood, Robert J. Woodford, and William G. Hartley., eds. *Documents: Vol. 2: July 1831–January 1833.* In THE JOSEPH SMITH PAPERS series, edited by Dean C. Jessee, Ronald K. Esplin, and Richard Lyman Bushman. Salt Lake City: Church Historian's Press, 2013.

Goodson, Stephanie Smith. "Plural Wives." In *Mormon Sisters: Women in Early Utah*, edited by Claudia L. Bushman, 89–111. Cambridge, MA: Emmeline Press, Ldt., 1976.

Gordon, Sarah Barringer. *The Mormon Question: Polygamy and the Constitutional Conflict in Nineteenth-Century America.* Chapel Hill, NC: The University of North Carolina Press, 2002.

Grow, Matthew J., Ronald K. Esplin, Mark Ashurst-McGee, Gerrit J. Dirkmaat, and Jeffrey D. Mahas, eds. *Administrative Records: Council of Fifty, Minutes, March 1844–January 1846.* In the THE JOSEPH SMITH PAPERS series, edited by Ronald K. Esplin, Matthew J. Grow, and Matthew C. Godfrey. Salt Lake City: Church Historian's Press, 2016.

Grow, Matthew J., and Ronald W. Walker, eds. *The Prophet and the Reformer: The Letters of Brigham Young and Thomas L. Kane.* New York: Oxford University Press, 2015.

Grua, David W., and William V. Smith, "The Tarrying of the Beloved Disciple: Intertextuality and the Textual History of the Account of John (D&C 7)." In *Creating Scripture: Joseph Smith's Translation Projects and the Making of Mormonism*, edited by Michael Hubbard MacKay, Mark Ashurst-McGee, and Brian M. Hauglid. Salt Lake City: University of Utah Press, forthcoming.

Gunderson, Robert C. "I Have a Question." *Ensign*, February 1984, 31.

Hales, Brian C. "Encouraging Joseph Smith to Practice Plural Marriage: The Accounts of the Angel with a Drawn Sword." *Mormon Historical Studies* 11, no. 2 (September 2010): 55–71.

———. *Joseph Smith's Polygamy*, 3 vols. Salt Lake City: Greg Kofford Books, 2013.

———. *Modern Polygamy and Mormon Fundamentalism: The Generations after the Manifesto.* Salt Lake City: Greg Kofford Books, 2006.

Hall, Marshall. *Commentaries on some of the more important of the Diseases of Females.* London, 1827.

Hardy, B. Carmon. *Doing the Works of Abraham, Mormon Polygamy: Its Origin, Practice, and Demise.* Kingdom in the West: The Mormons and the American Frontier. Norman, OK: Arthur H. Clark, 2007.

———. *Solemn Covenant: The Mormon Polygamous Passage.* Chicago: University of Illinois Press, 1992.

Harline, Paula Kelly. *The Polygamous Wives Writing Club: From the Diaries of Mormon Pioneer Women.* New York: Oxford University Press, 2014.

Hartley, William G. "Common People: Church Activity During the Brigham Young Era." In *Nearly Everything Imaginable: The Everyday Life of Utah's Mormon Pioneers*, edited by Ronald W. Walker and Doris R. Dant. 249–95. Provo, UT: Brigham Young University Press, 1999.

Hatch, John P., ed. *Danish Apostle: The Diaries of Anthon H. Lund, 1890–1921.* Salt Lake City: Signature Books, 2006.

Haws, J. B. *The Mormon Image in the American Mind: Fifty Years of Public Perception.* New York: Oxford University Press, 2013.

Heath, Harvard S., ed. *In the World: the Diaries of Reed Smoot.* Salt Lake City: Signature Books, 1997.

Hedges, Andrew H., Alex D. Smith, and Richard Lloyd Anderson, eds. *Journals, Vol. 2: December 1841–April 1843.* In The Joseph Smith Papers series, edited by Dean C. Jessee, Ronald K. Esplin, and Richard Lyman Bushman. Salt Lake City: Church Historian's Press, 2011.

Hedges, Andrew H., Alex D. Smith, and Richard Lloyd Anderson, eds. *Journals, Vol. 3: May 1843–June 1844.* In The Joseph Smith Papers series, edited by Ronald K. Esplin, and Matthew J. Grow. Salt Lake City: Church Historian's Press, 2015.

Hettinger, T. S. "It's the Law." *The Friend*, February, 1997.

Hicks, Michael. *Mormonism and Music: A History.* Chicago: University of Illinois Press, 2003.

Higbee, Marilyn, ed. "'A Weary Traveler': The 1848–50 Diary of Zina D. H. Young." *Journal of Mormon History* 19, no. 2 (Fall 1993): 86–125.

Hinckley, Gordon B. "Daughters of God." *Ensign*, November 1991, 97.

———. "Stand Strong Against the Wiles of the World." *Ensign*, November 1995, 98–107.

Hinton, Wayne. "John D. T. McAllister: The Southern Utah Years, 1876–1910." *Journal of Mormon History* 29, no. 2 (2003): 106–136.

Historian's Office General Church Minutes: 1839–1845. CR 100 318, LDS Church History Library.

"History of Brigham Young." *Deseret News* 8, no. 3 (March 24, 1858): 1.

Hodges, Blair Dee. "Intellectual Disability in Mormon Thought and History, 1830–1900." MA thesis, Georgetown University, Washington, DC, 2013.

———. "'My Principality on Earth Began': Millennialism and the Celestial Kingdom in the Development of Mormon Doctrine." *Dialogue: A Journal of Mormon Thought* 46, no. 2 (Summer 2013): 40–54.

Holzapfel, Richard Neitzel, and Christopher C. Jones. "'John the Revelator': The Written Revelations of John Taylor." In *Champion of Liberty: John Taylor*, ed. Mary Jane Woodger. Provo, UT: Religious Studies Center, Brigham Young University, 2009.

Homestead, Melissa J. *American Women Authors and Literary Property, 1822–1869.* New York: Oxford University Press, 2008.

How, Thomas Y. *A Vindication of the Protestant Episcopal Church.* New York: T. & J. Swords, 1816.

Howard, Richard P. "The Changing RLDS Response to Mormon Polygamy: A Preliminary Analysis." *John Whitmer Historical Association Journal* 3 (1983): 14–28.

Howe, Daniel Walker. *What Hath God Wrought: The Transformation of America, 1815–1848.* New York: Oxford University Press, 2007.

Howe, Mary. "Professional and Business Opportunities for Women." *Young Woman's Journal* 3, no. 1 (October 1891): 24–5.

Humez, Jean M. *Harriet Tubman: The Life and the Life Stories.* Madison, WI: The University of Wisconsin Press, 2003.

Huntington, Oliver B. "History and Life of Oliver B. Huntington, Also His Travels & Troubles, written by himself." June 12, 1842:5, Oliver Boardman Huntington papers, L. Tom Perry Special Collections and Manuscripts, Harold B. Lee Library, Brigham Young University, Provo, Utah.

Hyde, Orson. "Orson Hyde, Certificate About the Twelve, circa 1845 March," Brigham Young Office Files, Box 74, fd. 18, CR 1234 1, LDS Church History Library.

Ivins, Stanley. "Notes on Mormon Polygamy." *Western Humanities Review* 10, no. 3 (1956): 229–39.

Jeffrey, Duane E. "Seers, Savants and Evolution: The Uncomfortable Interface." *Dialogue: A Journal of Mormon Thought* 8, no. 3–4 (Autumn–Winter 1973): 41–75.

Jensen, Richard L. "Forgotten Relief Societies, 1844–67." *Dialogue: A Journal of Mormon Thought* 16, no. 1 (Spring 1983): 105–25.

Jensen, Robin Scott. "'Rely Upon the Things Which are Written': Text Context and the Creation of Mormon Revelatory Records." MA thesis, University of Wisconsin-Milwaukee, 2009.

Jensen, Robin Scott, and Benjamin Park, "Debating Succession, March 1846: John E. Page, Orson Hyde, and the Trajectories of Joseph Smith's Legacy." *Journal of Mormon History* 39, no. 1 (Winter 2013): 181–205.

Jensen, Robin Scott, Richard E. Turley Jr. and Riley M. Lorimer, eds. *Revelations and Translations, Vol. 2: Published Revelations.* In THE JOSEPH SMITH PAPERS series, edited by Dean C. Jessee, Ronald K. Esplin, and Richard Lyman Bushman. Salt Lake City: Church Historian's Press, 2011.

Jensen, Robin Scott, Robert J. Woodford, and Steven C. Harper, eds. *Revelations and Translations: Manuscript Revelation Books, Facsimile Edition.* In THE JOSEPH SMITH PAPERS series, edited by Dean C. Jessee, Ronald K. Esplin, and Richard Lyman Bushman. Salt Lake City: Church Historian's Press, 2009.

Jenson, Andrew. *Historical Record,* 9 Vols. Salt Lake City: Deseret News, 1886–1890.

Jessee, Dean C. "Howard Coray's Recollections of Joseph Smith." *BYU Studies* 17, no. 3 (Spring 1977): 341–47.

———. "Joseph Knight's Recollection of Early Mormon History." *BYU Studies* 17, no. 1 (Autumn 1976): 29–39.

Jessee, Dean C., Mark Ashurst-McGee, and Richard L. Jensen, eds. *Journals, Vol. 1: 1832–1839.* In THE JOSEPH SMITH PAPERS series, edited by Dean C. Jessee, Ronald K. Esplin, and Richard Lyman Bushman. Salt Lake City: Church Historian's Press, 2008.

Johnson, Benjamin F. Letter to George F. Gibbs, October 1903. MS 25079, LDS Church History Library.

Johnson, Benjamin Franklin. *My Life's Review.* 85–86. Independence: Zion's Printing and Publishing Co., 1947.

Johnson, Melvin C. *Polygamy on the Pedernales: Lyman Wight's Mormon Villages in Antebellum Texas, 1845–1858.* Logan, UT: Utah State University Press, 2006.

Jones, Christopher C. "Mormonism in the Methodist Marketplace: James Covel and the Historical Background of Doctrine and Covenants 39–40." *BYU Studies Quarterly* 51, no. 1 (2012): 67–98.

———. "'We Latter-Day Saints are Methodists': The Influence of Methodism on Early Mormon Religiosity." MA thesis, Brigham Young University, Provo, UT, 2009.

Joseph Smith's Last Sermon as Issued by Elder John Taylor, Nauvoo, Ill. Salt Lake City: Presbyterian Teachers' Association, 1903.

Journal History of the Church 1896–2001, CR 100 137, LDS Church History Library.

Journal of Discourses, 26 vols. London and Liverpool: LDS Booksellers Depot, 1854–86.

Kenney, Scott G., ed. *Wilford Woodruff's Journal, 1833–1898 Typescript,* 9 vols. Salt Lake City: Signature Books, 1983.

Kerber, Linda K. *Women of the Republic: Intellect and Ideology in Revolutionary America.* Chapel Hill: The University of North Carolina Press, 1980.

Kimball, Edward L. *Lengthen Your Stride: The Presidency of Spencer W. Kimball.* Salt Lake City: Deseret Book, 2005 (Working Draft).

Kimball, Heber C. Letter to Parley P. Pratt, June 17, 1842. Parley P. Pratt Correspondence 1842–1855, MS 897, fd. 1, LDS Church History Library.

———. "Remarks." *Deseret News* 6, no. 49 (February 11, 1857): 4.

Kimball J. Golden. Diary, MS 1354, Box 2, fd. 3, LDS Church History Library.

Kimball, Sarah. "Auto-Biography." *Woman's Exponent* 12, no. 7 (September 1, 1883): 51.

Kimball, Stanley B., *Heber C. Kimball: Mormon Patriarch and Pioneer.* Chicago: University of Chicago Press, 1981.

———, ed., *On the Potter's Wheel: The Diaries of Heber C. Kimball.* Salt Lake City: Signature Books, 1987.

Kimball, Vilate M. Letter to Heber C. Kimball, October 11, 1840. Vilate M. Kimball letters, 1840, MS 18732, LDS Church History Library.

Kimnach, Wilson H., ed. *Sermons and Discourses, 1743–1758.* Vol. 25 in THE WORKS OF JONATHAN EDWARDS series. New Haven, CT: Yale University Press, 2006.

King, Hannah. "Procreation." *Woman's Exponent* 14, no. 7 (September 1, 1885): 51.

Kingsbury, Joseph C. Diary of Joseph C. Kingsbury. Special Collections, Marriott Library, University of Utah, Salt Lake City.

———. Testimony in United States testimony 1892, United States Court of Appeals (8th circuit), Box 1, fd. 10, page 178, MS 1160 LDS Church History Library.

Kramer, Bradley H. "Keeping the Sacred: Structured Silence in the Enactment of Priesthood Authority, Gendered Worship, and Sacramental Kinship in Mormonism." PhD diss., University of Michigan, 2014.

Krueger, Christine L. *The Reader's Repentance: Women Preachers, Women Writers, and Nineteenth-Century Social Discourse.* Chicago: University of Chicago Press, 1992.

Lambert, Charles. Autobiography. MSS 927, L. Tom Perry Special Collections and Manuscripts, Harold B. Lee Library, Brigham Young University, Provo, Utah.

Larson, A. Karl and Katherine Miles Larson, eds., *The Diary of Charles Lowell Walker.* 2 vols. Logan, UT: Utah State University Press, 1980, 1:464–65.

Larson, Stan. *A Ministry of Meetings: The Apostolic Diaries of Rudger Clawson.* Salt Lake City: Signature Books, 1993.

Latter-day Revelations: Selections from the Book of Doctrine and Covenants of the Church of Jesus Christ of Latter-day Saints. Salt Lake City: Church of Jesus Christ of Latter-day Saints, 1930.

Laub, George. Journal, MS 9628, LDS Church History Library.

Launius, Roger D. *Joseph Smith III: Pragmatic Prophet.* Urbana, IL: University of Illinois Press, 1995.

LeBaron, E. Dale. *Benjamin Franklin Johnson: Friend to the Prophets.* Provo, UT: Grandin, 1997.

Lee, John D. *Mormonism Unveiled; or The Life and Confessions of the Late Mormon Bishop, John D. Lee.* St. Louis, MO: Brand, 1877.

Lepore, Jill. *The Mansion of Happiness: A History of Life and Death.* New York: Vintage Books, 2013.

"Letter from Elder W. H. Kelley." *The True Latter Day Saints' Herald* 29 (March 1, 1882): 67.

Lewis, Catherine. *Narrative of Some of the Proceedings of the Mormons; Giving an Account of Their Iniquities, With Particulars Concerning the Training of the Indians by Them, Description of the Mode of Endowment, Plurality of Wives, &c., &c.* Lynn, MA: Catherine Lewis, 1848.

Lindman, Janet Moore. "'Bad Men and Angels from Hell': The Discourse of Universalism in Early National Philadelphia." *Journal of the Early Republic* 31, no. 2 (Summer 2011): 259–82.

Lyman, Edward Leo, ed. *Candid Insights of a Mormon Apostle: The Diaries of Abraham H. Cannon, 1889–1895.* Salt Lake City: Signature Books, 2010.

MacKay, Michael Hubbard, Gerrit J. Dirkmaat, Grand Underwood, Robert J. Woodford, and William G. Hartley, eds. *Documents, Vol. 1: July 1828– June 1831* in THE JOSEPH SMITH PAPERS series. Salt Lake City: Church Historian's Press, 2013.

MacKinnon, William P. *At Sword's Point, Part 1: A Documentary History of the Utah War to 1858.* Norman, OK: University of Oklahoma Press, 2016.

Madsen, Carol Cornwall, ed. *In Their Own Words: Women and the Story of Nauvoo.* Salt Lake City: Deseret Book, 1994.

———. "Schism in the Sisterhood: Mormon Women and Partisan Politics, 1890– 1900." In *New Views of Mormon History*, edited by Davis Bitton and Maureen Ursenbach Beecher. 212–241. Salt Lake City: University of Utah Press, 1987.

Madsen, Truman G. *Eternal Man.* Salt Lake City: Deseret Book, 1966.

Marquardt, H. Michael. *Early Patriarchal Blessings of the Church of Jesus Christ of Latter-Day Saints.* Salt Lake City: Smith-Petitt Foundation, 2007.

Mauss, Armand L. *All Abraham's Children: Changing Mormon Conceptions of Race and Lineage.* Urbana, IL: University of Illinois Press, 2003.

———. *The Angel and the Beehive: The Mormon Struggle with Assimilation.* Urbana, IL: University of Illinois Press, 1994.

Maxwell, Neal A. "My Servant Joseph." *Ensign,* May 1992, 37–39.

McConkie, Bruce R. "Be Valiant in the Fight of Faith." *Ensign,* November 1974. https://www.lds.org/ensign/1974/11/be-valiant-in-the-fight-of-faith.

———. "The Keys of the Kingdom." *Ensign,* May 1983, 21–22.

———. *Mormon Doctrine* 2nd ed. Salt Lake City: Bookcraft, 1966.

McConkie, Joseph Fielding. "A Historical Examination of the Views of the Church of Jesus Christ of Latter-Day Saints and the Reorganized Church of Jesus Christ of Latter-Day Saints on Four Distinctive Aspects of the Doctrine of Deity Taught by the Prophet Joseph Smith." MA thesis, Brigham Young University, 1968.

McKenzie, Steven L. *King David: A Biography.* New York: Oxford University Press, 2000.

Milewski, Melissa Lambert, ed. *Before the Manifesto: The Life Writings of Mary Lois Walker Morris.* Logan, UT: Utah State University Press, 2007.

Minute Book 1. MS 3432, LDS Church History Library.

Miura, Yuzuru. "David in Luke-Acts: His Portrayal in the Light of Early Judaism." PhD diss., University of Aberdeen, Scotland, 2007.

"The Mormon Creed." *Painesville Telegraph* 2, no. 44 (April 19, 1831): 4.

"The Mormons in Nauvoo: Three Letters from William Law on Mormonism." *The Salt Lake Tribune* 30, no. 91 (July 31, 1887): 6.

Morrill, Susanna. *White Roses on the Floor of Heaven: Mormon Women's Popular Theology, 1880–1920.* New York: Routledge, 2006.

"Mother in Heaven." Church of Jesus Christ of Latter-day Saints. Accessed December 1, 2017. https://www.lds.org/topics/mother-in-heaven.

Moyer, Jonathan H. "Dancing with the Devil: The Making of the Republican/Mormon Pact." PhD diss., University of Utah, 2009.

Nauvoo City Council Proceedings, 1841 February–1845 February. MS 3435, LDS Church History Library.

The Nauvoo Diaries of William Clayton 1842–1846, Abridged. Salt Lake City: privately published, 2010.

Nauvoo Expositor, Nauvoo, IL, single issue, June 7, 1844.

Nauvoo Stake High Council Court Papers. LR 3102 23, LDS Church History Library.

Nauvoo Stake High Council minutes. LR 3102 22, LDS Church History Library.

Nauvoo vs. O. F. Bostwick, February 26, 1844. Judicial Proceedings: Mayor's Court, MS 16800, LDS Church History Library.

Newell, Linda King. "The Emma Smith Lore Reconsidered." *Dialogue: A Journal of Mormon Thought* 17, no. 3 (Autumn 1984): 87–100.

Newell, Linda King, and Valeen Tippetts Avery. *Mormon Enigma: Emma Hale Smith.* Urbana, IL: University of Illinois Press, 1994.

Noll, Mark A. *America's God: From Jonathan Edwards to Abraham Lincoln.* New York: Oxford University Press, 2002.

"Not So Very Former." *Salt Lake Tribune*, March 4, 1910, 4.

Nuttall, L. John. Papers. MSS 790, L. Tom Perry Special Collections and Manuscripts, Harold B. Lee Library, Brigham Young University, Provo, Utah.

Oaks, Dallin H. "The Plan and the Proclamation." *Ensign*, November 2017. https://www.lds.org/ensign/2017/11/saturday-morning-session/the-plan-and-the-proclamation.

Oaks, Dallin H. and Joseph L. Bentley, "Joseph Smith and the Legal Process: In the Wake of the Steamboat Nauvoo." *BYU Law Review* 1976, no. 3 (1976): 735–82.

"Our Southern Settlements." *Deseret News* 16, no. 49 (January 15, 1868): 5.

"Outline of Instructions to Patriarchs." Delbert L. Stapley files, CR 601 5, Box 9, fd. 18, LDS Church History Library.

Pack, John. Autobiography-Reminiscence (1808–1849): Recollections of John, May 16, 1847. Accessed June 13, 2017. http://boap.org/LDS/Early-Saints/ JHPack.html.

Packer, Boyd K. "Our Moral Environment." *Ensign*, May 1992, 66–8.

———. "The Pattern of Our Parentage." *Ensign*, November 1984, 66–9.

Palmer, Madelyn Stewart Silver. "'Joyful Were My Feelings,' Sarah Maria Mousley Cannon (1828–1912)." In *Women of Faith in the Latter Days: Volume Two, 1821–1845*, edited by Richard E. Turley and Brittany Chapman. Salt Lake City: Deseret Book, 2012.

Park, Benjamin E. "Early Mormon Patriarchy and the Paradoxes of Democratic Religiosity in Jacksonian America." *American Nineteenth Century History* 14, no. 2 (2013): 183–208.

Partridge, George F., Martha S. Hall Haven, Jesse Haven, Sarah S. Hall Scott, and Isaac Scott. "The Death of a Mormon Dictator: Letters of Massachusetts Mormons, 1843–1848." *The New England Quarterly* 9, no. 12 (1936): 583–617.

Paulsen, David L., and Martin Pulido. "'A Mother There': A Survey of Historical Teachings about Mother in Heaven." *BYU Studies* 50, no. 1 (2011): 70–126.

Peck, Steven L. "Crawling Out of the Primordial Soup: A Step Toward the Emergence of an LDS Theology Compatible with Organic Evolution." *Dialogue: A Journal of Mormon Thought* 43, no. 1 (Spring 2010): 1–36.

———. "When Our Leaders Speak, The Thinking Has Been Done," By Common Consent, June 25, 2009. https://bycommonconsent.com/2009/06/25/when-our-leaders-speak-the-thinking-has-been-done/

Phelps, William W. Letter to Sally Phelps, May 26, 1835. William W. Phelps Collection, L. Tom Perry Special Collections Library, Brigham Young University, Provo, Utah.

"Plural Marriage in The Church of Jesus Christ of Latter-day Saints." The Church of Jesus Christ of Latter-day Saints. Accessed October 1 2014. https://www.lds.org/topics/plural-marriage-in-the-church-of-jesus-christ-of-latter-day-saints.

Poelman, Anne Osborn. *The Simeon Solution: One Woman's Spiritual Odyssey.* Salt Lake City: Deseret Book, 1994.

"Popular Idea of Mormonism." *Presbyterian Home Mission Monthly* 23, no. 12 (October, 1909): 279–80.

Potter, David M. with Don E. Fehrenbacher. *The Impending Crisis: America Before the Civil War, 1848–1861.* New York: Harper Colophon, 1976.

Pratt, Belinda. *Defence of Polygamy, By a Lady of Utah, in a Letter to Her Sister in New Hampshire.* Council Bluffs, Iowa Territory: Belinda Marden Pratt, 1854.

Pratt, Orson. "Celestial Marriage." *The Seer* 1, no. 2 (February, 1853): 25–31.

———. "Christian Polygamy in the Sixteenth Century." *The Seer* 1, no. 12 (December 1853): 183.

———. "The Preexistence of Man." *The Seer*, 1, no. 3 (March 1853): 37–39.

Pratt, Parley P. *The Autobiography of Parley Parker Pratt, One of the Twelve Apostles of the Church of Jesus Christ of Latter-day Saints, Embracing His Life, Ministry and*

Travels, With Extracts, in Prose and Verse, From His Miscellaneous Writings. New York: Russell Brothers, 1874.

———. "Celestial Family Organization." *The Prophet* 1, no. 41 (March 1, 1845): 1–2.

———. Letter to Elizabeth Brotherton, October 7, 1843. Parley P. Pratt collection, Box 1, fd. 16, MS 2248, LDS Church History Library.

———. *"Mormonism!" "Plurality of Wives!" An especial chapter, for the especial edification of certain inquisitive news editors, etc.* San Francisco, n.p., 1852.

———. "Proclamation to the Church of Jesus Christ of Latter-Day Saints: Greetings." *Latter-Day Saints' Millennial Star* 5, no. 10 (March 1845): 151.

"President Smith's Testimony." *The Salt Lake Tribune* (March 5, 1905): 26.

Quinn, D. Michael. "The Council of Fifty and Its Members, 1844 to 1945." *BYU Studies* 20, no. 2 (Winter 1980): 163–98.

———. "LDS Church Authority and New Plural Marriages, 1890–1904." *Dialogue: A Journal of Mormon Thought* 18, no. 1 (Spring 1985): 9–105.

———. *The Mormon Hierarchy: Extensions of Power.* Salt Lake City: Smith Research Associates, 1997.

———. *The Mormon Hierarchy: Origins of Power.* Salt Lake City: Signature Book, 1994.

Ralph, Peter and Graham Coop. "The Geography of Recent Genetic Ancestry across Europe." *PLOS Biology* (May 7, 2013). Available at https://doi.org/10.1371/journal.pbio.1001555.

Raynes, Marybeth and Erin Parsons. "Single Cursedness: An Overview of LDS Authorities' Statements about Unmarried People." In *Multiply and Replenish: Mormon Essays on Sex and Family*, edited by Brent Corcoran, 217–27. Salt Lake City: Signature Books, 1994.

"Record of the Female Relief Society Organized the 9th of Feby in the City of Great Salt Lake 1854." Louisa R. Taylor Papers, L. Tom Perry Special Collections and Manuscripts, Harold B. Lee Library, Brigham Young University, Provo, Utah.

Reeve, W. Paul. *Religion of a Different Color: Race and the Mormon Struggle for Whiteness.* New York: Oxford University Press, 2015.

Reichmann, Edward. "The Rabbinic Conception of Conception: An Exercise in Fertility." *Tradition: A Journal of Orthodox Jewish Thought* 31, no. 1 (1996): 33–63.

Relief Society Minute Book, 1842 March –1844 March. MS 3424, LDS Church History Library.

Report of the Semi-Annual Conference of the Church of Jesus Christ of Latter-day Saints. Salt Lake City: Church of Jesus Christ of Latter-day Saints, semiannual.

"Resolutions." *Nauvoo Expositor* (June 7, 1844): 2

Revelations Collections, circa 1829–1876, MS 4583, Box 1, LDS Church History Library.

"Revelation Received 27 July 1842." Revelations Collections, circa 1829–1876, MS 4583, Box 1, fd. 104, LDS Church History Library.

Rhodes, Douglas L. T., Steve Olson, and Joseph T. Chang. "Modelling the Recent Common Ancestry of all Living Humans." *Nature* 431 (2004): 562–66.

Richards, Franklin D. "Scriptural Items." MS 4409, LDS Church History Library.

Richards, Willard. Letter to Brigham Young, July 18, 1843, Brigham Young Office Files, CR 1234, Box 41, fd. 28, LDS Church History Library.

————. "Pocket Companion written in England." MS 1490, Box 2, fd. 6, LDS Church History Library.

Riess, Jana K. "Heathen in Our Fair Land: Anti-polygamy and Protestant Women's Missions to Utah." PhD diss., New York: Columbia University, 2000.

Roberts, B. H. *Succession in the Presidency of the Church of Jesus Christ of Latter-day Saints,* 2nd ed. Salt Lake City: Cannon & Sons, 1900.

Rogers, Brent M. *Unpopular Sovereignty: Mormons and the Federal Management of Early Utah Territory.* Lincoln: University of Nebraska Press, 2017.

Rogers, Jedediah S., ed. *The Council of Fifty: A Documentary History.* Salt Lake City: Signature Books, 2014.

Romig, Ron. "The Temple Lot Suit After 100 Years." *John Whitmer Historical Association Journal* 12 (1992): 3–15.

Rowley, Dennis. "The Ezra Booth Letters." *Dialogue: A Journal of Mormon Thought* 16, no. 3 (Autumn 1983): 135–41.

Russel, Robert. *Russel's Sermon on the Unpardonable Sin* (London, 1692).

Salt Lake City School of the Prophets Minutes, February 12, 1870, School of the Prophets Salt Lake City records, minutes, 1870–1872, CR 390 6, LDS Church History Library.

Schmidt, Leigh Eric. *Hearing Things: Religion, Illusion, and the American Enlightenment.* Cambridge, MA: Harvard University Press, 2000.

Schnibbe, Karl-Heinz, Alan F. Keele and Douglas F. Tobler, *When Truth was Treason: German Youth Against Hitler: The Story of the Helmuth Hübener Group.* Urbana: University of Illinois Press, 1995.

Sheen, Isaac. *Melchisedic and Aaronic Herald* 1, no. 2 (March 1849): 1–2; no. 9 (April 1850): 3.

Sherlock, Richard. "'We Can See no Advantage to a Continuation of the Discussion': The Roberts/Smith/Talmage Affair." *Dialogue: A Journal of Mormon Thought* 13, no. 3 (Fall 1980): 63–78.

Sherwood, Salmon. "The Mormons." *Daily Missouri Intelligencer* (April 20, 1833): 1.

Shields, Steven L. *Divergent Paths of the Restoration,* 4th ed. rev. and enl. Independece, MO: Herald Houase, 1990.

Shipps, Jan, and John W. Welch, eds. *The Journals of William E. McLellin, 1831–1836.* Provo, Urbana and Chicago: BYU Studies and University of Illinois Press, 1994.

Sjodahl, J. M. "Temple Marriage an Antidote Against Divorce." *Improvement Era* 30, October 1927, 1098–1100.

Smith, Alexander H. Letter to Samuel H. B. Smith, November 19, 1866. Erwin P. (Buddy) Youngreen collection 1840–1938, Box 2, fd. 13, MS 17756, LDS Church History Library.

Smith, Christopher C. "The Inspired Fictionalization of the 1835 United Firm Revelations." *Claremont Journal of Mormon Studies* 1, no. 1 (April 2011): 15–31.

Smith, Daymon Mickel. "The Last Shall be First and the First Shall be Last." PhD diss., University of Pennsylvania, 2007.

Smith, E. Gary. "The Patriarchal Crisis of 1845." *Dialogue: A Journal of Mormon Thought* 16, no. 2 (Summer 1983): 24–36.

Smith, George D., ed. *An Intimate Chronicle: The Journals of William Clayton.* Salt Lake City: Signature Books, 1995.

———. *Nauvoo Polygamy: "... But We Called It Celestial Marriage."* Salt Lake City: Signature Books, 2008.

Smith, Heman C. *The Truth Defended, or A Reply to Elder D. H. Bays' Doctrines and Dogmas of Mormonism.* Lamoni, IA: Board of Publication of the Reorganized Church of Jesus Christ of Latter Day Saints, 1901.

Smith, Hyrum. Sermon, April 8, 1844. General Church Minutes, CR 100 318, LDS Church History Library.

Smith, James E., and Phillip R. Kunz. "Polygyny and Fertility in Nineteenth-Century America." *Population Studies* 30, no. 3 (1976): 465–80.

Smith, Joseph. Diary. MS 155, Box 1, fd. 7, LDS Church History Library.

———. "An Investigation of the Priesthood from the Scriptures." (Holograph, Robert B. Thompson) Joseph Smith Collection, 5 October 1840, Box 1 Supplement Folder 2, MS 155, LDS Church History Library.

———. Journal. Joseph Smith Collection, MS 155, LDS Church History Library.

———. Letter to Nancy Rigdon, Joseph Smith Collection, Correspondence, 1829–1844, MS 155, Box 2, fd. 5, LDS Church History Library.

———. Letter to Newel K. Whitney, Elizabeth Ann Whitney, August 18, 1842. MS 155, Box 2, fd. 5, LDS Church History Library.

———. Sermon, October 3, 1841. CR 100 318, Box 1, fd. 1, LDS Church History Library.

———. Sermon, October 5, 1840. Joseph Smith Collection, 1827–1844, MS 155, Box 4, fd. 4, LDS Church History Library.

Smith, Joseph F. "Celestial Marriage." *Ogden Herald*, May 21, 1886, 2.

———. Diary, MS 1325, Box 4, fd. 1, LDS Church History Library.

———. *Gospel Doctrine: The Sermons and Writings of President Joseph F. Smith*, edited by John A. Widtsoe, Osborn J. P. Widtsoe, Albert E. Bowen, and Franklin S. Harris. Salt Lake City: Deseret News Press, 1919.

———. Letter to _____, May 25, 1912. First Presidency Letterpress Copybooks, Scott G. Kenney collection, MS 587, Special Collections, Marriott Library, University of Utah, Salt Lake City.

———. Letter to _____, May 29, 1912. First Presidency Letterpress Copybooks, Scott G. Kenney collection, MS 587, Special Collections, Marriott Library, University of Utah, Salt Lake City.

———. Letter to A. Saxey, January 9, 1897. Joseph F. Smith letterpress copybooks, MS 1325, Box 33, fd. 1, LDS Church History Library.

———. Letter to George A. Smith, July 11, 1872. MS 1325, Box 10, fd. 8, LDS Church History Library.

———. Letter to Joseph F. Smith Jr, September 14, 1899. Joseph F. Smith letterpress copybooks, MS 1325, Box 33, fd. 3, LDS Church History Library.

———. Letter to Joseph Richards Smith, September 13, 1899. MS 1325, Box 33, fds. 2, 3, LDS Church History Library.

———. Letter to Thomas H. Blackburn, June 15, 1899. Joseph F. Smith letterpress copybooks, MS 1325, Box 33, fd. 2, LDS Church History Library.

———. "President Smith Speaks Again." *Deseret Evening News* (June 23, 1903): 12.

———. "Unchastity, The Dominant Evil of the Age." MS 1325, Box 45, fd. 8, LDS Church History Library.

Smith, Lucy Meserve. Statement, May 18, 1892. George A. Smith papers, Special Collections, Marriott Library, University of Utah, Salt Lake City.

Smith, Merina. *Revelation, Resistance and Mormon Polygamy.* Logan, UT: Utah State University Press, 2013.

Smith, William. "A Proclamation." *Warsaw Signal* 2 (October 29, 1845): 1.

Smith, William V. "A Documentary Note on a Letter to Joseph Smith. Romance, Death, and Polygamy: The Life and Times of Susan Hough Conrad and Lorenzo Dow Barnes." *Dialogue: A Journal of Mormon Thought* 49, no. 4 (Winter 2016): 87–108.

———. "Early Mormon Priesthood Revelations: Text, Impact, and Evolution." *Dialogue: A Journal of Mormon Thought* 46, no. 4 (Winter 2013): 1–84.

———. *The King Follett Sermon: A Social History.* Forthcoming (2018).

———. *Every Word Seasoned with Grace*: *A Textual Study of the Funeral Sermons of Joseph Smith.* Forthcoming.

Smith, William V. et al., eds. "The Parallel Joseph." Book of Abraham Project. Accessed August 31, 2017. http://www.boap.org/LDS/Parallel/.

Smith-Rosenberg, Carroll, and Charles E. Rosenberg. "The Female Animal: Medical and Biological Views of Woman and Her Role in Nineteenth-Century America." *The Journal of American History* 60, no. 2 (September 1973): 332–56.

Snow, Eliza R. Letter to Sister East, April 23, 1883. Eliza R. Snow letters, 1883–1884, MS 2325, LDS Church History Library.

———. "My Father in Heaven." *Times and Seasons* 6, no. 16 (November 15, 1845): 1039.

———. "A Synopsis." *Woman's Exponent* 3, no. 23 (1875): 178–9.

Snow, Lorenzo. "St. George Sermon." *Deseret Evening News* (June 3, 1899): 3.

Soby, Leonard. "Statement, November 14, 1883." MS 4635, fd. 1, LDS Church History Library.

Spencer, Emily. "Strong Minded Women." *The Woman's Exponent* 3, no. 23 (May 1, 1875): 179.

Spencer, Orson. *Patriarchal Order, or Plurality of Wives!* Liverpool: S. W. Richards, 1853.

Speth, Linda E. "The Married Women's Property Acts, 1839–1865: Reform, Reaction, or Revolution?" In *The Law of Sex Discrimination,* 2nd ed., edited by Beth Anne Wolfson, Carla M. Palumbo, and J. Ralph Lindgren, 12–15. New York: Wadsworth, 2011.

Staines, William C. "Report, circa 1854." CR 100 396, Box 1, fd. 49, LDS Church History Library.

———. "Statement." Joseph Smith Collection, 1827–1844, MS 155, Box 4, fd. 4, LDS Church History Library.

Staker, Mark Lyman. *Hearken, O Ye People: The Historical Setting of Joseph Smith's Ohio Revelations.* Salt Lake City: Greg Kofford Books, 2009.

Stapley, Jonathan A. "Adoptive Sealing Ritual in Mormonism." *Journal of Mormon History* 37, no. 3 (Summer 2011): 53–118.

———. "Last Rites and the Dynamics of Mormon Liturgy." *BYU Studies Quarterly* 50, no. 2 (2011): 96–128.

———. *The Power of Godliness: Mormon Liturgy and Cosmology*. New York: Oxford University Press, 2018.

Stapley, Jonathan A., and Kristine Wright. "Female Ritual Healing in Mormonism." *Journal of Mormon History* 37, no. 1 (Winter 2011): 1–85.

Stapley, Jonathan A., and Kristine L. Wright. "'They Shall Be Made Whole': A History of Baptism for Death." *Journal of Mormon History* 34, no. 4 (Fall 2008): 69–112.

Sternberg, Meir. *The Poetic of Biblical Narrative: Ideological Literature and the Drama of Reading*. Bloomington: Indiana University Press, 1987.

Stoker, Patricia H. "'The Lord Has Been My Guide': Cordelia Calista Morley Cox (1823–1915)." In *Women of Faith in the Latter Days: Volume 2, 1821–1845*, edited by Richard E. Turley Jr. and Brittany A. Chapman. Salt Lake City: Deseret Book, 2012.

Tait, Lisa Olsen. "Between Two Economies: The Business Development of the *Young Woman's Journal*, 1889–1900." *Journal of Mormon History* 38, no. 4 (Fall 2012): 1–54.

Talbot, Christine. *A Foreign Kingdom: Mormons and Polygamy in American Political Culture, 1852–1890*. Chicago: University of Illinois Press, 2013.

Talmage, James E. Letter to Elder Charles R. Brashear, November 27, 1922. James E. Talmage collection, 1879–1933, MS 1232, Box 3, fd. 11, LDS Church History Library.

Taylor, John. Letter to A. Kimball, November 19, 1886. First Presidency Letterpress Copybooks, Scott G. Kenney collection, MS 587, Special Collections, Marriott Library, University of Utah, Salt Lake City.

———. Letter to John Rogerson, January 20, 1884. First Presidency Letterpress Copybooks, Scott G. Kenney collection, MS 587, Special Collections, Marriott Library, University of Utah, Salt Lake City.

———. Letter to Moses Thatcher, September 25, 1877. First Presidency (John Taylor) correspondence: Letters, 1877, Letters, 1877 T–Z, Box 1, fd. 16, CR 1 180, LDS Church History Library.

Taylor, Samuel W., and Raymond W. Taylor. *The John Taylor Papers: Records of the Last Utah Pioneer*. 2 vols. Redwood City, CA: Taylor Trust Publisher, 1984–85.

Taysom, Stephen C. "The Last Memory: Joseph F. Smith and *Lieux de Memoire* in Late Nineteenth-Century Mormonism." *Dialogue: A Journal of Mormon Thought* 48, no. 3 (Fall 2015): 1–24.

———. "A Uniform and Common Recollection: Joseph Smith's Legacy, Polygamy, and the Creation of Mormon Public Memory." *Dialogue: A Journal of Mormon Thought* 35, no. 3 (Fall 2002): 121–52.

Tchuenche, Jean M. "An Age-Physiology Dependent Population Dynamics Model with Polygamy." *Folia Mathematica* 13, no. 1 (2006): 42–55.

Thompson, Mercy Fielding. Autobiography, (ca. 1880) MS 4580, LDS Church History Library.

Thompson, William. Affidavit, August 23, 1854. CR 100 396, LDS Church History Library.

"To the Public." *Nauvoo Neighbor Extra*, June 17, 1844, 1.

Trembath, Kent R. *Evangelical Theories of Inspiration: A Review and Proposal.* New York: Oxford University Press, 1987.

Tullidge, Edward William. *The Women of Mormondom.* New York: Tullidge & Crandall, 1877.

Turley Nancy R., and Lawrence R. Turley. *The Theodore Turley Family Book.* Mesa, AZ: self-published, 1978.

Turner, John G. *Brigham Young: Pioneer Prophet.* Boston: Harvard University Press, 2012.

———. "More than a Curiosity: Mormonism and Contemporary Scholarship." *The Journal of Religion* 94, no. 2 (April 2014): 229–41.

———. *The Mormon Jesus: A Biography.* Cambridge, MA: The Belknap Press, 2016.

Ulrich, Laurel Thatcher. *A House Full of Females: Plural Marriage and Women's Rights in Early Mormonism, 1835–1870.* New York: Alfred A. Knopf, 2017.

Underwood, Grant. "Revelation, Text, and Revision: Insights from the Book of Commandments and Revelations." *BYU Studies* 48, no. 3 (2009): 67–84.

Van Wagenen, Michael Scott. *The Texas Republic and the Kingdom of God.* College Station, TX: Texas A&M University Press, 2002.

Van Wagoner, Richard S. *Mormon Polygamy: A History.* Salt Lake City: Signature Books, 1989.

Waggoner, J. H. "The Parallel Joseph." *Advent Review and Sabbath Herald* 36, no. 22 (November 15, 1870): 175.

Walker, Charles Lowell. Journals, 1854–1899, 12 vols. Microfilm Collection, Harold B. Lee Library, Brigham Young University, Provo, UT.

Ward, Maurine Carr, ed. *Winter Quarters: The 1846–1848 Life Writings of Mary Haskin Parker Richards.* Logan: Utah State University Press, 1996.

Warner, Susan L. "Sharing Time: I Believe in Obeying the Law." *Liahona*, October 1995, https://www.lds.org/liahona/1995/10/sharing-time-i-believe-in-obeying-the-law.

The Wasp (Nauvoo, IL) (May 7, 1842): 3. Reprint, *The Wasp.* ed., Peter L. Crawley. Salt Lake City: Greg Kofford Books, 2004.

Watson, Elden J., ed. *Brigham Young Addresses: A Chronological Compilation of Known Addresses of the Prophet Brigham Young*, 5:52–54

Watt, Ronald G. "The Beginnings of 'The Journal of Discourses': A Confrontation Between George D. Watt and Willard Richards." *Utah Historical Quarterly* 75, no. 2 (Spring 2007): 134–48.

Wenger, Kaimipono David. "'The Divine Institution of Marriage': An Overview of LDS Involvement in the Proposition 8 Campaign." *Journal of Civil Rights and Economic Development* 26, no. 3 (Spring 2012): 705–51

"Why was the Manifesto Issued?" *Young Woman's Journal* 4, no. 6 (March 1893): 275–78.

White, Eugene E. *Puritan Rhetoric: The Issue of Emotion in Religion.* Carbondale, IL: Southern Illinois University Press, 1972.

White, Jean Bickmore, ed. *Church, State, and Politics: The Diaries of John Henry Smith*. Salt Lake City: Signature Books, 1990.

Whitney, Elizabeth Ann. "Autobiography." *Woman's Exponent* 7, no. 14 (December 15, 1878): 105

Whitney, Orson F. *The Life of Heber C. Kimball, an Apostle: The Father and Founder of the British Mission*. Salt Lake City: Kimball Family, 1888.

Whittaker, David J. "The 'Articles of Faith' in Mormon Literature and Thought." In *New Views of Mormon History: Essays in Honor of Leonard J. Arrington*, edited by Davis Bitton and Maureen Ursenbach Beecher. Salt Lake City: University of Utah Press, 1987.

———. "Mormons and Native Americans: A Historical and Bibliographical Introduction." *Dialogue: A Journal of Mormon Thought* 18, no. 4 (1985): 33–64.

Wilcox, Linda P. "Mormon Motherhood: Official Images." In *Sisters in Spirit: Mormon Women in Historical and Cultural Perspective*, edited by Maureen Ursenbach Beecher and Lavina Fielding Anderson, 208–226. Urbana: University of Illinois Press, 1992.

Wilson, James P. *A Free Conversation on The Unpardonable Sin*. Philadelphia: Towar, J. & D.M. Hogan, 1830.

Winchester, Elhanan. "The Outcasts Comforted; A Sermon Delivered at the University of Philadelphia, January 4, 1782, to the Members of the Baptist Church, Who Have Been Rejected by Their Brethren, for Holding the Doctrine of the Final Restoration of All Things, Published at the Earnest Desire of the Hearers." Philadelphia, 1782.

Widtsoe, John A. *Evidences and Reconciliations: Aids to Faith in a Modern Day*. Edited by G. Homer Durham. Salt Lake City: Bookcraft, 1960.

———. General Correspondence (1947). John A. Widtsoe papers, Box 73, fd. 8, CR 712 2, LDS Church History Library.

Woodford, Robert J. "The Historical Development of the Doctrine and Covenants." PhD diss. Brigham Young University, 1974.

Woodruff, Wilford. Book of Revelations, MS 23152, LDS Church History Library.

———. "The Law of Adoption." *The Utah Genealogical and Historical Magazine*, October 1922, 145–52.

———. Letter to Samuel Roskelley, June 8, 1887, Samuel Roskelley Collection, Box 2, book 4, Merrill-Cazier Library, Utah State University, Logan, UT.

Young, Brigham. Journal, 1844 September 28– 1846 February 3. Box 71, fd. 4, CR 1234 1, LDS Church History Library.

———. Letter to William Smith, August 10, 1845. CR 1234 1, Brigham Young Office files, reel 24, box 16, fd 3, LDS Church History Library.

———. Remarks, December 9, 1847. Church Historian's Office General Church Minutes, Box 1, fd. 60, CR 100 318, LDS Church History Library.

———. Sermon, October 8, 1866. Historian's Office Reports of Speeches 1845–1885. CR 100, 317, box 5, fd. 20, LDS Church History Library.

Zeitzen, Miriam Koktvedgaard. *Polygamy: A Cross-Cultural Analysis*. New York: Berg Publishers, 2008.

Scripture Index

Subject Index

Also available from
GREG KOFFORD BOOKS

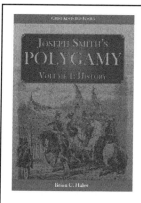

Joseph Smith's Polygamy, 3 Vols.

Brian Hales

Hardcover
Volume 1: History 978-1-58958-189-0
Volume 2: History 978-1-58958-548-5
Volume 3: Theology 978-1-58958-190-6

Perhaps the least understood part of Joseph Smith's life and teachings is his introduction of polygamy to the Saints in Nauvoo. Because of the persecution he knew it would bring, Joseph said little about it publicly and only taught it to his closest and most trusted friends and associates before his martyrdom.

In this three-volume work, Brian C. Hales provides the most comprehensive faithful examination of this much misunderstood period in LDS Church history. Drawing for the first time on every known account, Hales helps us understand the history and teachings surrounding this secretive practice and also addresses and corrects many of the numerous allegations and misrepresentations concerning it. Hales further discusses how polygamy was practiced during this time and why so many of the early Saints were willing to participate in it.

Joseph Smith's Polygamy is an essential resource in understanding this challenging and misunderstood practice of early Mormonism.

Praise for *Joseph Smith's Polygamy*:

"Brian Hales wants to face up to every question, every problem, every fear about plural marriage. His answers may not satisfy everyone, but he gives readers the relevant sources where answers, if they exist, are to be found. There has never been a more thorough examination of the polygamy idea." —Richard L. Bushman, author of *Joseph Smith: Rough Stone Rolling*

"Hales's massive and well documented three volume examination of the history and theology of Mormon plural marriage, as introduced and practiced during the life of Joseph Smith, will now be the standard against which all other treatments of this important subject will be measured." —Danel W. Bachman, author of "A Study of the Mormon Practice of Plural Marriage before the Death of Joseph Smith"

Modern Polygamy and Mormon Fundamentalism: The Generations after the Manifesto

Brian C. Hales

Paperback, ISBN: 978-1-58958-109-8

Winner of the John Whitmer Historical Association's Smith-Pettit Best Book Award

This fascinating study seeks to trace the historical tapestry that is early Mormon polygamy, details the official discontinuation of the practice by the Church, and, for the first time, describes the many zeal-driven organizations that arose in the wake of that decision. Among the polygamous groups discussed are the LeBaronites, whose "blood atonement" killings sent fear throughout Mormon communities in the late seventies and the eighties; the FLDS Church, which made news recently over its construction of a compound and temple in Texas (Warren Jeffs, the leader of that church, is now standing trial on two felony counts after his being profiled on America's Most Wanted resulted in his capture); and the Allred and Kingston groups, two major factions with substantial membership statistics both in and out of the United States. All these fascinating histories, along with those of the smaller independent groups, are examined and explained in a way that all can appreciate.

Praise for *Modern Polygamy and Mormon Fundamentalism*:

"This book is the most thorough and comprehensive study written on the sugbject to date, providing readers with a clear, candid, and broad sweeping overview of the history, teachings, and practices of modern fundamentalist groups."
—Alexander L. Baugh, Associate Professor of Church History and Doctrine, Brigham Young University

Mormon Polygamous Families: Life in the Principle

Jessie L. Embry

Paperback, ISBN: 978-1-58958-098-5
Hardcover, ISBN: 978-1-58958-114-2

Mormons and non-Mormons all have their views about how polygamy was practiced in the Church of Jesus Christ of Latter-day Saints during the late nineteenth and early twentieth centuries. Embry has examined the participants themselves in order to understand how men and women living a nineteenth-century Victorian lifestyle adapted to polygamy. Based on records and oral histories with husbands, wives, and children who lived in Mormon polygamous households, this study explores the diverse experiences of individual families and stereotypes about polygamy. The interviews are in some cases the only sources of primary information on how plural families were organized. In addition, children from monogamous families who grew up during the same period were interviewed to form a comparison group. When carefully examined, most of the stereotypes about polygamous marriages do not hold true. In this work it becomes clear that Mormon polygamous families were not much different from Mormon monogamous families and non-Mormon families of the same era. Embry offers a new perspective on the Mormon practice of polygamy that enables readers to gain better understanding of Mormonism historically.

From Above and Below:
The Mormon Embrace of Revolution,
1840–1940

Craig Livingston

Paperback, ISBN: 978-1-58958-621-5

**2014 Best International Book Award,
Mormon History Association**

Praise for *From Above and Below*:

"In this engaging study, Craig Livingston examines Mormon responses to political revolutions across the globe from the 1840s to the 1930s. Latter-day Saints saw utopian possibilities in revolutions from the European tumults of 1848 to the Mexican Revolution. Highlighting the often radical anti-capitalist and anti-imperialist rhetoric of Mormon leaders, Livingston demonstrates how Latter-day Saints interpreted revolutions through their unique theology and millennialism."
--Matthew J. Grow, author of *Liberty to the Downtrodden: Thomas L. Kane, Romantic Reformer*

"Craig Livingston's landmark book demonstrates how 21st-century Mormonism's arch-conservatism was preceded by its pro-revolutionary worldview that was dominant from the 1830s to the 1930s. Shown by current opinion-polling to be the most politically conservative religious group in the United States, contemporary Mormons are unaware that leaders of the LDS Church once praised radical liberalism and violent revolutionaries. By this pre-1936 Mormon view, 'The people would reduce privilege and exploitation in the crucible of revolution, then reforge society in a spiritual union of peace' before the Coming of Christ and His Millennium. With profound research in Mormon sources and in academic studies about various social revolutions and political upheavals, Livingston provides a nuanced examination of this little-known dimension of LDS thought which tenuously balanced pro-revolutionary enthusiasms with anti-mob sentiments."
--D. Michael Quinn, author of *Elder Statesman: A Biography of J. Reuben Clark*

Mormonism in Transition: A History of the Latter-day Saints, 1890–1930, 3rd ed.

Thomas G. Alexander

Paperback, ISBN: 978-1-58958-188-3

More than two decades after its original publication, Thomas G. Alexander's Mormonism in Transition still engages audiences with its insightful study of the pivotal, early years of the Churcah of Jesus Christ of Latter-day Saints. Serving as a vital read for both students and scholars of American religious and social history, Alexander's book explains and charts the Church's transformation over this 40-year period of both religious and American history.

For those familiar with the LDS Church in modern times, it is impossible to study Mormonism in Transition without pondering the enormous amount of changes the Church has been through since 1890. For those new to the study of Mormonism, this book will give them a clear understanding the challenges the Church went through to go from a persecuted and scorned society to the rapidly growing, respected community it is today.

Praise for Mormonism in Transition:

"A must read for any serious student of this 'peculiar people' and Western history." – STANLEY B. KIMBALL, *Journal of the West*

"Will be required reading for all historians of Mormonism for some time to come." – WILLIAM D. RUSSELL, *Journal of American History*

"This is by far the most important book on this crucial period in LDS history." – JAN SHIPPS, author of *Mormonism: The Story of a New Religious Tradition*

"A work of careful and prodigious scholarship." – LEONARD J. ARRINGTON, author of *Brigham Young: American Moses*

"Clearly fills a tremendous void in the history of Mormonism." – Klaus J. Hansen, author of *Mormonism and the American Experience*

Hearken, O Ye People:
The Historical Setting of Joseph Smith's Ohio Revelations

Mark Lyman Staker

Hardcover, ISBN: 978-1-58958-113-5

2010 Best Book Award - John Whitmer Historical Association

2011 Best Book Award - Mormon History Association

More of Mormonism's canonized revelations originated in or near Kirtland than any other place. Yet many of the events connected with those revelations and their 1830s historical context have faded over time. Mark Staker reconstructs the cultural experiences by which Kirtland's Latter-day Saints made sense of the revelations Joseph Smith pronounced. This volume rebuilds that exciting decade using clues from numerous archives, privately held records, museum collections, and even the soil where early members planted corn and homes. From this vast array of sources he shapes a detailed narrative of weather, religious backgrounds, dialect differences, race relations, theological discussions, food preparation, frontier violence, astronomical phenomena, and myriad daily customs of nineteenth-century life. The result is a "from the ground up" experience that today's Latter-day Saints can all but walk into and touch.

Praise for *Hearken O Ye People*:

"I am not aware of a more deeply researched and richly contextualized study of any period of Mormon church history than Mark Staker's study of Mormons in Ohio. We learn about everything from the details of Alexander Campbell's views on priesthood authority to the road conditions and weather on the four Lamanite missionaries' journey from New York to Ohio. All the Ohio revelations and even the First Vision are made to pulse with new meaning. This book sets a new standard of in-depth research in Latter-day Saint history."

-Richard Bushman, author of *Joseph Smith: Rough Stone Rolling*

"To be well-informed, any student of Latter-day Saint history and doctrine must now be acquainted with the remarkable research of Mark Staker on the important history of the church in the Kirtland, Ohio, area."

-Neal A. Maxwell Institute, Brigham Young University

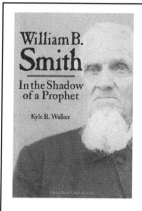

William B. Smith:
In the Shadow of a Prophet

Kyle R. Walker

Paperback, ISBN: 978-1-58958-503-4

Younger brother of Joseph Smith, a member of the Quorum of the Twelve Apostles, and Church Patriarch for a time, William Smith had tumultuous yet devoted relationships with Joseph, his fellow members of the Twelve, and the LDS and RLDS (Community of Christ) churches. Walker's imposing biography examines not only William's complex life in detail, but also sheds additional light on the family dynamics of Joseph and Lucy Mack Smith, as well as the turbulent intersections between the LDS and RLDS churches. *William B. Smith: In the Shadow of a Prophet* is a vital contribution to Mormon history in both the LDS and RLDS traditions.

Praise for *William B. Smith*:

"Bullseye! Kyle Walker's biography of Joseph Smith Jr.'s lesser known younger brother William is right on target. It weaves a narrative that is searching, balanced, and comprehensive. Walker puts this former Mormon apostle solidly within a Smith family setting, and he hits the mark for anyone interested in Joseph Smith and his family. Walker's biography will become essential reading on leadership dynamics within Mormonism after Joseph Smith's death." — Mark Staker, author *Hearken, O Ye People: The Historical Setting of Joseph Smith's Ohio Revelations*

"This perceptive biography on William, the last remaining Smith brother, provides a thorough timeline of his life's journey and elucidates how his insatiable discontent eventually tempered the once irascible young man into a seasoned patriarch loved by those who knew him." — Erin B. Metcalfe, president (2014–15) John Whitmer Historical Association

"I suspect that this comprehensive treatment will serve as the definitive biography for years to come; it will certainly be difficult to improve upon." — Joe Steve Swick III, Association for Mormon Letters

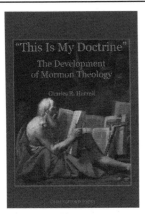

"This is My Doctrine":
The Development of Mormon
Theology

Charles R. Harrell

Hardcover, ISBN: 978-1-58958-103-6

The principal doctrines defining Mormonism today often bear little resemblance to those it started out with in the early 1830s. This book shows that these doctrines did not originate in a vacuum but were rather prompted and informed by the religious culture from which Mormonism arose. Early Mormons, like their early Christian and even earlier Israelite predecessors, brought with them their own varied culturally conditioned theological presuppositions (a process of convergence) and only later acquired a more distinctive theological outlook (a process of differentiation).

In this first-of-its-kind comprehensive treatment of the development of Mormon theology, Charles Harrell traces the history of Latter-day Saint doctrines from the times of the Old Testament to the present. He describes how Mormonism has carried on the tradition of the biblical authors, early Christians, and later Protestants in reinterpreting scripture to accommodate new theological ideas while attempting to uphold the integrity and authority of the scriptures. In the process, he probes three questions: How did Mormon doctrines develop? What are the scriptural underpinnings of these doctrines? And what do critical scholars make of these same scriptures? In this enlightening study, Harrell systematically peels back the doctrinal accretions of time to provide a fresh new look at Mormon theology.

"This Is My Doctrine" will provide those already versed in Mormonism's theological tradition with a new and richer perspective of Mormon theology. Those unacquainted with Mormonism will gain an appreciation for how Mormon theology fits into the larger Jewish and Christian theological traditions.

Re-reading Job: Understanding the Ancient World's Greatest Poem

Michael Austin

Paperback, ISBN: 978-1-58958-667-3
Hardcover, ISBN: 978-1-58958-668-0

Job is perhaps the most difficult to understand of all books in the Bible. While a cursory reading of the text seems to relay a simple story of a righteous man whose love for God was tested through life's most difficult of challenges and rewarded for his faith through those trials, a closer reading of Job presents something far more complex and challenging. The majority of the text is a work of poetry that authors and artists through the centuries have recognized as being one of--if not the--greatest poem of the ancient world.

In *Re-reading Job: Understanding the Ancient World's Greatest Poem*, author Michael Austin shows how most readers have largely misunderstood this important work of scripture and provides insights that enable us to re-read Job in a drastically new way. In doing so, he shows that the story of Job is far more than that simple story of faith, trials, and blessings that we have all come to know, but is instead a subversive and complex work of scripture meant to inspire readers to rethink all that they thought they knew about God.

Praise for *Re-reading Job*:

"In this remarkable book, Michael Austin employs his considerable skills as a commentator to shed light on the most challenging text in the entire Hebrew Bible. Without question, readers will gain a deeper appreciation for this extraordinary ancient work through Austin's learned analysis. Rereading Job signifies that Latter-day Saints are entering a new age of mature biblical scholarship. It is an exciting time, and a thrilling work." — David Bokovoy, author, *Authoring the Old Testament*

Authoring the Old Testament
Genesis – Deuteronomy

David Bokovoy

Authoring the Old Testament: Genesis–Deuteronomy

David Bokovoy

Paperback, ISBN: 978-1-58958-588-1
Hardcover, ISBN: 978-1-58958-675-8

For the last two centuries, biblical scholars have made discoveries and insights about the Old Testament that have greatly changed the way in which the authorship of these ancient scriptures has been understood. In the first of three volumes spanning the entire Hebrew Bible, David Bokovoy dives into the Pentateuch, showing how and why textual criticism has led biblical scholars today to understand the first five books of the Bible as an amalgamation of multiple texts into a single, though often complicated narrative; and he discusses what implications those have for Latter-day Saint understandings of the Bible and modern scripture.

Praise for *Authoring the Old Testament*:

"*Authoring the Old Testament* is a welcome introduction, from a faithful Latter-day Saint perspective, to the academic world of Higher Criticism of the Hebrew Bible. . . . [R]eaders will be positively served and firmly impressed by the many strengths of this book, coupled with Bokovoy's genuine dedication to learning by study and also by faith." — John W. Welch, editor, *BYU Studies Quarterly*

"Bokovoy provides a lucid, insightful lens through which disciple-students can study intelligently LDS scripture. This is first rate scholarship made accessible to a broad audience—nourishing to the heart and mind alike." — Fiona Givens, co-author, *The God Who Weeps: How Mormonism Makes Sense of Life*

"I repeat: this is one of the most important books on Mormon scripture to be published recently. . . . [*Authoring the Old Testament*] has the potential to radically expand understanding and appreciation for not only the Old Testament, but scripture in general. It's really that good. Read it. Share it with your friends. Discuss it." — David Tayman, The Improvement Era: A Mormon Blog

Search, Ponder, and Pray:
A Guide to the Gospels

Julie M. Smith

Paperback, ISBN: 978-1-58958-671-0
Hardcover, ISBN: 978-1-58958-672-7

From the author's preface:

During my graduate studies in theology, I came to realize that there is quite a bit of work done in the field of biblical studies that can be useful to members of the Church as they read the scriptures. Unfortunately, academic jargon usually makes these works impenetrable, and I was unable to find many publications that made this research accessible to the non-specialist. In this book, I have endeavored to present some of the most interesting insights of biblical scholars—in plain language.

It was also important to me that I not present the work of these scholars in a way that would make you feel obligated to accept their conclusions. Since scholars rarely agree with each other, I can see no reason why you should feel compelled to agree with them. My hope is that the format of this book will encourage you to view the insights of scholars as the beginning of a discussion instead of the end of an argument. In some cases, I have presented the positions of scholars (and even some critics of the Church) specifically to encourage you to develop your own responses to these arguments based on your personal scripture study. I certainly don't agree with every idea in this book.

I encourage you to read the Introduction. Although I have endeavored to keep it as short as possible, there are several issues related to the interpretation of the scriptures that should be addressed before you begin interpreting.

It is my experience that thoughtful scripture study leads to personal revelation. I hope that through the process of searching the scriptures, pondering these questions, and praying about the answers, you will be edified.

Life is full of unanswered questions. Here are over 4,500 more of them.

Beholding the Tree of Life: A Rabbinic Approach to the Book of Mormon

Bradley J. Kramer

Paperback, ISBN: 978-1-58958-701-4
Hardcover, ISBN: 978-1-58958-702-1

Too often readers approach the Book of Mormon simply as a collection of quotations, an inspired anthology to be scanned quickly and routinely recited. In Beholding the Tree of Life Bradley J. Kramer encourages his readers to slow down, to step back, and to contemplate the literary qualities of the Book of Mormon using interpretive techniques developed by Talmudic and post-Talmudic rabbis. Specifically, Kramer shows how to read the Book of Mormon closely, in levels, paying attention to the details of its expression as well as to its overall connection to the Hebrew Scriptures—all in order to better appreciate the beauty of the Book of Mormon and its limitless capacity to convey divine meaning.

Praise for *Authoring the Old Testament*:

"Latter-day Saints have claimed the Book of Mormon as the keystone of their religion, but it presents itself first and foremost as a Jewish narrative. *Beholding the Tree of Life* is the first book I have seen that attempts to situate the Book of Mormon by paying serious attention to its Jewish literary precedents and ways of reading scripture. It breaks fresh ground in numerous ways that enrich an LDS understanding of the scriptures and that builds bridges to a potential Jewish readership." — Terryl L. Givens, author of *By the Hand of Mormon: The American Scripture that Launched a New World Religion*

"Bradley Kramer has done what someone ought to have done long ago, used the methods of Jewish scripture interpretation to look closely at the Book of Mormon. Kramer has taken the time and put in the effort required to learn those methods from Jewish teachers. He explains what he has learned clearly and carefully. And then he shows us the fruit of that learning by applying it to the Book of Mormon. The results are not only interesting, they are inspiring. This is one of those books that, on reading it, I thought 'I wish I'd written that!'" — James E. Faulconer, author of *The Book of Mormon Made Harder* and *Faith, Philosophy, Scripture*

Made in the USA
Monee, IL
26 March 2020